Medi...

Five Ways to Master your Mind, Body and Spirit

BY

ABÚ-JALÁL NJ BRIDGEWATER

(FIVE WAYS TO BE SERIES, BOOK 2)

(Abergavenny, UK: Jaha Publishing)

ISBN: 978-0-9957369-2-4

Table of Contents

Dedication & Acknowledgements

This book is dedicated to my grandfather, Freddie, who passed away when I was young, as well as to my grandmother, Laura.

I would especially like to thank my wife, Grace, and my son, Jalál, whose love and support have strengthened me throughout the writing and editing of this book.

Thanks to the many teachers in my life, who have encouraged me to learn, grow and educate myself.

Special thanks must also go to my mother, Carolyn, who proofread this book, and to my father, Leslie, for inspiring me to think for myself and express my thoughts and ideas through art and writing.

Seek Wisdom – A Poem

Seek wisdom, reader, deep within thine heart—

That treasure-trove of gems and gold divine.

Made in the image of the Lord thou art,

A mirror polished shines with light sublime.

Seek knowledge deep within that ocean wide,

That stretches 'neath the realm of boundless light.

Pearls, gems and diamonds bright its depths do hide,

That beam with endless beauty, matchless might.

Seek truth, dear friend, from scriptures—ancient Writ,

That hold the keys to every insight grand.

From one Light all things are most firmly knit.

All things are generated from His Hand.

Seek peace and happiness within thy mind.

No trouble shall descend upon that place.

Intone the holy Names—all sins unwind,

And see that holy vision—divine Face.

Thus counsels thee Abú-Jalál with wisdom, love!

Set feet upon the path of Truth—of holy dove!

- Abú-Jalál NJ Bridgewater

Preface:

Meditation as a 'Way to Be'

What is existence? What is my inner reality? How can I achieve a state of balance—of true equanimity? These are questions which man has struggled with for thousands of years. Before we go onto the subject of meditation, let us briefly examine these questions. Human beings are endowed with the power of reason, which allows us to investigate and perceive spiritual truths that lie at the heart of all things. A famous French philosopher by the name of René Descartes (1596 – 1650 CE) famously questioned whether reality itself was an illusion and concluded that, even if it was, *he* was not. He famously surmised: "I supposed that all the objects (presentations) that had ever entered into my mind when awake, had in them no more truth than the illusions of my dreams. But immediately upon this I observed that, whilst I thus wished to think that all was false, it was absolutely necessary that I, who thus thought, should be somewhat; and as I observed that this truth, I think, therefore I am (COGITO ERGO SUM), was so certain and of such evidence that no ground of doubt, however extravagant, could be alleged by the sceptics capable of shaking it, I concluded that I might, without scruple, accept it as the first principle of the philosophy of which I was in search."[1] Since Descartes was the one experiencing reality, even if reality itself was unreal, the one experiencing it was not. He knew, through his own perception,

4

that he existed. While this may settle the question of the existence of a person, it does not explain what the 'inner reality' of that person is. Is it merely a collection of nerves and electrical signals within an organ, itself housed within a skull? Are we merely prisoners of our skeletons, or are we something *much*, much more?

As Descartes observes, the reason most people are unable to discern the true reality of man is that we confine ourselves to senses, and the senses are material. They cannot perceive what exists beyond the level of physical or material reality. The inner reality of man, however, is entirely spiritual, existing above the realm of the body or the senses. Referring to those who are unable to grasp the concept of spiritual reality, Descartes writes: "They never raise their thoughts above sensible objects, and are so accustomed to consider nothing except by way of imagination, which is a mode of thinking limited to material objects, that all that is not imaginable seems to them not intelligible..." Descartes realized that this awareness of his own existence had its origins in something more perfect than himself—something which possessed all the perfections of which he could conceive and, furthermore, something upon which he depended.[2]

If we can perceive the existence of something negative, the opposite must exist. Heat implies the existence of cold, and cold implies the existence of heat. However, the negative is only an absence of the positive. Therefore, there is no such thing as absolute cold, since cold is merely the lack of heat, but the existence of cold indicates that there must be heat. If there is imperfection, the opposite must be true: there must also be absolute perfection. Since perfection cannot exist in multiplicity, there must, therefore, be only one Absolute Perfect Being, which possesses all the attributes of perfection. There is no need for the existence of an absolutely-evil being, since evil and other negative attributes are merely the absence or lack of perfect attributes. This Perfect Being, therefore, is the Most Just, the Most Wise, the All-Knowing, the Eternal, without Beginning or End, everlasting and changeless, existing above and beyond the world of the imperfect. As St. Thomas Aquinas argues in his *Summa Theologica*; "Now the maximum in any genus is the cause of all in that genus; as fire, which is the maximum heat, is the cause of all hot things. Therefore, there must also be something which is to all beings the cause of their being, goodness, and every other perfection; and this we call God."[3]

Everything that exists is contingent and dependent on that Being, just as the rays of light are dependent on the Lamp which emits them. Everyone is aware of his own imperfections; therefore, we know that we are created beings, dependent on the power and might of an Absolute Being which created—and continues to generate—all of us. Creation is not a one-off event that occurred at some distinct time in the past. Rather, creation is a continuous process of generation which has no beginning or end. We are constantly emanating from the Source of all creation, which lies at the heart and core of all things. What is the reason for the creation of all things? According to the great mystical works and scriptures of the past, the answer is: Love. The famous Persian mystic poet, Jalālu'd-Dīn Muhammad Rūmī (1207 – 1273 CE)—known simply as Rūmī or *Mawlānā* ('our master')—recounts the story of the Prophet David, who asked God why He had created humanity. The origin of this story is a hadith (oral saying) from the Prophet Muhammad (upon whom be peace), who recounted it to his followers.[4] This is Rūmī's rendition of the sacred tale, from his *Dīvān-i-Shams-i-Tabrīz*:

"David said: 'O Lord, since you have no need of us,

Say, then, what wisdom was there in creating the two worlds?'

God said to him: 'O temporal man, I was a hidden treasure;

I sought that that treasure of loving kindness and bounty should be revealed.

"I displayed a mirror—its face the heart, its back the world—

Its back is better than its face—if the face is unknown to you.'

When straw is mixed with clay, how should the mirror be successful?"[5]

- Jalālu'd-Dīn Rūmī, *Dīvān-i-Shams-i-Tabrīz*, VI.

According to the Andalusian Sufi mystic and philosopher, Abū-Bakr Muhammad ibn 'Abdu'llāh, known as Ibn al-'Arabī (1165 – 1240 CE), God loved His creation before anything existed

7

(i.e. in the beginning which has no beginning), and then God called everything into being through the primal command of 'Be!', so that He might be known through every type of knowledge.[6] Ibn al-'Arabī, in commenting on the Qur'ānic verse, **"And wherever ye are, He is with you; and God beholdeth all your actions,"**[7] explains that God is with His creatures wherever they are, both in the state of existence and non-existence (or pre-existence), because they are the objects of His divine knowledge. Since God has loved His creation even before they existed, He is constantly concerned for the welfare of all of them.[8] The creation of the universe, however, did not occur at one fixed point in time. God says in the Qur'ān (28:88): **"Everything is perishable, except His face."**[9] The process of creation is eternal, without beginning or end, just as God's love for us is eternal, without beginning or end. Even though we each have a beginning in time as individuals, God's love for us is without beginning or end, just as souls continue to exist forever in an eternal progression towards the Divine Being. In his work, *Bezels of the Wisdom* (Arabic *Fusūs al-Hikam*), Ibn al-'Arabī states that the Absolute, i.e. God, cannot be known until we ourselves are known.[10] And how can we know ourselves, except through meditation or contemplation?

Human beings are created in the image and likeness of their Creator. As it says in the Book of Genesis (1:26) in the Pentateuch: **"And God said, Let us make man in our image, after our likeness."**[11] Uniquely upon man has God conferred the capacity to mirror forth and manifest all of His Divine Attributes, such as might and power, justice and mercy, forgiveness and magnanimity. Only in man can all these attributes be reflected, and the Light of God can shine clearly and resplendently therein. In Ibn al-‘Arabī's own summary of the *Bezels of the Wisdom*, he relates that the Name (and Attributes) of God number either 99 or 1,001, but that, in reality, they are limitless and infinite, because of the infinity of possible beings in creation.[12] Thus the Attributes of God can be manifested in each and every atom of existence, in each creature—however small and insignificant—and, most of all, in man himself. As God says in the Qur'ān: **"And He taught Adam the names of all things."**[13] Adam here represents humanity as a whole, but, also, most particularly, the Great Teacher, or the Perfect Teacher, who brings wisdom to humanity. Since the Divine Being cannot be known directly—He can only be known through His Names and Attributes—it is necessary for there to be a Divine Teacher who can manifest all the Names and Attributes in his Person. Adam, here, signifies that Perfect Teacher. The Perfect Teachers bring us guidance on how to live our lives, how to treat our fellow humans, and how to attain spiritual enlightenment.

> **"Confucius was travelling once over Mount T'ai when he caught sight of an aged man roaming in the wilds. He was clothed in a deerskin, girded with a rope, and was singing as he played on a lute. 'My friend,' said Confucius, 'what is it that makes you so happy?' The old man replied: 'I have a great deal to make me happy. God created all things, and of all His creations man is the noblest. It has fallen to my lot to be a man: that is my first ground for happiness..."[14]**

9

- Liezi (Lieh-tzu), *The Book of Lieh-Tzu*, Book I: Cosmogony.

The Perfect Teacher is a human being who perfectly manifests and reflects all the Divine Attributes. He is like a perfect Mirror which reflects the Light of the sun, i.e. God. In like manner, we are imperfect mirrors which reflect the names and attributes of God to a lesser degree. The part of us which reflects this Divine Light is the soul—our individual realities—which exist above and beyond our physical forms. We can only attain true balance and equanimity by refining our souls, by cleansing the dust and dross from off the mirrors of our hearts, and by meditating on the essence of reality. **Meditation, therefore, is key to unlocking the hidden potentialities that lie within us.** We are all treasuries full of untapped wisdom, glorious gems and pearls, which are hidden deep within us. Our hearts are full of gems of inestimable value, of true wisdom and understanding, of incredible potential, new insights and discoveries, boundless creativity and infinite love. We are thus the greatest resources in the whole of creation, full of such power and might that the whole world can shine with the light within us. That light is none other than a spark from the Divine Light which shines in deathless splendour upon the inner reality of all created things—which forever shines from the exalted heights of eternity and illumines the farthest reaches of the universe. Meditation can help us to unlock these inner resources—this wondrous inner power and might—and help us to understand the true purpose of our lives, as well as how to attain true happiness and inner peace.

"The study of the Vedas, austerity, (the pursuit of) knowledge, purity, control over the organs, the performance of meritorious acts and meditation on the Soul, (are) the marks of the quality of Goodness."[15]

- *The Laws of Manu*, Chapter XII, v. 31.

What is meditation? Webster's dictionary (1913) defines meditation as "The act of meditating; close or continued thought; the turning or revolving of a subject in the mind; serious contemplation; reflection; musing."[16] In the *Mahabharata*, the meditating *yogin* (yoga practitioner) is referred to as remaining motionless, neither hearing, nor smelling, nor even thinking, and desiring nothing.[17] Meditation is described in a similar manner in *Srimad-Bhagavatam*, where Shukadeva, a son of the famous sage Vyasadeva, began to meditate outside the royal palace. The text describes him as standing motionless, "like a log of wood" as he meditated on *moksha* (spiritual liberation, or enlightenment). It furthermore states that "he began to think the light and darkness as same; the greatly ascetic S'ûka became merged in Dhyâna (meditation) and remained at one place motionless."[18] A royal minister, on seeing Shukadeva, greeted him with folded hands and took him into the antechamber. There, he was shown beautiful gardens with fruit-laden trees, before he was taken to a beautiful palace. In that palace, women who were skilled in the art of *kāmashastra* (amorous pleasure) played musical instruments and prepared various dishes for him, worshipping and revering the sage with great devotion. Shukadeva was young and attractive, so all the ladies who saw him were struck with Cupid's arrow. Nevertheless, Shukadeva looked at each one of them as a son looks upon a mother, oblivious to their sensual charms. His mind was calm and undisturbed, and he occupied his time in meditation.[19] This detachment and calm serenity was, from the perspective of ancient India, the ultimate goal of meditation, since this indicates a state of God-consciousness and inner, spiritual awareness that allows the individual to transcend material attachments and exist on a plane of pure equanimity and inner balance.

> **"There is no profit in vexing oneself by austerities, but meditate on the Buddha and weigh his righteous law. We are encompassed on all sides by the rocks of birth, old age, disease, and death, and only by considering and practicing the true law can we escape from this sorrow-piled mountain. What profit, then, in practicing iniquity?... Exhibit true superiority by virtuous conduct and the exercise of reason; meditate deeply on the vanity of earthly things, and understand the fickleness of life. Elevate the mind, and seek sincere faith with firm purpose."[20]**

- Gautama Buddha, *Buddha, The Gospel*, Jetavana, The Vihara.

Meditation, then, is not merely the act of "serious contemplation." Rather, it involves concentrating one's attention on the inner reality of all things. This includes both the inner reality of our own selves, which is the heart or soul of man—the mirror of the Divine Being, as well as the inner reality of all created things, each of which mirrors forth an attribute of its Creator. Just as the flower displays the attribute of beauty, the lion displays the attribute of might, and the buffalo the attribute of perseverance. Rocks show the attribute of steadfastness and permanence, while water shows the attribute of magnanimity and air the attribute of all-encompassment. Gravity shows the attribute of attraction, and electricity the attribute of power. All things display and mirror the attributes of the Divine. Therefore, meditation is focus on the external and the internal, but not on the base forms. It involves contemplating the reality within all the forms of existence. True mindfulness, then, is not merely being aware of one's own body or form, but also being aware of the reality within all things, which generates all things.

The ancient Indian sage, Patañjali (c. 2nd century BCE), defines meditation (or yoga) as "the suppression of the functions of internal organ." [21] This verse has also been translated as "restriction (or stilling) of the fluctuations of the mind." [22] Bærensten (2015) argues that this definition may be appropriate for neuroscientific research on meditation. He notes that Patañjali belonged to a dualistic philosophical tradition which regards meditation as a spiritual phenomenon, rather than a physical phenomenon. However, he notes that Patañjali believed there to be an intimate relationship between the spiritual and material states of mind.[23] Nevertheless, regardless of the mental benefits or effects of meditation, the primary goal of meditation is achievement of a state of awareness—or mindfulness—which is

13

above material attachments. By suppressing our material attachments, we become free from the bondage of the material world and our minds and spirits can soar to the lofty heights of spiritual awareness. In the Bhagavad-Gita, Lord Krishna, an ancient Teacher and Avatar (may my life be a sacrifice for his being), teaches that the **"highest way"** is followed by **"he who shuts the gates of all his senses, locks desire safe in his heart, centres the vital airs upon his parting thought, steadfastly set; and, murmuring OM, the sacred syllable—emblem of Brahman—dies, meditating Me. For who, none other gods regarding, looks ever to Me, easily am I gained by such a yogi."**[24] He further states that, by meditating on God, or on Krishna as the Perfect Teacher and Mirror of God, one can overcome all their evil deeds and attain to the true goal of existence, which is the knowledge and love of God. He says: **"Him (i.e. God) meditating still, Him seeking, with Him blended, stayed on Him, the souls illuminated take that road which has no turning back—their sins flung off, by strength of faith. [Who will have this Light; who hath it sees]."**[25]

> **"The syllable Om is the manifest greatness of Brahman,**[1] **thus said one who well grounded (in Brahman), always meditates on it. Therefore by knowledge, by penance, and by meditation is Brahman gained... he who worships Brahman by**

---

[1] The Ultimate Reality, i.e. God.

14

these three (by knowledge, penance, and meditation), obtains bliss imperishable, infinite and unchangeable."[26]

- *Maitrâyana Brâhmana Upanishad*, Fourth Prapâthaka, v. 4, p. 301.

The purpose of this book is to give an introduction to meditation as a way to achieve equanimity, true happiness and inner peace. I will present five ways to meditate in order to achieve this state of balance, drawn from various religious and spiritual traditions. I will also briefly describe the history of meditation, as well as its benefits. All of this will be presented within the framework of the philosophy of equanimity, which I have described in my previous book, *Mindfulness: Five Ways to Achieve Real Happiness, True Knowledge and Inner Peace*, which I highly recommend reading before you continue. While it is not necessary to read the previous book in order to benefit from this one, it will help you to understand, in much more detail, the steps you should take to improve your life and become truly detached, mindful, magnanimous and happy. In that book, I presented the Five 'Ways to Be', which are ways in which to achieve that ideal state of balance. As I explained in the first book, "What I mean here by 'ways' is paths, or steps, which are, in reality, all parts of one path. They all lead to one goal but we must tread through each one of these paths before we can reach a state of true balance, which I call equanimity. In Buddhism, this is called the Middle Path, and in Islam is referred to as the Straight Path. The Greek philosopher, Plato, refers to this path as the 'heavenly way.'"[27]

These 'Five Ways to Be' are the following: (1) Detachment and Virtue, (2) Radiant Acquiescence, (3) Magnanimity, (4) Contemplation, and (5) Enkindlement. I have gleaned these from many spiritual and philosophical texts, and they represent the "essence and core of the highest philosophies and codes of wisdom throughout all ages of history."[28] For each one of these 'Ways to Be', I have also identified a practice, which helps us to attain to each state of being. These are the following: (1) the Path of Virtue, (2) Prayer, (3) Generous Giving, (4) Meditation, and (5) Fasting of the Heart. The fourth 'Way to Be', contemplation, relates to reflection or focus on the essence of reality. Meditation, the fourth practice, is the practical expression of that concept. Even though meditation is just one of the five practices, it is a thread which links all five, because true meditation includes and embraces the practice of detachment, and it enhances and encourages the development of virtue. Likewise, true meditation promotes generosity, and its highest form is enkindlement—or enlightenment—which involves the practice of 'fasting of the heart'.

"Behold, I stand poor and naked before Thee, requiring grace, and imploring mercy. Refresh the hungry suppliant, kindle my coldness with the fire of Thy love, illuminate my blindness with the brightness of Thy presence... Oh that Thou wouldst altogether by Thy presence, kindle, consume, and transform me into Thyself; that I may be made one spirit with Thee, by the grace of inward union, and the melting of earnest love! Suffer me not to go

away from Thee hungry and dry; but deal mercifully with me, as oftentimes Thou hast dealt wondrously with Thy saints. What marvel if I should be wholly kindled from Thee, and in myself should utterly fail, since Thou art fire always burning and never failing, love purifying the heart and enlightening the understanding."[29]

- Thomas à Kempis, *The Imitation of Christ*, Chapter XVI, v. 2- 3.

The term 'fasting of the heart' comes from the writings of the Chinese philosopher, Zhuangzi (Zhuang Zhou) (c. 4th century BCE), as translated by Herbert Giles.[30] It refers to a negative state, in which one is detached from all things, including one's own individuality. By becoming like an empty room, free from attachment to everything which surrounds it, we can then communicate with the Divine, which finds shelter within the mirror of our hearts. This attainment to a state of emptiness of self, or extinction of the lower self, is the central goal of meditation. As the Persian poet, Abū-Muhammad Muslihu'd-Dīn bin 'Abdu'llāh Shīrāzī (1210 – 1292 CE), known as Saadi, eloquently writes: "I behold whom I love without an intervention. Then a trance befalls me; I lose the road; it kindles fire, then quenches it with a sprinkling shower. Wherefore thou seest me burning and drowning."[31] Further explanation on this topic can be found in Chapter XIV of *Mindfulness*. I have also written an article on Equanimity Blog, entitled "How can we achieve true happiness and inner peace?", which gives a summary of the teachings contained in that book. I would highly recommend that you check it out. Also, you can subscribe to our mailing list for updates on future articles or publications, including any other books in the *Five Ways to Be* series.

This book will focus on Five Ways to Meditate, viz. (1) Mindfulness Meditation, (2) Loving-Kindness Meditation, (3) Mantra Meditation, (4) Contemplation on the Divine Word, and (5) Meditation on the Divine Being. As an additional service to my devoted readers, I have also provided a bonus chapter, which contains a brief description of other meditation techniques, including Zazen (Zen meditation), walking meditation, and other forms of meditation. The last chapter will contain steps for further development, and some additional quotations on meditation will be provided at the end of the book. In addition, I have provided a bibliography containing the sources used to write this book, as well as other useful books for you to continue your studies. Furthermore, you can also find a list of my other publications at the end of the book, with links to their product pages on Amazon. I have written works of non-fiction, e.g. , *Mindfulness: Five Ways to Achieve Real Happiness, True Knowledge and Inner Peace*, as well as works of fiction, e.g. Green Monk of Tremn, Part I: An Epic Journey of Mystery and Adventure, which constitutes the first part of the first volume of the *Coins of Amon-Ra Saga*. If you enjoy science fiction and fantasy, space and alien adventures, then I highly recommend that you check it out. If you would you like to be kept up-to-date on my latest publications, I would encourage you to sign up to my mailing list. When you sign up to the list, you will receive a free bonus chapter of additional inspirational quotations to help you on your spiritual journey.

I congratulate you for deciding to learn about meditation, and encourage you to continue reading until the end. Perseverance on the path to spirituality and self-realization is essential. Every step you take on the spiritual path will lead you closer to the one Beloved who created all things and fills our souls with the Light of eternity. Our hearts are lamps hidden within the depths of material veils—veil upon veil, wrapt in the illusions of material pleasure and confusion. Only by emptying ourselves of the all preconceptions—by washing ourselves clean with the burnish of spiritual Truth, can we receive the Light of God within us. Only by removing the veils which conceal the Light of the Sun of Truth can the fire of His love burn within the depths of our hearts. Only by enkindling ourselves can we burn away the thick partition which separates us from the horizon of eternity. Only by looking within, meditating on our higher being, our innermost soul, can we see the Face of God shining within the mirror of divinity. When we can envision all things submerged in the ocean of oneness, then we can recognize the attributes of the Divine in all created things; then can we truly know that the Divine Being exists—and then can that Divine Being fill us with His power and might. Then can we shine with deathless splendour within the darkness of the physical realm, like torches lit upon the summit of a lofty mountain. Well has the famous Persian poet, Shamsu'd-Dīn Muhammad Hāfez-e-Shīrāzī (1325/26 – 1389/90 CE), known simply as Hāfez, written:

"From Canaan Joseph shall return,

Whose face a little time was hidden: weep no more!...

O stricken heart! joy shall return again,

Peace to the love-tossed brain—oh, weep no more!...

And yet behind the veil Love's fire may burn—

Weep'st thou? let hope return and weep no more!...

And guide thine ark to the desirèd shore!

The goal lies far, and perilous is thy road,

Yet every path leads to that same abode

Where thou shalt drop thy load—oh, weep no more!"[32]

- Hāfez-e-Shīrāzī, *Teachings of Hafiz*, XXIX.

Ponder these words on the Path—the Middle Way—as you begin your journey of self-discovery and self-realization. The key is in the lock—turn it and open the door.

Abú-Jalál N.J. Bridgewater

∞∞∞∞∞∞∞∞∞∞∞∞∞∞∞∞∞∞∞∞∞∞∞∞∞∞

I. The History and Origins of Meditation

Ancient Origins – Indus Valley Civilization

How ancient is meditation and where did it come from? Meditation, it seems, is an ancient as humanity itself—or at least as ancient as religion. The practice of rhythmic chanting, or the repetitive chanting of specified phrases (i.e. mantras), is present in all cultures and religions across the world. In fact, one of the earliest indications of the practice of meditation can be found in the Indus Valley civilization, which flourished c. 3,300 – 1300 BCE in the north-western regions of South Asia, in what are now areas of Afghanistan and Pakistan. It was originally believed that the Aryan tribes which invaded South Asia around 1500 BCE completely dominated the indigenous populations, giving rise to the Aryan/Vedic civilization of ancient India. However, the discovery of the Indus Valley civilization in the 1920s and 1930s challenged this concept.[33] The 'Proto-Siva' seals depict a deity with horns, suggesting the trident and fertility aspect of the Hindu god, Shiva, though it has also been suggested that the figure represents Agni.[34] In particular, seal #420 depicts a figure seated on a low platform with an erect, frontal posture, almost seeming to be seated in a lotus position. This seal, also called the Pashupati seal, appears to represent Shiva as *Pashupati*, i.e. 'lord of the animals', or Rudra, who is associated with yoga. Dhyanksy (1987) identifies the Pashupati seal with the ancient

21

practice of yoga meditation. He notes that yoga has always been an oral tradition, and suggests that the practice of yoga may derive from the ancient Indus Valley civilization. The Pashupati seal is depicted below.

Figure 1. Pashupati Seal

1

We may never know whether or not yogic meditation began during the Bronze Age in the Indus Valley civilization. What we do know is that every ancient society had some form of ritual practice which enabled shamans or spiritual leaders to gain access to the 'spirit world,' which may be equated to their higher consciousness or being. Various methods of attaining a trance-like state were practiced, most likely as a form of divination, in order to obtain knowledge about the future, the hunt, or to summon spirits to provide rain, plentiful crops or fertility. These ritual practices were intimately associated with early forms of religion. As we learned in the first book in this series, religions have their origin in those Perfect Men who appear from time-to-time throughout history (and pre-history), who perfectly mirror the Divine Being and express His Will for humankind. The names of many of these Perfect Beings are known, including Abraham, Moses, Krishna, Zoroaster and Buddha. Many more there are, also, whose names we do not know. Did an ancient Prophet or Perfect Teacher inspire the development of the Indus Valley civilization? Since the ancient script of that civilization has not yet been deciphered and we do not have any records of their history, we may never know the answer to that question. However, in the case of the ancient Sumerian and Babylonian civilizations, we do have evidence of ancient Teachers, e.g. the Apkallu—the Seven Sages who lived before the Flood.35 The first of these was called Adapa/Uan (or Oannes in Greek), equivalent to the Biblical Prophet Adam:

> **"He [Oannes] taught them to construct cities, to found temples, to compile laws, and explained to them the principles of geometrical knowledge. He made them distinguish the seeds of the earth, and showed them how to collect the fruits; in short, he instructed them in every thing which could tend to soften manners and humanize their lives. From that time, nothing material has been added by way of improvement to his instructions."36**

> - Extract from Alexander Polyhistor, quoted in *The Chaldean Account of Genesis*

24

The Avatars and Perfect Teachers

In ancient India, there are legends and records of ancient Teachers who are called Avatars. The Sanskrit word *avatāra*, which is usually written as Avatar in English, literally means 'descent' or 'appearance',[37] i.e. the Descent or Appearance of the Divine in the form of a human being. Of the many Avatars mentioned in the Hindu Scriptures, two of the most important are Rama and Krishna. Rama, a prince, appeared in an earlier age, before the advent of Krishna. His legend and wisdom is preserved in the *Ramayana*, one of the most important epic tales of ancient India. The story of Krishna is preserved in the *Mahabharata*, as well as in the *Bhagavata Purana* and other source texts. While Hinduism holds that both of these individuals were fully divine, i.e. literal incarnations of God, I posit that this is not the case. Rather, as we explained in *Mindfulness: Five Ways to Achieve Real Happiness, True Knowledge and Inner Peace*, the Divine Being is utterly transcendent and unknowable.[38] Like the sun in the heavens, it is impossible to know the Uncreated Being directly. Instead, we need to take a perfect and spotless Mirror and face it towards the sun. When we look at the Mirror, we see the perfect reality, beauty and power of the sun. In like manner, a Perfect Teacher, a Divine Teacher, is a Perfect Man, who possesses all the attributes and qualities of the Divine Being, but that Divine Being does not descend into the man. Rather, all the attributes, power and majesty of the Divine Being is reflected and manifested through the Perfect Teacher. In this sense, Rama and Krishna are Perfect Teachers through whom we can gain access to the Divine and attain to true knowledge and understanding.

"Death is the end of life, and all,

Now firmly joined, apart must fall.

One fear the ripened fruit must know,

To fall upon the earth below;

So every man who draws his breath

Must fear inevitable death."[39]

- Rama, quoted in *The Ramayana*, Canto CV

The ancient wisdom imparted by Rama and Krishna constitute the spiritual pillars of Hinduism and the practice of yoga. In the *Bhagavad-Gita*, the 'Song of the Lord', Krishna imparts his central teachings to his friend and disciple, Arjuna. He says: **"Unto pure devotion devote thyself: with perfect meditation comes perfect act, and the right-hearted rise—more certainly because they seek no gain—Forth from the bands of body, step by step, to highest seats of bliss. When thy firm soul hath shaken off those tangled oracles which ignorantly guide, then shall it soar to high neglect of what's denied or said, this way or that way, in doctrinal writ. Troubled no longer by the priestly lore, safe shall it live, and sure; steadfastly bent on meditation. This is Yoga and Peace!"**[40] Central to Krishna's religion and philosophy, then, is the practice of meditation. While the exact date of the Bhagavad-Gita's composition is unknown, it is believed to have been written after the classical Upanishads.[41] The war which is described in the Mahabharata, and during which

Krishna instructs Arjuna, may have taken place in the 9th century BCE (according to Basham 1954),[42] which gives us a reasonable date for the life of Krishna, who was contemporary with the composition of many of the Upanishads. Upinder Singh gives a date for the battle of around 1000 BCE, which bring Krishna's dating further back to the 11th century BCE.[43] The Upanishads are philosophical texts in Hinduism, which were composed after the ancient Vedas but before the Puranas.

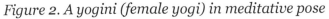
Figure 2. A yogini (female yogi) in meditative pose

[2]

---

[2] Image source: Exhibit in the Arthur M. Sackler Gallery, Washington, DC, USA. Photograph uploaded 12 February 2013, 17:09:50 by Daderot. CCo 1.0 Universal (CCo 1.0). Available online at: https://upload.wikimedia.org/wikipedia/commons/f/fd/Yogini%2C_So uth_India%2C_Tamil_Nadu%2C_Kaveripakkam%2C_10th_century_A

The Upanishads

Krishna's name first appears in the Chandogya Upanishad, dated between the 8th and 6th centuries BCE, where he is called 'Krishna, the son of Devāki.' It says: "Ghora Ângirasa, after having communicated this (view of the sacrifice) to Krishna, the son of Devăki—and he never thirsted again (after other knowledge)—said: 'Let a man, when his end approaches, take refuge with this Triad: 'Thou art the imperishable,' 'Thou art the unchangeable,' 'Thou art the edge of Prâna.'"[44] This chapter of the Upanishad then goes on to quote the Rig-Veda, the oldest of Hindu scriptures, which says: **"Perceiving above the darkness (of ignorance) the higher light (in the sun), as the higher light within the heart, the bright source (of light and life)... we have reached the highest light, yea, the highest light."**[45] The Chandogya Upanishad clarifies that the divine light, the Light of God, is within all human beings, and it is through meditation that we can access this Light. As it further says: **"Now that light which shines above this heaven, higher than all, higher than everything, in the highest world, beyond which there are no other worlds, that is the same light which is within man."** [46] The central theme of this Upanishad is meditation—reflection on all things in order to gain an awareness of the divine light which permeates the whole of creation. It says:

"Let a man meditate on the syllable Om, called the udgitha; for the udgitha (a portion of the Sâma-veda) is sung, beginning with Om... He is indeed the udgitha (Om=Brahman), greater than great (parovariyas), he is without end. He who knowing this meditates on the udgitha, the greater than great, obtains what is greater than great, he conquers the worlds which are greater than great... He who knows the udgitha, and meditates on it thus, his life in this world will be greater than great, and also his state in the other world, yea, in the other world."[47]

- *Chandogya Upanishad*, Prapâthaka I, Khanda 1, v. 1; Khanda 9, v. 4.

What is the mysterious Brahman referred to in the Upanishads? Some attempt is made to explain it in the Talavakâra-Upanishad (or Kena-Upanishad), where it is described as follows: "It is different from the known, it is also above the unknown, thus we have heard from those of old, who taught us this. That which is not expressed by speech and by which speech is expressed, that alone know as Brahman, not that which people here adore. That which does not think by mind, and by which, they say, mind is thought, that alone know as Brahman, not that which people here adore... He by whom it (Brahman) is not thought, by him it is thought; he by whom it is thought, knows it not. It is not understood by those who understand it, it is understood by those who do not understand it. It is thought to be known (as if) by awakening, and (then) we obtain immortality indeed. By the Self

30

we obtain strength, by knowledge we obtain immortality."[48] In other words, Brahman is a higher, Divine Being—the ultimate Reality, the Source of all being and all light and power.

> **"Brahman says to him: 'Who am I?' He shall answer: 'That which is, the true' (Sat-tyam)... Whatever victory, whatever might belongs to Brahman, that victory and that might he obtains who knows this, yea, who knows this."[49]**

- Kaushîtaki-Upanishad, 1 Adhyâya, v. 6 – 7.

Figure 3. Patañjali, depicted as the King of the Nāgas (serpents)

[3] Image source: Patañjali as an incarnation of Adi Sesha. Uploaded to Wikipedia by en:Rpba; created on 6 September 2006 (Creative Commons Attribution-Share Alike 3.0 Unported). Available online at: https://upload.wikimedia.org/wikipedia/commons/4/47/Patanjali.jpg (accessed 14/05/2017). For more information on the license, see: https://creativecommons.org/licenses/by-sa/3.0/deed.en

<u>Yoga and Meditation</u>

The term 'yoga' derives from the Sanskrit word *yuj*, which means 'to add', 'join', or 'unite'.[50] Yoga may find its origins in the ascetic practices of the ancient Vedas. According to Geoffrey Samuel (2008), yogic practices may have developed within the ascetic circles of the *śramana* movements, roughly around the 6th – 5th centuries BCE.[51] The *śramana* movements include Jainism, Buddhism, and other ancient movements. These movements emphasised self-denial, strict *ahimsā* (non-violence) and vegetarianism. They also incorporated the popular concepts of *samsāra* (the cycle of birth and death) and *moksha* (liberation from *samsāra*).[52] Yoga was synthesised in the Yoga Sūtras of Patañjali—196 sutras (i.e. aphorisms) compiled by the sage, Patañjali some time before 400 CE. In this famous text, in the very first Sutra, he defines yoga as follows: "Yoga is *Samâdhi*, Meditation; but (this meditation) is a property of the internal organ, common to all its various stages."[53] In Sutra 2, he further states that "Yoga is the suppression of the functions of internal organ."[54] Patañjali also lists the five *yamas* (or moral imperatives) of Hinduism, which are the foundation of true yogic practice, viz. *ahimsā* (non-violence), *satya* (truthfulness), *asteya* (not stealing), *brahmacārya* (chastity), and *asparigraha* (non-avarice).[55] I would also translate the last of these as 'detachment', which is one of the *Five Ways to Be* we have described in the previous book in this series. Furthermore, all of these fall under the category of virtue, the development of which is essential for happiness and spiritual development. The other elements of yoga we will not describe here, for the sake of brevity.

"He who knows at the same time both knowledge and not-knowledge, overcomes death through not-knowledge, and obtains immortality through knowledge. All who worship what is not the true cause, enter into blind darkness: those who delight in the true cause, enter, as it were, into greater darkness... He who knows at the same time both the cause and the destruction (the perishable body), overcomes death by destruction (the perishable body), and obtains immortality through (knowledge of) the true cause. The door of the True is covered with a golden disk. Open that, O Pûshan, that we may see the nature of the True."56

- *Vâgasaneyi-Samhitâ-Upanishad (Îsâ-Upanishad)*, v. 11 – 12, 14 – 15.

There are several different types of yoga, e.g. hatha yoga, raja yoga, karma yoga, bhakti yoga, and jnana yoga. Hatha yoga deals with training the body through various exercises. This is what we traditionally think of when we hear the word 'yoga'. Raja yoga relates to mental training; karma yoga focuses on perfection through work (e.g. altruistic work); bhakti yoga aims at perfection through devotion to God; and jnana yoga focuses on union with God through the development of wisdom.57 Traditionally, yogic philosophy teaches that the ultimate goal of existence is to merge into the divine, i.e. an all-pervading universal spirit, of which each person is part and parcel.58 This notion derives from some verses of the Upanishads, e.g. "Verily, in the beginning, all this was Self, one only; there was nothing else blinking whatsoever. He thought: 'Shall I send forth worlds?' He sent forth these worlds..."[59] In other words, in the beginning, there was one Being, and that Being generated the worlds. This has been interpreted as pantheism, or the idea that God is within everything, or that everything is part and parcel of God.

I would argue that this understanding of yoga is incorrect. Rather than being part and parcel of the divine, I would argue that all things are, in fact, mirrors of the divine. Our souls, our higher spiritual nature, is created by the Divine Being but distinct from it. In fact, it manifests and mirrors the attributes of the Divine Being, such as mercy, power, strength, compassion, kindness, love, etc. Even though we are all imperfect beings, we are all capable of mirroring *all* the attributes of the Perfect Being (though to a limited degree). The mirror of God is our heart—or soul—which can be described as our 'innermost being'. When we meditate or pray, we are communing with this innermost being, which, in turn, reflects the light and power of the Divine Being. Our hearts can thus be compared to lamps, which are lighted by the flame of the Light of God. The very fact that God asked Himself (according to the Upanishads), 'Shall I send forth worlds?' implies that the worlds are something other than God.

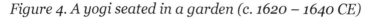

Figure 4. A yogi seated in a garden (c. 1620 – 1640 CE)

---

4 Image source: A yogi seated in a garden, North Indian or Deccani miniature painting, c. 1620-40. Date: 1620 – 1640 CE. Public domain image. Available online at: https://upload.wikimedia.org/wikipedia/commons/7/70/A_yogi_seated _in_a_garden.jpg (accessed 15/05/2017).

Gautama Buddha

In my previous book, *Mindfulness: Five Ways to Achieve Real Happiness, True Knowledge and Inner Peace*, Chapter I – First Way to Be, we looked at the story of Siddhartha Buddha, also known as Gautama Buddha. We began with the tale of Buddha's origin as the son of King Suddhodhana and his wife, Queen Māyā-devī, and how he encountered the 'Three Woes'.[60] If you have not already read the previous book, I would highly recommend that you do so before proceeding, as it gives a good foundation for the topic of meditation. Nevertheless, we will briefly mention the story of Siddhartha here. Siddhartha Gautama was born in what is now Nepal, and lived sometime between the 6th and 4th centuries BCE.[61] This would make him contemporary with the development of yoga meditation and some of the Upanishads. He thus appeared after the time of the Great Teacher Krishna, but before the coming of Jesus Christ (may the peace and blessings of God be upon them both). He was said to have lived during the reign of Bimbisara (c. 558 – c. 491 BCE), ruler of the Magadha Empire, and he died during the early years of the reign of Ajātasattu (r.c. 492 – c. 460 BCE), Bimbisara's successor.[62] Bimbisara and Ajātasattu both belonged to the Haryanka dynasty of Magadha in northern India. Siddhartha belonged to the Shakya clan, which existed on the eastern fringe of the Indian subcontinent during the 5th century BCE, while his father, Suddhodhana, was a chieftain, oligarch or ruler of the tribe.[63] The traditional birthplace of Siddhartha was Lumbini, which is in modern-day Nepal, and he was raised in the Shakya capital, Kapilavastu.

Siddhartha belonged, like Rama and Krishna before him, to the Kshatriya, or 'warrior' caste, one of the four Hindu castes (the others being the priestly or Brahmin caste, the merchant caste, and the worker or peasant caste). His family tree traces back to the mythical king, Okkaka, the Pali equivalent of the Sanskrit Ikshvaku. The Puranas also give Siddhartha's ancestry back to Rama (another descendant of Ikshvaku), thus connecting the two Great Teachers in one family tree. [64] Krishna was the son of Vasudeva, a descendant of Yadu, of the lunar (or moon) dynasty, while Rama and Buddha were descendants of the solar dynasty (*Suryavansha*) of ancient India.[65] In any case, when Siddhartha was young, according to traditional accounts, there was a prophecy regarding his future. The prophecy went, "If he stays in his home, he will become a great monarch, but if he goes away into homelessness, he will become a Buddha, a teacher of mankind."[66] Since his father longed to keep him with him, he surrounded his son with luxury, so that he might be contented and remain at home. He was not allowed to catch sight of any ugliness, pain or suffering.

One day, when Siddhartha departed from the palace in order to visit some beautiful gardens, he rode his chariot down through the city (guided by his charioteer, Channa). Suddenly, however, he encountered a shrunken old man, with white hair and dim eyes, who begged for alms. When he asked the reason for this man's appearance, he was told: "Prince, this is old age; this man has lived many years. All men become like him if they live long enough." On another occasion, he caught sight of another man lying in the road, suffering from great pain, his face swollen and discoloured. When asked what the cause of his suffering was, he was told: "This is sickness; from day to day we cannot tell if we shall be struck down by disease and be even as this man." On the third occasion that he rode in his chariot, Siddhartha encountered some men carrying a still and lifeless body on their shoulders, while women wailed loudly and bitterly. When he asked what they were doing and what they were carrying, Channa informed him: "O Prince, all men will be like that still shape when life shall have passed away; that which you see is Death." Finally, on one last occasion, he ventured forth in his chariot and encountered a man wearing plain clothes of a dull orange hue, with a shaven head and face. The man carried an alms-bowl and went from house to house, begging for food. When he noticed the man's peaceful and happy expression, he asked Channa for the cause of his contentment. He replied: "The man that you see, O Prince, is a good and righteous man who has forsaken the world, and, having given up all he had, is obliged to beg his food from day to day." It was then that Siddhartha resolved within himself: "I will do as this man has done; I will give up everything I possess and go into the wilderness. So shall I find peace of mind and learn the wisdom which shall teach mankind how to overcome the miseries of mortal life."[67]

After practising many austerities, Siddhartha eventually resolved to meditate on the cause of suffering and the path to true peace and happiness. Seating himself beneath the Bodhi Tree (a sacred fig tree), also called a peepal tree, located at Bodh Gaya, in what is now the Gaya district of the Indian state of Bihar, he began to meditate. He seated himself cross-legged, with his back to the trunk and his face towards the east, determining not to move from that spot until he had grasped the highest wisdom. It was then that he was tempted by Mara, equivalent to the Biblical concept of Satan—the spirit of evil—which tried to deter him from his quest. Edith Holland describes his moment of Enlightenment, when he had overcome Mara and attained true wisdom and understanding, in the following words: "Like a man who comes forth from a dark prison into the glorious light, where each object appears in clearness and certainty, so the mind of the perfectly enlightened Buddha passes into the region where all truth becomes clear, all secrets of light and death stand revealed in the light of the supreme wisdom."[68] He then set about preaching his new doctrine, explaining the origin of suffering, which is attachment to material things, and how to achieve happiness by following the Middle Path. He summarised his teachings in the following words, addressing his first monks (*bhikkhus*): **"Now this, O bhikkhus, is the noble truth concerning the way which leads to the destruction of sorrow. Verily! it is the noble eightfold path; that is to say: right views; right aspirations; right speech; right behavior; right livelihood; right effort; right thoughts; and right contemplation."**[69] The Eightfold Path is further explained in *Mindfulness: Five Ways to Achieve Real Happiness, True Knowledge and Inner Peace.*[70]

With regards to the origins of Buddhist meditation practices, Wynne (2007) argues that there is a strong case for a Brahminic origin of 'formless meditation,'[71] i.e. the *arūpajhānas*, the four successive levels of meditation on non-material objects.[72] Wynne bases this on schemes of 'element meditation' found in

40

both Buddhist and Brahminic literature, in which the *yogin* (practitioner of yoga) must become mindful and aware of the four elements which compose the human being.[73] In the Buddhist practice, the bhikkhu (monk) becomes aware that the body contains the four elements of earth, water, fire and air, which are just elements, not a singular being. They are merely material elements—not a soul or self.[74] According to Hirakawa (2007), Siddhartha was taught the practice of attaining a 'state of nothingness' through meditation (*dhyāna*) by the famous sage, Ārāda Kālāma, who was a master of meditation. Unsatisfied with this practice, however, Siddhartha went on to study under Udraka Rāmaputra, who had attained a trance state of neither perception nor non-perception. This practice also proved unsatisfactory for Siddhartha. Both of these practices are, however, according to Hirakawa (2007), listed in the early Buddhist list of 'four formless trances'. It seems that Buddha valued meditation but placed a higher value on wisdom, as meditation alone was incapable of allowing one to realize the Truth. Together with morality, meditation and wisdom form the triad of the 'Threefold Teaching' of the Buddha.[75] The Buddhist practice of meditation then, it seems, had antecedents in the practice of contemporary Hindu ascetics, which may have had an earlier origin in the Teachings of Krishna (may his being fill us with joy and peace).

<u>Meditation and Contemplation in Ancient Greece</u>

In ancient Greece, often referred to as the cradle of Western civilization, we find many of the earliest European thinkers and philosophers. Notable among these was the ancient sage, Socrates (470/469 – 399 BCE), who was the teacher of Plato and dubbed the wisest of all men by the Oracle at Delphi—the sacred voice of the ancient Greek gods. Yet, as Socrates himself admitted, he himself possessed no wisdom or knowledge save what God had bestowed upon him and only that celestial, Higher Being possessed true knowledge and wisdom. He, as quoted by Plato, said: "...the truth is, O men of Athens, that God only is wise."[76] He furthermore states: "He, O men, is the wisest, who, like Socrates, knows that his wisdom is in truth worth nothing. And so I go about the world, obedient to the god, and search and make enquiry into the wisdom of any one, whether citizen or stranger, who appears to be wise; and if he is not wise, then in vindication of the oracle I show him that he is not wise; and my occupation quite absorbs me, and I have no time to give either to any public matter of interest or to any concern of my own, but I am in utter poverty by reason of my devotion to the god."[77] In other words, Socrates made it his mission to uncover truth and expose falsehood and, by so doing, reveal true wisdom. That wisdom, indeed, originated not from man but from the light radiated from the Divine Being, which illumines all things. As Plato says in *The Republic*, "And is there anything more akin to wisdom than truth?"[78]

As Linda Johnsen points out *in Lost Masters: Rediscovering the Mysticism of the Ancient Greek Philosophers*, some of the ancient Greek philosophers were influenced by ancient Indian civilization. She relates that Apollonius of Tyana visited ancient India in the first century CE, leaving an account of his travels.[79] Johnsen notes a particular similarity between the

Hindu practice of yoga and the spiritual practices described by the Neoplatonic philosopher Plotinus (c. 204/5 – 270 CE) in the *Enneads*.[80] In speaking of the highest reality, i.e. God, Plotinus writes: "The first Principle is infinite because He is one, and nothing in Him could be limited by anything whatever... Since He has neither parts nor form, He has no figure. Not by mortal eyes therefore must you seek to grasp this principle such as reason conceives of Him. Do not imagine that He could be seen in the way that would be imagined by a man who believes that everything is perceived by the senses, and thus annihilate the principle which is the supreme reality."[81] The practice of meditation and spiritual discipline, however, traces back much further than Plotinus. Indeed, one of the earliest Greek philosophers, Pythagoras of Samos (c. 570 – c. 495 BCE), who founded the movement later called Pythagoreanism, established a complete pattern of life which included ascetic practices, vegetarianism, common meals and the practice of music and gymnastics.[82]

"It is also said, that Pythagoras was the first who called himself a philosopher. ...The most pure and unadulterated character, is that of the man who gives himself to the contemplation of the most beautiful things, and whom it is proper to call a philosopher."[83]

- Iamblichus, *Life of Pythagoras*

According to Riedweg (2008), the daily practice of Pythagoreans included self-reflection in the morning and evening.[84] In the *Golden Verses of Pythagoras*, one of the sacred texts of Pythagoreanism, there are two verses which adherents were advised to sing before getting up: "Never suffer sleep to close thy eyelids, after thy going to bed, till thou hast examined by thy reason all thy actions of the day."[85] This act of self-reflection allowed the practitioners of Pythagoreanism to reflect on their actions, purify their characters and improve their conduct, much as we advised in the first book in this series. In discussing this process of reflection and purification, we wrote: "We should recognise our shortcomings, ask for the spiritual effects of those shortcomings to be cleansed and washed away, and ask for guidance in living a more morally-consistent and virtuous life. This is a more holistic way of looking at the concept of sin and forgiveness. It is not a case of merely trying to make up for one's wrongs. It is a way of trying to heal one's own soul and then improve, starting from a clean slate. The way to truly achieve forgiveness is with genuine contrition and a desire to do what is right. We should endeavour to develop virtues and avoid vices within us and try to do what is right. Only with reformation of character and a sincere desire to change can this be fully achieved."[86] Self-reflection is essential to this process of self-purification for, without it, we are unable to recognise what needs improving.

Figure 5. Pythagoreans celebrating sunrise, by Fyodor Bronnikov (1827 – 1902)

87

Riedweg explains that ethical perfection was not the sole aim of Pythagorean meditation. Rather, it also served as a form of mental training to improve the faculty of memory.[88] Furthermore, meditation allowed for an understanding of the 'hidden mysteries' of creation. As the Golden Verses relate: "Sacred nature reveals to them the most hidden mysteries. If she impart to thee her secrets, thou wilt easily perform all the things which I have ordained thee. And by the healing of thy soul, thou wilt deliver it from all evils, from all afflictions."[89] According to Wallace (2014), Pythagoras practiced silent meditation, with the primary focus of his meditation being the harmony of the heavenly spheres. Wallace also proposes that Pythagoras may have been influenced by Indian beliefs, transmitted via Persia and Egypt. Wallace furthermore states that Pythagoras was an admirer of Judaism and its veneration of one God.[90] The ancient biographer, Hermippus of Smyrna, writes that Pythagoras was influenced by the doctrines of the Jews and Thracians.[91] According to Iamblichus, in his *Life of Pythagoras*, Pythagoras also travelled to Sidon, an ancient Phoenician city in what is now Lebanon, where he was "initiated in all the mysteries of Byblus and Tyre, and in the sacred operations which are performed in many parts of Syria."[92] Doubtless, he would have come across Jewish teachings during his sojourn in ancient Phoenicia. This search for knowledge, Iamblichus assures us, was not "for the sake of superstition," but, rather, "from a love and desire of contemplation."[93] The concepts and practices of Pythagoras, therefore, have truly ancient origins stretching back to the ancient Phoenicians, Hebrews and, perhaps, ancient India.

Jewish and Christian Meditation

Early on in the history of Christianity, meditation and quiet contemplation became central elements of the religious life. As Kaplan (1988) explains in *Meditation and the Bible*, the origins of Biblical meditation may trace back to the Hebrew Psalms, which use the term *hagah, higayon, hagig* or *hagut* to refer to meditation.[94] Kaplan gives the example of Psalms 19:15, which states: **"Let the words of my mouth, and the meditation (*hagayon*) of my heart, be acceptable in thy sight, O LORD, my strength, and my redeemer."**[95] The term *hagah*, he notes, refers both to thought and to speech. In the Book of Joshua (1:8), we are told: **"This book of the law shall not depart out of thy mouth; but thou shalt meditate (*hagah*)** therein day and night."[96] Likewise, in Psalm 1:2, the command is given to meditate on the Torah (the Jewish scripture, also called the Pentateuch) every day and night: **"But his delight is in the law of the LORD; and in his law doth he meditate (*hagah*) day and night."**[97] Kaplan (1988) suggests that this refers to a sort of mantra meditation, in which one constantly repeats and reviews the Torah until it becomes part of his own being. This may have inspired various Jewish mystical texts, such as the *Hekhalot*.[98]

Elsewhere in the Psalms, it is even suggested that one meditate using the harp: **"It is a good thing to give thanks to the LORD, and to sing praises unto thy name, O Most High: To shew forth thy lovingkindness in the morning, and thy faithfulness every night, upon an instrument of ten strings, and upon the psaltery; upon the harp with a solemn sound."**[99] Kaplan points out that that verse uses the Hebrew word *higayon*, referring to 'meditation on the harp'. This would appear to suggest that the harp was played while one meditated by chanting/repeating verses from the Torah. [100] Recitation of the Psalms themselves, being prayers and invocations of the Divine, were a form of meditation, as they allowed one to focus on the Divine attributes and attain a state of higher consciousness as a result.

The practice of Christian meditation, as well as self-denial and isolating oneself from one's fellow man in order to commune with the spirit, seem to derive from Jesus Christ himself. We know almost nothing at all about the childhood and upbringing of Jesus Christ, except that he was apparently born at Bethlehem in

Judea,[101] was born of a virgin,[102] and was possessed of innate knowledge, which enabled him to dispute with the doctors of religion at Jerusalem.[103] Thereafter, the Gospel narrative finds him appearing before John the Baptist, a Prophet who had come to prepare the way for his mission. After being baptised by the Prophet John, Jesus repaired to the wilderness for a period of forty days, in which he fasted and communed with his Creator. There, like Gautama Buddha, he was tempted by Satan (or Mara) and attained enlightenment. Like Buddha before him, Jesus then set out on a mission to teach his fellow man about the true way to live—the true path to salvation, happiness and inner peace. This message is contained in his famous Sermon on the Mount,[104] where he explains the moral basis and spiritual teachings which lie at the heart of his *kerygma*, or 'core teaching'. Jesus taught using parables, and avoided literalistic interpretations of scripture. For Jesus, life meant spiritual life, i.e. turning one's heart to God, while death meant spiritual death, i.e. turning one's heart away from God. He opposed the fossilized religious institutions of his day, taught that man could attain a state of new birth, or baptism by fire (i.e. enlightenment), and that this was attainable only by accepting and following his teachings. As he says (peace be upon him): **"He that hath my commandments, and keepeth them, he it is that loveth me: and he that loveth me shall be loved of my Father, and I will love him, and will manifest myself to him."**[105]

This is not a statement of the exclusivity of Christianity, nor does it imply that Christianity is the only path to God; rather, it is a statement that only by following the teachings of the great and Perfect Teacher, Jesus Christ, could one gain access to divine knowledge and wisdom. Only by believing in him and following those teachings could one truly be said to love God. As a perfect Mirror of God, Jesus reflected all the attributes and qualities of the Divine Being in the utmost perfection, so only by turning to that Mirror can we see God, and He will "manifest" Himself to us. He likewise said: **"I am the way, the truth, and the life: no man cometh unto the Father, but by me."**[106] In other words, only by following the Perfect Teacher can one find the true Path to God, the Straight Path, and enter the Divine Presence. This applies also to Krishna, Zoroaster and Gautama Buddha, as well as to the Prophet Muhammad (may the peace and blessings of God be upon all of them). All the Perfect Teachers are the Way, the Truth and the Life, and they are all Mirrors of the same Sun of Truth.

The true reality—the Divine Light—can only be found within our innermost selves. Thus, in the Book of Revelation (3:20), Jesus Christ tells his followers to open the doors of their hearts and find him within them, standing ready to fill each person with the water of life. He says: **"Behold, I stand at the door, and knock: if any man hear my voice, and open the door, I will come in to him, and will sup with him, and he with me."**[107] This reflects, again, the non-literalistic teaching of early Christianity, in which symbols and parables represent higher realities. Jesus dwells within the hearts of those who believe in him, even though he is not physically present. Likewise, he says: **"For where two or three are gathered together in my name, there am I in the midst of them."**[108] Again, the presence of Jesus Christ is non-physical and non-literal. Other concepts, such as the Return of Christ, resurrection, hellfire and heaven, are also non-literal concepts which refer to spiritual, and not literal, places and events.

The practice of early Christians was to gather together in houses, or in the catacombs beneath Rome, as Christianity was a proscribed religion, and to break bread and drink wine in remembrance of Jesus. This practice, now known as the Eucharist (from the Greek word *eucharistia* 'thanksgiving'), or the Lord's supper, comes from several verses in the Gospels,[109] where Jesus refers to himself non-literally as the **"bread of life"**, stating that **"he that cometh to me shall never hunger; and he that believeth on me shall never thirst."**[110] Elsewhere, he states that he is **"the living bread which came down from heaven: if any man eat of this bread, he shall live forever."**[111] This is a mystical concept, and not a literal one, as Jesus did not literally descend from heaven (he was born of Mary), and his followers did not literally live forever. He also added: **"And whosoever liveth and believeth in me shall never die. Believest thou this?"**[112] Since millions of Christians have died throughout the ages, we know that the concepts of life, death, rebirth, resurrection and return are all mystical and spiritual in meaning, rather than literal.

The practice of the Eucharist, then, would have had a deep, spiritual meaning for early Christians, who believed that they were reaching a state of spiritual ecstasy and rebirth by letting Jesus enter their hearts. St. Paul explains the early ritual of the church, in which the practice of the Eucharist was preceded by self-examination, rather like the Pythagorean practice. In First Corinthians 11:28, Paul writes: "But let a man examine himself, and so let him eat of *that* bread, and drink of *that* cup. For he that eateth and drinketh unworthily, eateth and drinketh damnation to himself, not discerning the Lord's body."[113] The practice involved "discerning the Lord's body", i.e. being aware of the spiritual essence of Christ entering within one's heart. Rather than a mere rite performed for the sake of ritual, the Eucharist was a deeply meditative act which involved contemplation on Christ, who must be consumed within one's own Being, just as one consumes the bread and wine. In addition, the early Christians recited the Lord's Prayer (or 'Our Father'), which Jesus revealed as an example of how to pray. In this prayer, we ask for the kingdom of God to be revealed on earth, as it is in heaven[114]—In other words, for the Names and Attributes of God to so influence the world as to transform it into a mirror of the Kingdom of God in the realm above. He says (and may his words endure for eternity):

> **"But thou, when thou prayest, enter into thy closet, and when thou hast shut thy door, pray to thy Father which is in secret; and thy Father which seeth in secret shall reward thee openly... Lay not up for yourselves treasures upon earth, where moth and rust doth corrupt, and where thieves break through and steal: But lay up for yourselves treasures in heaven, where neither moth nor rust doth corrupt, and where thieves do not break through nor steal: For where your treasure is,**

51

there will your heart be also. The light of the body is the eye: if therefore thine eye be single, thy whole body shall be full of light."[115]

- Jesus Christ, Matthew 6:6, 19 – 22.

According to Mermis-Cava (2009), Father John Main, a Roman Catholic and Benedictine monk who advocated (or sought to revive) the practice of Christian meditation, based his ideas on the practices of the 'Desert Fathers'—i.e. those Christian ascetics who went into the desert to pray, meditate and commune with God. In particular, he based his ideas on the teachings of John Cassian, who lived in the Fourth Century BCE. Cassian described the Catholic method of prayer as prayer without images, consisting in repetition of a single verse, i.e. mantra meditation.[116] The early Christian monks were called *monachoi* in Greek (sg. *monachos* 'one, alone'), deriving from the Syriac concept of the *īhīdāyā*—an individual who had renounced married life and vowed to live separately according to the Christian ideal of celibacy.[117] Boisvert (1992) writes that the central idea around which Christian monasticism revolved was that of *monotropos* ('having a single aim'), i.e. having a total desire to commit oneself to God. The Desert Fathers of the first few centuries of the Christian era sought to embody this concept in their words and deeds. Another key concept was the idea of always keeping death before one's eyes, as embodied in the Latin phrase: *mortem cotidie ante oculos suspectam habere* ('to keep death before one's eyes daily').[118]

Islamic Meditation

There have been many other forms and types of meditation throughout history, including Jain meditation, Taoist meditation, Sikh meditation, etc. but we will not describe these in detail here. The sacred texts of many religions have, however, been influential in preparing the sections on specific methods of meditation later in this book. However, we will now focus our attention on the history of Islamic meditation. There are currently over 1.6 billion Muslims on the planet, which accounts for approximately 23% of the world population.[119] According to Lipka (2017), there are some 3.3 million Muslims in the US, while, by the year 2050, it is estimated that 10% of the European population will be Muslim.[120] Furthermore, in the United Kingdom, there are now over 3 million Muslims.[121] In comparison, as of 2015, there were roughly 2.04 billion Christians (32% of the world's population), 950 million Hindus, and 350 million - 1.6 billion Buddhists.[122] The meditative and devotional practices of these four religions have, therefore, left an indelible mark on the daily practice and routines of countless millions of adherents.

Meditation is integral to the history and practice of Islam. It finds its origins in the practice of the Prophet Muhammad himself, who was known in his hometown for his trustworthiness, honesty and his meditative practices. Instead of worshipping the pagan gods of his hometown, Muhammad was known as a *ḥanīf* (pl. *ḥunafā'*), which refers to individuals who did not practice idol worship but, instead, believed in the one God of the Prophet Abraham.[123] Although a merchant by occupation, Muhammad spent a considerable amount of his time on spiritual retreats, cloistered within a cave on Mount Hirā', which was on the outskirts of the city. There, far away from the Quraysh (his tribe) and their pagan practices, as well as the hustle and bustle of the merchant town, he was able to dwell in solitude, peace and quiet, and commune with his own soul. He would take provisions with him on his trips and stay a few nights, sometimes returning home to take more provisions before once again seeking spiritual comfort in the mountain cave. It was during one night, near the end of the month of Ramadan, when he was forty years' old, that he suddenly beheld an angel in human form, who commanded him to recite. He replied, saying that he was not a reciter. The angel then wrapped him in its embrace and squeezed until he could endure no more. Releasing him, it again commanded that he recite.[124] He repeated his objection. The angel embraced him again, and this was repeated a third time, until the angel, who was called Gabriel, told him the following words:

>**"RECITE thou, in the name of thy Lord who created;**
>
>**Created man from clots of blood:**
>
>**Recite thou! For thy Lord is the most Beneficent,**
>
>**Who hath taught the use of the pen;**
>
>**Hath taught Man that which he knoweth not."**[125]
>
>- The Qur'ān 96:1 – 5.

This was the beginning of Muhammad's prophetic mission. Like Gautama Buddha and Jesus Christ before him, Muhammad had experienced a transcendent event—a divine call—which shook him to the very fibre of his being. That same Archangel Gabriel, who had appeared to Jesus's mother, Mary, and announced that she would conceive and bear a son (even though she was a virgin),[126] had now reappeared after almost 600 years, in the western region of ancient Arabia. We will not describe, in detail, his life and mission here. That will, perhaps, be the topic of another volume. For now, suffice it to say that the Prophet Muhammad founded a new religious community and instituted devotional practices that have endured to this day. These include obligatory prayers (called *salāh* in Arabic), which are preceded by ablutions, and consist of various movements and recitations. The prayers are preferably congregational and consist of standing, bowing and prostration, facing towards the sacred shrine at Mecca. In addition to five obligatory prayers, which must be said daily, Muhammad also instituted a number of optional, supererogatory prayers, such as the Sunnah prayer, which can be said at any time of the day, and the *nafl* prayer.[127] According to the Prophet Muhammad, these prayers draw one nearer to God. They are, therefore, important in increasing one's awareness of and connection to the Divine.

Islamic meditation developed in its fullest form, however, through the development of Islamic mysticism—or Sufism—which first developed in the 9th century in Baghdad. The Prophet Muhammad was born in Mecca in 570 CE, received his first revelation in 610 CE, and immigrated to Medina in 622 CE. He finally passed away in 632 CE, having completed the revelation of the Qur'ān, establishing a pattern of life for his followers to continue.[128] Several generations had now passed, and Baghdad was the capital of the Abbasid caliphate (750 – 1258 CE). The Sufi practices of asceticism had clear parallels in Christian communities, e.g. the Desert Fathers we have already referred to. However, in discussing the origins of the Sufis, Green (2012) argues that, rather than talking of borrowings or adaptations of ideas from different religious traditions, we should see these common practices as part of a 'semiotic *koinê*', common to Jews, Christians and Muslims of the era.[129] In fact, the term *sūfī* (deriving from the Arabic *sūf*, meaning 'wool'), may have originally referred to Christian ascetics in Iraq during the Abbasid era.[130]

The ultimate goal of Sufism is the same as that of Buddhism, viz. to die to oneself (Arabic *fanā'*) and attain reunion with the Divine (referred to as the state of Nirvana in Buddhism). The definition of Sufism (Arabic *tasawwuf*), according to the Persian mystic, al-Junayd of Baghdad (835 – 910 CE), is to die (*fanā'*) to oneself and live in God,[131] recalling the Qur'ānic verse: **"There is no god but He! Everything shall perish except Himself!"**[132] This continuance in a 'life-in-Him' is referred to as *baqā'* (Arabic for 'continuance'), while the life of this world, which is full of misery and affliction, is referred to as *balā'* ('trial').[133] Hāfez frequently refers to this suffering in separation from the Divine Beloved in his mystic poetry where he writes, for example, that "a dart from thy bent brows has wounded me—ah, come! my heart still waiteth helplessly, has waited ever, till thou heal its pain."[134] Here the Divine Beloved is the one who has wounded Hāfez's heart by causing him to be separated within the physical world. Only by reunifying with this mystic Beloved in the world to come could Hāfez's pain be soothed and his love requited. As we described in the previous book, Sufi meditation takes the form of repetition of the Divine Names of God.[135] We will not repeat the details of this practice here, as it will be described in more detail later on this book. The reader may also refer to what I have written on the subject of Sufi meditation in *Mindfulness: Five Ways to Achieve Real Happiness, True Knowledge and Inner Peace*, Chapter XV. Fasting of the Heart – Steps for Further Development.

In the next chapter, we will mention some of the benefits of practising meditation.

Questions for Reflection:

The following are some questions that will help us to reflect on what we have learned in this chapter:

1. What was the earliest civilization to apparently practise meditation?

2. What is an Avatar?

3. How does the sage, Patañjali, define meditation?

4. What is Brahman?

5. What is the central message of the story of Gautama Buddha's enlightenment?

6. What was the Pythagorean practice of daily self-reflection?

7. How did Jesus Christ instruct that we should pray?

8. What is the ultimate goal of Sufism?

∞∞∞∞∞∞∞∞∞∞∞∞∞∞∞∞∞∞∞∞∞∞∞∞∞∞∞

II. The Benefits of Meditation

"One, O Bharata, by oneself directing one's mind and senses to the path of meditation, succeeds in bringing them under perfect control by steadfast yoga. The felicity that he feels who has succeeded in controlling his mind and senses is such that its like can never be obtained through Exertion or Destiny. United with such felicity, he continues to take a pleasure in the act of meditation. Even in this way yogins attain to Nirvana which is highly blessed."[136]

- *The Mahābhārata*, Book 12, Section CXCV.

Introduction

The defining characteristic of a human being is the faculty of reason. As Aristotle states in *Nicomachean Ethics*: "For man, therefore, the life according to reason is best and pleasantest, since reason more than anything else is man. This life therefore is also the happiest."[137] Reason enables us to investigate the deepest mysteries of the universe and unravel the hidden laws of nature. It enables us to understand the functioning of the human body, to develop cures for infectious diseases, to solve problems of poverty and want, to develop new solutions to provide food and energy for the world, to build houses and cities, and to structure the whole fabric of society. Our capacity for reason has enabled us to go from naked hunter gatherers wandering across the Great Rift Valley of Eastern Africa, to developing stone tools and weapons for hunting, harnessing the power of fire, and establishing the first villages and cities. It enabled us to discover agriculture and invent writing. It enabled us to develop irrigation in the Fertile Crescent, so that we could harness the potential of the River Nile and the Tigris and Euphrates. It enabled us to conquer space, explore the depths of the oceans, and discover the very fabric of space, time, energy and matter. Far from merely possessing the power of cognition, human beings also possess a capacity for compassion, mercy, justice, kindness and other spiritual qualities which, combined with this capacity for reason, enable human beings to become veritable mirrors of the Divine. We are capable not only of transcending the limitations of the material world, but also of establishing harmonious lives and harmonious societies, based on spiritual principles. We are capable of transforming ourselves, our communities and the societies in which we live. Furthermore, we have the potential and power to transform the entire world around us.

How can we transform ourselves in order to release this inner potential within us? Meditation is a powerful tool that enables us to look within ourselves and discover the concealed gems which lie hidden in the profoundest depths of our hearts. It is a key which can unlock the mysteries which lie hidden within our souls. Meditation involves intense reflection, both within and without ourselves, as well as the purification of our minds from material attachments. As we learned in the Preface and the previous chapter, meditation is the "restriction (or stilling) of the fluctuations of the mind."[138] Beyond that, meditation is, actually, a

60

way of life. It is a conditioning of the mind to such a degree that one is meditating while walking, working, eating, drinking, and even when in a state or repose and relaxation.

Figure 6. The Diamond Sutra (printed in 868 CE)

139

According to the Diamond Sutra, the oldest extant printed book in the world, Gautama Buddha discussed the concept of *dhyāna* (i.e. meditation) with his disciple, Subhuti. Subhuti was, in fact, one of the Ten Great *Srāvakas* ('disciples') of the Buddha, rather like the Twelve Apostles of Jesus Christ. On the one hand, Buddha explained, **"Those who practise Dhyana should dwell in solitude and, sitting erect, should remain motionless, seeking to quiet the mind,"** while, on the other hand, **"Dhyana is not at all to be confined to sitting erect in meditation; one's mind should be concentrated at all times, whether sitting, standing, moving, working; one should constantly discipline himself to that end."**[140] This will enable the practitioner of meditation to enter a state of *samādhi* ('a state of intense concentration'), which is equivalent to the Sufi concept of *fanā'* ('death to oneself / annihilation of the ego'). As Buddha further explains in the Diamond Sutra, **"Gradually entering into the state of Samadhi, he will transcend all hindrances and become strengthened in faith, a faith that will be immovable."**[141]

Meditation produces a number of benefits to the individual, as well as society, though we will focus here on the individual benefits. These include physical benefits, such as physical relaxation and improved concentration, as well as mental, emotional and spiritual benefits, such as improved creativity, self-understanding, mindfulness and tranquillity. [142] It leads to moderation of temper, control over one's feelings, and self-mastery. [143] Meditation also destresses the body, leading to rejuvenation and increased vitality.[144] It keeps one's head clear and transparent, and, as Shaku (1906) argues, "logical accuracy depends greatly on the dispassionateness of the arguing mind, and scientific investigation gains much from the steadiness of the observing eye."[145] However, as Feuerstein (2006) remarks, the highest purpose of meditation is not physical, but spiritual, and involves the achievement of *samādhi*, the ultimate purpose of which is self-realization and liberation from the bonds of the material world. [146] The following are the main benefits of meditation:

1. Achieving a state of mindfulness

The term 'mindfulness' is becoming more and more popular and relevant in the hectic, materialistic world in which we live today. This is partly due to the introduction of mindfulness-based stress reduction (MBSR), which was first introduced in 1979 at the Stress Reduction Clinic at the University of Massachusetts Medical Center, which is located in Worcester, Massachusetts.[147] According to Williams & Kabat-Zinn (2013), mindfulness-based cognitive therapy has also been introduced in the NHS in the UK. [148] The origin of the practice, however, is rooted in the Buddhist practice of 'mindfulness meditation', which we will describe in the next chapter. The introduction of mindfulness meditation techniques into mainstream therapeutic practices indicates not only the relevancy and efficacy of the techniques, but also their ability to be adapted and applied within a secular, clinical setting.

Bhikku Bodhi (2013) states that mindfulness is the main factor in the practice of *satipatthāna*, which is the best-known system of meditation in Buddhism. Bodi explains that the term *sati* is translated as 'mindfulness', while *sampajañña* is translated as 'comprehension,' or 'clear comprehension', which are two elements of the practice. Bodhi (2013) distinguishes these two terms by stating that mindfulness means 'lucid awareness of the phenomenal field', i.e. an awareness of outward or external phenomena. Development of this level of awareness occurs in the early stages of the practice. Clear comprehension, which is the next stage of awareness, involves interpreting the 'presentational field' in a meaningful way. In other words, one is able to interpret and understand what one perceives, including what we perceive physically, emotionally etc. This leads, eventually, to the development of 'direct insight' (*vipassanā*) and 'wisdom' (*paññā*).[149] The attainment of wisdom, according to Buddha, leads to peace of mind. The wise, being aware of the impermanence of all things, do not grieve and lament. Rather, they attain a state of mental and emotional composure and inner peace. Buddha tells us:

> **"So the world is afflicted with death and decay, therefore the wise do not grieve, knowing the terms of the world. In whatever manner people think a thing will come to pass, it is often different when it happens, and great is the disappointment; see, such are the terms of the world... He who seeks peace should draw out the arrow of lamentation, and complaint, and grief. He who has drawn out the arrow and has become composed will obtain peace of mind; he who has overcome all sorrow will become free from sorrow, and be blessed."[150]**

- Gautama Buddha, *Buddha, The Gospel*, The Mustard Seed.

Achievement of a state of mindfulness, furthermore, helps us to develop an alert awareness of what is going on in the world, and within ourselves, heightening our concentration and memory in the process.[151] Fontana & Slack (2007) also point out that mindfulness heightens our awareness of the effect we have on other people and our environment.[152] Furthermore, as I remarked in the first book in this series: "As more people learn how to live in equanimity and mindfulness, we will gradually be able to overcome the hate, violence and discord which so plagues the world we now live in. Inner harmony, peace and prosperity are, ultimately, the necessary prerequisite to world harmony, peace and prosperity... As long as we live discordant lives, we will never be able to live in harmony with one another."[153] When we achieve a state of mindfulness, we become aware of ourselves and the true meaning of things, and are thus able to make a more positive impact on the world around us.

2. Spiritual development

Too often, in the modern materialistic world in which we live, do we tend to accept the notion that the material world is all that exists. We look upon the houses on our street, the rocks on the path, the river which flows through our village, or the sun, moon and stars, and see them as 'real', 'true' or 'important'. We believe that our bodies, which are composed of flesh and bone, are lasting and not subject to dissolution or decomposition. We regard our jobs as permanent, our properties as secure and our health as lasting. We cannot contemplate our own death or physical extinction, nor can we imagine the death of those we love who surround us and are important in our lives. This focus on the material is called materialism, and it is a whole way of looking at reality. It is the basis of materialistic philosophies, such as Marxism, scientism, analytical behaviourism, mechanism, objectivism, etc.

Materialism proposes that the whole of existence is material and can be explained using material means, e.g. through science alone. Philosophically, materialism is the reductionist position that mental properties, i.e. thoughts, feelings, etc., are nothing more than physical properties.[154] If we are only material creatures, then our lives serve no other purpose than reproduction, which is the biological imperative, and the acquisition of resources for ourselves and our families. As such, we would be little more than machines functioning to achieve the blind design of a random universe, ultimately purposeless, without a framework or morality, and existing for the sake of existence. If, after all, reality is material, then there would be no higher purpose other than to continue existing. Since physical life must come to an end, life would be pretty bleak if this were true. This concept, however, is gradually coming to the end of its lifespan as more and more scientists and others are becoming aware of science's limitations to describe the totality of existence.[155] In reality, the world, and all that is within it, is nothing more than a shadow of actual reality, which is fundamentally spiritual. As Buddha (may his glorious essence illumine our souls) says in the Diamond Sutra: **"The phenomena of life are like a dream, a phantasm, a bubble, a shadow, the glistening dew, a lightning flash; thus should they be contemplated by an enlightened disciple."**[156]

Meditation helps us to us to develop our real selves. In reality, as countless philosophers and religious teachers throughout the ages have averred, man is essentially a spiritual being. We are much more than the sum our physical atoms, or the collected experiences of a lifetime. We are eternal beings, full of inner nobility and unlimited potential. While our physical selves are transitory and impermanent, and our egos and material attachments are temporary, our true selves persist for all eternity, because they are singular and indivisible, rather than composite and perishable. While prayer and supplication is communion with a Higher Being, meditation is communion with our own souls. As such, it helps us to realize our own true nature and uncover the hidden gems that lie deep within the depths of our souls. It allows us to uncover our true, spiritual reality. It allows us to develop the spiritual qualities which are essential for a life of equanimity and balance, such as mindfulness, kindness, tolerance, peace, love, compassion, mercy and forgiveness. It makes us more forbearing, more respectful, more hard-working and patient. It makes us more loving to others, more generous and more reverent. If we are—truly—spiritual beings, then we can transcend the material reality of our lives and develop those spiritual capacities which lie latent and unused within the treasury of our inner being.

3. Achievement of a state of enkindlement

The verb 'to kindle' literally means to set something afire, to light something. The noun for this is 'enkindlement'. Enkindlement here, however, refers to spiritual fire—to the death to ourselves and life in God that Sufis refer to as *fanā'* and *baqā'* respectively. It is a new rebirth, being born again in the spirit, a baptism of fire which cleanses us of our impurities and shortcomings and fills us with a burning love for the Divine Being. Fire is a cleansing force, eliminating and destroying one's material attachments and ego, leaving only the higher essence—the soul, which is a mirror of its Creator. As Jalālu'd-Dīn Rūmī relates in his masterful *Masnavī*:

"Till man destroys 'self', he is no true friend of God.

Once a man came and knocked at the door of his friend.

His friend said, 'who art thou. O faithful one?'

He said, 'Tis I.' He answered, 'There is no admittance.

There is no room for the 'raw' at my well-cooked feast.

Naught but fire of separation and absence

Can cook the raw one and free him from hypocrisy!

Since thy 'self' has not yet left thee,

Thou must be burned in fiery flames.

The poor man went away, and for one whole year

Journeyed burning with grief for his friend's absence.

His heart burned till it was cooked; then he went again

And drew near to the house of his friend...

His friend shouted, 'Who is that at the door?'

He answered, 'Tis Thou who art at the door. O Beloved!'

The friend said, 'Since 'tis I, let me come in,

There is not room for two 'I's' in one house.'[157]

- Jalālu'd-Dīn Rūmī, *The Masnavi*, Story XI.

This does not mean that the seeker and his Beloved are literally one and the same, or of one 'essence'. Rather, there are two individuals, but the object of one's love is so wondrous, so luminous, so absolute, that there can be no thought of self in its presence. This Beloved, of course, refers to the Divine Being, the Creator of our bodies and souls, which generates all things through its Primal Will. Every atom of existence mirrors one of His Names and Attributes, and our souls are mirrors which can reflect and manifest all these divine qualities and potentialities. We can only truly achieve our objective, and enter the state of *samādhi* referred to in the Buddhist scriptures, if we strip ourselves of all notions of 'self' and 'individuality' and burn brightly with the fire of love. This fire is kindled when we realize, firstly, our separation from the Divine Beloved, and, secondly, our utter non-existence in the face of that Absolute Existence. Thirdly, we must acknowledge our inability to grasp that Divine Beloved or fathom His existence. Fourthly, we must acknowledge that the only way to attain to that Divine Beloved, and seek reunion with Him, is to recognize the Perfect Teacher which manifests all the divine Names and Attributes, e.g. Krishna, Buddha, Christ, etc. Fifthly, we must follow the teachings of that Perfect Teacher, who gives us the instructions we need to burn away all our material attachments and limitations.

Meditation allows us to dissolve the material attachments, including the attachment to ego and self, which hinder us from attaining unto our true Beloved. The material world is like a prison or cage, and the body can be compared to the chains and fetters which keep us attached to that cage. Meditation is the key which allows us to unloose these chains and fetters and open the door of the cage which holds us within. Meditation allows us to focus our love within, to the mirror of our hearts, and to see therein the Light of the Beloved. Our hearts are like candles—only the flame of the love of God can kindle them. Then, when that flame burns brightly within us, we can shine like lamps in the darkness of the world, like torches burning brightly on the summits of a lofty peak, while all the world around us rests in impenetrable darkness. Yet, as we burn brightly, so will other torches light up and be enkindled. Others will seek a way out from the darkness, and, seeing us burning brightly on the horizon, will climb these snow-capped peaks and set ablaze their own innermost selves, burning away all vain imaginings and illusions, and clinging to the true essence of reality—the ultimate Reality which underpins and infuses all created things. As Rumi says so eloquently: "If you desire to rise above mere names and letters, make yourself free from self at one stroke! Like a sword be without trace of soft iron; like a steel mirror, scour off all rust with contrition; make yourself pure from all attributes of self, that you may see your own pure bright essence!"[158] This is the greatest benefit of meditation.

4. Self-understanding

In the *Book of Proverbs* (14:8), we read: **"The wisdom of the prudent is to understand his way: but the folly of fools is deceit."**[159] This roughly corresponds with the inscription on the ancient Greek Temple at Delphi, which read: "Know thyself, and thou wilt know the universe..."[160] In the Bhagavad-Gita, Lord Krishna says: **"When the completely controlled mind rests serenely in the Self alone, free from longing after all desires, then is one called steadfast, (in the Self). 'As a lamp in a spot sheltered from the wind does not flicker,'—even such has been the simile used for a Yogi of subdued mind, practising concentration in the Self."**[161] The self, here, refers to the higher self, not the lower ego. Knowledge of this higher self is the same as knowledge of God, as the true self is purified from any taint of material attachments or limitations. These limitations only pertain to the body and the ego, both of which are part of the lower self.

The word ego, which exists in both Greek and Latin, literally means 'I', as in the Ancient Greek phrase, *egō eimi* 'I exist/am'. In John 6:20, Jesus says to his companions (after the Resurrection): ***egō eimi, mē phobeisthe***, meaning **'It is I; be not afraid.'**[162] However, I am here using the term 'ego' to refer to a person's sense of self-esteem or self-importance.[163] In other words, it is that self within us, which insists on its own needs, wants and desires. It is the insistent self which desires its own advancement at the expense of others. This is the driving force behind crime, war, exploitation and injustice in the world. This 'self' is, in reality, illusory and impermanent, as it exists only on the level of material reality. Material reality itself, as Buddha taught, is illusory, existing only in the sense that we perceive it to exist. It is, in fact, a shadow of the Absolute Existence, which exists above and beyond all things. As Lord Buddha (peace be upon him) says: **"How transient are all component things! Growth is their nature and decay: they are produced, they are dissolved again: and then is best,—when they have sunk to rest."**[164]

To know one's true self, or higher self, is the greatest of achievements. The true self, which is the soul, is not composed of different elements. It is one, singular, indivisible reality—and hence eternal. Buddha states that all **"component things"** are transient, but not that which is singular in its nature. The ego is a composition of our hopes, desires, prejudices and self-conceptions, which can deteriorate, evolve and dissolve just like a lump of sugar in a cup of tea. The true self, which is eternal and mighty, can neither dissolve nor cease to exist. When we meditate, we commune with this higher self and begin to understand what it is—who we truly are. We begin to understand our true reality, our true inner essence, which rests like a diamond sealed within the midst of an ocean of ice. It is not subject to pain or suffering, to distress or despair. Rather, it is protected from all things, free and untouchable, ethereal and placeless. As such, we are never in any danger, nor can we ever be truly harmed or hurt. To realize this is to free ourselves of all fear and unhappiness, all pain and suffering, and to embrace the reality of our innermost essence. As Jesus Christ (may he guide and protect us) declared, when asked when the Kingdom of God would come, said: **"Neither shall they say, Lo here! or, lo there! for, behold, the kingdom of God is within you."**[165] At another time, according to the Gospel of John (14:20), he also taught his disciples: **"At that day**[5] **ye shall know that I *am* in my Father, and ye in me, and I in you."**[166]

5. Self-control and control over one's thoughts

Self-discipline is the result of gaining mastery over oneself. Self-mastery is the key to perfection. Even though perfection is not truly attainable, the path to perfection, which is as long as the universe is broad, is self-control, self-refinement, and self-mastery. Buddha says: **"He is called 'elder' in whom dwell truth and righteousness, harmlessness and self-control and self-mastery, who is without taint and wise."** [167] Meditation requires focus and concentration, the ability to reflect intently within oneself and sever oneself from passion and material attachments. Through constant practice, one can learn to master one's behaviour, one's thought processes, one's goals, as well as learning to refine one's character, conduct and speech. Just as we need to polish a mirror until it can shine resplendently, so must we also make the constant effort to scrub and polish the

---

5 That is, after his passing.

mirror of our hearts. Meditation enables us to cleanse the heart through constant effort and determination.

> **"Mental and bodily equilibrium are to be sought within oneself."**[168]

- Liezi (c. 350 BCE), *Book of Lieh-Tzü*, Book VII.

According to Nukariya (1913) in *The Religion of the Samurai*, the goal of mental training is to achieve "absolute control over Self."[169] He writes that, "to get Enlightened, we must establish the authority of Self over the whole body. We must use our bodies as we use our clothes in order to accomplish our noble purposes... It is not a matter of theory, but of practice. You must train your body that you may enable it to bear any sort of suffering, and to stand unflinched in the face of hardship."[170] As the Greek-speaking Stoic philosopher, Epictetus (c. 50 – 135 CE), teaches us: "For freedom is secured not by the fulfilling of men's desires, but by the removal of desire."[171] When we have mastery over ourselves, we are free from the cage of desire and passion, which rules over us like a tyrant. There is no greater slavery than to be slaves to our own lower selves. There is no greater freedom that to overthrow this tyrant and assert control over the body and the five senses. What greater freedom is there than this?

6. Improved concentration

Another benefit of meditation is improved concentration and focus. Concentration is the result of detachment to external things. Focus means turning away from all that is unimportant and concentrating one's attention on that which is most important. As Lord Krishna (peace be upon him) says in the *Bhagavad-Gita*: **"For the man of meditation wishing to attain purification of heart leading to concentration, work is said to be the way: For him, when he has attained such (concentration), inaction is said to be the way."**[172] Furthermore, in the same chapter, he—may the world be a sacrifice for his glory—states: **"The Yogi should constantly practise concentration of the heart, retiring into solitude, alone, with the mind and body subdued, and free from hope and possession."**[173]

Improved concentration allows us to focus better at work, at home, and in our personal lives. We live at a time when people are constantly distracted by the buzz of their mobile phones, the distraction of social media and various applications, as well as the constant race to satisfy material needs and acquire material possessions. By focusing on what is most important, we can live in the moment and spend better quality time with the ones we love. We can turn away from that which is less important, such as frivolous pursuits and unnecessary chatter, gossip and hearsay, and focus on providing a service to our fellow men, helping and loving our families and serving our communities in a spirit of joy and happiness. Meditation is like a knife which cuts through the frivolity, vanity and materialistic morass of modern civilization, melting away—like butter—all that is impermanent and unimportant.

7. Memory enhancement

Memory allows us to understand where we have come from, so that we can know where we are going. According to Fontana & Slack (2007), forgetfulness results from a failure in concentration on what is happening. This is often caused by the interference of our conscious minds, especially when worried or anxious. Meditation, however, enables us to increase our memory by increasing our awareness.[174] According to Madigan (2015), when meditation practitioners pay attention and focus on their breathing, they activate high-level mental operations which are essential to working memory.[175] Researchers at the University of Copenhagen taught mindfulness meditation to a group of students and compared the results against groups which had not received the same treatment. Remarkably, only the group which had received training in mindfulness meditation showed improvement in attention and memory.[176]

In one study (Alexander et al. 1989),[177] 73 seniors, who had a mean age of 81 years, were divided into three groups based on meditation techniques used, with one control group which received no intervention.[178] The three techniques were transcendental meditation (TM), mindfulness meditation, and a relaxation technique. According to Marciniak et al. (2014), the groups were measured before and immediately after meditation, as well as at 18 months and 36 months, with the results showing improvements in cognitive flexibility, memory and verbal fluency in the group using transcendental meditation, followed by the group using mindfulness meditation. The group using a relaxation technique and the control group received the worst results. These results indicate that various forms of meditation can be useful in improve mental acuity and memory, even among the elderly. Furthermore, according to van Vugt (2015), mindfulness meditation not only improves one's attention, but it also enhances working memory, both verbal and non-verbal. Van Vugt suggests that the meditation may improve the practitioner's ability to encode stimuli, increase the stimuli which can be held at one time, or, perhaps, decrease the degradation of memory over a period of time.[179] In short, numerous studies indicate that meditation has a positive effect on memory.

8. Increased creativity

According to Gelb (2014), mindfulness meditation can serve as an effective aid to creativity, helping us to harness and retain insights which result from the many connections and associations which our minds produce.[180] Gelb also discusses what he calls 'qi-cultivation practices', which encourage the natural movement of *qi*—the vital energy which animates the body according to Chinese philosophy [181] —within one's body and between one's body and the field of energy which surrounds us all. [182] These methods, according to Gelb (2014), involve movements, breathing patterns and visualizations which empower the individual to flow with creativity.[183] Ching & Ching (2014), likewise, argue that, when this vital life force flows through the body smoothly, when our emotions are unblocked and our minds are focused, creativity can flourish.[184] Furthermore, according to Ching & Ching (2014), those who practice meditation or contemplative prayer can sense the *qi* force flowing through their bodies, through others and throughout the universe, thus increasing their focus, concentration and stamina. [185] It allows them to become aware of their creative energies and focus these in the practice of art and other forms of self-expression.

In a survey of various studies on mindfulness and creativity, Sinclair & Seydel (2016) have found that mindfulness training significantly improves both divergent and convergent thinking on the part of participants. They argue that creativity is affected more by the motivational intensity of one's emotions than one's moods, whether positive or negative. By becoming mindful and aware of the motivational intensity of our emotions, we can understand the quality of our creative output. [186] Furthermore, Sinclair & Seydel (2016) argue that mindfulness allows us to overcome rigid and narrow ways of thinking by becoming aware and cognizant of reality as it is. [187] When we are in a state of mindfulness, we do not try to filter reality; rather, we become intensely aware of our situation and the reality which surrounds us, absorbing information, solving problems and releasing the creative mind from the cage of conventionality. As Buddha says in the Lankāvatāra Sutra:

"Thoughtfulness will give way to mindfulness wherein discriminated meanings and logical deductions and rationalisations will give way to intuitions of significance and spirit."[188-]

9. Physical relaxation and stress relief

This is, perhaps, one of the main reasons that people in the West turn to meditation. As Western countries (and many other lands) are increasingly engulfed in the sea of materialism, consumerism and wage slavery, we are filled with stress and anxiety, impatience and hopelessness, depression and despair. We find little fulfilment in the day-to-day activities of our humdrum lives and, even those who are most successful at the game of material acquisition often find themselves empty and unhappy. Their bodies are worn down by the stress of constant busyness and a hectic work-life, while they are unable to balance their home life, intimate relationships and social life in a way which can produce inner balance and equanimity. Many, therefore, turn to medicinal methods of stress relief, such as anti-depressants or drugs (e.g. tobacco, alcohol, marijuana or narcotics), or turn to frivolous activities and digital entertainment. As Buddha says: **"They that are serious do not die; they that are frivolous are always dead."** [189] Yet others turn to alternative practices, such as meditation, martial arts and yoga to relieve stress, improve the balance of their mind, body and soul, and achieve a sense of inner well-being and peace.

Meditation is an ideal practice to achieve a state of deep relaxation and inner repose. Not only does it allow one to shut out the noise and clamour of the chaotic and forlorn civilization in which we now live, but it also allows us to find a reservoir of inner strength and might which we did not even know we possessed. It allows us to tap into that ancient and eternal source of power which flows from the innermost essence of our hearts—a spiritual energy which transcends the material realm and has its ultimate origin in the Primal Will which generates all created things. Meditation allows us to find our inner nobility, to realize our true worth and exalted nature, and to understand our real purpose and ultimate goal in life—which is to develop those divinely-inherited qualities and attributes which constitute the nature of the true human being, and to use our divinely-gifted powers and abilities to serve humanity and improve the world around us. As Jesus Christ said in the Sermon on the Mount: **"Blessed are the peacemakers: for they shall be called the children of God."**[190] We can, by turning to that Divine Source which feeds and strengthens us with the water and bread of life,[191] become conduits of divine energy and potentiality, helping others to achieve that same balance and inner happiness which we have achieved. We can feel more relaxed, free of stress, and more peaceful, if only we focus our attention on the powers which lie within us.

10. Improved health, happiness and tranquillity

Meditation can have a profound effect on one's physical health and well-being. It can also help one to feel happiness and tranquillity. The physical and emotional aspects of a human being are intricately linked, with happiness having a positive effect on physical health, and vice versa. Physical health helps us to feel good about ourselves and be happy. Meditation is a key practice in keeping and maintaining the balance between these two elements within the individual. According to Gregory (2014), a number of benefits have been identified of mindfulness meditation, which have helped healthcare practitioners to develop empathy, compassion and acceptance. [192] Miller (2013) states that meditation can improve health-related outcomes in a number of conditions, *inter alia*, anxiety, depression, sleep disturbance, asthma, cancer, hypertension, chronic pain, coronary artery disease, etc.[193] She, furthermore, states that meditation has many physiological effects, such as positive effects on the immune and neurological systems and the ability to activate the autonomic nervous system.[194] According to Hartz (2012), mindfulness-based cognitive therapy encourages the 'clients' to develop a sense of present centeredness, allowing them to deal with the present situation (i.e. the moment in which they are now living), rather than the past or future. They thus develop an attitude of non-striving and acceptance, which helps them to overcome depression and anxiety, which often result from rumination on one's problems. By achieving a state of mindfulness, Hartz (2012) informs us, one can overcome depression through awareness and acceptance of the reality of one's life, including the negative thoughts and feelings that one experiences. [195] Furthermore, mindfulness meditation has been shown to help overweight/obese adults to make healthier choices in terms of eating and losing weight (Spadaro 2008),[196] and it can help us to get better sleep, since, Emet (2012) argues, while the unconscious mind controls our ability to sleep, it is the conscious mind which prepares us for sleep. [197] As the health benefits of meditation continue to be explored, I am sure additional insights and new approaches will be discovered to enhance the efficacy of meditation for health improvement. In addition, the role of meditation in achieving happiness and tranquillity merits further research.

> **"Without knowledge there is no meditation, without meditation there is no knowledge: he who has knowledge and meditation is near unto Nirvâna... as soon as he has considered the origin and destruction of the elements of the body, he finds happiness and joy which belong to those who know the immortal (Nirvâna)... The Bhikkhu (i.e. monk), full of delight, who is calm in the doctrine of Buddha will reach the quiet place (Nirvâna), cessation of natural desires, and happiness."[198]**

- Gautama Buddha, *The Dhammapada*, Chapter XXV., v. 372, 374, 381.

In the next chapter, we will discuss the First Way to Meditate: Mindfulness Meditation.

Questions for Reflection:

The following are some questions that will help us to reflect on what we have learned in this chapter:

1. According to the Diamond Sutra, how is meditation a way of life?

2. What is *samādhi* and how can it be achieved?

3. What are some of the benefits of meditation for the individual?

4. What is 'enkindlement'? How does meditation help us to achieve it?

5. What is the real purpose and ultimate goal of life?

∞∞∞∞∞∞∞∞∞∞∞∞∞∞∞∞∞∞∞∞∞∞∞∞∞∞

III. The First Way to Meditate – Mindfulness Meditation

"Let a brother, O mendicants, be mindful and thoughtful; this is our instruction to you... Herein, O mendicants, let a brother, as he dwells in the body, so regard the body that he, being strenuous, thoughtful, and mindful, may, whilst in the world, overcome the grief which arises from bodily craving—while subject to sensations, let him continue so to regard the sensations that he, being strenuous, thoughtful, and mindful, may, whilst in the world, overcome the grief arising from the craving—which follows our sensation—and so also as he thinks or reasons or feels let him overcome the grief which arises from the craving due to ideas, or reasoning, or feeling...

"He acts, O mendicants, in full presence of mind whatever he may do, in coming out and coming in, in looking and watching, in bending in his arm or stretching it forth, in wearing his robes or carrying his bowl, in eating and drinking, in consuming or tasting, in walking or standing or sitting, in sleeping or waking, in talking and in being silent.

"Thus let a brother, O mendicants, be mindful and thoughtful; this is our instruction to you."[199]

- Gautama Buddha, *Mahâ-Parinibbâna-Suttanta*, Chapter II, v. 13 - 15.

Introduction

In an article on Equanimity Blog, entitled 'How can we achieve true happiness and inner peace?', I have defined right mindfulness as "attaining a higher awareness of what surrounds us, and our own inner beings, such that we recognize and remain aware of our whole bodies and what we are doing, our breathing, and the reality around us. We remain aware of the impermanence and insignificance of the material world and remember the essential nobility of man and our inner, spiritual nature."[200] Mindfulness meditation is an ancient Buddhist method of meditation which is becoming increasingly popular in the West. According to Gethin (2011), the Buddhist term, called *sati* in Pali, was first translated as 'mindfulness' by T.W. Rhys Davids in 1881. [201] Other translations of the word include 'memory', 'recollection', 'remembrance', or 'calling to mind'.[202] Rhys Davids remarks that "*sati* is literally 'memory,' but is used with reference to the constantly repeated phrase 'mindful and thoughtful' (*sato sampajāno*); and means the activity of mind and constant presence of mind which is one of the duties most frequently inculcated on the good Buddhist." [203] One definition of mindfulness, contained in the Milindapañha, explains that *sati* has two characteristics, *apilāpana* ('calling to mind'), i.e. calling to mind wholesome and unwholesome qualities so that one can know which ones to pursue or avoid, and *upaganhana* ('taking possession'), i.e. taking possession of those qualities which are beneficial.[204] In other words, this means the practice of avoiding vices and adopting virtues as a result of deep reflection on the nature of vice and virtue, as well as awareness of one's own qualities, strengths and shortcomings.

"But be thou at all times mindful of the Lord, and thou shalt never sin. For if such an evil thought should arise in thy heart, thou shouldst be guilty of a great sin; and they who do such things follow the way of death. Look therefore to thyself, and keep thyself from such a thought; for where chastity remains in the heart of a righteous man, there an evil thought ought never to arise."[205]

- *The Second Book of Hermas*, Command IV, v. 2.

According to developed Theravāda systematic thought,[6] called *abhidhamma*, mindfulness is more than just present-centred awareness of one's thoughts, feelings and sensations; rather, it also includes the concepts of *apilāpanatā* ('absence of floating') and *asammussanatā* ('absence of forgetfulness'). [206] Other elements of *sati* include *anussati* ('recollection'), *patissati* (recall), *saranatā* (remembrance), and *dhāranatā* ('keeping in mind').[207] Floating refers to when the mind bobs up and down like a gourd floating in water, while mindfulness alone allows us to plunge deep into the object of our awareness.[208] Forgetfulness does not refer to mere forgetting or lack of memory but, rather, to being

---

[6] Theravāda is a school or sect of Buddhism.

87

absentminded and forgetful, e.g. of one's duty to guard against the attachment of the senses.[209] Since this implies detachment from the material world, which is a spiritual practice deeply rooted in religion, I would argue that the true practice of mindfulness meditation cannot be fully secularized. Rather, it is intimately connected to the practice of right conduct, right thought, right speech, and the other moral principles of the Noble Eightfold Path of the Buddha. For more information on the Noble Eightfold Path, see Chapters II and III of *Mindfulness: Five Ways to Achieve Real Happiness, True Knowledge and Inner Peace.* [210] In brief, however, let us quote the words of the glorious Buddha, Siddhartha Gautama—may his spirit bless us with kindness and compassion, wisdom and understanding:

> **"There are two extremes, O Bhikkhus (monks), which the man who has given up the world ought not to follow—the habitual practice, on the one hand of those things whose attraction depends upon the passions, and especially of sensuality... and the habitual practice, on the other hand, of asceticism (or self-mortification), which is painful, unworthy, and unprofitable.**
>
> **"There is a middle path, O Bhikkhus, avoiding these two extremes, discovered by the Tathâgata[7]— a path which opens the eyes, and bestows understanding, which leads to peace of mind, to**

---

7 i.e. the Buddha.

the higher wisdom, to full enlightenment, to Nirvâna! What is that middle path, O Bhikkhus, avoiding these two extremes, discovered by the Tathâgata—that path which opens the eyes, and bestows understanding, which leads to peace of mind, to the higher wisdom, to full enlightenment, to Nirvâna? Verily! it is this noble eightfold path, that is to say: Right views; Right aspirations; Right speech; Right conduct; Right livelihood; Right effort; Right mindfulness; and Right contemplation.

"This, O Bhikkhus, is that middle path, avoiding these two extremes, discovered by the Tathâgata— that path which opens the eyes, and bestows understanding, which leads to peace of mind, to the higher wisdom, to full enlightenment, to Nirvâna!"[211]

- Gautama Buddha, *Dhamma-Kakka-Ppavattana-Sutta*, v. 2 – 4.

Mindfulness meditation has, however, been adapted by Kabat-Zinn and other practitioners as an education and training tool for people who suffer from psychological and emotional stress, as well as chronic health problems (Crane et al. 2016). Kabat-Zinn defines mindfulness as "the awareness that arises through paying attention on purpose in the present moment, and non-judgmentally."[212] Kabat-Zinn went on to publish a series of books on mindfulness, including *Wherever You Go, There You*

Are: Mindfulness Meditation in Everyday Life.[213] In this book, he explains that the key to mindfulness is appreciation of the present moment, instead of taking life for granted.[214] Too many people, Kabat-Zinn (2001) argues, are lacking in awareness of how our mind works and how it can influence our perceptions and actions, thus limiting our perspective on our reality as human beings and how we are connected one to another. Kabat-Zinn argues, furthermore, that, while mindfulness meditation is a Buddhist practice, one does not have to be Buddhist to practice it. Rather, he says, it is simply 'the art of conscious living.'[215] From this perspective, mindfulness practices are ideologically and religiously neutral, since they are universally-applicable and relate to a systematic process of self-observation, self-inquiry and mindful action.[216] How does he recommend that we practice mindfulness? I would summarize Kabat-Zinn's practice as follows: first of all, we must pay attention, being aware of what we are doing; secondly, we can focus our attention on the present moment by bringing our awareness to our breathing; thirdly, we commit to be present in every moment, observing ourselves and our surroundings without reaction or judging; fourthly, we can take up a formal meditation practice every day; and, fifthly, we should avoid the temptation to constantly talk about meditation, advertising our own experience of meditation.[217]

The main therapies which have been developed based on mindfulness include Mindfulness-Based Stress Reduction (MBSR) and Mindfulness-Based Cognitive Therapy (MBCT), drawing on a confluence of sources, including the contemplative tradition of Buddhism, as well as advances in medicine, psychology and education.[218] According to Crane et al. (2016), these programs are characterized by the development of a focus on the present moment, 'de-centring,' and 'an approach orientation'. It also fosters the development of positive qualities, such as equanimity, joy, compassion and wisdom.[219] Some of the common features of the practice of mindfulness which Crane et al. (2016) identify include an acknowledgement that habitual reactive patterns, fear, denial and 'discrepancy-based thinking' both create and exacerbate one's experience of stress, and that the development of greater awareness of one's self and others can lead to freedom from reactivity.[220] Gethin (2011) observes that, in the practice of MBSR and MBCT, the definition of mindfulness used is somewhat minimalist, being based on one particular tradition of Buddhism.[221] In the Buddhist context, he explains, there are four ways of establishing mindfulness, which are achieved through abandoning the 'five hindrances' and developing the 'seven constituents of awakening.'[222] This chapter will focus on the traditional Buddhist practice of mindfulness meditation, rather than the mindfulness-based therapies pioneered by Kabat-Zinn.

The Buddhist Practice of Mindfulness Meditation

According to Nyanaponika Thera (2005), Buddha described *satipatthāna* ('the way of mindfulness') as *ekāyano maggo*, i.e. the 'only way'. As such, mindfulness may also be described as *dhamma-hadaya*, i.e. the 'heart of the entire doctrine.'[223] The aim and highest goal of mindfulness, Thera explains, is nothing short of attainment of the highest goal of Buddha's teaching itself, which is Nirvāna ('enlightenment'). This is the final achievement of detachment from the material world

91

and liberation from suffering. [224] The first thing we should remember, Thera (2005) informs us, is that the mind is the starting point while the mind of the liberated saint is the culminating point of the journey to perfection.[225] As Buddha says in the *Dhammapada*: **"All that we are is the result of what we have thought: it is founded on our thoughts, it is made up of our thoughts. If a man speaks or acts with an evil thought, pain follows him, as the wheel follows the foot of the ox that draws the carriage. All that we are is the result of what we have thought: it is founded on our thoughts, it is made up of our thoughts. If a man speaks or acts with a pure thought, happiness follows him, like a shadow that never leaves him."**[226] The mind is the source of all evil, and it is also the source of all good, as all actions find their ultimate origins in the mind. As such, Thera (2005) identifies three key elements of the Buddha's 'doctrine of the mind', viz. to know the mind, to shape the mind, and to free the mind.[227] The key to achieving these three things is meditation.

Figure 7. Bronze figure of a Yogi in meditation

8

The Basics – Location, Setting and Posture

Now, let us begin the practice of mindfulness meditation (MM). There is no better way to understand it than to try it, so here are some steps that you can follow. We will begin by outlining mindfulness meditation in its most basic form. The following steps have been adapted from several sources, including the five steps outlined by Thích Nhât Hanh (b. 1926), a Vietnamese Buddhist monk and peace activist, who has published more than 100 books, including more than 40 in English, [228] Joseph Goldstein's *Mindfulness: A Practical Guide to Awakening*, and Nyanaponika Thera's *The Heart of Buddhist Meditation*. Hanh belongs to the Zen tradition of Buddhism, called *Thiên* in Vietnamese and *Chán* in Chinese, [229] all of which derive from the Sanskrit term for meditation, *dhyāna* (Pali *jhāna*).[230] Before we begin, however, we need to ensure that we have the right posture and environment in which to meditate. We should meditate in a quiet location, away from the hustle and bustle of the world, preferably in one's own bedroom or some other quiet place. It could be in a garden, a park or even on the beach or by the lakeside. In the Bhagavad-Gita, Krishna says: **"Sequestered should he sit, steadfastly meditating, solitary, his thoughts controlled, his passions laid away, quit of belongings."**[231]

Meditation can be performed while sitting or standing, but let us first focus on the posture of sitting. Traditionally, one meditates on the floor, usually on a thick mat for comfort, with an erect posture, with a straight back and relaxed shoulders. If we are unable to maintain this posture, we can rest with our backs against the wall. The traditional method of sitting involves crossing our legs. For many neophytes, this may prove difficult, but, with continued practice, it becomes easier to do. For now, if you find this difficult, you can sit on your knees or with legs outstretched.

Figure 8: The Easy Pose (sukhasana)

9

The easiest way to cross our legs is called the 'easy pose,' in which our legs are loosely crossed with both feet resting below the opposite knee or thigh. The *sukhasana* ('easy pose') simply involves sitting cross-legged with both feet laying on the floor in a relaxed position.[232] The following steps are adapted from Mehdi (2016). We should first, sit straight with feet outstretched before us. Next, we cross our legs in such a manner that our knees are bent and legs tucked into our torso. Our feet should be relaxed, with the outer edges resting on the floor and the inner edges on the arch of your shins. There should be a comfortable space between the pelvis and our feet. We should next place our palms on our lap, one resting on the other, or rest them on our knees.[233] According to Renjie (2017b), the benefits of this pose include that it keeps the spine straight, and it creates a clear channel for one's breath. [10] The Shambhala Buddhist practitioner and teacher, Rinzler (2015), recommends this method in his online article on meditation postures. Other methods include the half lotus, the full lotus, the Burmese position and the *seiza*.

---

[10] See: Qiao Renjie (2017b) *Yoga: 25 Yoga Poses for Weight Loss, Health, and Inner Peace* (ebook). Available online at: https://www.amazon.com/dp/B071F9Y6CY/ (accessed 18/05/2017), 23. Easy Pose (Sukhasana), p. 84.

Figure 9: The half lotus position

The half lotus is similar to the quarter lotus, but with one foot resting on the opposite thigh. This is slightly more difficult but still manageable for the beginner.

---

[11] Image source: Srila Bhaktivinoda Thakur (1838 – 1914 CE). Uploaded on 3 April 2008 (public domain image). Available online at: https://upload.wikimedia.org/wikipedia/commons/5/5e/Bhaktivinoda_Thakura .jpg (accessed 18/05/2017).

Figure 10: The full lotus position (padmasana)

Next comes the 'full lotus,' which is the one most people associate with meditation and yoga. It involves crossing one's legs with both feet resting on the opposite thighs.[234] Kaiten Nukariya (1913), an expert on Zen Buddhism, gives the following instructions for performing this posture:

"Seat yourself on a thick cushion, putting it right under your haunch. Keep your body so erect that the tip of the nose and the navel are in one perpendicular line, and both ears and shoulders are in the same plane. Then place the right foot upon the left thigh, the left foot on the right thigh, so as the legs come across each other. Next put your right hand with the palm upward on the left foot, and your left hand on the right palm with the tops of both the thumbs touching each other. This is the posture called the crossed-leg sitting."[235]

- Kaiten Nukariya, *The Religion of the Samurai*, Chapter VIII.

Figure 11: The Burmese position

The Burmese position, which is similar to the 'easy pose' mentioned above, involves sitting in a cross-legged position with the left heel inside your right thigh and your right heel lightly

---

[13] Image source: Medita PoA 2014-10-25. Created by Eugenio Hansen, OFS, 1 January 2010 (own work). (CC BY-SA 4.0). Available online at: https://upload.wikimedia.org/wikipedia/commons/a/a3/Medita_PoA_2014-10-25_17.JPG (accessed 18/05/2017). For more information on the license, see: https://creativecommons.org/licenses/by-sa/4.0/deed.en

touching the top of your left foot, calf or ankle, such that it sits in front of you.[236] If you do not feel comfortable, you can sit on the front half of a cushion or pillow, and a pillow or blanket can also be used to give extra support to your knees, if necessary.

Figure 12: The seiza method

The *seiza* method is also quite simple. Instead of sitting on one's legs, the practitioner should prop a cushion or yoga mat under the thighs and kneel on another thick mat or yoga mat.[237] This pose is also known as the *virasana* or 'hero pose'.[238] For more information on meditation poses and yoga poses used in

[14] Image source: Jimbo Wales wearing Kimono, taken in Kyoto, Japan, 13 March 2007. Image by Azuncha – self-published (CC BY-SA 3.0). Available online at: https://upload.wikimedia.org/wikipedia/commons/0/0b/JimmyWales_wearing _Kimono.jpg (accessed 18/05/2017). For more information on the license, see: https://creativecommons.org/licenses/by-sa/3.0/

meditation, check out *Yoga: 25 Poses for Weight Loss, Health and Inner Peace*, by Qiao Renjie (2017b).

The second point of posture mentioned by Rinzler is to elongate one's spine. As Nukariya states above, the body should be "so erect that the tip of the nose and the navel are in one perpendicular line," and "both ears and shoulders are in the same plane."[239] Rinzler gives the analogy of an arrow or a stack of coins, one on top of another, as if a rod were placed through one's head and down through to the bottom.[240] This helps to keep us alert and focused.

Figure 13: Buddhist monk in meditation

15

The third point of posture is to rest one's hands on one's lap. Nukariya instructs that we should rest our right hand with

---

palm facing upwards on our left foot (in the full lotus position), while our right hand, in the same manner, rests on our left foot. The two thumbs should touch one another.[241] However, it should be noted that Kilung Rinpoche (2015) suggests that we drop our palms down on our thighs, as sitting with our palms facing downwards tends to relax the flow of energy as it circulates throughout our bodies.[242] Rinpoche also mentions that the great, 14th century Tibetan Buddhist Dzogchen teacher, Longchenpa (Longchen Rabjam) was known for using this position.[243]

Figure 14: Longchen Rabjampa (1308 – 1364)

Fourth, we should relax our shoulders—letting all the muscles in our shoulders and back relax. The shoulders should be pushed back, helping to establish a strong back and an open chest. Fifth, we should tuck in our chin. Sixth, we should relax our face muscles so that the jaw hangs open, with the tongue against the roof of the mouth to allow for clear breathing and to slow down our swallowing, which can distract us from our meditation. Seventh and lastly, we should 'relax our gaze'. This means that we should gaze two to four feet ahead of us—slightly downwards—in an unfocused manner. Rinpoche advises that, if you start to feel sleepy, then it is useful to lift your gaze slightly. If we feel energetic, however, it may be useful to lower the gaze a bit.[244] Our eyes remain open, but we do not focus on anything in particular. The point is to stay mindful of the world we live in, and it also helps to avoid falling asleep.[245]

> **"The ice is mindful of that extreme cold,**
>
> **And even in winter that crop is mindful of the summer.**
>
> **In like manner, O son, every member of your body**
>
> **Tells you tales of God's bounties to your body."[246]**
>
> - Rūmī, *The Masnavī*, Book VI., Story V.

Mindfulness Meditation – Steps

Step 1: Mindful Breathing

In the *Mahā-Satipatthāna-Sutta*, which Clarke (1896) translates as 'The Four Intent Contemplations,' Gautama Buddha (peace be upon him) asked his disciples rhetorically: **"And how, O priests, does a priest live, as respects the body, observant of the body?"** [247] He then gives us the answer: **"Whenever, O priests, a priest, retiring to the forest, or to the foot of a tree, or to an uninhabited spot, sits him down cross-legged with body erect and contemplative faculty intent, and contemplates his expirations, and contemplates his inspirations..."** [248] The practitioner of mindfulness thus lives **"unattached, nor clings to anything in the world."**[249] Mindfulness of breathing may seem a simple step, but it is a potent one. When we breathe in, we remain mindful that our inhalation and exhalation are inhalation and exhalation. When we breathe in, we acknowledge that it is our breath, and when we breathe out, we acknowledge that we are breathing out. This sounds incredibly simple—and it is, but it has a profound effect. What recognizes the inhalation is our mind, and the breathing—in itself—is the object of our mindfulness. To be mindful, we must be mindful of something. That s*omething* is called 'the object of mindfulness'.[250] According to Thera (2005), rather than being an exercise in breathing, as practised in yoga, mindfulness in breathing means simply the quiet observation of the natural flow of our breathing, including the length or shortness of breath. Regular practice will result in a calmer, more equalizing flow of breath without conscious effort to regulate it.[251]

Mindfulness of breathing allows us to develop our ability to concentrate, quieten our mental unrest and irritation and obtain a higher level of focus.[252] Hanh (2015) points out that this helps us to stop our mental discourse—to stop *thinking* and focus, instead, on the way we breathe. Not only that, but we start to enjoy our inhalation, and the practice becomes pleasant and joyful. We realise that we are alive—we are breathing—and appreciate the great miracle that is life. [253] This acknowledgement—this recognition—brings us to a state of happiness and acceptance—of radiant tranquillity—as we achieve the first level of mindfulness. Buddha says:

> **"O priests, a priest, in making a long expiration thoroughly comprehends the long expiration he is making, and in making a long inspiration thoroughly comprehends the long inspiration he is making, and in making a short expiration thoroughly comprehends the short expiration he is making, and in making a short inspiration thoroughly comprehends the short inspiration he is making, and trains himself to be conscious of all his expirations, and trains himself to be conscious of all his inspirations, and trains himself to quiet his expirations, and trains himself to quiet his inspirations."[254]**

- Gautama Buddha, *Mahā-Satipatthāna-Sutta*

In Hinduism, the practice of controlling one's breathing is referred to as *prānāyāma*, which literally means the control of *prāna*,[255] i.e. the cosmic energy which permeates the universe, similar to the Chinese concept of *qi* which we mentioned earlier. According to Vivekananda (1920), in his book on *rāja yoga*, the entire universe is made of one substance, called *ākāśa*, and everything is manufactured or created by the power of *prāna*. Both of these are infinite and omnipresent, but all the material forms eventually dissolve and return to *ākāśa*, from which they are again manifested in innumerable forms.[256] Vivekananda taught that *prāna* is "the vital life force in every being, and the finest and highest action of Prâna is thought."[257] Thought, therefore, is a manifestation of this life-energy which flows through everything.

The first step in controlling *prāna*, and thus controlling one's thoughts, is the control of one's lungs. Vivekananda recommends breathing in a measured way, in and out, in order to harmonise the system. As the breath starts to become rhythmic and harmonious, one will find that the whole body becomes rhythmic and harmonious. This leads to a complete state of relaxation, and can be accompanied by the mental (or verbal) repetition of the sacred syllable *Om*, or another sacred word.[258] The Hindu practice is not strictly related to the Buddhist practice of mindfulness meditation, but I mention it here because of its relation to the positive results of focusing on breathing. I do not see any hard and fast divisions between the various religious traditions, which are all inspired by the same mystic Force which governs and generates all created things.

The next exercise is to focus on one's breath, concentrating on each inhalation and exhalation. If we breathe in for three or four seconds, then our mindfulness lasts three or four seconds. When we breathe out, we mentally follow our breath as it passes out of the body. In both our inhalation and exhalation, the mind is always present. Uninterrupted mindfulness on one's breathing leads to improved concentration.[259]

Step 2: Mindfulness of Postures

"But again, O priests, a priest, in walking thoroughly comprehends his walking, and in standing thoroughly comprehends his standing, and in sitting thoroughly comprehends his sitting, and in lying down thoroughly comprehends his lying down, and in whatever state his body may be thoroughly comprehends that state.

"Thus he lives, either in his own person, as respects the body, observant of the body, or in other persons, as respects the body, observant of the body, or both in his own person and in other persons, as respects the body, observant of the body; either observant of origination in the body, or observant of destruction in the body, or observant of both origination and destruction in the body; and the recognition of the body by his intent contemplation is merely to the extent of this knowledge, merely to the extent of this contemplation, and he lives unattached, nor clings to anything in the world.

"Thus, O priests, does a priest live, as respects the body, observant of the body."[260]

- Gautama Buddha, *Mahā-Satipatthāna-Sutta*.

The next exercise is to become aware of one's body and posture as one is breathing. We become aware and mindful that the body is there. Our heart is beating, our blood is flowing, we have eyes, ears, a nose, mouth, etc. Our mind and body become one reality, as we become fully aware and fully cognizant of who we are and the wonders of life which surround us. Being mindful of one's mind and body allows us to be fully present. Often, we are present in body but absent in mind. By becoming mindful of the body, we recognise that the two are interconnected and we truly live in the moment. Hanh (2015) then advises us to release the tension in our bodies. We consciously make the decision to release our tension and then say to ourselves: 'I release the tension in my body.'[261]

In *Mindfulness: A Practical Guide to Awakening*, Goldstein (2013) observes that noticing our movement from one posture to the next helps to strengthen the continuity of our mindfulness. [262] The practice is simplicity itself. We simply maintain an awareness of our different postures as we sit, stand, walk, etc. When we stand, we know how we stand. When we walk, we pay attention to how we walk. This also tells a lot about our states of mind throughout the day. If we rush, for example, it could be that we are in a state of anticipation. Goldstein also remarks that mindfulness of posture helps us to remain aware of the *anicca*, ('impermanence') of our movements. It also helps us to remember the *dukkha* ('unsatisfactoriness') of the material world. Almost all movements, we soon realize, are intended to alleviate pain or discomfort. When we focus on our movements, we thus become continually aware of our movements, we likewise become aware of the impermanence within our lives, that all things change and pass away, and that there is no point in being attached to anything material. We become selfless as we observe the body as something we do not truly own.[263] We should look upon the body objectively, just as one looks upon the posture and movement of a puppet. Our attention should constantly return to that of the body, whenever our focus wanders away from the objects of mindfulness.[264] Like a pair of clothes, we will eventually have to discard the body when it is worn out and no longer functional. This frees us from the need to possess, covet and envy others, and stops us from desiring material things.

Step 3: Mindfulness of Activities

> **"But again, O priests, a priest, in advancing and retiring has an accurate comprehension of what he does; in looking and gazing has an accurate comprehension of what he does; in drawing in his arm and in stretching out his arm has an accurate comprehension of what he does; in wearing his cloak, his bowl, and his robes has an accurate comprehension of what he does; in eating, drinking, chewing, and tasting has an accurate comprehension of what he does; in easing his bowels and his bladder has an accurate comprehension of what he does; in walking, standing, sitting, sleeping, waking, talking, and being silent has an accurate comprehension of what he does."[265]**

> - Gautama Buddha, *Mahā-Satipatthāna-Sutta*

This next step, according to Goldstein, involves *sampajañña* ('clearly knowing'), which is also translated as 'clear comprehension.'[266] This involves extending our focus to all the different functions of the body—to our postures, movement, dressing, eating, drinking, speaking, silence, wakefulness and sleep, etc. Thera (2005) discusses four kinds of clear comprehension: (1) clear comprehension of purpose, (2) clear comprehension of suitability, (3) clear comprehension of the domain of meditation, and (4) clear comprehension of reality.[267]

Goldstein refers to these as four ways of training oneself to develop this quality of mind. The first is to clearly know the purpose of doing an action before we do it, understanding whether it is *truly* beneficial to ourselves or others. This allows us to clearly examine our motivations and helps us to develop a clear level of discernment. Since we often act on impulse or without thought regarding the true reason behind our actions, we often lack a clear awareness of *why* we really do what we do.

The second training is to know the suitability of an action. Is our action wholesome or unwholesome? Will it lead to suffering, or will it help others? Will it lead to vice or the practice of virtue? This relates quite directly to the Buddha's teachings on right speech, right thoughts and right actions. As mentioned in the previous book in the *Ways to Be* series: "Our intentions should be threefold: detachment from all things, good will towards all things, and harmlessness towards all things. These are the three things that should be our focus when dealing with others, or with the world at large, including the environment and animals. If we intend to detach ourselves, to renounce all that is ephemeral, then we are freeing ourselves from the cause of suffering. We abandon lust, idleness and delusion. If we have good will for all things, then we will help and truly love other human beings, we will care for and be compassionate to animals and other creatures, and we will care for the environment in which we live. Good will is all-embracing, like a river which has burst its banks. The water of good will flows over all things and encompasses all things. It is the basis of real love, which is attraction to the inner reality of things."[268]

The third training is to clearly understand the proper 'domain of meditation', which Goldstein refers to as the 'proper pastures' of our meditation practice. In the *Satipatthāna Sutta*, the Buddha outlines four fields of mindfulness, viz. the body, feelings, mind and the categories of experience. In other words, we should focus our mindfulness on these four areas, so that we can remain mindful and thus avoid attachment to the material world.

Lastly, the fourth training is to develop clear comprehension of the reality of things. Goldstein calls this 'non-delusion,' i.e. seeing clearly the impermanent, unreliable and selfless nature of all phenomena in existence.[269] Everything that exists, from the smallest atom of creation even until the most massive star in the sky, will cease to exist. Every particle of creation had a beginning, in the moment that time and space in our universe exploded into existence, and every atom in existence will eventually break down and be disintegrated, because all composite or component things are subject to dissolution. Our bodies are not truly 'selves'—they will disintegrate after a mere span of several decades, when we die either from natural or

116

unnatural causes. Even throughout that time, they continually change and are renewed. The cells within our bodies die and are renewed all the time, and our sense of self alters from one moment to the next as we move along a continuum of time. Are we the same self that we were 10 years ago, or 20 years ago, or five minutes ago? The self is as illusory as the bodies we live in. The only thing that endures is our higher reality—the soul—and the only way to achieve true liberation is to die to ourselves (*fanā'*, i.e. the annihilation of self and passion) and live in that higher reality which is called Nirvāna, *baqā'* or the Paradise of reunion with the Divine Beloved. This is true knowledge and true understanding.

Step 4: Mindfulness of the Parts of the Body

We then focus our attention on the actual component parts of the body. By visualizing the parts of the body, we gradually become aware of the impermanent nature of each part and develop a growing sense of detachment from the body and its imperfections.[270] What is there to be attached to? What is truly lasting about a biological organism, which is nothing more than a collection of animate cells composed of inanimate matter? And what animates these cells but a temporary impulse which, when the cell has reached the end of its lifespan, fizzles out and leads to inevitable disintegration? Our physical bodies are nothing more than the sum of their parts. Buddha tells us:

> **"But again, O priests, a priest, considers this body upwards from the soles of the feet, and downwards from the crown of the head, enclosed by skin, and full of all manner of uncleanness,**

117

saying, 'There is in this body hair of the head, hair of the body, nails, teeth, skin, flesh, sinew, bone, marrow of the bones, kidneys, heart, liver, pleura, spleen, lungs, intestines, mesentery, stomach, faeces, bile, phlegm, pus, blood, sweat, fat, tears, lymph, saliva, snot, synovial fluid, urine.'"[271]

- Gautama Buddha, *Mahā-Satipatthāna-Sutta*

As we contemplate the body and all its constituent parts, Goldstein informs us, we become cognizant of the impermanence and contingent nature of all of them. We understand that what we call the body is, in reality, an interdependent structure consisting of the various organs, bones and other elements which make up one functioning system.[272] This body cannot be called a 'self'; rather, it is simply a vehicle for the soul. As Krishna informs us: **"The elements, the conscious life, the mind, the unseen vital force, the nine strange gates of the body, and the five domains of sense; desire, dislike, pleasure and pain, and thought, deep-woven, and persistency of being; these all are wrought on Matter by the Soul!"** [273] When we recognize that the body is simply a collection of matter which is vitalized and moved by some higher power—a higher self—then we realize that it is, in reality, nothing more than a suit of clothes which, when put it aside, will dissolve into each of its constituent parts. How often have we looked upon a skeleton or a mummy in a museum, and reflected that we are nothing more than *that*? Those bones—that skeleton—is the same as the skeleton which holds our body together. What difference is there? And in a hundred year's time, what will be left of our bodies and the constituent parts which constitute them? The flesh will have long since rotted away and all that will remain, if anything remains, are the mouldering bones which rest within our graves. For some, nothing but ashes will remain, blown away by the wind and dissolved into the earth, air and water.

Step 5: Mindfulness of the Four Elements

"But again, O priests, a priest takes this body, whatever it may be doing, or however it may be situated, and considers it according to the elements of which it is composed, saying, 'There are in this body the elements earth, water, fire, and wind." Just as, O priests, a skilful butcher, or butcher's apprentice, having slaughtered a heifer, divides her into pieces, and stations himself at a place where four roads meet; in exactly the same way, O priests, a priest takes this body, whatever it may be doing, or however it may be situated, and considers it according to the elements of which it is composed, saying, 'There are in this body the elements earth, water, fire, and wind.'"[274]

- Gautama Buddha, *Mahā-Satipatthāna-Sutta*

The next step is to meditate on the four elements. This meditation reduces the body into the four primary elements of matter, which helps us to understand, at a deeper level, the impermanence of the physical form. [275] Thera (2005) also mentions 'cemetery contemplations', which involves observing the forms of dead bodies, bringing one's awareness to the self-deception that body belongs to you. Rather, the body is a temporary vehicle which is discarded at the moment of death. In the same *Sutta*, Buddha says: **"But again, O priests, a priest, if perchance he sees in a cemetery a decaying body being eaten by crows, or being eaten by eagles, or being eaten by vultures, or being eaten by dogs, or being eaten by jackals, or being eaten by various kinds of insects, he compares his own body, saying, 'Verily, my body also has this nature, this destiny, and is not exempt.'"**[276] When we contemplate death, we realize that there is no real difference between the knucklebone of a thief or a pauper and the knucklebone of a king or emperor. What was the difference between the two? The pauper lived his days in distress and poverty, not enjoying any of the fruits of material existence, while the king lived in the most opulent of palaces, enjoying every delight and frivolity. But both states of being were temporary, and the king's state of being was actually worse than the pauper's, the reason being that pauper was not attached to material pleasures which he did not experience, while the king was attached to material pleasures and lost them at the moment of death. In the end, the fate of both was the same, and the king's life was wrapped up like a scroll which is discarded and cast into a furnace. Buddha tells us:

> **"Soon will this body lie upon the ground, deserted, and bereft of sense, like a log cast aside."**[277]

> - Gautama Buddha, *The Dhammapada*, v. 41.

According to Goldstein (2013), the earth element represents solidity and hardness, the water element represents cohesion and fluidity, the fire element represents both hot and cold temperature, and the air element represents expansion and extension. Meditating on these four elements also helps to avoid the conceit of imagining 'I am,' 'I was,' and 'I will be', which are each rooted in ignorance and the notion of a continuing ownership of the body. When we see the body as a mere collection of elements, this conceit vanishes and we realise that this sense of selfhood in the material form is illusory.[278] As the Greek-speaking philosopher, Plotinus (c. 204/5 – 270 CE), writes in the *Enneads*: "All that we see, and describe as having existence, we know to be compound; hand-wrought or compacted by nature, nothing is simplex."[279] Material forms, by their nature, are combined and dissolved and have no real permanence. Even the most basic building blocks of matter, such as atoms, can be split and divided. Furthermore, most of their composition is empty space, filled with fields and forces that can be dispersed or divided. Since everything material is compound and subject to disintegration, the only true reality is spiritual, since the spirit is simplex and uncompounded.

Step 6: Mindfulness of Feelings

The Pali term *vedanā* refers to 'feeling,' meaning any sensation, whether physical or mental, pleasant or unpleasant. Feelings give rise to passion and passion to unwholesome attachment and activities. When one becomes aware of one's feelings, Thera (2005) instructs us, we can allow them to gradually fade away and give room for another feeling to arise, so that we are never carried away by the winds of self and passion.[280] We can also extend our awareness to the feelings of others, allowing us to observe them and compare them with our own feelings.[281] Buddha says

> **"And how, O priests, does a priest live, as respects sensations, observant of sensations? Whenever, O priests, a priest, in experiencing a pleasant sensation thoroughly comprehends the pleasant sensation he is experiencing, and in experiencing an unpleasant sensation... an interested and indifferent sensation..."[282]**

- Gautama Buddha, *Mahā-Satipatthāna-Sutta*.

We become mindful when we recognise each pleasant feeling and acknowledge that feeling, and when we recognise each unpleasant feeling and acknowledge *that* feeling—and even neutral feelings; we acknowledge these as well.[283] As we recognise the coming and going, the passing and fleeting nature of our feelings and emotions, we begin to lose attachment to them, since they are ephemeral and evanescent, like a soap bubble on a clear summer's day, or a mist rising and disappearing as the sun's rays lift over the horizon on a cool, crisp morn. All feelings, whether pleasant, unpleasant or neutral, are impermanent and pass away. When we recognise this, we become immune to the ebb and flow of pleasure and pain, which rise and fall like the tide. We transcend material limitations and the strictures of our minds, and enter a state of peacefulness and tranquillity. As Krishna says in the Bhagavad-Gita: **"Yea! whoso, shaking off the yoke of** flesh lives lord, not servant, of his lusts; set free from pride, from passion, from the sin of 'Self,' toucheth tranquillity!"[284] It takes time and effort to become detached from one's body, feelings, and material concerns. In the Dhammapada, Buddha refers to this gradual process of purifying mind and body through detachment: **"Let a wise man blow off the impurities of his self, as a smith blows off the impurities of silver one by one, little by little, and from time to time."**[285]

Step 7: Mindfulness of the Mind

"And how, O priests, does a priest live, as respects the mind, observant of the mind? Whenever, O priests, a priest, in having a passionate mind thoroughly comprehends that passionate mind, or in having a mind free from passion . . . a mind full of hatred . . . a mind free from hatred . . . an infatuated mind . . . a mind free from infatuation . . . an intent mind . . . a wandering mind . . . an exalted mind . . . an unexalted mind . . . an inferior mind . . . a superior mind . . . a concentrated mind . . . an unconcentrated mind . . . an emancipated mind . . . an unemancipated mind thoroughly comprehends that unemancipated mind... Thus, O priests, does a priest live, as respects the mind, observant of the mind."[286]

- Gautama Buddha, *Mahā-Satipatthāna-Sutta.*

Next comes contemplation of one's state of mind. Here, we become aware of the state our conscious minds. We observe the state of our minds, allowing the facts to speak for themselves, rather than becoming enmeshed in introspection, self-justifications and self-accusations which do not lead to fruitful results.[287] This will, according to Thera (2005), help us to assess our progress and our failures.[288] According to Goldstein (2013), the Buddha emphasizes the importance of recognizing three unwholesome roots of mind, viz. greed/lust, hatred (including anger), and delusion/ignorance. We should recognize these three unwholesome attributes and their absence. We should also appreciate and be aware of their absence, when they are absent, and appreciate the peace and openness of mind that this brings us.[289]

Contemplation of mind also includes awareness of the rising and passing of various states of mind. According to Anālayo (2003), the Buddha identified categories for the contemplation of the mind, including four ordinary and four higher states of mind. The four ordinary states of mind he lists are lustful (*sarāga*), angry (*sadosa*), deluded (*samoha*) and distracted (*vikkhitta*), while the four higher states of mind are great (*mahaggata*), unsurpassable (*anuttara*), concentrated (*samāhita*) and liberated (*vimutta*).[290] According to Thepyanmongkol (2012), the practice of Dhamma (Sanskrit *Dharma*) or 'religion' is not pure unless it is practised without lust (*virāgadhamma*).[291] Lust is attachment to sexual desire, which leads us to impurify our minds and actions. It is one of the strongest forms of attachment to material objects and, hence, one of the biggest barriers to attaining a state of inner peace and liberation. Too often, in our modern world, we are bombarded with sexuality and are taught the mantra that sexuality in all its forms should be embraced openly. However, this embrace of sexual attachment leads to suffering, and only detachment can bring us true liberation. Anger, likewise, leads to pain and suffering, as do delusion and distractedness, which are the opposites of wisdom and mindfulness.

The term 'great', here, refers to what Nyanaponika and Hecker (2012) call the 'exalted liberation of mind' (*mahaggatā cetovimutti*), which involves widening one's inner perception from a limited extent to a vast extent.[292] The term 'unsurpassable' refers to a state of unsurpassable equanimity and mindfulness. The 'concentrated' state of mind refers to a person who has achieved full concentration and absorption. Finally, the 'liberated' mind refers to achieving a state of full liberation or 'awakening', in which one has overcome lust, anger, delusion, etc. forever. However, it can also mean temporary freedom or liberation from defilements during the process of meditation. This state of freedom of the mind is called *cetovimutti*.[293] Krishna tells us: **"Only with him, great Prince! whose senses are not swayed by things of sense—only with him who holds his mastery, shows wisdom perfect."**[294]

Step 8: Mindfulness of Thought / Mental Contents

Now, we come to the contemplation of mental contents, i.e. the contents of thought.[295] This involves, first of all, being mindful of and thus overcoming the 'five hindrances', which are: (1) sensuality, (2) anger or ill-will, (3) sloth and torpor, (4) restlessness and remorse, and (5) doubt. The practitioner becomes aware of each of these hindrances and whether they are present within himself. He or she also comes to realise how these hindrances arise and how to abandon them. [296] Material attachments are the cause of sorrow, misery and pain. Only by detaching oneself from the material world can one truly attain freedom and independence. True freedom is not the freedom to do whatever one wants. That kind of liberty belongs to the realm of animals, which function according to instinct, passion and the law of brute strength. Human beings, however, being possessed of higher reason and wisdom, are meant to live a life of nobility, unencumbered by the cords and chains of material attachment. As we learned in *Mindfulness: Five Ways to Achi,eve Real Happiness, True Knowledge and Inner Peace*, "real freedom is to be detached from the material and aware of spiritual reality. Attachment to the material world is a barrier between the soul—the inner being of each human—and the vast and limitless potentialities of the spiritual world... We can imagine that we are all like birds trapped within a cage. Imagine also that the door of the cage is closed, but not locked. Most of us are unaware that there is a door, and even those that are aware of the door think that it is locked. All that is required to escape from the cage is to push open the door and leave behind the cage and all that is contained therein."[297]

Buddha explains:

"Whenever, O priests, a priest, having existing in himself a sensual disposition thoroughly comprehends the sensual disposition as existing in himself, or not having existing in himself a sensual disposition thoroughly comprehends the sensual disposition as not existing in himself, and thoroughly comprehends how a sensual disposition not yet arisen may arise, and thoroughly comprehends how a sensual disposition already arisen may be abandoned, and thoroughly comprehends how a sensual disposition that has been abandoned may be kept from arising again in the future; or having existing in himself a malevolent disposition . . . a slothful and torpid disposition . . . a proud and unmannerly disposition . . . a doubting disposition thoroughly comprehends the doubting disposition as existing in himself, or not having existing in himself a doubting disposition thoroughly comprehends the doubting disposition as not existing in himself, and thoroughly comprehends how a doubting disposition not yet arisen may arise, and thoroughly comprehends how a doubting disposition already arisen may be

127

abandoned, and thoroughly comprehends how a doubting disposition that has been abandoned may be kept from arising again in the future."[298]

- Gautama Buddha, *Mahā-Satipatthāna-Sutta*.

Next, the practitioner turns his or her attention to the 'five aggregates' or 'five attachment-groups', which are: (1) 'thus its material form', (2) 'thus its origin or arising of material form', (3) 'thus the disappearance of its material form', (4) 'thus internally/its formations', and (5) 'thus its consciousness.'[299] In other words, we reflect on the nature of matter, its outward form, its origin, how it disappears, its internal structure and the nature of consciousness. This is basically a reflection on the nature of material reality and the composition and decomposition of things. For example, when we think of a silver goblet, how does it come to be? The goblet begins as an idea in the mind of the artificer, who conceives the idea of a goblet in the realm of his imagination. Then it is formed from the base substance, i.e. silver, by the craft and skill of the artificer's hand. We reflect on the composition and inner nature of the goblet, which is silver. Next, after many years of use, it is melted down by a silver merchant, who returns it to formless metal.

Likewise, if we imagine the human body, it has its origins in sexual reproduction, when the sperm and egg meet and form the embryo, which is the beginning of man's existence. This embryo becomes a babe, and the babe becomes a child. The child grows into a man, the man grows to his prime—and then he declines until he reaches old age, disease and, eventually, death.

We reflect on both the outward and inward form of the body. After many years, the body decomposes and returns to its basic elements of minerals, water and carbon. Consciousness, which is a manifestation of the soul, is an eternal element within man. It is the inner nobility of man which transcends his physical form and lasts beyond the extinction of his material body. It pervades all he thinks and conceives and imagines. It is the origin of the goblet, and it is the sustaining force which sets his body in motion.

Buddha says:

"Whenever, O priests, a priest grasps the nature of form, and how form arises, and how form perishes; the nature of sensation, and how sensation arises, and how sensation perishes; the nature of perception, and how perception arises, and how perception perishes; the nature of the predispositions, and how the predispositions arise, and how the predispositions perish; the nature of consciousness, and how consciousness arises, and how consciousness perishes."[300]

- Gautama Buddha, *Mahā-Satipatthāna-Sutta*.

Thirdly, the practitioner will focus on the 'six bases', i.e. the six internal and external sense-bases: the eye, ear, nose, tongue, body and mind; and the material form, mind, smell, tastes, tactile object and mental object. (1) He must, firstly, understand the eye; (2) he must understand the material form which is visible; (3) he must understand the ten-fold fetter that arises from dependence on the eye and forms, e.g. desire, resentment, pride, speculation, doubt, belief in rites and ceremonies, the desire to keep on living, envy, avarice and ignorance; (4) he must understand how the fetter came to be; (5) he must understand how one can abandon this fetter; and (6) he must understand how the future non-arising of the fetter comes to be.[301] What is the fetter? It is the chains and ropes which bind us—it is also the cage we referred to earlier. Desire, resentment, pride, as well as ideological attachments, attachments to rites and rituals, attachment to man-made dogmas and theologies, fantasies and illusions—all of these hold us back and keep us in a state of ignorance. As long as we worship the idle fancies of our vain imaginings—as long as we believe that the material world is the true reality and hold to the false belief that matter is the one reality of existence, then we will be bound in thick chains and fetters. Our attachment springs from desire, and desire springs from the insistent self within us. Our ignorance springs from false learning and the negative influences of society, friends, ideologues and the mass media which promotes the vicious doctrine of materialism.

Fourthly, the mindfulness practitioner must understand the seven factors of enlightenment. Kornfield (2010) lists the seven factors of enlightenment in his book, *Living Dharma: Teaching and Meditation Instructions from Twelve Theravada Masters*. Three of these, Kornfield tells us, are passive elements: (1) concentration of mind, (2) tranquillity or quietness of mind, and (3) detachment and balance of mind (in the face of change). The next three are energetic elements: (4) effort or volition to be mindful, (5) silent investigation of what is happening, and (6) rapture or intense zeal in spiritual practice. The seventh factor, according to Kornfield, is the key to spiritual practice and its development leads to automatic development of the other six factors. This factor is (7) mindfulness.[302] All progress depends on, firstly, the intention to improve oneself. This is followed by focus on our objective, singleness of purpose, and constant effort. What should be our objective? The seven factors of enlightenment are the path to true happiness and equanimity—these should be our objectives. We must learn to concentrate our mind, attain an inner stillness and peace, and detach ourselves from material things. This requires effort, conscious investigation, and an intense zeal or desire to follow the spiritual path. Lastly, we will attain a state of true mindfulness and equanimity.

The final step in mindfulness meditation is for the practitioner to understand the Four Noble Truths, which are: (1) understanding what suffering is, (2) understanding the origin of suffering, (3) understanding the end of suffering, and (4) understanding the way which leads to the end of suffering and to the attainment of Nirvāna.[303] Suffering, we should understand, is the reality of physical existence, viz. birth, old age, disease, death and everything connected with these elements of suffering. The origin of suffering is attachment to the material world. The end of suffering comes when we break free from the chains and fetters of material attachment. Lastly, the way to end suffering is to follow the Middle Way of the Buddha, which is called the Straight Path in Islam, and the Narrow (or Strait) Gate in Christianity, which leads to the state of Nirvāna. Nirvāna is freedom from attachment to the material world and annihilation of the lower self. It is death to oneself and entrance into the Divine Presence, the life in love and servitude to God. Jesus Christ said: **"Enter ye in at the strait gate: for wide is the gate, and broad is the way, that leadeth to destruction, and many there be which go in thereat: Because strait is the gate, and narrow is the way, which leadeth unto life, and few there be that find it."**[304]

Buddha summarises these truths as follows:

"Whenever, O priest, a priest knows the truth concerning misery, knows the truth concerning the origin of misery, knows the truth concerning the cessation of misery, knows the truth concerning the path leading to the cessation of misery... And what, O priests, is the noble truth of misery? Birth is misery; old age is misery; disease is misery; death is misery; sorrow, lamentation, misery, grief, and despair are misery; to wish for what one cannot have is misery; in short, all the five attachment-groups are misery... And what, O priests, is the noble truth of the origin of misery? It is desire... desire, namely, for sensual pleasure, desire for permanent existence, desire for transitory existence.

"And what, O priests, is the noble truth of the cessation of misery? It is the complete fading out

**and cessation of this desire, a giving up, a loosing
hold, a relinquishment, and a non-adhesion."**[305]

- Gautama Buddha, *Mahā-Satipatthāna-Sutta.*

<u>Conclusion</u>

When we finish this last step in realization, we have
completed the eight progressive steps of mindfulness meditation.
Eddy (2012) writes that the process of *satipatthāna* ('the way of
mindfulness') involves a progressive pattern of examination,
moving from coarse objects, e.g. body parts, to subtle objects of
awareness, e.g. one's mind and feelings. Eddy argues that this
process of developing an expanding field of awareness leads to
changes in our subjective field of experience, changes to our sense
of self, and changes in our worldview as an internal frame of
reference, and each of these changes are interdependent.[306] As we
continue to expand our fields of mindfulness, we come to embrace
not only awareness of ourselves and others, but also the wider
world around us. Ultimately, self-transformation is related to
world-transformation and the two are intimately interlinked.
Transformation begins at a single point and then expands in
greater and greater circles until it embraces the totality of things.
Every journey begins with a single step, but the step is the totality
of the journey. Likewise, every book begins with a single letter,
and each letter with a single point, and the point is the totality of
the book. Jesus tells us: **"Then said he, Unto what is the
kingdom of God like? and whereunto shall I resemble it?
It is like a grain of mustard seed, which a man took, and**

cast into his garden; and it grew, and waxed a great tree; and the fowls of the air lodged in the branches of it."[307]

When asked what causes the ruin of the world, Buddha replied: **"Ignorance causes the ruin of the world. Envy and selfishness break off friendships. Hatred is the most violent fever, and the Buddha is the best physician."** And when asked what is able to reform the world, he replied: **"Blessing! Neither fire, nor moisture, nor wind can destroy the blessing of a good deed, and blessings reform the whole world."**[308] And what leads to good deeds? Buddha informs us: **"This trembling, wavering mind, so difficult to guard and to control—this the wise man makes straight as the fletcher straightens his shaft... Good it is to tame the mind, so difficult to control, fickle, and capricious. Blessed is the tamed mind. Let the wise man guard his mind, incomprehensible, subtle, and capricious though it is. Blessed is the guarded mind. There is no fear in him, the vigilant one whose mind is not befouled with lust, nor embittered with rage, who cares nought for merit or demerit. Let him who knows that his body is brittle as a potsherd, make his mind strong as a fortress; let him smite Mara with the sword of wisdom, and let him guard his conquest without dalliance."**[309] Only by purifying one's mind can we transform ourselves and others, and this can only be achieved through attaining to a state of mindfulness. It is the mind, after all, which affect and acts upon the world. Let us conclude this chapter with the words of Lord Buddha (may he bless us with mindfulness), who says:

"Mind it is which gives to things their quality, their foundation, and their being: whoso speaks or acts with purified mind, him happiness accompanies as his faithful shadow."[310]

- Buddha, *The Dhammapada*, v. 2.

In the next chapter, we will discuss the Second Way to Meditate: Loving-Kindness Meditation.

Questions for Reflection

The following are some questions that will help us to reflect on what we have learned in this chapter:

1. What is the definition of 'mindfulness?'

2. How should we seat ourselves when meditating?

3. What are the eight steps in mindfulness meditation?

4. What is the path that we should follow if we want to attain to Nirvāna?

∞∞∞∞∞∞∞∞∞∞∞∞∞∞∞∞∞∞∞∞∞∞∞∞∞∞∞

IV. The Second Way to Meditate Loving-Kindness Meditation (*Metta* Meditation)

"May every being experience happiness, peace, and mental enjoyment! Whatever sentient being may exist, erratic or stationary, or whatever kind, long, or tall, or middle-sized, or short, or stout, seen or unseen, near or remote, born or otherwise existing, may every being be happy! In whatever place they may be, let no one deceive or dishonour another! Let there be no desire from wrath or malice to injure each other! As a mother protects with her life the child of her bosom, so let immeasurable benevolence prevail among all beings! Let unbounded kindness and benevolence prevail throughout the universe, above, below, around, without partiality, anger or enmity!"[311]

- Gautama Buddha, *Karanīya-Metta-Sutta*, v. 3 - 8

Introduction

L oving-kindness, which is called *mettā* in the Pāli language, *maitrī* in Sanskrit and *maħabbah* in Arabic, [312] is the practice of friendliness, amity, good-will and benevolence towards others. [313] The eighteenth-century Dzogchen teacher, Jigme Lingpa, defined loving-kindness as 'wishing happiness for others' and compared it to the love that a mother has for her only child, giving up care for her own body, wealth and the benefits of virtuous deeds in order to care for her child, even going so far as to tolerate hardships for its sake. [314] This love, therefore, is pure love—an unadulterated love that requires no requital. The Persian Sūfī mystic, Qutbu'd-Dīn Ardishīr al-'Ibbādī (d. 1152 CE) described *mahabbah* as being a level of pure friendship, cleansed of all aberrations, in which one becomes totally devoted to obtaining his friend's satisfaction. This is thus a higher level of love, above and beyond mere affection or attraction. For al-'Ibbādī, however, it was still not the highest form of love. Beyond *mahabba* lies the state of *'ishq*, which is passionate love for the beloved, and this is only attained from melting one's friendship in the 'crucible of adversity,' when one has attained a state of *fanā'* ('annihilation'), [315] which we have already referred to in previous chapters. Attainment to that station is the ultimate goal of Sufism.

In his sermon at Rajagaha, Gautama Buddha described loving-kindness in the following words: **"Gifts are great, the founding of *viharas*[17] is meritorious, meditations and religious exercises pacify the heart, comprehension of the truth leads to Nirvana, but greater than all is loving-kindness. As the light of the moon is sixteen times stronger than the light of all the stars, so loving-kindness**

---

[17] A Buddhist monastery.

is sixteen times more efficacious in liberating the heart than all other religious accomplishments taken together. This state of heart is the best in the world. Let a man remain steadfast in it while he is awake, whether he is standing, walking, sitting, or lying down."[316] The practice of loving-kindness, therefore, may be understood as the highest and noblest practice of the Middle Way of the Buddha. So potent is it that it can shine brighter than the moon and the stars and is more beneficial than the founding of monasteries and other religious establishments. So important is it that it should permeate every aspect of our lives, including all our activities while standing, walking, sitting or lying down. What greater thing can there be, therefore, than the practice of loving-kindness in our daily lives?

Thus did Jesus Christ—may my life be a sacrifice for his radiant and all-encompassing Spirit—instruct and command his followers**: "But love ye your enemies, and do good, and lend, hoping for nothing again; and your reward shall be great, and ye shall be the children of the Highest: for he is kind unto the unthankful and to the evil."**[317] Likewise, he says: **"But I say unto you, That ye resist not evil: but whosoever shall smite thee on thy right cheek, turn to him the other also... Love your enemies, bless them that curse you, do good to them that hate you, and pray for them which despitefully use you, and persecute you; that ye may be children of your Father in heaven. He causes his sun to rise on the evil and the good, and sends rain on the righteous and the unrighteous."**[318] Love, indeed, is the essence of life—it is the defining characteristic of the true man—

the true human being—and the mortar through which the bricks and stones of society should be cemented and bound together. Love is the building block of the family and the principle upon which social welfare and community-building function and develop. Loving-kindness is the way we should treat one another, with love, compassion, generosity, tolerance, forbearance and forgiveness.

Loving-kindness meditation (or *mettā* meditation) is a training of one's thoughts and deeds in order to benefit the whole of mankind.[319] Thondup (2009) explains that loving-kindness meditation involves opening our hearts to love all men, thus filling our lives with inner peace and joy. World peace, he argues, as well as true happiness, can only ever come from loving-kindness.[320] Thondup advises that we should visualize Buddha as the 'Buddha of Loving-Kindness' (*Avalokiteśvara*), feeling his boundless and unconditional love within us. As this loving-kindness touches our hearts, and permeates our inner essence, we become awakened to the reality that all created things are bathed within the limitless ocean of Buddha's love.[321] Why should we focus on this image of the Buddha of Loving-Kindness? And what is this image? First of all, it is not a physical image. We are not imagining a statue or painting of Buddha, but the attributes of Buddha as the embodiment and fountainhead of loving-kindness. If we are Jewish, or Christian, or Hindu, or Muslim, then why should we focus on Buddha?

Loving-kindness meditation developed within the Buddhist tradition, so the terminology used by adherents of this practice refers to the Buddha. However, there is no actual difference between the Prophet Zoroaster, the Prophet Moses, Gautama Buddha, Srī Krishna Vāsudeva, Jesus Christ or the Prophet Muhammad (may their love and benevolence rain down upon us). They are all mirrors of the same sun and daysprings of the same eternal Light. They are all Perfect Teachers from the same school and emissaries of the same deathless and eternal King. We can focus on any one of these supernal, eternal beings, who are the essence of loving-kindness, compassion and mercy. There is no difference between focusing on Buddha as the source of loving-kindness, or focusing on God as the source of loving-kindness— one is the mirror, the other the sun. In the Lotus Sutra, Avalokiteśvara is thus invoked: **"Think, O think with tranquil mood of Avalokitesvara, that pure being; he is a protector, a refuge, a recourse in death, disaster, and calamity. He who possesses the perfection of all virtues, and beholds all beings with compassion and benevolence, he, an ocean of virtues, Virtue itself, he, Avalokitesvara, is worthy of adoration."[322]**

The meaning of the Sanskrit word *Avalokiteśvara* is the 'Lord who gazes/looks down' (i.e. at the world).[323] The Sanskrit term Īśvara (also spelled Ishvara) is used to refer to God, the Supreme Being, and the Master of all. According to *Encyclopædia Britannica*, Ishvara means the concept of a personal God, whereas Brahman is the equivalent impersonal concept. Vaishnavas (followers of Vishnu) also use the term Bhagavan, which is translated as Lord.[324] Avalokiteśvara is an embodiment of the concept of the Buddha as the Manifestation and Mirror of the Divine Being—the eternal God. While much is made in the West of

141

Buddhism as a non-theistic religion, Avalokiteśvara is an example of the theistic terminology used in Buddhist literature. As Buddha says, referring to the Divine Being: **"There is, O monks, an unborn, unoriginated, uncreated, unformed. Were there not, O monks, this unborn, unoriginated, uncreated, unformed, there would be no escape from the world of the born, originated, created, formed. Since, O monks, there is an unborn, unoriginated, uncreated and unformed, therefore is there an escape from the born, originated, created, formed."**[325] According to Steele (2000), this is a reference to the ultimate reality of Nirvāna (Pāli *Nibbāna*), which is the attainment of *anatta* ('non-self'), a state which involves bliss and permanence. Steele observes that the terminology used by Buddha to refer to Nirvāna does not speak of actual extinction, but of infinite happiness, absolute purity and peace.[326] A similar concept can be found in St. Paul's statement in the New Testament: **"Yet not I, but Christ liveth in me."**[327] In other words, St. Paul has died to himself and lives in Christ. As such, the true meaning of attaining Nirvāna is identical to the Sūfī concept of *fanā'*, i.e. the death of one's lower self and *baqā'*, which is reunion with the Divine Beloved, the Unborn, the Uncreated, the Unformed, whom the Qur'ān refers to as: **"God the eternal! He begetteth not, and He is not begotten; and there is none like unto Him."**[328]

The Buddha tells us that he who **"acts with kindness, who is calm in the doctrine of Buddha, will reach the quiet place (Nirvâna), cessation of natural desires, and happiness."**[329] There are four qualities which, above all, loving-kindness meditation aims to cultivate, and these are referred to as the *brahma-viharas* ('heavenly abodes') in Pāli: *metta* (love), *karuna* (compassion), *mudita* ('sympathetic joy'), and *upekkha* ('equanimity').[330] According to Salzberg (2004), loving-kindness, or *metta*, is the first and most important of the *brahma-viharas*, as the other three—compassion, sympathetic joy and equanimity— find their origin in loving-kindness. She is keen to point out that *metta* is not passion or sentimentality, as love is commonly understood in the West, but, rather, love which is unconditional, open and unobstructed, and she gives the example of water poured from one vessel to another.[331] She writes that *metta* is all-embracing—it is our ability to embrace ourselves and the whole world. We thus become open to everything and extend the healing force of love throughout the universe. This helps to expand our minds to encompass the entirety of life, including all its pleasures and pains. This can be accomplished, Salzberg argues, because of the Buddhist principle that mind (or *citta* in Pāli, meaning both heart and mind) is naturally radiant and pure, and it is only through *kilesa* ('defilement') of *citta* ('mind', 'heart') that we suffer.[332] These defilements include anger, fear, guilt, and greed.[333] According to Buddha: **"Anger, drunkenness, obstinacy, bigotry, deception, envy, self-praise, disparaging others, superciliousness and evil intentions constitute uncleanness."**[334]

One way to overcome these defilements, purify our hearts and attain the four *brahma-viharas*, is to practice loving-kindness meditation. In Sanskrit, loving-kindness is called *maitri*. The Blessed Buddha said: **"As a mother, even at the risk of her** own life, protects her son, her only son—so let every man cultivate *maitri* without measure among all beings. Let him cultivate *maitri* without measure toward the whole world, above, below, around, unstinted and unmixed with any feeling of difference or opposition. Let a man remain steadfastly in this state of mind all the while he is awake, whether he be standing, walking, sitting, or lying down. This state of heart (*chetovimukti*) is the best in the world."[335] Loving-kindness meditation, therefore, is not confined to sitting down and thinking about loving-kindness. On the contrary, as with mindfulness meditation, which we have discussed in the previous chapter, meditation is about achieving a mind-set, an awareness, a consciousness that is constant, pervasive and uninterrupted. We should manifest loving-kindness to all who cross our paths. We should regard all things with loving-kindness and practice it as our way of life. Loving-kindness is our essence, our being, our occupation. Our hearts should flow with *maitri* (or *metta*)—with loving-kindness—like an endless fountainhead whose source is none other than the higher being, our higher self, which is immortal and divine.

I have written a brief summary of loving-kindness meditation, which appears in Chapter XI of *Mindfulness: Five Ways to Achieve Real Happiness, True Knowledge and Inner Peace*, Second Step – Focus on Loving-Kindness. [336] I would recommend that you read that section first and try to practice the method explained. The steps outlined below for practising loving-kindness meditation are based on the following works: *Loving-Kindness: The Revolutionary Art of Happiness* by Sharon

Salzberg (2004),[337] Ven Pannyavaro's article on 'Loving-Kindness Meditation' on *BuddhaNet*,[338] as well as the Karanīya-Metta-Sutta of the Buddha, translated by D.J. Gogerly (1872) and published posthumously in the *Journal Asiatique*. Study the following steps and put them into practice on a daily basis. Thus will you be enabled to develop a state of loving-kindness that pervades your mentality, your consciousness and your actions throughout your life.

Step 1: Realize Your Inner Nobility & Love Yourself

The first step in loving-kindness meditation is to develop loving acceptance of yourself. Each of the steps in loving-kindness meditation should take at least 5 to 15 minutes, so focus on this step for at least a good five minutes. We should overcome any feelings of self-doubt and negativity while developing loving-kindness towards others.[339] Salzberg (2004) recommends that we begin by sitting comfortably, closing our eyes and letting go of analysis and expectation. For a period of 5 to 15 minutes, we should call to mind something we have done or said which is a good action, e.g. a time when we did something generous, caring, etc. As we experience each of these memories, we should feel happy about this remembrance.[340] Even if we cannot think of anything positive that we have done, we should turn to a quality that we possess that we like, e.g. patience, love, forbearance, kindness, etc. And even if we cannot do this, Salzberg argues, we should reflect on the 'primal urge toward happiness' that exists within us. Even if negative experiences arise, we should not be

145

disheartened. Rather, we should let go of these negative emotions and start again. [341] I would suggest we start by repeating the following phrases, through you can use any other phrases that you prefer:

- I will be happy and healthy
- I will love and be loved
- I will be strong and noble
- I will be helpful and kind
- I will be a servant of humanity
- My heart is a mirror of the Divine Light
- My soul is filled with the fire of love

By focusing on positive statements such as these, we teach ourselves to *love* ourselves. We come to respect our inner nobility and we extend compassion to our own selves. Just as everyone throughout the world is suffering from the forces of materialism and material attachment, so we are also suffering from those influences. Therefore, we must be compassionate to ourselves as we are also compassionate to others. In the previous book, we wrote: "Our happiness can transcend all physical limitations and suffering, because it is spiritual happiness. The fruit of happiness is loving-kindness... We should learn to develop kindness, not just to others, but to ourselves as well. We should try not to feel unworthy or dejected. Rather, we should recognize our own inner nobility. We are all oceans full of great value—great treasures hidden in the profoundest depths. We should avoid all feelings of negativity, self-loathing and self-doubt, all tendencies towards 'beating ourselves up' and feelings of worthlessness. We are spiritual beings—we are eternal beings—we are souls created in the image of the Higher Being which fashioned us—the All-Highest Being, the All-Knowing, the All-Wise. Feel loving-kindness for yourself. Be aware of your own being and focus on the peace and tranquillity within you. You can focus on an image, such as light pouring through your inner being."[342]

"So God created man in his own image, in the image of God created he him; male and female created he them."[343]

- Genesis 1:27

Always remember this: we are all noble beings. Nobility does not depend on one's ancestry or birth. It does not have any relation to wealth, influence or breeding. You are not an animal, nor are you insignificant, mundane or impotent. On the contrary—you are noble. You are noble. I repeat this because it is true, and you should never forget it. You are a noble being—a spiritual being. You are not the sum of your bodily parts. You are not your brain or your mind. The lower self of your body is transitory and illusory. The material world is a shadow of real existence. Your body is a shadow of reality. You are, in reality, a spirit—a soul—an immortal and noble being. You are a soul. You are a human being. Love yourself because your true self is full of loving-kindness. Love yourself because your reality is pure and worthy of love. You are full of gems of inestimable value. You are full of divine power and might. You possess all the virtues and attributes of God, which are latent within the innermost essence of your being—but you need to find these gems and share them with mankind.

"I am the Spirit seated deep in every creature's heart;

From Me they come; by Me they live; at My word they depart!...

Living or lifeless, still or stirred, whatever beings be,

None of them is in all the worlds, but it exists by Me!"[344]

- Krishna, *The Bhagavad-Gita*, Chapter X

You are a treasure-trove full of limitless energy, potential and boundless power. But you need to release these treasures and unfold this power by channelling the force within you. Love your higher being—your true reality—and realize that this is who you truly are. You are not material—you are spiritual. You are in charge of your body, you are in charge of your potential, you are able to become virtuous, powerful, spiritual and benevolent. Focus on what you truly are and forget all that you thought you were. You are created in the image of God—in His own image created He you. As Krishna states above, speaking in the voice of God, we exist only by the grace of God. He is our source and our origin and His Light can shine within us. As Epictetus has written: "Why then are you ignorant of your high birth? Why do you not know whence you have come?"[345] Cleanse the mirror of your heart, so that the Light of God may shine within. When you have realized your inner nobility, and attained to a state of loving-kindness towards yourself, move on to the next step.

"And He [i.e. God] is the Oft-Forgiving,

Full of loving-kindness."[346]

- Qur'ān 85:14

Step 2: Extend Your Loving-Kindness to Respected Individuals

There are four types of people to whom we should develop loving-kindness: a respect and beloved person, a dearly-loved family member or friend, a neutral person and, lastly, a hostile person.[347] We can achieve this through four means: visualization, reflection and repeating an internalized mantra or phrase. [348] Alidina (2015) recommends repeating simple phrases such as 'may I feel well', 'may I feel happy', 'may I feel healthy', or 'may I not suffer.'[349] This is then extended to others by changing the pronoun from 'I' to 'you', and, at the next stage, from 'you' to 'we', e.g. 'may we feel well', 'may we feel happy', 'may we feel healthy', etc.[350] Lastly, we expand this to include all plants, animals, and the whole universe, by replacing 'we' with 'all.'[351] Let us, however, take each one of these step-by-step together. Once we have accepted our own inner nobility and begun to feel love for ourselves, we should extend our loving-kindness to someone whom we greatly respect or admire, e.g. a teacher, respectable person, role model, etc. Salzberg (2015) characterizes these various objects of loving-kindness as 'concentric circles of connection', and writes that, with each step, we strengthen our ability to feel compassion for others.[352] She refers to this as our 'muscle for compassion.' Let us then move to the second of these concentric circles—expressing love for respected individuals (e.g. a spiritual teacher).

We can do this through visualization (i.e. seeing a mental image of the person in question, smiling at you or being joyful), reflection on the positive qualities of the person and the kind acts he or she has done for us, and through auditory repetition (i.e. repeating a positive statement to oneself, e.g. 'loving-kindness') while thinking of the person. Focus on this individual or individuals for at least five minutes. The respected individual(s) we focus on should have had an impactful or important influence in our lives. It could be a mentor, a teacher, a guru or some other person we regard highly. Why should we do this? Because gratitude is essential to life, and, by extending loving-kindness, we are simultaneously extending gratitude to those whom we love and admire. As Thomas à Kempis writes: "Be thankful, therefore, for the least benefit and thou shalt be worthy to receive greater. Let the least be unto thee even as the greatest, and let that which is of little account be unto thee as a special gift."[353] I suggest the following phrases:

- May my teacher(s) be happy and well
- May my teacher(s) be healthy and joyful

- May they feel loving-kindness and joy
- May they feel inner peace and equanimity

While this gratitude (and loving-kindness) may be most fully extended to God, who is the Source of all blessings and munificence, we may also extend it to the truest of spiritual teachers. And while we all encounter many guides and influences in life, the truest guide is a spiritual teacher, who lives the life that he preaches and embodies the teachings which he conveys. As Bhishma says in the Mahabharata: "One *Acharya* ['preceptor', i.e. spiritual master] is superior to ten Brahmanas learned in the Vedas... In my opinion, however, the preceptor is worthy of greater reverence than the father or even the mother. The father and the mother are authors of one's being. The father and the mother, O Bharata, only create the body. The life, on the other hand, that one obtains from one's preceptor, is heavenly. That life is subject to no decay and is immortal."354

And who is a greater preceptor—a greater spiritual master—than those Great Teachers who appear in every age and give us spiritual teachings which lead us to emancipation from material attachment and suffering? Should we not extend our loving-kindness to Gautama Buddha, the great Tathāgata,[18] who achieved true enlightenment and blessed the world with the Four Noble Truths and the Eightfold Path or Middle Way, which provide the steps and principles needed to attain liberation from suffering and material bondage? Should we not extend our loving-

---

[18] 'One who has thus come', a title of the Buddha.

kindness to the incomparable Lord Srī Krishna, who is also known as Govinda, Syāmasundara and Muralīdhara,[355] and who blessed the world by revealing the Bhagavad-Gita—the 'Song of the Lord?' He taught us the principles of *bhakti-yoga*, which is the cultivation of love and devotion to God—or pure devotional service to God.[356] Should we not extend our loving-kindness to the Prophet Zoroaster, who taught us to have good thoughts, good words and good deeds? Should we not also extend our loving-kindness to the Great Teachers of the Holy Bible, viz. the Prophet Abraham, Moses and Jesus Christ, who gave us teachings of fairness, justice, love and peace? Should we not also extend our loving-kindness to the Prophet Muhammad, who taught the way of submission to the Divine, the unity of the Great Teachers, and the brotherhood of man? May the peace, prayers and blessings of God—glorified be His Glory—be upon each one of these Perfect Teachers. The following phrases are an example:

- Peace and blessings be upon all the Great Teachers
- Peace and blessings be upon all the Great Prophets
- Peace and blessings be upon all the Suns of Truth

Focus all your loving-kindness and good will upon these holy souls.

"Of all good virtues, lovingkindness stands foremost.... It is the source of all merit.... It is the mother of all Buddhas.... It induces others to take refuge in the incomparable Bodhi. The loving heart of a Bodhisattva is annoyed by one thing,

that all beings are constantly tortured and threatened by all sorts of pain."[357]

- Devala's Mahâpurusa, quoted in *Outlines of Mahayana Buddhism.*

Step Three: Extend Your Loving-Kindness to Loved Ones

Next, we should focus our loving-kindness on those whom we love, whom we are close to and for whom we have bonds of affection. This can include our wives, husbands, parents, children and other family and friends. These are the people who mean the most to us in our day-to-day lives and for whom we already have bonds of affection and love. Why then do we need to extend our loving-kindness to such people? Because there are different levels of love. The basest form of love is mere physical attraction, which is based on sensory perception and animal instincts. This, it should be understood, is not actually 'love,' but merely passion or attraction. Next, there is love in the form of affection. We have affection for a fiancée or wife, but this can dissipate over time and eventually be extinguished. This is also not true or real love. Real love, and real loving-kindness, refer to love which is truly selfless, where we wish not only for others what we wish for ourselves, but in which we also strive to give others more of ourselves than we give to ourselves. In other words, we sacrifice ourselves for that other individual or individuals and, in so doing, testify to our love through our actions and deeds. By wishing loving-kindness for those whom we love, therefore, we are extending a love which is selfless and kind, which is noble and pure, full of good-will, compassion, mercy and beneficence. It is a divine form of love, which is higher than mere affection or familial bonds.

You can do this by simply wishing them 'may he/she be happy' or by extending the phrases already used for oneself to one's loved ones, e.g.:

- May they be happy and healthy
- May they love and be loved
- May they be strong and noble
- May they be helpful and kind
- May they serve humanity

Thus, just as we have learned to truly love ourselves, we extend those same good wishes to those who love us and whom we love most.

"Only that Love that seeks no personal gratification or reward, that does not make distinctions, and that leaves behind no heartaches, can be called divine."[358]

- James Allen, *The Way of Peace.*

Step Four: Extend Loving Kindness to Neutral Persons

We should look upon all human beings, and all created things, with the eye of equanimity. Krishna calls this the 'eye of evenness.' [359] In describing the perfect yogi, i.e. the perfect practitioner of *bhakti-yoga*, or devotional service to God, Krishna says that he **"looks with equal regard upon well-wishers, friends, foes, neutrals, arbiters, the hateful, the relatives, and upon the righteous and the unrighteous alike."**[360] How can someone develop this 'eye of equanimity?' The answer is simple: by seeing the divine attributes in each and every human being, and in each and every atom and particle of existence. As Krishna says: **"He who sees Me in all things, and sees all things in Me, he never becomes separated from Me, nor do I become separated from him. He who being established in unity, worships Me, who am dwelling in all beings, whatever his mode of life, that Yogi abides in Me."**[361] Thus, as we look upon all created things with equanimity, so too do we regard neutral persons whom we know with equanimity. By neutral persons, we mean people whom we neither love nor hate, but towards whom we have a neutral regard. We should not look upon them any differently than any other people, except that we should extend loving-kindness to them. As such, I recommend using the same phrases that we have already used above, while bringing to mind all those for whom we have no particular love nor hate.

"If you are given to hatred or anger you will meditate upon gentleness and forgiveness, so as to become acutely alive to a sense of your harsh and foolish conduct. You will then begin to dwell in thoughts of love, of gentleness, of abounding forgiveness; and as you overcome the lower by the higher, there will gradually, silently steal into your heart a knowledge of the divine Law of Love with an understanding of its bearing upon all the intricacies of life and conduct. And in applying this knowledge to your every thought, word, and act, you will grow more and more gentle, more and more loving, more and more divine. And thus with every error, every selfish desire, every human weakness; by the power of meditation is it overcome, and as each sin, each error is thrust out, a fuller and clearer measure of the Light of Truth illumines the pilgrim soul."[362]

- James Allen, *The Way of Peace*

Step Five: Extend Loving-Kindness to Enemies

This may be the most difficult step, because it involves extending one's loving-kindness to those for whom we feel or harbour negative emotions, e.g. enemies. In the Gospels, Jesus Christ—may my soul be offered up in his service—teaches that loving one's enemies is essential for spiritual progress. He says—and this is the essence of true religion and philosophy:

"But I say unto you which hear, love your enemies, do good to them which hate you, bless them that curse you, and pray for them which despitefully use you. And unto him that smiteth thee on the one cheek offer also the other; and him that taketh away thy cloak forbid not to take thy coat also. Give to every man that asketh of thee; and of him that taketh away thy goods ask them not again. And as ye would that men should do to you, do ye also to them likewise.

"For if ye love them which love you, what thank have ye? for sinners also love those that love them. And if ye do good to them which do good to you, what thank have ye? for sinners also do even the same. And if ye lend to them of whom ye hope to receive, what thank have ye? for sinners also lend to sinners, to receive as much again. But love ye your enemies, and do good, and lend, hoping for nothing again; and your reward shall be great, and ye shall be the children of the Highest: for he is kind unto the unthankful and to the evil. Be ye therefore merciful, as your Father also is merciful."[363]

- Jesus Christ, Luke 6:27 – 36

It is not enough to extend love to one's friends, or those who have done us no harm; on the contrary, the Kingdom of God can only be established when we extend our love to those who actively do us wrong or oppose us. Every action has a result, which can be positive or negative. If we do something good—a righteous deed—the results of that action will be positive. If we help someone, for example, that action will result in happiness and good-will, and the positive results will multiply and extend to others. We may improve someone's life, and they go on to improve other people's lives. We may help someone who goes on to help others. Or we may simply bring joy and hope to someone who is sad and hopeless. In any case, by doing good, we create ripples of goodness which affect all created things and which echo through the depths of eternity. As Ignatius of Antioch (c. 35 – 108 CE) tells us in his Epistle to the Ephesians (3:1 -2): "Pray also without ceasing for other men: for there is hope of repentance in them, that they may attain unto God. Let them therefore at least be instructed by your works, if they will be no other way. Be ye mild at their anger; humble at their boasting; to their blasphemies return your prayers; to their error, your firmness in the faith; when they are cruel, be ye gentle; not endeavouring to imitate their ways."364

On the other hand, if we do an evil deed, or return evil for evil, or hate for hate, this causes negative ricochets, which also echo throughout the stretches of time and space. The results of good and evil actions accumulate over time, and their influence leads to result after result through the generations. Furthermore, every action also has a spiritual impact, which can either lead to our own spiritual development or retardation. This is the essence of the principle of *karma*. If we do good, our souls will progress and grow in power, but if we do evil, our souls will regress. And if our actions are neutral, having neither good nor evil results, then we simply make no progress. As Ignatius explains in his letter to the Smyrnæans (3:19): "For inasmuch as ye are perfect yourselves, you ought to think those things that are perfect. For when you are desirous to do well, God is ready to enable you thereunto."365 Likewise, in his Epistle to the Trallians (2:7), he writes: "Let us therefore do all things, as becomes those who have God dwelling in them; that we may be his temples, and he may be our God: as also he is, and will manifest himself before our faces, by those things for which we justly love him."366

Now, in this stage of the meditation, you should extend your loving-kindness to enemies, using the phrases already mentioned above, viz.:

- May they be happy and healthy
- May they love and be loved
- May they be strong and noble
- May they be helpful and kind
- May they serve humanity

To our enemies and those who do us harm, we feel no malice, nor any feelings of negativity whatsoever. We see in all human beings a mirror of the Divine Light, shining with the Face of the Divine Being. We see the innermost reality of things, and do not look upon the physical element. As Krishna tells Arjuna in the Bhagavad-Gita, the true yogi should look with the "eye of evenness" on all things, and he **"looks with equal regard upon well-wishers, friends, foes, neutrals, arbiters, the hateful, the relatives, and upon the righteous and the unrighteous alike."**[367] When we see the everlasting and eternal attributes of the Divine Being manifest within the core of all created things, it is impossible to hate that essence. We extend loving-kindness, in other words, for the sake of the Divine Light which sheds it effulgence, liberally, upon all people—upon the good and the evil alike. As Jesus tells us, we should love our enemies that we **"may be the children"** of God, **"for he maketh his sun to rise on the evil and on the good, and sendeth rain on the just and on the unjust."** [368] And, likewise, God says in the Qur'ān (5:8): **"Stand steadfast to God as witnesses with justice; and let not ill-will towards people make you sin by not acting with equity. Act with equity, that is nearer to piety, and fear God; for God is aware of what ye do."**[369]

Step Six: Extend the Circle Outwards, Embracing the Whole Universe

Lastly, we extend our loving-kindness in the widest of the concentric circles, i.e. to the whole universe and all created things. As we explained in the previous book, we should "think of all four individuals together and then extend the circle of loving-kindness outwards, embracing the whole of humanity with your love. Extend your loving-kindness from your local community, to your region, your nation and, finally, the entire world and universe."[370]

Imagine loving-kindness welling up within your heart, like water gushing forth from a mighty spring which shoots up from the depths of everlasting holiness within the innermost core of your being. That water is celestial—divine—having its origin in the mighty river of divine bounty, which flows from the ocean of divine power and might. This ocean is measureless, eternal and infinitely profound. Its water is the very water of life, which nourishes and sustains all created things, and its essence is the essence of mercy, compassion, forgiveness and grace. The eternal streams which flow out from this ocean embrace all things, giving life to that which is dead, and providing forgiveness and blessings to the hopeless and lost. You are an eternal spring—the source of life-giving water for humanity—and a channel of this divine water for the whole universe and all the worlds—all the galaxies and galactic clusters—and all the realms which exist therein. Flow out—gush forth—with that eternal, all-sustaining water. Our hearts are, indeed, temples of light, which illuminate the world in all their splendour. As Barnabus writes in his general epistle (5:18): "For, my brethren, the habitation of our heart is a holy temple unto the lord."[371]

Figure 15. Twenty-five Bodhisattvas descending from Heaven

[19] Image source: Twenty-five Bodhisattvas Descending from Heaven, Japan, Kamakura period, Pair of hanging scrolls; gold and mineral pigments on silk, Kimbell Art Museum. Japanese painting, c. 1300. Public domain image. Created c. 1300 CE. Available online at: https://upload.wikimedia.org/wikipedia/commons/b/b3/Twenty-Five_Bodhisattvas_Descending_from_Heaven%2C_c._1300.jpg

The following phrases are useful to say during this step of the meditation:

- May all people be happy and healthy
- May all people love one another and be loved
- May all people be strong and noble
- May all people be helpful and kind
- May all people serve one another
- May all plants, animals and created beings be filled with loving-kindness
- May all created things be immersed in the ocean of love
- May the whole universe be immersed in compassion and loving-kindness
- May the Light of God shine on all created things

We can also use the Buddha's own phrases from the Karanīya-Metta Sutta:

"May every being experience happiness, peace, and mental enjoyment!

"Whatever sentient being may exist, erratic or stationary, or whatever kind, long, or tall, or middle-sized, or short, or stout, seen or unseen, near or remote, born or otherwise existing, may every being be happy!

"In whatever place they may be, let no one deceive or dishonour another!

"Let there be no desire from wrath or malice to injure each other!

"As a mother protects with her life the child of her bosom, so let immeasurable benevolence prevail among all beings!

"Let unbounded kindness and benevolence prevail throughout the universe, above, below, around, without partiality, anger or enmity!"[372]

- Gautama Buddha, *Karanīya-Metta-Sutta*, v. 3 – 8

We should imagine ourselves flowing with loving-kindness, extending from our hearts outward, to those we respect, to our loved ones, to those for whom we have neutral feelings, to our enemies, to our communities, countries and the world. We should extend our loving-kindness to animals, trees, nature and the whole universe, that our love may flow outwards throughout the vastness of eternity, just as light pours forth from the limitless stars of heaven. We should be like Avalokiteśvara, the bodhisattva of compassion, who is described in the Lotus Sutra as **"he who possesses the perfection of all virtues, and beholds all beings with compassion and benevolence, he, an ocean of virtues"** the **"great cloud of good qualities and of benevolent mind"** who **"quenchest the fire that vexes living beings,"** and who **"pourest out nectar."**[373] Let us reflect on the words of the Chinese Confucian philosopher, Mencius (372 – 289 BCE):

"He whose goodness is part of himself is what is called real   man.

He whose goodness has been filled up is what is called beautiful man.

He whose completed goodness is brightly displayed is what is called a great man.

When this great man exercises a transforming influence, he is what is called a sage.

When the sage is beyond our knowledge, he is what is called a spirit-man."[374]

- Mencius, Book 7, Part II, Chapter 25, v. 4 - 8

We should also look to the example of the Prophet Muhammad (upon whom be peace), who endured years of persecution from his fellow countrymen in his native town of Mecca. Once, for example, as he was praying in his house, one of his enemies threw a sheep's uterus filled with blood and excrement over him. On another occasion, as he was coming from the sacred Kaaba (cube-shaped temple) of Mecca, a man took a handful of dirt and threw it in his face and over his head.[375] He did not respond to either aggression and, when he returned home, his daughter washed him clean while weeping. He comforted her by saying, **"Weep not, little daughter, God will protect thy father."**[376]

Our love should encompass all created things, just as the love of God and His Prophets and Messengers encompasses all things with the ocean of eternal mercy and compassion. As John the Evangelist advises his fellow believers in the New Testament: **"Beloved, let us love one another: for love is of God; and every one that loveth is born of God, and knoweth God. He that loveth not knoweth not God; for God is love... No man hath seen God at any time. If we love one another, God dwelleth in us, and his love is perfected in us."**[377]

Conclusion

If we follow the steps above, we can develop an attitude of loving-kindness. The purpose of loving-kindness meditation is, ultimately, to change our attitude and behaviour in order to live in accordance with the Middle Way, the Straight Path, which leads to inner perfection, peace and happiness—both within oneself and within one's family, community and the wider world. While loving-kindness meditation finds its origin in Buddhist practices, it is, in reality, an element of all religions and true philosophies. As we have seen in the quotations cited above, all the Great Teachers have advocated loving-kindness, and true loving-kindness is the essence of true religion.

As we are all noble mirrors of the Divine, created in the image of God, so we should see the Divine in all human beings, and the whole of creation. For this reason, we should love all created beings, having compassion on all things. We should be kind to our fellow human beings, tolerant, forbearing, patient and forgiving. We should overlook the faults of others, be patient in adversity and look upon all people with a kind and friendly face. Our inward life should conform to our outward life, i.e. our hearts should flow with loving-kindness just as we express loving-kindness towards others in word and deed.

We should, furthermore, have compassion on the whole of nature, on plants and animals, on the smallest creatures and the largest, on our environment and the world around us. We should be respectful of the environment and the rights of animals, and we should be loving and kind to trees, plants and all other living things. Our loving-kindness should expand in outward, concentric circles, embracing ourselves, our friends, loved ones and acquaintances and, ultimately, the entire universe. Thus may we become the recipients and the bestowers of divine blessings and abundant joy and happiness.

"For thy lovingkindness is before mine eyes: and I have walked in thy truth... Because thy lovingkindness is better than life, my lips shall praise thee."[378]

- Psalm 26:3; 63:3

To summarize the main points of this chapter:

- Loving-kindness (*mettā, maitrī* or *maḥabbah*) is selfless love, amity, good-will and benevolence towards others

- We can visualize Buddha as the 'Buddha of Loving-Kindness' (*Avalokiteśvara*), feeling his boundless and unconditional love within us

- As we are all mirrors of God, we should recognize our own inner nobility and the nobility of all human beings

- Loving-kindness meditation aims to cultivate the four 'heavenly abodes' of love, compassion, sympathetic joy and equanimity

- The first step is to love ourselves and feel loving-kindness towards ourselves

- The next step is to extend our loving-kindness to someone we respect, such as a teacher or mentor, or to the Great Teachers of every age (e.g. Krishna, Buddha, Christ, Muhammad, etc.)

- The third step is to extend our loving-kindness to those whom we love, such as family members and close friends

- The fourth step is to extend our loving-kindness to those for whom we have neutral feelings

- The fifth step is to extend our loving-kindness to those who do us harm (e.g. enemies, persecutors, etc.)

- The sixth step is to extend our loving-kindness to our community, nation, world, all life-forms and nature, and, ultimately, the entire universe

In the next chapter, we will discuss the Third Way to Meditate: Mantra Meditation.

Questions for Reflection:

The following are some questions that will help us to reflect on what we have learned in this chapter:

1. What is 'loving-kindness?'

2. What are the four 'heavenly abodes?'

3. In what way are we 'treasure-troves full of limitless energy, potential and boundless power?'

4. What is the first step in loving-kindness meditation?

5. What is the third step in loving-kindness meditation?

6. What is the third step in loving-kindness meditation?

7. What is the fourth step in loving-kindness meditation?

8. What is the fifth step in loving-kindness meditation?

9. What is the sixth step in loving-kindness meditation?

10. What is the ultimate purpose of loving-kindness meditation?

∞∞∞∞∞∞∞∞∞∞∞∞∞∞∞∞∞∞∞∞∞∞∞∞∞

V. The Third Way to Meditate – Mantra Meditation

"SAY: Call upon God (Allāh), or call upon the God of Mercy (Ar-Rahmān), by whichsoever ye will invoke him: He hath most excellent names."[379]

"And to God alone belong all perfect attributes. So call on Him by these attributes."[380]

"The seven heavens praise Him, and the earth, and all who are therein: Neither is there any thing which doth not celebrate his praise; but ye understand not their celebration thereof: He is gracious and merciful."[381]

"All that is in the Heavens and all that is on the Earth praiseth God! He, the Mighty (al-'Azīz), the Wise (al-Hakīm)!"[382]

- Qur'ān 17:110, 7:180, 17:44; 59:1

"Praise ye the LORD. Praise, O ye servants of the LORD, praise the name of the LORD. Blessed be the name of the LORD from this time forth and for evermore. From the rising of the sun unto the going down of the same the LORD'S name is to be praised. The LORD is high above all nations, and his glory above the heavens."[383]

- Psalm 113:1 - 4

"My holy name should be remembered and meditated upon repeatedly. Matsya, Kūrma, Varaha, Narasimha, Vāmana, Paraśurāma, Rāma, Krishna, Buddha, and also Kalkī: [20] These ten names should always be meditated upon by the wise... Of him who gives voice to the auspicious name 'Krishṇ a' tens of millions of great sins are quickly reduced to ashes... Hari,[21] meditated upon even by one who has evil thoughts, takes away sins: fire burns, even though accidentally touched... One should worship the Achyuta, Keśava, Nārāyana, Kṛ ishna, Dāmodara, Vāsudeva, Hari, Śrīdhara, Mādhavam, Gopīkāvallabham, Rāmachandra, the Lord of Jānakī."[22][384]

- Veda-Vyāsa, *The Garuda Purāna*, Chapter VIII, v. 9 – 12, 14, 17.

---

[20] Names of the 10 main Avatars of Vishnu.

[21] A name of God.

[22] Names of God.

Introduction

A mantra is a word, phrase or series of words which are repeated (silently or out loud) over and over again, or in a fixed number of recitations, in order to produce a change in spiritual awareness. In this chapter, we will use this phrase to refer to repetition of the Names of God, or the names of the Great Teachers who have appeared throughout the ages, in order to achieve a state of God-consciousness and inner spiritual awareness. This state of God-consciousness may be referred to as 'enlightenment'. In the Five Ways to Be series, we refer to this as a state of 'enkindlement', i.e. when the Light of God shines within the mirror of one's heart. We will briefly look at mantra meditation in several key traditions, including Vaishnavism, Mahayana Buddhism and Sufi Islam, each of which have strong mystical traditions and a practice of mantra meditation. The use of the term 'meditation' or *dhyāna*, in the context of mantra meditation, does not refer to mere introspection, nor does it necessarily require a seated pose or posture. Rather, it refers to the use of recitation as a means of focus on the Divine Being. By repeating certain key Names of God and phrases over and over again, we focus on the mind on the inner reality of each Name and phrase. It can be compared to submerging a cube of sugar in a boiling pot of water. The water represents the mantra, and the sugar represents our mundane thoughts, which are preoccupied with the day-to-day concerns of life, material hopes and aspirations, and the general worries, concerns and attachments of material reality. When we submerge our minds in the boiling water of the mantra, all these material concerns and preoccupations are dissolved and become one with the water. Their substance is changed from the solidity of materiality to the liquidity of spiritual reality.

> "Om. Therefore the reciter of the Mantra 'Om-namo-Nārāyanāya,' reaches the Vaikuntha world...[23] It is effulgent like lightning, shining like a lamp... He who meditates upon that sole Nārāyana[24] who is latent in all beings, who is the causal Purusha, [25] who is causeless, who is Parabrahman, [26] the Om, [27] who is without pains and delusion and who is all-pervading—that person is never subject to pains."[385]

- *Thirty Minor Upanishads*, Ātmabodha-Upanishad of Rgveda.

---

[23] The celestial realm of Lord Vishnu, i.e. God. Vishnu literally means the 'All-Pervasive'.

[24] Another name of Vishnu. Narayana brought the universe into existence.

[25] Another word for the Creator.

[26] The 'Highest Brahman', i.e. God.

[27] A sacred sound used in meditation.

Mere repetition of a mantra is not enough, however. Repetition on its own may be compared to cold water, which has little effect on the solid lump of sugar. Rather, we must heat the water with the key element—which is the fire of love. Only when this fire of love has been enkindled in our hearts can the water boil and the mantra take effect. In other words, simply repeating the word 'God', 'God', 'God', over and over again, will have little effect if it is not accompanied by a passionate longing for the Divine Beloved. This longing—this passionate desire—is the essence of true enkindlement. This passionate desire is called *'ishq* in Arabic, and the one who possesses this love—the lover—is called an *'āshiq*. It may seem paradoxical that mantra meditation leads to a state of enkindlement, while a state of enkindlement is necessary to achieve true mantra meditation. However, all that is required, in reality, is a seed of love in one's heart. When a flame is ignited, it begins as a mere spark. When that flame is given fuel, which are the divine teachings, and it is blown upon with the wind of spirituality, then it grows bit-by-bit, until it reaches the fullness of a hearty flame; meditation begins with a spark of love, and the process of practising it leads to a greater and greater flame of enkindlement. The ultimate goal of mantra meditation is absorption in the Divine Love, which is referred to as *fanā'* in Sufism, which is death to one's self, or annihilation of the lower self. The true self, the divine soul, remains intact, as it can never be destroyed. In reality, this is the essence of the Buddhist concept of Nirvāna, which is annihilation of the lower self and true awareness of the higher self, which the Hindu scriptures refer to as the *Ātman* (Pali *atta*).[386] Fozdar (1995) argues that Buddha did not actually deny the existence of the soul. Rather, he distinguished between the 'real-self' and the 'non-self', [387] as mentioned in the *Dhammapada*: **"Self is the lord of self, who else could be the lord? With self well subdued, a man finds a lord such as few can find."**[388]

Why is mantra meditation so potent? The reason is simple. The origin of all things is One, the Primal Will, also known as the Primal Word. In the language of the New Testament, it is referred to as the Logos (Koine Greek for 'Word'). As the Gospel of John says (1:1 - 3): **"In the beginning was the Word, and the Word was with God, and the Word was God. The same was in the beginning with God. All things were made by him; and without him was not any thing made that was made."**[389] The Word is the Source of all existence, not simply through one act of creation, but through perpetual generation. All things emanate from the Primal Will, like light emanating from a lamp. The Lamp is the One Source of all existence and we, along with all other created things, are the emanation of that primeval and pre-existent Being. This Primal Will is not something which can be defined with scientific definitions. It exists above and beyond the realm of Its creation and is, hence, eternally transcendent and exalted above place, time, ascent, descent, location, matter or energy. The source of the light of existence is exalted far, far beyond the light itself. And that Primal Will has Its own origin in the Everlasting Essence, which is the utterly inaccessible reality of God. As the *Sarvasāra-Upanishad* states: **"What is Brahman? Brahman is that which is free from**

all vehicles, which is the Absolute Consciousness devoid of particularities."[390]

From this Everlasting and Eternal Essence proceeded the Primal Will, the Primal Word, which was uttered in the time before time, in the beginning which has no beginning. And then that Word brought all things into existence in a time before time, i.e. it has always been bringing creation into existence. Creation has no beginning and no end, just as the Primal Will has no beginning and no end. It is, as Buddha says: **"There is, O Bhikkhus, an unborn, unoriginated, uncreated, unformed. Were there not, O Bhikkhus, this unborn, unoriginated, uncreated, unformed, there would be no escape from the world of the born, originated, created, formed. Since, O Bhikkhus, there is an unborn, unoriginated. uncreated, unformed, therefore is there an escape from the born, originated, created, formed."**[391] According to Fozdar (1995) this Uncreated, Unoriginated, Causeless Cause represents the '*Element or Causeless Cause*' from which all Buddhas and Dharmas originate, i.e. God.[392] He further states that this Unoriginated being is the source from which all things emanate and they are all subject to one law, whether it be called 'Dharma, or Karma or religion.'[393] Krishna, likewise says: **"It is called neither being nor non-being... Without and within (all) beings; the unmoving and also the moving; because of Its subtlety incomprehensible; It is far and near... The Light even of lights, It is said to be beyond darkness; Knowledge, and the One Thing to be known, the Goal of knowledge, dwelling in the hearts of all."**[394]

The Rig-Veda, also, refers to this being as **"that One wherein abide all things existing."** 395 Why is all of this relevant? Because this Primal Will has infused all created things with Its own Names and Attributes (i.e. the Names and Attributes of God). Every leaf, every flower, every stem, every rock, every star, every galaxy, every galactic cluster—from the smallest proton and particle of existence to the greatest bodies of energy and power within the universe, all things are inherently possessed of at least one of these attributes. Stars are the sources of energy, light and power, which are all attributes of the Divine Being. Atoms and particles, likewise, operate under the power of attraction and unity, which are divine attributes. The whole of creation is a mirror of the Divine—and so are we.

> **"And he taught Adam the names of all things, and then set them before the angels, and said, 'Tell me the names of these, if ye are endued with wisdom.'"396**
>
> - Qur'ān 2:31

We, being human beings, are created in the image of our Creator. We are, as Genesis informs us, created **"in his own image, in the image of God created he him; male and female created he them."**397 Krishna likewise says: **"he sees, who sees the Lord Supreme, existing equally in all beings, deathless in the dying. Since seeing the Lord equally existent everywhere, he injures not Self by self, and so goes to the highest Goal."**398 And in the Qur'ān (59:24), we find this verse, **"He is God, the Creator, the**

Maker, the Former. He hath most excellent names. Whatever is in heaven and earth praiseth Him: And He is the Mighty, the Wise."[399] As such, we are capable of mirroring forth all the Names and Attributes of God within our innermost selves. Each of the Names of God is a key to understanding these attributes and, by meditating on them, we can attain to a greater understanding of their power, embosom them within our innermost hearts, and internalize these attributes. It allows us to become receptacles of the Word of God, which will pulsate through our beings like vital blood pulsating through a living creature. These names have immense spiritual power, being capable of changing and refining our character, redirecting us to the Divine Source, and enabling us to become channels of divine energy and power.

In the *Śrī Caitanya-Caritamrita* the Vaishnava saint, Krsnadāsa Kavirāja Gosvami (b. 1496 CE), quotes several sacred Hindu scriptures which refer to the power of the divine Name. Quoting the Haribhakti-Vilasa, he states that "whosoever utters the holy name of the Lord once, brings it once on his mind's eye or allows it only once to enter his ears, is certainly saved" and this applies "whether the name is correctly or incorrectly pronounced."[400] The same verse furthermore states that "the very touch of the holy name is able to kill the effects of sin in men."[401] Krsnadāsa also quotes another Vaishnava saint called Svarupa Damodara Gosvami who, in the *Bhaktirasamrita Sindhu*, writes that "the name of the holy Lord is like the Sun," and the very touch of it drives in one moment the "darkness of heaps of sins contracted in the courses of life."[402] He does condition this, however, by stating that the name must, firstly, "enter your heart or the labyrinth of your ears," and, secondly, "you must have your mind and heart adorned by faith."[403] Thus, as we have stated above, without the fire of love, mere repetition is ineffective.

Mantra Meditation in Vaishnavism

> **"The Supreme Deity, called by the name of Hari, resides in the hearts of those who have succeeded in dispelling all doubts."[404]**

> - Veda-Vyāsa, *The Mahabharata*, Book 12: Santi Parva, Part 3, Section CCCL.

The term Vaishnavism refers to the branch of Hinduism which focuses on the worship of Vishnu, which is a Name of God referring to His Attribute as the Divine Preserver. Literally, Vishnu means the 'All-Pervasive,' from the verb *viś*, which means 'to pervade.'[405] The worship of Vishnu goes back to the very earliest origins of Hinduism, and various hymns to Vishnu are found within the Rig-Veda, which is the earliest of the Vedas. For example, in Hymn CLIV, we find: **"I will declare the mighty deeds of Visnu, of him who measured out the earthly regions... Who verily upholds the threefold, the earth, the heaven, and all living creatures."**[406] The Rig-Veda also refers to the abode of Vishnu as being the **"sublimest mansion."**[407] In particular, however, a Vaishnava is a devotee of Lord Srī Krishna (also spelled Krsna) Vasūdeva, the author of the Bhagavad-Gita (may he bestow his grace and blessings upon us), who is regarded by Hindus as an Avatar of Lord Vishnu. The term

Avatar refers to a 'descent' or manifestation of God in the form of a human being. While most Hindus take this to mean a literal incarnation of God, we will use this concept here to refer to a perfect Mirror of God. Since all humans are capable of mirroring God's attributes to a limited degree, might we not also understand that there can be a Perfect Mirror of God's Names and Attributes? The Divine Teachers, who appear in every age, are Perfect Teachers and Perfect Mirrors of the Divine, being conduits of His Will, Purpose and Divine Power. Krishna was thus the perfect vessel of the Divine Will and His Mirror on earth.

"Of him who gives voice to the auspicious name 'Krishna' tens of millions of great sins are quickly reduced to ashes. Even the dying Ajāmila reached heaven by pronouncing the name Hari,[28] which had been given to his son. How much more then is its effect when it is pronounced with faith!"[408]

- Veda-Vyāsa, *The Garuda Purāna*, v. 12 – 13.

The name Krishna (or Krsna) means, according to A.C. Bhaktivedanta Swami Prabhupada (1896 - 1977), the 'All-Attractive One.'[409] In the Mahabharata, Sanjaya defines the name Krishna as follows: **"...he is called Krishna because he**

---

[28] The story of Ajāmila can be found in Canto 6 of the *Srimad-Bhagavatam*. See: http://prabhupadabooks.com/sb/6/1 (accessed 12/04/2017).

uniteth in himself what are implied by the two words *Krishi* which signifieth 'what existeth' and *na* which signifieth 'eternal peace'." [410] In his commentary on the *Srī Brahma Samhitā*, Prabhupada's teacher, Bhaktisiddhanta Sarasvati Gosvami (1874 - 1937) also writes that "the very name 'Krsna' implies His love-attracting designation."[411] Literally, however, Krishna means the 'Dark One,' as stated in the Mahabharata: **"I till the Earth, assuming the form of a large plough-share of black iron. And because my complexion is black, therefore am I called by the name of Krishna. I have united the Earth with Water, Space with Mind, and Wind with Light. Therefore am I called Vaikuntha..."** [412] Krsnadāsa Kavirāja states that the Name of Krishna has particular potency in cleansing the heart of sin. He writes that "the Name of Lord Shree Krishna, in the first place, dissipates all sin, and, in the next place, manifests Devotion, which is the source of Divine Love."[413] As we mentioned in *Mindfulness: Five Ways to Achieve Real Happiness, True Knowledge and Inner Peace*, one well-known mantra, which was popularized in 16th century India by Chaitanya Mahaprabhu (1486 – 1534 CE), is known as the 'Hare Krishna' mantra or *mahā-mantra*.[414] It was later popularized in the West through the efforts of A.C. Bhaktivedanta Swami Prabhupada, who founded the International Society for Krishna Consciousness (ISKCON). The mantra consists of 16 words and goes as follows: **Hare Krishna, Hare Krishna / Krishna, Krishna, Hare Hare / Hare Rāma, Hare Rāma / Rāma, Rāma, Hare, Hare**. It invokes the names Krishna and Rāma, who were both Avatars of Vishnu, as well as the vocative form of the Divine Name, Hari, which means 'He who removes illusion.'[415] In a lecture delivered in 1966, Prabhupada explained that the word 'Hara' means 'energy, internal energy,' of which Hare is the vocative form, addressing God's energy.[416] Krishna, as already mentioned, means the 'All-Attractive One.' Rāma is the name of the Avatar of Vishnu who appeared prior to Krishna. According to Prabhupada, the meaning of Rāma is the 'highest pleasure', [417] 'unlimited happiness', [418] or the 'reservoir of pleasure.'[419]

> **"The name of Hari, coming within the range of hearing, takes away the sins of men... My holy name should be remembered and meditated upon repeatedly... Hari, meditated upon even by one who has evil thoughts, takes away sins: fire burns, even though accidentally touched... Hence one should remember the name of Mahā Visnu, [29] which effaces multitudes of sins, and should read or listen to the Gītā [30] and the Hymn of the Thousand Names."[420][31]**
>
> - *The Garuda Purāna*, v. 8 – 9, 14, 25.

---

[29] In Vaishnavism, *Mahā-Vishnu* is God the Creator—the Absolute Being.

[30] The Bhagavad-Gita.

[31] For the thousand names, see *The Mahabharata*, Book 13: Anusasana Parva, Part 2, Section CXLIX. Available online at: http://www.sacred-texts.com/hin/m13/m13b114.htm (accessed 12/04/2017).

The mantra is also mentioned in the *Kalisantārana-Upanishad*, which states: **"Hearken to that which all S'rutis (the Vedas) keep secret and hidden, through which one may cross the samsāra (mundane existence) of Kali [i.e. the age of Kali]... Again, Nārada asked Brahmā: 'What is the name?' To which Hiranyagarbha (Brahmā) replied thus: (the words are:) '1. Harē, 2. Rāma, 3. Harē, 4. Ramā, 5. Rāma, 6. Rāma, 7. Harē, 8. Harē, 9. Harē, 10. Krshna, 11. Harē, 12. Krshna, 13. Krshna, 14, Krshna, 15. Harē, 16. Harē. These sixteen names (words) are destructive of the evil effects of Kali. No better means than this is to be seen in all the Vedas."**[421] The following anecdote is meant to give an indication of the power of this mantra. It relates to a Vaishnava saint by the name of Haridāsa Thakur, who was a disciple of the afore-mentioned Chaitanya Mahaprabhu. It is said that, in his youth, Haridāsa led a life of penance and spiritual training. He was a Muslim by birth but his original, Islamic name is lost to history. The name Hari-dāsa literally means 'Servant of Hari,' which is a name of God.[422] He was given this title by the Vaishnava saint, Advaita Acharya (1434 – 1449 CE), who instructed him to recite Krishna's names. His activities, however, were looked upon with great annoyance by the ruling authorities of the region where he preached. In particular, Rāmachandra Khān, the *zeminder*,[32] disliked the Vaishnavas and

---

[32] From the Persian *zamīn-dār* ('land-owner'). They collected land revenue during the Mughal rule in India.

could not bear the fact that Haridāsa was a devotee. As such, he decided that he would devise a means to defame the saint.[423]

Rāmachandra Khān could find no fault in the behaviour of this saint. Therefore, he decided to tempt him with the charms of a beautiful woman. Gathering together some 'public women,' he pointed out Haridāsa and urged them to 'shake him from his saintliness.' One of the most beautiful of these women at once declared her willingness to carry out this mission. "That is nothing hard for me," she said. "For, I shall cause diversion in him in three days." Adorning herself with the finest clothes and ornaments, she reached the dwelling-place of the Vaishnava saint and, with a soft and sweet tone, said: "You, Oh Saint! are very fair. And this is the very flush of your youth. What woman will control her passions at the sight of your beautiful person? So my heart, Oh Saint! yearns for association with you. And I cannot bear this life unless I obtain the touch of your beautiful person."[424]

Haridāsa considered what she said and replied: "Yes. I shall promise thee what thou desirest. But let me first finish saying the *fixed number of the holy name*. So sit you here till then before me. And hear you the holy name pronounced. *I shall fulfil your desire when I shall have finished with the holy name*."[425] The woman sat on the floor and waited as he chanted, and chanted, and chanted, until morning dawned and she had to stand up and leave. Again, she returned the next day, at night, and—again—sat as he chanted the name 'Hari.' As she was about to leave, he informed her: "Every month, Oh woman, I utter the holy name

'Hari' a crore[33] of times and I perform a sacrifice. This number is almost complete. Yea, I thought it would end to-day. So I uttered the holy name all night. But I could not finish it. I am, however, sure it will be finished tomorrow. And so I shall be able to end my vow to-morrow. When I have done it, I shall have intercourse with you to your heart's content."[426] The woman again left and returned to the Khan, explaining what had happened.

On the third night, he came again and sat as Haridāsa yet again chanted the name of God again and again and again. Pausing to speak to the woman, he informed her that he would finally finish his chanting that day, reaching the designated number. This time, however, she also repeated the name 'Hari,' again and again, and, as a result, her heart was opened. She returned to Rāmachandra Khan and explained what had happened. Then, she returned to Haridāsa Thakur and confessed her sins, informing him of her instructions from the Khān. She begged him for forgiveness, saying: "Oh Lord! And as a woman I have committed infinite sins. Be merciful and save this wretched sinner." [427] And Haridāsa replied to her: "Give all your property, all that you have got at home away to the Brahmins. Come to this house and rest here... and utter ye the *holy name* with intermission. For, if you do this, you will ere long attain the holy feet of Krishna."[428] She followed his instructions, giving up all her wealth, shaving her head and wearing only a single piece of cloth. She took up residence in Haridāsa's house, sometimes fasting and

---

[33] Crore = 100 lakhs = 10,000,000.

187

sometimes sustaining herself by chewing certain things. Finally, she became a great saint, renowned among Vaishnavas, who paid her homage and respect.[429] This was the transformative effect of hearing the mantra, especially through the influence of a saintly individual who *lived* what he *preached.*

> **"I am desirous of hearing those names of Hari, that Supreme Lord of all creatures. Indeed, by listening to those names, I shall be sanctified and cleansed even like the bright autumnal moon..."[430]**

> **"Hear, O king, the thousand names, possessed of great efficacy in destroying sins, of that foremost one in all the worlds that Master of the universe, viz., Vishnu. All those names derived from His attributes, secret and well-known, of the high-souled Vasudeva which were sung by Rishis, I shall recite to thee for the good of all. They are, Om! He that enters all things, besides Himself, He that covers all things, He unto whom sacrificial libations are poured, the Lord of the Past, the Present, and the Future, the Creator (or Destroyer) of all existent things, the upholder of all existent things, the Existent, the Soul of all, the Originator of all things..."[431]**

- Veda-Vyāsa, *The Mahabharata*, Book 12: Santi Parva, Part 3, Section CCCXLII; Book 13: Anusasana Parva, Part 2, Section CXLIX.

Mantra Meditation in Buddhism

In Buddhism, mantra meditation is particularly mentioned as a method of deliverance from material bondage by the Pure Land school of East Asia. It was prophesied that the teachings of Buddha would one day disappear from the world, with some saying this would happen after two thousand years, and others saying it would disappear after only five hundred years. [432] However, according to Lopez (2004), they were all agreed that the teachings would face a gradual decline, both in the quality of the doctrines and in the discipline of the followers. Despairing of the disparate teachings and texts which had reached them from India, Chinese Buddhists concluded that they were in the final stages of the decline of Buddha's teachings and, therefore, an alternative method of achieving liberation would be needed.[433] As such, the monk Daozhuo (562 – 645 CE) said that two paths existed: the path of the sages and the path of rebirth in the Land of Bliss, with only the latter being accessible in this age of degeneration.[434] The Chinese called this latter practice *nianfo*, meaning 'Buddha contemplation', being a translation of the Sanskrit term *buddhānusmrti* ('mindfulness of the Buddha'). [435] The practice involved reciting the name of Buddha Amitābha, who had come to liberate all those who sincerely sought freedom from the material world and entrance into his Pure Land.[436] The practice was taken up by popular preachers, including Shandao (613 – 681 CE), and the Japanese monk Hōnen (1133 – 1212 CE), who wrote a book entitled *On the Nembutsu Selected in the Primal Vow*.[437] In that work, he argues that the practice of *nembutsu*—the Japanese term for *nianfo*—is superior to all other practices, because all the myriad virtues—including the light of wisdom, the teaching of dharma, and the benefiting of all living things—have been gathered in the name of Amitābha (or Amida) Buddha.[438] Thus by repeating this name, one is, in effect, practising all the virtues laid out in the teachings of Gautama Buddha and one can attain full liberation.

> "And now, O Ânanda, stand up, facing westward, and having taken a handful of flowers, fall down. This is the quarter where that Bhagavat Amitâbha, the Tathâgata, holy and fully enlightened, dwells, remains, supports himself, and teaches the Law, whose spotless and pure name, famed in every quarter of the whole world with its ten quarters, the blessed Buddhas, equal to (the grains of) the sand of the river Gangâ,[34] speaking and answering again and again without stopping, extol, praise, and eulogize."[439]

- Gautama Buddha, *Buddhist Mahâyâna Texts*, The Larger Sukhāvatī-Vyūha, Description of Sukhāvatī, The Land of Bliss, § 39.

The name, Amitābha, refers to a *bodhisattva*, or 'liberated being' who strives to save the unliberated souls of this world from material bondage. Fozdar (1995), p. 109 argues that the various

---

[34] The River Ganges.

'qualitative super-personal Buddhas' described in later texts, such as Amitabha, Vairocana, Avalokitesvara, etc. are all 'emanations from the Adi-Buddha Vajrasattva' and are thus names and qualities used to describe the 'Infinite, the intangible *Absolute*.'[440] As we explained in Chapter XI of *Mindfulness: Five Ways to Achieve Real Happiness, True Knowledge and Inner Peace*, Amitābha is the Buddha of Unbounded Light, also known as Amita or Amida Buddha.[441] The name, Amitābha, means 'Infinite Light,' while His alternative name, Amitāyus, means 'Infinite Life.'[442] Yejitsu Okusa, in *Principal Teachings of The True Sect of Pure Land*, writes: "In the True Sect of Pure Land, we have the true, all-embracing love of Amida to save all beings from ignorance and pain. It is the net of boundless compassion thrown by the Buddha's own hand into the sea of misery, in which the ignorant rather than the wise, the sinful rather than the good, are meant to be gathered up. This love and compassion is eternally abiding with the Buddha, whose will to save all beings knows no temporal limitations; and on this account the Buddha is called *Amitāyus* (Eternal Life). His power to save is manifest in his light..."[443] The Japanese Pure Land Buddhist poet, Saichi Asahara (1850 – 1932) writes:

"Shining in glory is Buddha's Pure Land,

And this is my Pure Land!

'Namu-amida-butsu! Namu-amida-butsu!'"[444]

191

- Saichi Asahara, quoted in Daisetz Teitaro Suzuki (1957) *Mysticism, Christian and Buddhist*, Appendix VIII.

The 'Land of Bliss' described in the Buddhist scriptures is called Sukhāvatī.[445] This realm of existence is described in detail in a text called the Wonderful Panoply of the Land of Bliss, using such imagery as the 'world-system Blissful.' It describes a 'buddha-field' called Śāriputra, which is enclosed with seven railings, the same number of palm trees and nets of bells.[446] There are lotus ponds, each surrounded by four flights of steps made of precious metals and rocks, such as gold, silver, chrysoberyl and crystal. Within each pond, there are lotus flowers of many colours and, around each pond, there are gem trees.[447] While this sounds perfectly fanciful, it represents the concepts of purity, beauty and transcendence which describe the land of Pure Bliss which can be obtained through this form of mantra meditation. The same sutra promises that, whoever hears the name of Amitābha (here called Amitāyus) and brings it to mind, without distraction, and keeps it in mind for 1 – 7 nights, will be liberated at the moment of death. Furthermore, at the hour of death, Amitāyus will stand before him or her, surrounded by a host of other liberated souls, and he or she will then be reborn in Sukhāvatī.[448]

The practice of mantra meditation in Pure Land Buddhism consists of repeating the mantra, **Om amitābha hrīh,**[449] or **Namo Amitābhāya**[450] (in Sanskrit), **Namu Amida Butsu** (in Japanese), or **Nāmó Ēmítuófó** in Chinese.[451] All of these versions have the same effect, in that they call upon Amitābha as the Primal Will who enables us to attain enlightenment through His bounty and grace.[452] As Okusa clarifies: "While all other deeds of ours are more or less defiled, the reciting of 'Namu Amida Bu' is an act free from impurities; for it is not we that recite it, but Amida himself, who, giving us his own name, makes us recite it."[453] Buddha himself (peace and blessings be upon him) is quoted as saying:

> **"Amitābha, the unbounded light, is the source of wisdom, of virtue, of Buddhahood. The deeds of sorcerers and miracle-mongers are frauds, but what is more wondrous, more mysterious, more miraculous than Amitābha?... the repetition of the name Amitābha Buddha is meritorious only if thou speak it with such a devout attitude of mind as will cleanse thy heart and attune thy will to do works of righteousness."[454]**
>
> - Buddha, *The Gospel of Buddha*, LX.

There are various recordings of this mantra, in each of the above languages, available on YouTube. You can find some links to these recordings in Chapter XI of <u>our previous book</u>.[455]

Mantra Meditation in Christianity

"And the publican, standing afar off, would not lift up so much as *his* eyes unto heaven, but smote

upon his breast, saying, God be merciful to me a sinner."[456]

- Luke 18:13

Christianity has always contained a strong element of contemplation and personal prayer. This practice has its origins in the Gospels, where Jesus teaches his followers the Lord's Prayer (Matthew 6:9-13; Luke 11:2-4). Jesus specifies that prayer should not be done for the sake of looking spiritual. Rather, we must pray individually, so that we can attain God's pleasure. He says, in the Sermon on the Mount, which contains the core teachings and essence of Christianity: **"But thou, when thou prayest, enter into thy closet, and when thou hast shut thy door, pray to thy Father which is in secret; and thy Father which seeth in secret shall reward thee openly."**[457] In other words, prayer is between the seeker and his Beloved, or between the supplicant and his Creator. God gives spiritual rewards and blessings to those who perform their prayers, and other good deeds, in private, without any hope for reward or praise. Private prayer, contemplation and meditation, therefore, are perfectly in accord with the teachings of Jesus Christ.

"Rejoice evermore. Pray without ceasing. In every thing give thanks: for this is the will of God in Christ Jesus concerning you."[458]

- 1 Thessalonians 5:16 - 18

In the Gospel of Luke, likewise, he gives a parable to identify sincere prayer and forgiveness. There was a Pharisee, who stood by himself and prayed to God, saying: **"God, I thank thee, that I am not as other men are, extortioners, unjust, adulterers, or even as this publican. I fast twice in the week, I give tithes of all that I possess."**[459] There was a tax collector standing at some distance from the Pharisee, who was greatly ashamed at his sins. Looking up at heaven, he beat upon his breast and said: **"God be merciful to me a sinner."**[460] Jesus then explained that it was the tax collector, not the Pharisee, who received God's forgiveness and blessing. What does this tell us? That humility is essential for forgiveness and to receive divine grace and blessings. Hypocrisy and conceit are great barriers between the seeker and his Beloved.

> **"And whatsoever ye shall ask in my name, that will I do, that the Father may be glorified in the Son. If ye shall ask any thing in my name, I will do *it*."**[461]

- John 14:13 – 14

The early Desert Fathers of the 5th century CE used to practice a form of mantra meditation, using what has become known as the 'Jesus prayer.' This is essentially the verse from Luke 18:13—the tax collector's prayer—prefaced with the words 'Lord Jesus Christ, son of God.'[462] In the Discourse on Abba Philimon (6th – 7th century CE), from the *Philokalia*, the story is given of a brother, named John, who came to see one of the Desert Fathers, called Philimon.[463] Clasping the ascetic's feet, he asked him what he needed to do to be saved. Philimon replied that he must acquire a 'perfect longing for God.' Brother John enquired further, asking how he could attain this state of perfect longing. Philimon replied that he should, firstly, meditate for a while, deep within his heart, as this can cleanse his intellect. When John pressed him for further clarification, Philimon explained that he should, within his heart and mind, and with great awe and trembling, repeat the Jesus Prayer, i.e. **"Lord Jesus Christ, have mercy upon me."**[464] Philimon thus recommended this prayer as a form of silent mantra, which forms part of the essential practice of silent meditation. The purpose of this meditation, Philimon explained, was to attain a state of perfect longing for God, which is identical to the Sufi concept of longing for the Divine Beloved.

Mantra Meditation in Sufi Islam

"Blessed be the name of thy Lord, Possessed of Glory (al-Jalāl) and Honour (al-Ikrām)!"[465]

- Qur'ān 55:78

Sufi Islam (Arabic *tasawwuf*), which is the mystical branch of Islam, has a long tradition of practising *dhikr*, or 'remembrance of God.' The goal of Sufism is to attain to a state of reunion with the Divine Beloved, i.e. God. This involves annihilating one's lower self—the *nafs* as it is called in Arabic. This achievement is called *fanā'* (i.e. 'annihilation'). By annihilating our lower self, we also attain to reunion with God, which is called *baqā'* (lit. 'subsistence' or 'permanency'). It is so called because *baqā'* is a permanent state of reunion, esp. after death, in which one enters permanent union with the Divine. This should not be understood literally, as a form of pantheism—on the contrary, the *rūḥ*—the rational soul—remains intact. There is a clear distinction between the Creator and His creation. The form of 'union' referred to, therefore, is a union of love and nearness. By developing spiritual qualities, virtues and noble attributes—which are the very names and attributes of God—we can become near to God and receive His love. God's love is unceasing, unending, and eternally flowing. However, in order to receive His love, we have to turn unto Him with our hearts and souls, and seek reunion with the Divine Beloved. We can understand this through an analogy: our souls are like plants. If they are turned away from the light of the sun, the plants will be deprived of light, heat and energy, and will be unable to grow. However, when a plant is placed in the sunshine, it grows verdant and strong, tall and fruitful. In the same manner, if we turn away from God, ignore His teachings, live a life which is contrary to virtue, and deny His bounties and grace, then we are living in the darkness, unable to see or feel the light of the Sun of Truth. If we want to attain unto the bounties of God and feel His boundless love, then we must emerge from the shadows and step into the Light.

> **"God is the LIGHT of the Heavens and of the Earth. His Light is like a niche in which is a lamp - the lamp encased in glass – the glass, as it were, a glistening star. From a blessed tree is it lighted, the olive neither of the East nor of the West, whose oil would well-nigh shine out, even though fire touched it not! It is light upon light. God guideth**

whom He will to His light, and God setteth forth parables to men, for God knoweth all things."[466]

- Qur'ān 24:35

It is not easy, in this modern, materialistic world, to maintain a state of God-consciousness. We are often preoccupied with material concerns and, too often, we embrace that darkness that surrounds us. How, then, can we remain within the light? How can we attain a state of permanent God-consciousness? This has been the concern of Sufism since its beginning. And the great Islamic sages and mystics of the ages have come up with practices and methods to retain this state of God-consciousness, in order to achieve *fanā'* and *baqā'*. Not all these mystics have properly understood the nature of reunion with the Divine Beloved. Some have fallen into the fallacies of pantheism, monism and reincarnation. Others have believed they can literally become 'God.' Yet others have come to believe that they are 'above the law' (i.e. antinomianism) and not subject to the laws and precepts revealed by the Prophet Muhammad and other Prophets (peace be upon them all). These are all errors which result from an extreme interpretation of Sufi principles. Rather, we must maintain the separation between the Creator and His creation. We can become mirrors of the Divine—however imperfect—but we cannot literally *become* the Divine. Also, although we can see God's names and attributes in all things, God does not literally *enter* all things. He is eternally transcendent.

In order to attain a state of reunion with God, one must also follow the divine laws and teachings, because these help us to purify our hearts from the rust and dust of materialism, vices and imperfections. We are like birds which have descended from the heights of celestial glory and, becoming enamoured of the clay, have descended into the mud and filth of material existence. Here, our wings have become soiled and enmeshed in the clay and mud, and we are now unable to fly. However, by developing virtues—by becoming detached and acquiescent to the divine Will—we can clean our hearts and cleanse our wings from the dust and dross of material existence—and we can then again soar aloft in the celestial heights of spiritual purity and God-consciousness. It is important, therefore, while engaged on the spiritual path, to follow the teachings—the laws and precepts—of the Great Teachers who appear throughout the ages, e.g. Krishna, Gautama Buddha, Zoroaster, Jesus Christ, Muhammad, etc. For more information on this point, I would refer you to Chapters I through III of *Mindfulness: Five Ways to Achieve Real Happiness, True Knowledge and Inner Peace*.[467]

"Hail to thee, then O LOVE, sweet madness!

Thou who healest all our infirmities!"[468]

- Jalāl ad-Dīn Rūmī, *The Masnavi*, Book I.

The spiritual method of Sufism is based on four main practices: remembrance of God (Arabic *dhikr*), contemplation (*fikr*, lit. 'thought'), meditation (*murāqabah*), and self-examination (*muḥāsabah*).[469] Netton (2000) explains that *dhikr* is different from *fikr* in the sense that *dhikr* is sensory, while *fikr* is intellectual. *Fikr* involves an internalization of the sacred, while *dhikr* involves a focus on one of the Divine Names.[470] The first to describe the practice of *dhikr* was al-Tustari.[471] Although the concept of *dhikr*, or 'remembrance God (*Allāh*)', was a well-established Islamic concept, Abū-Muhammad Sahl ibn 'Abdu'llāh al-Tustari (c. 818 – c. 896 CE) gave it a new meaning—the practice of repetitive prayer, i.e. mantra meditation.[472] According to Sedgwick (2016), one account has al-Tustari learning this practice from his uncle while still a child. When his uncle asked if he remembered God who created him, al-Tustari asked how he should remember Him. The uncle replied, saying that he should, once he had changed into his nightclothes, repeat the phrase 'God is my witness' three times. When he had done this for three days straight, the uncle instructed him to say it seven times each night. When he had done this, the uncle instructed him to say it eleven times each night. The result of this practice was that the young boy began to experience, in his own words, a 'a sweetness in my inmost being.'[473] According to Keeler & Keeler's (2011) introduction to their translation of the Tafsīr al-Tustarī (al-Tustarī's commentary on the Qur'ān), the exact mantra which the uncle imparted was: ***Allāh-u ma'-ī, Allah-u nāẓir-ī, Allāh-u shāhid-ī*** (i.e. 'God is with me, God is watching over me, God is my Witness.')[474] These phrases have a scriptural basis in various verses from the Qur'ān, such as the following: (39:36): **"Is not God a sufficient protector of his servant?"**;[475] (50:16): **"We created man, and We know what his soul whispereth within him; and We are nearer unto him than his jugular vein"**;[476] (49:18): **"Verily, God knoweth the secrets of the**

200

Heavens and of the Earth: and God beholdeth what ye do;[477] (4:79): **"And God sufficeth for a witness."**[478]

Figure 16. A Sufi practising meditation

The spiritual practices of Sufism differ depending on the order or school of Sufism followed. In the practice of the Naqshabandi Sufi order, there are three categories of meditation: *dhikr* (remembrance of God), *nafi wa asbat* (negation and affirmation, i.e. a practice of breath-channelling exercise), and *murāqabah* (the visualization of the *shaykhk/pīr* through meditation).[479] Sufi orders generally have a *shaykh*, also called a *pīr*, who trains the disciples in various spiritual practices. In Naqshbandi-Mujaddidi practices, the *dhikr* is generally silent.[480] In the Suhrawardī Sufi practice, *murāqabah* takes the form of mindfulness meditation, which is aimed at focusing every part of the body (*al-badan al-insānī*), as well as one's breath or spirit (*rūḥ*) towards the ultimate goal of *fanā'*.[481] The practice of *dhikr* among Suhrawardī Sufis involves the constant repetition of the Qur'ān, the repetition of certain Qur'ānic verses (111 times), as well as benedictions on the Prophet, his companions and Suhrawardī shaykhs, including Shihābu'd-Dīn Yaḥyā al-Suhrawardī (1154 – 1191 CE) himself.[482] The goal of *dhikr*, according to the Suhrawardī Sufis, is to move us, in every shape and form, from the mundane reality which we believe to be true, to the realm of the divine presence (called *ḥazaratu'l-ḥaqq*).[483]

The most famous Sufi practice, perhaps, is that of the so-called 'whirling dervishes,' which is performed by the followers of

https://upload.wikimedia.org/wikipedia/commons/d/d4/Indischer_Maler_um_1630_001.jpg (accessed 15/05/2017).

the mystic poet, Jalāl ad-Dīn Muhammad al-Balkhī (Rūmī) (1207 – 1273 CE), called Mevlevi Sufis. According to one account, when Jalāl was just a child of seven years old, he used to recite the 108th sūrah ('chapter') of the Qur'ān, which states: **"TRULY we have given thee an ABUNDANCE; pray therefore to the Lord, and offer sacrifice.**[484] **Verily he who hateth thee shall be childless."**[485] Even as a child, he used to weep when he recited these words. Then, suddenly, one day, he had a vision of the Divine, in which he heard a voice saying: "O Jalālu-'d-Dīn By the majesty (*jalāl*) of Our glory, do thou henceforward cease to combat with thyself; for We have exalted thee to the station of ocular vision."[486] Thereafter, he vowed to devote himself to the Lord in the hope that he could help others to achieve a high spiritual station.[487]

The practice of Mevlevi whirling is called *samā'* (literally 'listening').[488] This is a ritual performed on certain dates (called *muqābalah*), in which Mevlevis listen to musical chanting of the *na't-i-sharīf* (i.e. poetry in praise of the Prophet Muhammad) while whirling in a circular fashion, hoping to attain to a state of *fanā'*, or annihilation of the lower self.[489] Each of these practices can be seen as deriving from the same origin and tradition as the Hindu and Buddhist practices of mantra meditation and may very well be influenced by them. All religions should be regarded as forming part of one, universal tradition of inspiration and devotion; and mantra meditation, regardless of its origins, is a universally-applicable practice which leads to spiritual awareness, insight and God-consciousness.

"In the Name of God. I praise and invoke the creator, Lord All-Wise,[36] the Radiant, Glorious, Omniscient, Maker, Lord of Lords, King over all kings, Watchful, Creator of the universe, Giver of daily bread, Powerful, Strong, Eternal, Forgiver, Merciful, Loving, Mighty, Wise, Holy, and Nourisher. May (His) just kingdom be imperishable. May the majesty and glory of the Lord All-Wise, the Beneficent Lord, increase."[490]

- The Prophet Zoroaster, *Avesta: Khorda Avesta*, Khwarshed Niyayesh

Step One: Self-Preparation

One should begin the process of mantra meditation by situating himself or herself in a state of spiritual awareness or receptivity. There is no point in simply repeating names without *meaning* or *feeling* what one is saying. A spiritual and reverent attitude, therefore, is essential. One may chant the Names of God in any location—any place whatsoever—as awareness of God and God-consciousness should be perpetual, unceasing and unending. We should constantly be aware of God's blessings and His attributes, which are manifest in all created things, from the smallest leaf and flower, from the tiniest ant and mite, to the

---

[36] Originally Ohrmazd, or Ahura Mazda. I have translated this as 'Lord All-Wise.'

largest objects in physical existence, viz. stars, galaxies, black holes and galactic clusters. All created things shine brilliantly with the Light of God and manifest at least one of His attributes, while human beings, being created in the image of their Creator, possess the capacity to manifest *all* the names and attributes within themselves, howbeit imperfectly.

If the meditation is performed alone, where one has the most freedom and comfort to chant the Names of God out loud, then it is best to ensure that the environment in which we chant is clean and free of clutter or other distractions. We should turn off any music, television or other noises, so that we can focus solely on chanting the holy Names. When we chant, we should focus solely on the sound and meaning of the Names as they are uttered by our tongues, free from any outward distractions—oblivious to our own selves, our needs and our physical wants. The Names themselves should take precedence and should dance on our tongues like a force of immense power. We should become like hollow reeds, free from self and passion, and instruments of the divine Will. We become instruments, blowing with the Word and Name of God, and channels of divine power and might. Furthermore, these holy Names give us divine inspiration, a feeling of loving-kindness, and develop within us a state of longing for the Divine Beloved, whose Name we call upon with earnestness and eager supplication.

Step Two: Choose the Mantra and Prayer Beads

The next step is to choose one's mantra, or the Names that one wishes to chant (silently or vocally). We have already mentioned the effectiveness of several mantras above, including the various forms of the Sanskrit name, Hari, including the Hare Krishna *mahā-mantra*, the Pure Land Buddhist mantra invoking the name of Amitabhā, the Jesus Prayer and the various invocations used by Sufi orders. All of these have their relative merits and benefits, as they all call upon the one, true God, either directly (e.g. by invoking God Himself), or indirectly, through the Great Teachers of every age. If we invoke the names Krishna, Rāma, Amitabhā or Jesus, we are calling upon the Great Teachers who are Mirrors of the Divine. Calling upon them is the same as calling upon God, just as following them, obeying their teachings, etc. is the same as following God, obeying His Teachings, etc. The argument can be made, however, that these names are also Names of God. Just as the name Krishna refers to an individual who lived thousands of years ago in India, the Name Krishna is also a Divine Attribute and can refer to God Himself. As we learned earlier in this chapter, Krishna can be interpreted to mean the 'All-Attractive One,' or the 'Dark One.'[491] The same may be said for Rāma and Amitābha. Amitābha means 'Infinite Light', and is not God Infinite Light? After all, the Qur'ān says (24:35): **"God is the LIGHT of the Heavens and of the Earth."**[492] Likewise, the name Jesus, which means 'YHWH is salvation,' contains the Name of God, and thus calling upon the name Jesus is also calling upon the Name of God directly. According to Wilkinson (2015), Jesus is the Greek version of the Hebrew Joshua (*Yehoshu'a*), which is often shortened to *Yeshu'a*.[493] The names that we choose to chant or glorify do not matter, as long as they are Names of God and invoke His numerous and mighty attributes.

When you have chosen your mantra, you may wish to keep track of how many times you repeat the mantra. This is important, because it allows us to maintain a regular spiritual practice. For example, in the case of al-Tustarī (mentioned above), he repeated the mantra, **Allāh-u ma'-ī, Allah-u nāẓir-ī, Allāh-u shāhid-ī**, eleven times each night. The followers of the Hare Krishna movement, under the direction of Prabhupāda, are told to chant 16 'rounds' of the Hare Krishna *mahā-mantra* every day, which takes approximately two hours. Adherents of the movement use *japa*-beads, which are usually made of *tulasi/tulsi* wood,[37] and each set contains 108 beads—a sacred number in Hinduism. According to Sarbadhikary (2015), the term *japa* refers to *manas-jap*, which means hearing the sounds in our mind's ear, while muttering or chanting aloud is referred to as *upanghsu*, and, when the Names of God are chanted in a group, this is known as *nam-kirtan*.[494] Islamic prayer beads, called a *misbaḥah* or *tasbīḥ*, contains 99 or 33 beads. If you choose to chant the Names of God in Arabic, this set of beads would be preferable. One method of recitation is called the Tasbīḥ of Fāṭimah, or 'Prayer of Fāṭimah' (the daughter of the Prophet Muhammad). According to the Shī'ī Imām, Ja'far

---

[37] *Ocimum tenuiflorum*, also known as 'holy basil'.

as-Sādiq (c. 702 – 765 CE), this practice consists of repetition of the phrase *Allāh-u-Akbar* ('God is Most Great') 34 times, *Al-ḥamdu li'llāh* ('Praise be to God') 33 times, and *Subḥāna'llāh* ('Glorified be God') 33 times.[495] According to a tradition preserved in *al-Kāfī*, this recitation should be followed by 1 recitation of the phrase *lā ilāha illa llāh* ('there is no God but God').[496] Whichever of these mantras—or others—you prefer, counting on beads is a useful way of keeping tracking of your progress, which should be daily and continuous. As St. Paul writes (1 Thessalonians 5:17): **"Pray without ceasing."**[497]

Step Three: Recite the Names of God

This step is, perhaps, the most obvious. What we should bear in mind, however, is that our recitation should be mindful. We learned about the practice of mindfulness meditation in Chapter III, and we should also extend the practice of mindfulness to our chanting of the holy names. We should remember, firstly, that we are uttering the Name of God, which is sacred. By being aware and mindful of its sacredness, we respect its sanctity. As Mary, the mother of Jesus, prayed in the Gospel of Luke (1:49): **"For he that is mighty hath done to me great things; and holy *is* his name."**[498] And in the Book of Psalms (135:3, 13), we read: **"Praise the LORD: for the LORD is good: sing praises unto his name; for it is pleasant... Thy name, O LORD, endureth for ever, and thy memorial, O LORD, throughout all generations."**[499] It is essential to remember the holiness of the Divine Names, therefore, and keep this in mind as we recite them.

Next, we must ensure that we are being mindful of the sound of each Name. Yes, all too often, words just slip off our tongues without being aware of what we are uttering. We often find ourselves thinking of other things and forget that we are even reciting anything at all. Therefore, we must focus on the transcendental sounds we are uttering, as we become instruments of the Divine, blowing with the spiritual names and attributes which flow through us.

Thirdly, we should, if possible, try to remember the meaning of what we are uttering. Thus, if we recite the name *Krishna*, we should remember that this means the 'All-Attractive One,' and if we recite the name *Allāh*, we should remember that this means 'God' or 'the-God'. If we recite the name *Amitābha*, we should remember that it means 'Infinite Light,' and if we recite the phrase *Allāh-u Akbar*, we should remember that this means 'God is Most Great'. Lastly, we should focus on God Himself, realizing that we are actually communing with the Divine. When we utter His Names, we are actually speaking to God, communicating with Him and calling upon Him. As such, we should be mindful and aware that we are in a state of communion with the Divine Beloved, who fills our hearts and our souls with the water of life and kindles the fire of love within the temple of our innermost being. As Rūmī says in the *Masnavī*: **"When love of God kindles a flame in the inward man, he burns, and is freed from effects. He has no need of signs to assure him of love, for love casts its own light up to heaven."**[500]

Remember: once you begin the practice of mantra meditation, you should continue to practise it every day, either keeping to the same minimum number of recitations, or increasing your recitations in order to develop a deeper and deeper spiritual awareness.

Conclusion

In this chapter, we have looked at the practice of mantra meditation within the context of Hinduism (in particular, Vaishnavism), Buddhism, Christianity and Sufism. We have found a number of important benefits of mantra meditation, including development of a state of God-consciousness, longing for the Divine Beloved and spiritual enkindlement. According to various scriptures, such as the Purānas, chanting or reciting the Names of God, or even listening to the Names of God, can bring about forgiveness, liberation from material attachment and spiritual progress. Mantra meditation is a universal tradition, which can be found in every major religion. Its efficacy and universality, therefore, cannot be overestimated. As we develop a regular, daily practice of mantra meditation, we can increase our spiritual awareness day-by-day, and achieve a state of inner bliss, happiness and fulfilment.

A word of caution, however: as we have already mentioned, mantra meditation does not mean mere repetition of names. It has some prerequisites, e.g. a "mind and heart adorned by faith"[501] and "great awe and trembling."[502] We should first have faith that what we are reciting is, indeed, the Name of God, and that there is a Divine Being which has created us and continues to sustain us. Otherwise, we are simply repeating names rather like a record player, which is unaware of what it is playing. The record player, however much it may play numerous and varied records, has no awareness of what it is playing, nor does it benefit from playing them. A human being, however, when engaged in true mantra meditation, should be aware of what he or she is doing, and the reality behind the Divine Names that he or she is chanting. Otherwise, like a plant which is placed in the shadows, we will be unable to receive our measure of divine light and love. We should thus practice mantra meditation in a state of faith and certitude that what we are reciting is truly divine. Also, we should recite in a state of mindfulness, aware of the sacredness of what we are chanting, being mindful of the sounds we are uttering, and being aware of the meaning of what we are reciting. Thus, we will attain the greatest benefit from our meditation.

Questions for Reflection:

The following are some questions that will help us to reflect on what we have learned in this chapter:

1. What is a 'mantra'?

2. Why is it not enough to simply repeat the mantra again and again?

3. What does it mean to be created in the image of God?

4. What do the names Krishna and Rāma mean?

5. What are some of the benefits of chanting the name 'Hari', according to the Purānas and other scriptures?

6. What does Amitābha mean?

7. What is the Jesus Prayer?

8. What was the mantra recited by al-Tustarī? How many times did he recite it each night?

9. What is the *Tasbīh of Fātimah*?

10. Why should we be mindful during mantra meditation?

In the next chapter, we will look at the Fourth Way to Meditate: Meditation on the Divine.

∞∞∞∞∞∞∞∞∞∞∞∞∞∞∞∞∞∞∞∞∞∞∞∞∞

VI. The Fourth Way to Meditate-Meditation on the Divine Word

" The grass withereth, the flower fadeth: but the word of our God shall stand for ever."[503]

- Isaiah 40:8

"In truth hath He sent down to thee 'the Book,' which confirmeth those which precede it: For He had sent down the Torah (Law), and the Evangel aforetime, as man's Guidance; and now hath He sent down the 'Illumination'[38]..."[504]

"For we have sent down to thee a Book explaining clearly everything, and a guidance, and a mercy, and glad tidings to the believers."[505]

"This Book have we sent down to thee that by their Lord's permission thou mayest bring men out of darkness into light, into the path of the Mighty, the Glorious."[506]

- Qur'ān 3:3 – 4; 16:89; 14:1

---

[38] i.e. the Qur'ān, here called the *Furqān* (discrimination/illumination).

Introduction

As we have moved through this book, we have, as it were, ascended step-by-step through stages of development in our practice of meditation. The first method explored was mindfulness meditation, which is foundational and cultivates a sense of spiritual awareness which permeates every aspect of our daily lives. In the second method, we developed a radiant loving-kindness, through which we become conduits of loving-kindness for all created things, from our own selves to the greatest bodies and formations of this mighty and limitless universe. In the third method, we have learned to focus on the divine Names and Attributes, which are mirrored resplendently in all created things. Each of these practices cultivate the essential spiritual qualities and virtues which cleanse the rust and dust from off the originally pure mirrors of our hearts, so that the Light of the Almighty and Transcendent Lord of the universe may shine therein. These practices are incomplete, however, if we do not also learn to focus on the source of guidance which allows us to bring our lives into conformity with the Primal Will—that central orb of the universe from which all things are created and perpetually generated.

"Nārāyana is the only one that is stainless, sinless, changeless, and unnameable, and that is pure and divine. There is no second... Nārāyana who pervades all elements, who is one only, who is the cause Purusha and who is causeless, is known as Parabrahman."[507]

214

- Nārāyana-Upanishad

Like light emanating from a lamp, we—our very souls and bodies, and the entire created universe—are emanating from this Primal Will, which is also called the Primal Word, the Logos, the Word of God, Bhagavan,[508] Parabrahman,[509] Ādi-Purusha,[510] the Tao, and the Way. In the Qur'ān, God says (glorified be His glory): **"He it is who has created the heavens and the earth in truth; and on the day when He says, 'BE,' then it is. His word is truth."**[511] The Will and purpose of this Divine Being is made manifest in the form of the divine scriptures which are revealed in every age. He says: **"We did send our apostles with manifest signs; and we did send down among you the Book and the balance, that men might stand by justice."**[512] In ancient India, this divine Word took the form of the Bhagavad-Gita, and in ancient Persia, it took the form of the Gathas and other Zoroastrian scriptures. It also became manifest in the Torah, the Psalms, the Tripitakas, the Gospels, the Qur'ān and other holy Texts. Some of these ancient scriptures have undergone changes—interpolations and textual corruptions—over time, but their central message has remained intact, and some of them, e.g. the Qur'ān, have been preserved intact, without alteration or corruption.

"To him that understandeth, that word sufficeth, and to repeat it often is pleasing to him that loveth it."[513]

- Thomas à Kempis, *The Imitation of Christ*, Ch. XXXIV

The scriptures of the world are vast, comprising volume after volume of sacred texts. How then can we meditate on the Divine Word? Where would we even begin? The natural response would be, that one should focus on the tradition with which one is most familiar. Thus, someone of Zoroastrian background might choose to meditate on the Gathas or the other parts of the Avesta, or perhaps even later Pahlavi texts. A Christian might meditate on the word of Jesus Christ, as expressed in the Four Gospels recorded in the New Testament. A Jew might decide to meditate on the precepts of the Torah, the divine hymns of David revealed in the Psalms, or other Prophetic writings, e.g. those of Isaiah, Jeremiah, Daniel, etc. This is, no doubt, a useful course of action. However, by restricting ourselves to one religious tradition, we are veiling ourselves from the numerous truths hidden within the other great scriptures. One might spend a lifetime studying the Bible and never once peruse the Bhagavad-Gita, or the Qur'ān. This is understandable if one has never been exposed to these other texts, but, in the enlightened age in which we now live, there should be no barriers restricting us from seeking truth unbridled and unhindered by prejudice or preconceptions. We should open ourselves to the possibility that Light can become manifest in more than one Lamp. Even though there are many Lamps (e.g. Krishna, Zoroaster, Buddha, Jesus, Muhammad, etc.), there is only one Light. If we become lovers of the Lamp only, we can easily become deniers of the Light. In fact, loving the Lamp while hating the Light nullifies our love for the Lamp. Can one claim to love a lamp while hating another lamp which radiates with the same light? Can we truly deny one of these Great Teachers and accept only the one with whom we are most familiar? That would make us deniers of the Light itself. To truly call ourselves lovers of the Light (i.e. the Divine Being), therefore, we must declare ourselves lovers of all the Great Teachers and their scriptures. We must feel the divine spirit flowing from all the great holy Texts, which all have their divine inspiration and origin in one source, which is the All-Highest. As God (exalted be His glory) says in the Qur'ān:

"If all the trees that are upon the earth were to become pens, and if God should after that swell the sea into seven seas of ink, His words would not be exhausted: for God is Mighty, Wise."[514]

- Qur'ān 31:27

Now that we have recognized the Light which is manifest in all the great scriptures, how should we go about meditating on them? Thomas à Kempis wrote: "It is Truth which we must look for in Holy Writ, not cunning of words. All Scripture ought to be read in the spirit in which it was written. We must rather seek for what is profitable in Scripture, than for what ministereth to subtlety in discourse. Therefore, we ought to read books which are devotional and simple, as well as those which are deep and difficult."[515] His advice is to meditate on all parts of the Bible, aiming to understand the text in the spirit in which it was written, rather than imposing our own ideas upon the text or taking verses out of context (a practice all too common these days). He also advised: "Men pass away, but the truth of the Lord endureth for ever. Without respect of persons God speaketh to us in divers manners. Our own curiosity often hindereth us in the reading of holy writings, when we seek to understand and discuss, where we should pass simply on. If thou wouldst profit by thy reading, read humbly, simply, honestly, and not desiring to win a character for learning. Ask freely, and hear in silence the words of holy men; nor be displeased at the hard sayings of older men than thou, for they are not uttered without cause."[516] Thus we should read the Holy Books with patience and an open mind, avoiding the imposition of our own ideas on the text, and avoiding the cardinal mistake of taking the texts too literally.

"It is the spirit that quickeneth; the flesh profiteth nothing: the words that I speak unto you, they are spirit, and they are life."[517]

- John 6:63

As we wrote in Chapter XI of <u>Mindfulness</u>, we should also bear in mind that many of the Great Teachers and Prophets spoke in parables, using symbolic language. Symbolic language was used because many of the listeners at the time did not have the spiritual capacity to understand the teachings without using symbols. Life, for example, means 'spiritual life', rather than physical life. Resurrection means attaining spiritual life, rather than literal resurrection of bodies, etc. Therefore, we should not take what these Great Teachers and Prophets have said literally, and should try to understand them in the original context. Thus, Jesus said: **"Therefore speak I to them in parables: because they** seeing see not; and hearing they hear not, neither do they understand."[518] It is best not to read too much every day but to focus on a small sample of scripture or a small passage."[519] For example, we can focus on a single verse or several verses. Each verse, and even each word within a verse, contains profound meanings. For example, the following verse from the Qur'ān is particularly moving and filled with great power: **"And whoso feareth God, to him will He grant a prosperous issue, and will provide for him whence he reckoned not upon it. And for him who putteth his trust in Him will God be all-sufficient. God truly will attain his purpose. For everything hath God assigned a period."**[520] If we enshrine this most exalted verse within our hearts and minds, then we can have no fear, because we know that God is protecting us, will grant us a prosperous issue and will help us to achieve what we need to achieve. And even if things happen which are contrary to our wishes, we can trust that God has the best plan for us, and will provide for us from His munificence. As Jesus says: **"Take no thought for your life, what ye shall eat, or what ye shall drink; nor yet for your body, what ye shall put on. Is not the life more than meat, and the body than raiment? Behold the fowls of the air: for they sow not, neither do they reap, nor gather into barns; yet your heavenly Father feedeth them. Are ye not much better than they?"**[521]

Another beautiful and incredibly potent verse from the Qur'ān is called the Light Verse, in which He says, glorified be His glory: **"God is the LIGHT of the Heavens and of the Earth.**

His Light is like a niche in which is a lamp - the lamp encased in glass - the glass, as it were, a glistening star. From a blessed tree is it lighted, the olive neither of the East nor of the West, whose oil would well nigh shine out, even though fire touched it not! It is light upon light. God guideth whom He will to His light, and God setteth forth parables to men, for God knoweth all things."[522]

Meditation on this verse can help us to realize, within the innermost depths of our souls, the power and majesty of that one Light which illumines the material and spiritual horizons—that one Being which belongs neither to the east nor the west, which is lighted from that blessed Tree, which is the Primal Will. Even as the physical sun illumines all the horizons of the world, and fills the earth with heat, light and splendour, so too does the spiritual Sun, which rises on the horizon of Truth, illumining all created things in spiritual splendour and glory. By its aid, we can develop spiritual insight, true knowledge, wisdom and understanding, and can rid ourselves from the veils of self and passion. By embracing the divine Light, we can transcend all divisions, all dogmas and prejudices, and recognize Truth wherever it may be found, in whatever Lamp or scripture, and in the Person of all the Great Teachers and Prophets who have appeared throughout the length and breadth of time. Meditating on this verse can produce profound insights.

> **"The Lord is my light and my salvation; whom shall I fear? the Lord is the strength of my life; of whom shall I be afraid?"**[523]

- Psalm 27:1

If one is to look at a wide range of scriptures, then it is useful to focus on those verses which contain the core teachings of the Great Teachers. In the Gospel, for example, the core teachings of Jesus Christ are contained in the Sermon on the Mount, which lays out the pattern of Christian life. Too often, these teachings are forgotten or overlooked, while his death and resurrection are emphasised within theological traditions that date back to the Reformation or earlier. The central aim and mission of Jesus was not, however, to simply die as part of a redemptive act. Rather, he came to renew the foundations of the Revelation of Moses and provide new teachings suitable for his age. Instead of applying the law of an 'eye for an eye, and a tooth for a tooth,' for example, he emphasised forgiveness and forbearance. He also altered some of the laws of the Torah by, for example, forbidding divorce and banning execution for adultery. His main contribution, however, was in emphasising spiritual concepts, including that of divine love and spiritual salvation. He condemned literalistic interpretations of scripture, emphasizing parables and symbolic language, e.g. the bread of life, blood, water of life, heaven as a state rather than a place, spiritual resurrection (not literal resurrection), etc. This method of symbolic interpretation was followed by St. Paul, who also taught that the resurrection was a non-literal, spiritual event involving 'celestial bodies,' rather than 'physical bodies'.[524] In addition to the Sermon on the Mount, it is useful to meditate on Jesus's parables, as well as his statements in the Gospel of John, which relate to the symbolic concepts of the bread of life, heaven, etc. The following verses are from the Sermon on the Mount:

"Blessed are the poor in spirit: for theirs is the kingdom of heaven. Blessed are they that mourn: for they shall be comforted. Blessed are the meek: for they shall inherit the earth. Blessed are they which do hunger and thirst after righteousness: for they shall be filled. Blessed are the merciful: for they shall obtain mercy. Blessed are the pure in heart: for they shall see God. Blessed are the peacemakers: for they shall be called the children of God. Blessed are they which are persecuted for righteousness' sake: for theirs is the kingdom of heaven. Blessed are ye, when men shall revile you, and persecute you, and shall say all manner of evil against you falsely, for my sake. Rejoice, and be exceeding glad: for great is your reward in heaven: for so persecuted they the prophets which were before you.

"Ye are the salt of the earth: but if the salt have lost his savour, wherewith shall it be salted? it is thenceforth good for nothing, but to be cast out, and to be trodden under foot of men. Ye are the light of the world. A city that is set on an hill cannot be hid. Neither do men light a candle, and put it under a bushel, but on a candlestick; and it giveth light unto all that are in the house. Let your light so shine before men, that they may see your good works, and glorify your Father which is in heaven."[525]

- Matthew 5:3 – 16

And the following are from the Gospel of St. John:

"And Jesus said unto them, I am the bread of life: he that cometh to me shall never hunger; and he that believeth on me shall never thirst."

"I am the living bread that came down from heaven. If anyone eats of this bread, he will live forever. And this bread, which I will give for the life of the world, is My flesh. The Jews therefore strove among themselves, saying, How can this man give us *his* flesh to eat? Then Jesus said unto them, Verily, verily, I say unto you, Except ye eat the flesh of the Son of man, and drink his blood, ye have no life in you."

- John 6:35, 6:51 – 53

These verses contain a number of mystic and spiritual truths that defy literal interpretation. The main failing of the Pharisees—that great failing which veiled them from Jesus Christ's true station as the Messiah promised in their scriptures—was their insistence on literal understanding and their failure to interpret his words symbolically, just as they insisted on a literal interpretation of the prophecies regarding the coming of the Messiah, the Anointed One of Israel. When he said that he was the bread of life, they thought he was speaking literally. He also said that they should drink his blood, which they regarded as a preposterous proposition. The reality is this: the bread of life is the core teaching of Jesus, which has descended from heaven. His blood, which is the water of life, is another term for that same divine teaching. By eating his flesh and drinking his blood is meant accepting his teachings and station, which allows for spiritual rebirth and true baptism (i.e. 'cleansing of one's heart and soul'). As Jesus says in the same Gospel: **"Verily, verily, I say unto thee, Except a man be born again, he cannot see the kingdom of God."**[526] And in the Gospel of Matthew, John the Baptist says, speaking of Jesus Christ: **"He that cometh after me is mightier than I, whose shoes I am not worthy to bear: he shall baptize you with the Holy Ghost, and *with* fire."**[527] Furthermore, as he says above, Jesus says: **"I am the living bread that came down from heaven."**[528] This indicates that heaven is not a place and that descent from and ascent to heaven cannot be taken literally, just as resurrection, life and death are all spiritual concepts that do not refer to the body or physical matter.

The following are some practical steps to help us study and meditate on the Divine Word:

STEP ONE – PURIFY YOURSELF

"Make thyself pure, O righteous man! any one in the world here below can win purity for himself, namely, when he cleanses himself with good thoughts, words, and deeds."[529]

- Zoroaster, *The Zend-Avesta*, Part I. The Vendîdâd, Fargard X, 19 (38).

The first step is to purify your mind and body. Why is this necessary? We may think that by meditating on the words of a scripture, we are simply reading a book, or parts of a book—but this is an incorrect understanding. When we study verses which are divine in origin, we are actually intimately approaching the Divine. The Primal Will, which is the source of Light and life for the entire universe, is revealed in the person of the Great Teachers—the Perfect Mirrors who appear in every age. These Perfect Teachers, in turn, act as channels of the Divine—as Mouthpieces which reveal the divine teachings and purpose of God for mankind. These teachings form a pattern of life which we should follow, which Buddha calls the Dharma, and which is known in Hinduism as *sanātana-dharma* (i.e. the 'eternal law/way'). The words which are revealed in scripture are infused with tremendous potency and meaning. The power latent in every single word is capable of transforming human character, building communities and societies, and bringing someone from a state of spiritual death and unhappiness to a state of spiritual life and happiness. This is why Jesus said: **"This is the bread which cometh down from heaven, that a man may eat thereof, and not die."**[530] And regarding those who turned away from the divine verses and rejected them, he said: **"Let the dead bury their dead: but go thou and preach the kingdom of God."** [531] Each revealed word is a mother word—like a sun, burning in the depths of eternity, filled with the essence of power and might. Every word is also like an ocean of immeasurable depths, in which one can dive into the profoundest meanings and inner wisdom. This ocean is full of limitless treasures hidden deep within its boundless immensity—pearls of great price, diamonds of everlasting splendour, jewels of eternal brilliance and glory, and gems of all-encompassing and unsurpassed radiance. Within this ocean is the knowledge of all things, the answer to all things, and the source of all things. As the Qur'ān (12:111) itself declares: **"This is no new tale of fiction, but a confirmation of previous scriptures, and an explanation of all things, and guidance and mercy to those who believe."**[532]

As such, let us ensure that we are clean in body, heart and mind. Let us cleanse ourselves of unclean clothes and wash our hands so that we do not touch the verses with an unclean hand. This helps us to purify our mind. As the body is the temple for the soul, so does the body represent the soul in its actions. When we purify ourselves physically, it is easier to purify our inner selves and wash off the dust and dross of attachment and illusion. St. Paul says: **"What? know ye not that your body is the temple of the Holy Ghost which is in you, which ye have of God, and ye are not your own?"**[533] If we regard the body as a temple, how can we allow ourselves to be unkempt, unclean or dishevelled? One often imagines religious ascetics wandering in the graveyards, covered in dust and grime—or one pictures the monk in cassock, stained with the dust of a long voyage, flagellating himself with a whip in order to atone for his sins. But such exaggerations of religion and spirituality do not really treat the body with the respect it deserves as the temple of the soul. If the body is the temple of the soul, it must be dignified, clean and

226

well taken care of, just as one would clean and preserve a temple built of stone or wood. Likewise, in our innermost minds, we should endeavour to remove impure thoughts and preoccupations, focusing instead on the Light of oneness. Mindfulness, loving-kindness and mantra meditation are all excellent methods to help cultivate pure-mindedness and spiritual thoughts. Paul says: **"Finally, brethren, whatsoever things are true, whatsoever things are honest, whatsoever things are just, whatsoever things are pure, whatsoever things are lovely, whatsoever things are of good report; if there be any virtue, and if there be any praise, think on these things."**[534]

If you have completed this step, proceed immediately to Step Two.

STEP TWO – RECITE THE VERSES

"Give attendance to reading, to exhortation, to doctrine."[535]

- 1 Timothy 4:13

Very often, it is easier to understand something when we hear it out loud. It is also easier to focus on something when it is read out loud. While this is not strictly necessary, the act of reading or reciting verses out loud is highly beneficial. When we utter words, we are more likely to internalize them, similar to the way mantras, when chanted out loud, help us to absorb the words we utter, and take us to a transcendental plane of awareness. By reciting the selected verses, we are allowing them to enter our hearts more deeply, just as if we are taking medicine. If we apply medicine externally, it affects our skin. When we swallow a tablet, it works from within. In the same manner, when we read a word silently, we may passively absorb its wisdom. When we say that same word, we internalize it, and it starts permeating our consciousness at a much greater depth. This is not always the case for mundane and ordinary words, but it is certainly the case for divine words which, as we said, are like suns burning brightly within the depths of outer space. As the Qur'ān (17:82) says: **"And we send down of the Koran that which is a healing and a mercy to the faithful."**[536] Let us take this divine medicine, and allow it to work on the depths of our innermost selves.

"RECITE thou, in the name of thy Lord who created... Recite thou! For thy Lord is the most Beneficent; Who hath taught the use of the pen; hath taught Man that which he knoweth not."[537]

- Qur'ān 96:1, 3 – 5

When we recite the words, we should do so with purity of mind and concentration, not haphazardly, or in a slovenly or indistinct manner. It is useful to practice chanting, which involves intoning the verses, rather like one might imagine a monk doing in Gregorian chant. However, one could also simply read with great depth of feeling, like a devotee of some famous poet reading with the utmost passion for the work. We should read with intention, since we want to hear the words and feel their beauty and rhythm. We should not read them simply for the sake of doing so. Intention is important, because it is the starting-point for all actions. If our intentions are pure, our activities are likely to be pure also. But if we have bad intentions, or are simply negligent, then our actions produce no fruit and we fail to achieve our purpose. Therefore, when we read the verses, we should do so with good intention, so that we can reap the utmost reward therefrom. In the Book of Proverbs (16:3), we read: **"Commit thy work unto the LORD, and thy thoughts shall be established."**538 By adorning ourselves with a good character and good behaviour, we also purify our thoughts and intentions.

STEP THREE – READ SILENTLY AND REFLECT

"Commune with your own heart upon your bed, and be still."539

- Psalm 4:4

Next, we should read the text again, this time silently, as we ponder the meaning of each word and sentence. We should try to understand the verse within its wider context. Thus, if we are reading about war or conflict, these verses should be understood within the historical context in which the verse was revealed. We should also ponder on both the obvious or outer meaning of the verse and its inner, more profound meaning. Thus, for example, let us consider the verse **"And the LORD said unto Noah, Come thou and all thy house into the ark; for thee have I seen righteous before me in this generation."**[540] What is the context for this verse? It occurs within the story of Noah and the Ark in the Book of Genesis, which is a parable and not a story of literal events. Was there an historical kernel from which this story developed? Perhaps. But the main point of the story is its spiritual significance, not its literal occurrence. The Prophet Noah was commanded by God to build an ark in order to preserve the righteous from the flood of God's anger and wrath. The people of the world at the time were sinful and negligent and had turned away from God's teachings, so God decided to eradicate mankind, with the exception of Noah and his 'house', i.e his family. However, when we meditate on the inner or true meaning of this verse, we come to a more profound conclusion.

> **"Verily, we sent Noah to his people, 'Warn thy people before there come to them a grievous torment!' Said he, 'O my people! verily, I am to you an obvious warner, that ye serve God and fear Him and obey me. He will pardon you your sins, and will defer you unto an appointed time; verily, God's appointed time when it comes will not be deferred, did ye but know!'"**[541]

- Qur'ān 71:1 – 4

Noah was a Prophet—a Great Teacher—who was sent to his people to deliver a message of virtue, monotheism and purity,

230

delivered in the language and terminology of his age. He brought divine teachings and, as so often happens when a Prophet or Messenger of God appears, these teachings were rejected by the leaders and priests of the age. As a result, God commanded Noah to build an ark. This ark is not a literal boat, but the spiritual covenant—the laws of God—which the true believers enter. When they enter this spiritual ark, they are preserved from death and destruction and enter a new world of spiritual happiness and inner peace. Noah's 'house' refers not only to his family but also to the company of his followers—those individuals who heeded his message and became believers in God and Noah's teachings. This story was preserved in the form of a parable or allegory, so that the profound spiritual concepts which underlie it could be passed down in a concise form. Symbols are useful for expressing deeper truths, but they can prove perilous for those who cling to literal interpretations, thus depriving themselves of the true water of life and inspiration. The Qur'ān states: **"These similitudes do We propose unto men, that they may consider."**[542] Those who open their eyes to inner meanings—to the unveiled truth—are possessed of spiritual sight and hearing, while those who cling to literal interpretations and outward meaning alone are deprived of sight. As Jesus said: **"Therefore speak I to them in parables: because they seeing see not; and hearing they hear not, neither do they understand."**[543]

231

STEP FOUR – MEDITATE ON THE IMPLICATIONS

"If ye love me, keep my commandments."[544]

- John 14:15

Every verse in the scriptures has a direct impact and relevance to the material world, and thus our daily lives. For example, when Jesus says: **"But those things which proceed out of the mouth come forth from the heart; and they defile the man."**[545] At the first level, when we understand the words, the structure and the basic meaning, this is a straightforward statement. What is the context? Jesus and his followers were criticized by the literalist scribes and Pharisees, who held to a prescriptive understanding of the Torah. They saw that the Apostles did not wash their hands before eating bread, which is one of the commandments of the Prophet Moses. Jesus, having divine authority, broke this tradition. Jesus turned their accusation around and accused the Pharisees and scribes of transgressing God's commandments. He said: **"Why do ye also transgress the commandment of God by your tradition?"**[546] He gave the example that the Torah says that a man who dishonours his father or mother should be put to death, but they allowed such offenders to go free. He then quotes the Prophet Isaiah, who says: **"This people draweth nigh unto me with their mouth, and honoureth me with *their* lips; but their heart is far from me. But in vain they do worship me, teaching *for* doctrines the commandments of men."**[547]

232

With this in mind, we can now understand that Jesus was talking about the fact that it is not what one eats which defiles a person, but that which they speak, because what one speaks has its origin in the intentions of the heart. Thus we understand the actual meaning of the verse, which emphasizes purity of heart and speech, and condemns hypocrisy and man-made traditions, laws and doctrines. Now comes the question of implications. What are the implications of this verse? That we should, firstly, avoid inventing or adhering to man-made traditions or doctrines. Secondly, we should avoid any trace of hypocrisy in our words or deeds. Thirdly, we should purify our hearts, so that what we speak is also pure. If we take this verse at literal or face value, then we only learn that it is okay to eat without washing one's hands, which is not the intention, true meaning or real implication of this verse. Rather, it is a higher teaching—a teaching of purification, true spirituality and virtuous conduct. We know that washing our hands is essential for good hygiene, but which is worse, an unclean hand or an unclean heart? That is the question we should ponder. When we follow this practice of meditating on the implications of verses, we gradually begin to understand God's purpose and true teachings, as laid out in the Bhagavad-Gita, the Dhammapada, the Bible, the Qur'ān and other scriptures.

STEP FIVE – APPLY THE TEACHINGS IN LIFE

> "By this shall all men know that ye are my disciples, if ye have love one to another."[548]

- John 13:35

Once we have come to an adequate understanding of the verse upon which we are meditating, and once we have understood its context, its outward and inward meanings, as well as the implications for our daily lives, let us then put these teachings into practice. A word of caution here: not every law or commandment one finds in the ancient scriptures is applicable in this day and age. This is why the issue of context is supremely important. Should we stone witches or wage war on the Amalekites (even if we could identify who a modern Amalekite might be)? The answer, to any rational individual, is obvious. Those laws and commandments were time-dependent and are no longer applicable. This is not a haphazard process of discerning and ignoring laws. As Jesus indicates in the verse already quoted above, it is not really up to us to decide which laws are or are not applicable in the modern age. Rather, it is the Great Teachers themselves who tell us whether a law from the past is applicable or not. Just as Jesus broke the Sabbath, forbade divorce and allowed his disciples to eat without first washing their hands, and as his disciples, Peter and Paul, were instructed in a vision to allow Gentile Christians to join the fold without practising circumcision or observing *kashrut* (Jewish dietary restrictions), the Prophet Muhammad allowed divorce, reinstated circumcision and reinstated certain dietary restrictions from the Torah. These laws and commandments change and evolve with each subsequent age, and are never stationary. At one time, unlimited polygamy is allowed—at another, polygamy is restricted or abolished. The main basis of each revelation, however, remains the same, and the same essential moral teachings, virtues and divine qualities, are taught in every age.

> **"Righteousness (Dharma) is so called because it upholds all creatures. In fact, all creatures are upheld by righteousness. Therefore, that is righteousness which is capable of upholding all creatures."**[549]

- Bhishma, *The Mahabharata*

With this in mind, one should try to apply the verses to our lives, refining our character and allowing ourselves to become modelled on the divine pattern laid out by those Greatest of Teachers, who have left a pattern and way of life for us to follow. In Chapter I of Mindfulness, we laid out the First Way to Be, which is detachment and virtue. In the second chapter, we outlined the path of virtue and, in the third, we described some steps for further development on the path of virtue, being broadly based on the Eightfold Path of the Buddha. In the first chapter, we wrote: "We can imagine that we are all like birds trapped within a cage. Imagine also that the door of the cage is closed, but not locked. Most of us are unaware that there is a door, and even those that are aware of the door think that it is locked. All that is required to escape from the cage is to push open the door and leave behind the cage and all that is contained therein. The cage represents all our attachments—material, emotional and ideological. Most of us are unwilling to consider even leaving the cage, because we believe it is all that is. What if, however, there is a whole world beyond the cage, even more magnificent and beautiful, full of limitless energy and boundless joy? What if we can escape from the cage of attachment and embrace a higher reality?"[550] We can, indeed, break this cage and soar aloft in the heights of spiritual eternity. How, one may ask? By following the path of virtue. For further advice and practical steps to achieve this, I would recommend that you read the first three chapters of *Mindfulness: Five Ways to Achieve Real Happiness, True Knowledge and Inner Peace*. And virtue cannot truly be obtained without devotion to the Divine Being—that is the highest path to liberation and spiritual freedom.

> **"Devotion alone leads him to the Supreme; devotion alone shows Him; in the power of devotion is the person; devotion only is the best (of means)."[551]**

> - *Mathara Sruti*, quoted by Madhvacarya (1238 – 1317 CE)

Conclusion

By following these simple steps, by embracing the power and majesty of the Divine Word, we can better ourselves and improve our lives. We can help to effect a change in the character of others, and we can gain inspiration to develop our communities, establish better relationships and improve our interaction with the wider world. As channels of the Primal Will, the Great Teachers who have appeared in every age reveal potent words and teachings which are the very bread and water of life, which can grant us true spiritual sight, hearing and life. To embrace the divine teachings and practise them in our lives is the true spiritual baptism—the baptism of fire—the spiritual rebirth. As Jesus says: "Verily, verily,

I say unto thee, Except a man be born again, he cannot see the kingdom of God."[552] And what is the Kingdom of God? It is the word and teachings of God—the Divine Being—the Dharma—the Dīn—which appears in every age. It is the Will of the Primal Being as manifested within the world of creation. And we establish that kingdom, first of all, by refining ourselves—by building our own characters and bringing our lives more and more into conformity with the teachings of the Great Teachers. We can achieve this by meditating, day by day, on selected verses of the divine scriptures, reading them within their wider context, understanding their inner and outer meanings, and learning their implications for our individual lives and the wider community. When we dive deep within the ocean of the Word, we will find the hidden gems of meaning which can fill our souls with life and light. As Veda-Vyāsa writes when referring to the Mahabharata: **"As the sacred Ocean, as the Himavat mountain,[39] are both regarded as mines of precious gems, even so is this Bharata (regarded as a mine of precious gems)... It is immeasurable, sacred, sanctifying, sin-cleansing, and auspicious."**[553][40]

---

[39] i.e. the Himalayan mountain.

[40] According to Madhvacharya, the Sastras (Hindu scriptures) include the "Rik, Yajus, Saman and Atharva Vedas, the Maha Bharata and the Mula Ramayana. And also whatever agrees with these is to be considered Sastra." – Madhvacharya, *The Vedanta Sutras with the commentary of Sri Madhvachara*, p. 12.

Meditate on these sacred verses—absorb their inner wisdom. Let the words sink within the fabric of your being, like a sword plunged deep within the earth. St. Paul says: "For the word of God is quick, and powerful, and sharper than any two-edged sword, piercing even to the dividing asunder of soul and spirit, and of the joints and marrow, and is a discerner of the thoughts and intents of the heart."[554] And in his epistle to the Romans, he writes: "All scripture is given by inspiration of God, and is profitable for doctrine, for reproof, for correction, for instruction in righteousness."[555] The goal of this meditation, then, is to learn the essence of wisdom, to uncover the hidden gems of knowledge, and to learn what constitutes true righteousness, right living and spiritual conduct. This will lead us to live happier, better and more productive lives. When we leave the shores of attachment and ignorance, and plunge into the depths of the great ocean of life— the great sea of eternal bliss and knowledge—the ancient and divine Word, we will have achieved the essence of true happiness and abiding joy. As Krishna tells Arjuna in the Bhagavad-Gita: **"As into the ocean,—brimful, and still,—flow the waters, even so the Muni**[41] **into whom enter all desires, he, and not the desirer of desires, attains to peace."**[556] Let us meditate, then, and embrace that path of peace.

> **"This book of the law shall not depart out of thy mouth; but thou shalt meditate therein day and night, that thou mayest observe to do according to**

---

[41] A holy man.

all that is written therein: for then thou shalt make thy way prosperous, and then thou shalt have good success."[557]

- Joshua 1:8

Questions for Reflection:

The following are some questions that will help us to reflect on what we have learned in this chapter:

1. In what way can the Word of God be compared to an ocean?

2. How does Thomas à Kempis recommend that we meditate on the Word?

3. Why do the Great Teachers speak in parables?

4. What is the bread of life referred to by Jesus Christ?

5. What kind of resurrection did St. Paul refer to?

6. What are the dangers of scriptural literalism?

7. What is the first step in meditation on the Word?

8. What is the second step?

9. What is the third step?

10. What is the fourth step?

11. What is the fifth step?

12. What is the goal of meditation on the divine Word?

13. In the next chapter, we will look at the Fifth Way to Meditate: Meditation on the Divine.

∞∞∞∞∞∞∞∞∞∞∞∞∞∞∞∞∞∞∞∞∞∞∞∞∞∞∞

VII. The Fifth Way to Meditate- Meditation on the Divine Being

"To Mercy, Pity, Peace, and Love,

All pray in their distress,

And to these virtues of delight

Return their thankfulness.

"For Mercy, Pity, Peace, and Love,

Is God our Father dear;

And Mercy, Pity, Peace, and Love,

 Is man, His child and care."[558]

- William Blake (1757 – 1827), The Divine Image

"Speak to Him thou for He hears, and Spirit with Spirit can meet—

Closer is He than breathing, and nearer than hands and feet."[559]

- Alfred, Lord Tennyson (1809 – 1892), The Higher Pantheism

"He to whom the Eternal Word speaketh is free from multiplied questionings. From this One Word are all things, and all things speak of Him; and this is the Beginning which also speaketh unto us."[560]

- Thomas à Kempis, *The Imitation of Christ*, Ch. III, 2.

"Let us meditate on the Supreme (Lord) from whom the creation, preservation, etc. of this world proceed..."[561]

- Veda-Vyāsa, *Srimad Bhagavatam*, First Skandha, Adhyaya 1, p. 1

Introduction

What is true meditation? Patañjali, as we learned in the Preface to this work, says that meditation involves controlling the functions or fluctuations of one's mind,[562] and Krishna states that the "highest way" is to shut the gates of all one's senses, lock desire safe within one's heart and meditate on him (i.e. the Divine).[563] Meditation is self-realization, which is, in reality, realization of the Divine within the essence of one's heart. As we polish the mirrors of our hearts—as we kindle the fire of love within the depths of our inner being—we come to realize the Divine Beloved which is mirrored in the world of creation—and in ourselves. As Jalālu'd-Dīn Rūmī writes: "For if a mirror reflects not, of what use is it? Knowest thou why thy mirror reflects not? Because the rust has not been scoured from its face. If it were purified from all rust and defilement, it would reflect the shining of the SUN Of GOD."[564] The whole universe reflects the innumerable attributes of the Divine. In the Rig-Veda, it is said that **"the souls stand as so many reflections with regard to the different forms of the Lord."** [565] If we are, indeed, reflections of the Divine Light, which radiates from the central Orb of existence, we should realize our inner nobility and meditate on that glorious cause of all things.

"SAY: Whose is the earth, and all that is therein;— if ye know? They will answer, 'God's.' SAY: Will ye not, then reflect?"[566]

- Qur'ān 23:84

In Chapter V, we learned the importance of mantra meditation, which involves repetition of the names of God. This helps us to maintain a state of God-consciousness, or awareness of the Divine. This is a form of remembrance of the Divine. In Chapter VI, we learned about meditation on the Divine Word, which involves studying the teachings of the Great Teachers who appear in every age. By studying the Bhagavad-Gita, the Dhammapada, the Bible, the Qur'ān, and other scriptures, we can learn our true purpose in life, how we should treat others, and how we should respect and honour the Divine Being who brought us into existence and continues to sustain us and generate us through His Primal Will. In the Narayana Tantra, we learn that **"contemplation is of two kinds, one of remembrance, the other of deep meditation."** [567] What is the goal of this meditation? According to the Brahmanda-purana, **"meditation should continue till the perception of Brahman rises; and the wisdom that has once dawned is never annulled."**[568] Brahman, as we learned, in a term used in the Hindu scriptures for the Divine Being, also called Hari in Sanskrit.

> **"In the Pippalada Sakha, the following is said, 'He that knows the Lord Hari who is unchangeable, blissful... who is perfect and the maker and protector of all, he is released from (fear, the bondage of life), when he has seen the Lord)."**[569]

> - Madhvacarya, *Commentary on the Vedanta-Sutra*, First Adhyaya, Fourth Pada.

It is not enough to simply be intellectually aware that we are created by a Higher Power, or that we are created in the image and likeness of God, for **"God created man in His own image, in the image of God created He him."**[570] These are, indeed, necessary steps in our gradual awareness of the true meaning of existence, but they are—on their own—insufficient. True knowledge, and true awareness, is to attain a state of love—or true longing—for the Divine Beloved. Inasmuch as we are all created by a heavenly Father, so must we also recognize and feel the love that He has for us. We are created for the sake of love, by a loving Creator, **"because God is love."**[571] When we recognize this profound truth, then we also realize that we must **"love one another: for love is of God; and every one that loveth is born of God, and knoweth God."**[572] The highest form of meditation, then, is to perceive the true Beloved within oneself and to love Him with true devotion. To profess one's love on the tongue is not enough. We must love the Divine Beloved through active service to Him. This is true devotion. When we perceive the Divine Lord in the mirror of our hearts, then we realize that He is the object of all devotion and love and the source of love. We thus become channels of His love and light for the whole world. When we become conduits of this heavenly love, then our hearts pour forth with loving-kindness and compassion. True devotion to the Divine Beloved is manifested in service, and the highest service is to serve our fellow human beings, who are made in the image and light of their Creator. As we see the Lord in every face, and every soul, then we realize that true brotherhood is not only possible, but necessary, for we are all children of one heavenly Father.

245

"I am in my Father, and ye in me, and I in you."[573]

- John 14:20

So how do we achieve this love for the Divine Beloved? And how do we perceive the Divine Being and realize His love for us? In Chapter XI of in *Mindfulness: Five Ways to Achieve Real Happiness, True Knowledge and Inner Peace*, we explained that meditation on the Divine Being means, essentially, "meditation on God and His attributes."[574] We further explained that, "in this state, we meditate on the sublimity of the Divine Being and His attributes, and commune with our spirits."[575] We can meditate, firstly, on the attributes of God, which are also His innumerable Names. This is similar to the process of mantra meditation. However, we focus more deeply on the meaning of these attributes and their reflection in the world of creation, including within ourselves. Thus, for example, the famous Vaishnava spiritual master and philosopher, Madhva Acharya (1238 – 1317 CE), who was a major proponent of the Dvaita (dualist) school of Vedanta philosophy, advised that we should meditate on the Lord "as Bliss, Intelligence, the Faultless and the Master." [576] He quotes the *Brahma Tarka*, which says: **"The meditation of Brahman[42] by all that seek release is, it is concluded, to be made with the comprehension that Brahman is the faultless, is bliss, is intelligence and is the master."**[577] Madhva Acharya further

---

[42] i.e. God.

instructs that "the Supreme Lord is to be contemplated necessarily with a comprehension of all the excellences and absence of defects declared by all the Vedas."[578] Thus, by comprehending these Divine Attributes, we can come to know and understand the Divine. And we can see these attributes both within ourselves, and in the world of nature around us. In all things, we see the hand of God and His might and power, and His attributes infused within every atom of existence. As the Qur'ān (47:3; 62:1) says: **"He is the First, and the Last; the Manifest, and the Hidden: And He knoweth all things"**[579] and **"ALL that is in the Heavens, and all that is on the Earth, uttereth the Praise of God, the King! the Holy! the Mighty! the Wise!"**[580] From the smallest ant to the greatest of heavenly bodies, all things mirror the attributes of God, and we can see God's attributes reflected in all things.

Meditation on the Divine Being can be achieved in five steps, as outlined below:

STEP ONE – PREPARATION, POSTURE AND ATTITUDE

"The radiant Dawns have risen up for glory, in their white splendour like the waves of waters."[581]

- *Rig-Veda*, Book 6, Hymn LXIV.

The best time to perform this meditation is early in the morning, when the sun has just dawned above the horizon, or before the moment of dawn. Alternatively, it could be performed at other quiet times, such as midnight, or after sunset. These are times when the world is quiet, tranquil and serene, and our souls can also feel the silence, serenity and tranquillity of the world around us, and within ourselves. As the prominent Quaker and founder of the city of Philadelphia, William Penn (1644 - 1718) advised, we should meditate in the morning in silence, and lift up our hearts unto God. He wrote: "So soon as you wake, retire your mind into a pure silence from all thoughts and ideas of worldly things, and in that frame wait upon GOD, to feel His good presence, to lift up your hearts to Him, and commit your whole self into his blessed care and protection."[582] The Psalms of David (57:8 – 9) declare: **"Awake my tongue, awake viol and harp: I will awake early. I will praise thee, O LORD, among the people,** *and* **I will sing unto thee among the nations."**[583] The Qur'ān (30:17 – 18), furthermore, advises: **"Glorify God therefore when ye reach the evening, and when ye rise at morn. And to Him be praise in the Heavens and on the Earth; and at twilight, and when ye rest at noon"**[584]

Before we begin meditation, we should try to achieve a state of reverence and devotion, as we are about to approach the Divine with our minds and souls. As such, we can wash our hands and face and cleanse our minds of impure thoughts and vain desires. As a preliminary, therefore, I would recommend that one practise mantra meditation in order to cleanse the mind and focus on the Divine. One can also practice mindfulness meditation, as this helps us to achieve a state of focus and alert awareness. We should also precede our meditation by first studying the attributes of God mentioned in the holy scriptures. This is essential, as we cannot meditate on something which we have not even considered. If we do not know that God is mighty, for example, how can meditate on the might of God? Thus Madhva Acharya quotes the following from the *Brahmanda-purana*: **"One should study scripture till ignorance is removed, should think till the doubt as to reasonableness is removed; meditation should continue till the perception of Brahman rises; and the wisdom that has once dawned is never annulled."**[585]

At the beginning of our meditation, we can sit silently, with a straight back and cross-legged, if possible, or leaning against a wall, as we have outlined in the previous chapters. If necessary, a chair could also be used. Sitting is essential, according to Madhva Acharya, quoting the *Narayana Tantra*, since deep meditation "is possible (only) in the sitting posture." [586] This is because movement is distracting, and we are too often focused on what is going on around us. He defines meditation as "uninterrupted course of conscious states" and argues that "this is possible only for him who sits up (in complete wakefulness), but not for him who is lying in bed overcome by sleep, or standing or walking; for then distraction would necessarily set in." Thus we should begin by sitting down in a meditative pose.

Next, we can say a mantra or prayer before we begin our silent meditation. This will open our hearts to the Divine before we revert to a state of silence and deep meditation. The following are some examples of phrases we could say: **"Om-namo-Nārāyanāya,"** [43] [587] **"Hare Krishna,"** [588] **"Hare Rāma,"** [589] **"Namo Amitābhāya,"** [590] **"The name of the LORD is a strong tower: the righteous runneth into it, and is safe,"** [591] **"So will I always sing praise unto thy Name,"** [592] **"Praise ye the LORD. O give thanks unto the LORD; for he is good: for his mercy endureth for ever,"** [593] **"Let every thing that hath breath praise the Lord. Praise ye the LORD,"** [594] **"Hallowed be thy name,"** [595] **"For God is my Lord, and your Lord, so worship Him,"** [596] **"In the Name of God, the Compassionate, the Merciful,"** [597] **"Blessed be the name of thy Lord, full of Majesty and Glory,"** [598] **"God! There is no God but He; the Living, the Self-Subsisting,"** [599] or **"God is the Light of the heavens and the earth."** [600] These are just examples, but we may choose whatever mantra or verse we are most comfortable with.

STEP TWO – AWARENESS OF THE DIVINE ATTRIBUTES IN CREATION

"Assuredly in the creation of the Heavens and of the Earth; and in the alternation of night and day; and in the ships which pass through the sea with what is useful to man; and in the rain which God sendeth down from Heaven, giving life by it to the

---

[43] "Om, salutations to Nārāyana (i.e. God)."

earth after its death, and by scattering over it all kinds of cattle; and in the change of the winds, and in the clouds that are made to do service between the Heaven and the Earth; are signs for those who understand."[601]

- Qur'ān 2:164

When we are in the right state of mind—a calm and receptive state, we should become aware of the Divine attributes in the world of creation. We should visualize the great bodies of water—the lakes, rivers, seas and oceans, which reflect the might and power of the Divine Word. We should imagine the trees, forest, mountains, hills and valleys, which shine with the splendour of the God's effulgent glory. We should visualize the sun in all its transcendent heat and radiance, which represents the eternal Sun of Truth which dawns on the horizon of eternity. We should imagine all the animals, fish and plants of this world, each of which grows and lives through the sustaining power of God's all-encompassing bounty and sustaining grace. We should see all people, from the street-sweeper on the street to the most sublime of kings, to be mirrors of the attributes of God, of His mercy, kindness, justice, fortitude, patience, tolerance, mercy and forgiveness. We should see, in every face, the Light of the splendour of that eternal Source of Light—the central Orb of the universe. Madhva Acharya advised that we should meditate on the Lord "as Bliss, Intelligence, the Faultless and the Master."[602] As quoted above, Madhva further states that "the Supreme Lord is to be contemplated necessarily with a comprehension of all the excellences and absence of defects declared by all the Vedas."[603]

251

So what are some of these attributes we should focus on? In the Mahabharata, God is described in the following manner:

"**Him who is the Veda of the Vedas, and the most ancient of all ancient objects, to him who is the energy of all energies, and the penance of all penances; to him who is the most tranquil of all creatures endued with tranquillity, and who is the splendour of all splendours; to him who is looked upon as the most restrained of all creatures that are restrained, and him who is the intelligence of all creatures endued with intelligence; to him who is looked upon as the deity of all deities, and the Rishi of all Rishis; to him who is regarded as the sacrifice of all sacrifices... to him from whom all the worlds start into existence, and unto whom all the worlds return when they cease to exist; to him who is the Soul of all existent creatures, and who is called Hara of immeasurable energy.**"[604]

- *The Mahabharata*, Book 13: Anusasana Parva, Part 1, Section XVII.

In the Bhagavad-Gita, Krishna gives the following summary of some of the principle divine virtues, which are the adornment of a true man:

"**Fearlessness, singleness of soul, the will always to strive for wisdom; opened hand and governed appetites; and piety... humbleness, uprightness, heed to injure nought which lives, truthfulness, slowness**

unto wrath, a mind that lightly letteth go what others prize; and equanimity, and charity which spieth no man's faults; and tenderness towards all that suffer; a contented heart, fluttered by no desires; a bearing mind, modest, and grave... with patience, fortitude, and purity; an unrevengeful spirit... such be the signs, O Indian Prince! of him whose feet are set on that fair path which leads to heavenly birth!"[605]

- Krishna, *The Bhagavad-Gita*, Ch. XVI.

These are the qualities of someone who is endowed with Divine virtues and attributes. These divine attributes exist in a latent form within every individual, and they can be cultivated through practice and determination. However, at this stage, we are simply recognizing these attributes in the world around us—and in our fellow human beings. We are recognizing kindness when we see kindness, we are recognizing love when we see love. We are focusing on the good and ignoring the bad. This is because good is, in reality, what really matters. Evil is simply the absence of good. When we focus on the good, we are focusing on something which really exists. The reality of our fellow human beings is not the sum of their vices and bad qualities, it is the good which they each possess and which we can see in them. These good attributes are the real fruits of their lives and what they can take with them when they die and pass on to another world—their true *karma*. Our evil deeds and bad qualities are like so much dross which are washed away in the rain of divine love and compassion. We should cultivate the good within ourselves, and overcome the bad qualities within us, while being forbearing of others and seeing the good in them. If someone has ten bad qualities and one good quality, we should focus on the good that is within them. Thus, we begin to see the attributes of God in every atom of existence, from the smallest ant or gnat to the greatest bodies of the universe—the stars, planets, galaxies and the whole universe, which is a mirror of the Divine Being. Always remember that the souls, indeed, **"stand as so many reflections with regard to the different forms of the Lord."**[606] Furthermore, let us feel gratitude for the divine blessings which pour down upon us from every aspect of God's creation. As He says in the Qur'ān (45:12 – 13):

"It is God who hath subjected the sea to you that the ships may traverse it at his bidding, and that ye may go in quest of the gifts of his bounty, and that ye may be thankful. And he hath subjected to you all that is in the Heavens and all that is on the Earth: all is from him. Verily, herein are signs for those who reflect."[607]

When we have finished practising this method of visualization, and we can start to see the attributes of God in all created things, we can move on to the next step, which is to see these attributes within oneself.

STEP THREE – AWARENESS OF THE DIVINE ATTRIBUTES WITHIN ONESELF

"Stuff not the ear of your mind with cotton.

Take the cotton of evil suggestions from the mind's ear,

That the heavenly voice from above may enter it,

That you may understand that riddle of His,

That you may be cognisant of that open secret.

Then the mind's ear becomes the sensorium of inspiration;

For what is this Divine voice but the inward voice?"[608]

- Jalāl ad-Dīn Rūmī, *The Masnavi*, Book I, Story VI.

Next, let us reflect on our own selves, which are channels of divine grace and bounty. In mindfulness meditation, we reflect on our breathing and the various parts of our body, expanding our awareness in concentric circles. The same goes for loving-kindness meditation, in which we expand our loving-kindness from ourselves to the rest of the world. In this meditation, however, you should focus deep within yourself, to the virtues and morals which define your inner self. Reflect, and reflect deeply, on those qualities which define your true self—i.e. love, compassion, kindness, truth, justice, honesty. What virtues do you already possess? What virtues have you cultivated within yourself? What virtues do you potentially possess? The answer to the last question is *all of them*. We are mirrors of the Divine—hence, we are able to reflect within ourselves *all* the Divine attributes—*all* the names of God. As we ponder, deeper and deeper within the depths of our hearts, we will find love, we will find virtue, we will find every good and divine quality hidden at the core of our being. Even if believe ourselves to be without virtue or merit—as full of vices and bad qualities—yet, even if this were true, we would find the hidden gems and diamonds of virtue buried deep within the mine our hearts. Find these virtues, visualize them as so many gems, diamonds and jewels of precious value, and release them from the rock which holds them. Let these virtues free; let them merge with your outer mind and being and let them define your character. You are an essence of virtue; you are an embodiment of divine qualities; you are the recipient of divine bounties and grace; you are the channel of divine love for all mankind. When you recognize your inner nobility—that you are made in God's image and are a reflection of the Divine—then you can *live* these qualities and virtues within your own day-to-day life.

"Knowledge of self is the key to the knowledge of God, according to the saying: 'He who knows himself knows God,' and, as it is Written in the Koran, 'We will show them Our signs in the world and in themselves, that the truth may be manifest to them.' Now nothing is nearer to thee than thyself, and if thou knowest not thyself how canst thou know anything else?"[609]

- Al-Ghazālī, *The Alchemy of Happiness*, Chapter I.

Open the door of your heart. As Jalālu'd-Dīn Rūmī says, "Stuff not the ear of your mind with cotton."[610] When we close the doors of our heart, the Light cannot flow through us. This happens when we turn away from virtue and embrace the insistent self—the lower self—within us. Sanā'ī says: "Abandon talk, and bid farewell to thy lower self."[611] This self is that which urges us to serve our personal whims and desires at the expense of others. The higher self, which is buried deep within us, is that which flows with loving-kindness and virtue. While the lower self is annihilated at the moment of death, the higher self is eternal and indestructible. However, its growth and development depend on the extent to which it is immersed in the Divine Light. And this can only be achieved if we cleanse our hearts from the rust and grime of illusion and attachment. We must open our ears to spiritual truth by opening our hearts within, embracing the Light in whatever Lamp it may appear. We must realize that we are conduits of that Light, and channels of everlasting power and might. We are full of inner potential, divine splendour and deathless beauty. Rūmī says: "For if a mirror reflects not, of what use is it? Knowest thou why thy mirror reflects not? Because the rust has not been scoured from its face. If it were purified from all rust and defilement, it would reflect the shining of the Sun of God."[612] Jesus said: **"He that hath ears, let him hear,"**[613] and **"having eyes, see ye not? and having ears, hear ye not? and do ye not remember?"**[614] The key is to close our eyes and ears to material attachment, and open them to the heavenly horizon of Truth and Light, which flow unceasingly from the Primal Will.

STEP FOUR – AWARENESS OF THE DIVINE ATTRIBUTES WITHIN THE GREAT TEACHERS

> **"Think, O think with tranquil mood of Avalokitesvara, that pure being; he is a protector, a refuge, a recourse in death, disaster, and calamity. He who possesses the perfection of all virtues, and beholds all beings with compassion and benevolence, he, an ocean of virtues, Virtue itself, he, Avalokitesvara, is worthy of adoration."[615]**

> - *Saddharma-Pundarīka*, Chapter XXIV., v. 25 - 26

It is not enough to simply be aware of the Divine Light illuminating all created things—and ourselves—because we, being limited and imperfect mirrors, are incapable of guiding ourselves. Though we can become channels of Divine Light, we cannot understand it through our own minds and limited conceptions. Therefore, we are in need of guidance—divine guidance—which can only come from a pure and perfect Mirror of God, which acts as the Representative of God on earth and the Mouthpiece of God, and which is the Source of Divine Guidance for all mankind. Such individuals appear only rarely on the earth—perhaps once every millennium, or roughly every 500 – 1000 years. Lord Krishna says: **"as often as there is a decline of virtue [Dharma], and an insurrection of vice and injustice [Adharma], in the world, I make myself evident; and thus I appear, from age to age, for the preservation of the just, the destruction of the wicked, and the establishment of virtue."**[616] In this verse, Krishna promises that, whenever and whenever (Sanskrit *yada yada*) there is a decline in religion (Sanskrit *dharma*) and a predominance of irreligion (Sanskrit *adharma*), at that time (Sanskrit *tada*), he manifests himself (Sanskrit *atmanam srjami aham*).[617] Krishna does not give a specific time for his appearances, simply stating that he appears whenever and wherever there is a decline in true religion, which is called Dharma (or *Dhamma* in Pali) in both Hinduism and Buddhism. When he says that he manifests himself, this does not refer to the individual Krishna. Rather, he is here referring to the Primal Will, the Word of God, the *Logos*, which becomes manifest through a perfect Mirror in every age. As John (1:1, 14) says: **"In the beginning was the Word , and the Word was with God, and the Word was God... And the Word was made flesh, and dwelt among us, (and we beheld his glory, the glory as of the only begotten of the Father,) full of grace and truth."**[618] Thus, the meaning of this verse is that, in every age—every 500 – 1000 years or more—a pure Mirror of God, a Manifestation of the Primal Will, appears in the world to re-establish the divine teachings and bring new laws, commandments and teachings which are suitable for that day and age.

Krishna describes his purpose as **"the preservation of the just, the destruction of the wicked, and the** establishment of virtue."[619] These Great Teachers preserve the just by giving them divine guidance and Light, they oppose the oppressors and evil-doers of society and judge them with divine justice, and they re-establish the foundation of morality, virtue and good conduct. Jesus Christ, likewise, describes his purpose in the following words: **"For judgment I am come into this world, that they which see not might see; and that they which see might be made blind."**[620] His mission was to give sight to the spiritually blind and salvation to those who embraced His truth, who possess seeing eyes. As Al-Ghazālī (c. 1058 – 1111 CE) writes: "There are two kinds of eye, an external and an internal... the former belongs to one world, the World of Sense, and that internal vision belongs to another world altogether, the World of the Realm Celestial."[621] The goal of the Great Teacher is to give sight to those who are unaware of spiritual truth, and hence blind. Likewise, those who claim to see—the religious leaders and clerics of every age—are blind because they fail to see the Light which dwells within this Great Teacher. When the Pharisees saw Jesus, they saw only a man—a *tektōn* (i.e. carpenter or builder), who was the son of Joseph, from an obscure town called Nazareth. They failed to see that he was the *Logos*, the Word, made flesh—a pure and spotless Mirror of the Divine. Likewise, when Buddha appeared, many people confused him for an ordinary human being. Some Western students of Buddhism even believe that he claimed nothing more than humanity. Buddha clarified this misconception by saying: **"Do not call the Tathagata by his name nor address him as 'friend,' for he is the Buddha, the Holy One. The Buddha looks with a kind heart**

equally on all living beings, and they therefore call him 'Father.' [622] Likewise, in the Qur'ān (33:40) it is said: **"Muhammad is not the father of any man among you, but he is the Apostle of God, and the seal of the prophets: and God knoweth all things."** [623]

With this in mind, we should meditate on the Great Teachers as the sum of all perfections, all virtues and divine attributes—as the Fountainheads of all wisdom, truth and knowledge—as the Sources of Divine Guidance and grace—as the Mainsprings of eternal life and light—as the Mouthpieces of the Creator of all things—and as the Perfect Mirrors of God. They manifest and express the Primal Will, the Logos, in human form. Even though they are themselves human beings, with individual souls, minds and personalities, they are also Perfect Mirrors of the Divine Will and can thus be called Manifestations of the Divine. All of these Great Teachers, we should also remember, are one in purpose and mission, and are Mirrors of the same Light. Even though the Mirrors are many, the Sun of Truth is one. Even though the Lamps are many, the Light is one. Al-Ghazālī writes: "The Lamp itself is the transcendental Light of Prophecy..." [624] Thus, when we look at these Mirrors, we see one Light and one Sun.

When we see the Mirror, we see God within the Mirror, even though God does not literally descend into the Mirror. Thus, when we look at Moses, as a Perfect Mirror of the Divine, then we see the Divine Being shining within him. Likewise, when we look at Jesus Christ, we see the same Light and the same Sun of Truth. Thus, Moses and Jesus are, from that perspective, one and the

261

same. As Jesus says: **"For had ye believed Moses, ye would have believed me: for he wrote of me."**[625] The same may be said of Krishna and Buddha, or Zoroaster and Muhammad. In the Qur'ān, God says: **"We make no distinction between any of His Apostles [*rusul*]."**[626] They are all one and the same. Thus, when Krishna says that he manifests himself in every age, this means that the same Sun of Truth becomes manifest in a new Mirror, or the same Light appears in a new Lamp. As lovers of the Truth and the Light, we should recognise the Truth and Light in every one of these Great Teachers, and we should recognize all the divine attributes and perfections which appear within them.

When we have finished reflecting on these profound truths, we should move on to Step Five, which is the highest stage of spiritual realization—love and devotion to the Divine Beloved.

STEP FIVE – LOVE AND DEVOTION TO THE DIVINE BELOVED

"The BELOVED is all in all, the lover only veils Him;

The BELOVED is all that lives, the lover a dead thing.

When the lover feels no longer LOVE's quickening,

He becomes like a bird who has lost its wings. Alas!

How can I retain my senses about me,

When the BELOVED shows not the light of His countenance?"[627]

- Jalāl ad-Dīn Rūmī, *The Masnavi*, Book I, Prologue

The highest form of love, and the ultimate purpose of existence, is to love our Creator, the Divine Being, God (glorified be His glory), who is our most intimate Friend and our true Beloved. As we were created through love and on account of love, so must we also reciprocate that love for God. Like plants in the shade, we must come into the light in order experience the heat and life-giving power of the sun. Likewise, we must come out of the shell of ignorance and despair and enter into the light of God's love, so that we may experience that ever-flowing, eternal and unconditional love which He has for all created things, especially man, who is made in His own image and capable of reflecting all His divine names and attributes. When we love God, our lives are full of life and joy. When we turn away from Him, we may have material comforts, but we are devoid of true happiness and inner peace. When we love someone, we cannot feel settled or happy when we are away from them. There is no happiness, no repose or satisfaction, when we are separated from our beloved. Likewise, when we become mired in material attachments and imprisoned within the cage of self and passion, we are separated from the Divine Beloved, who is our true Lover. We must break free from the cage of material attachments, clean our wings from the oil and dross of this world, and soar aloft in the atmosphere of divine love. This love, which is called *ʿishq* in Arabic or *bhakti* in Sanskrit, is expressed through service to the Divine and devotional practice, such as meditation, chanting the Divine Names and prayer. As the *Mathara Sruti* states: **"Devotion alone leads him to the Supreme; devotion alone shows Him; in the power of devotion is the person; devotion only is the best (of means)."**[628] Madhva Acharya explains: "As the Supreme Being of His own accord shows Himself in consideration of the soul's devotion and bestows upon him final beatitude; devotion becomes the foremost of all means."[629] Madhva is thus saying that, if we express our love for the Divine through devotion, we will perceive the Supreme Being and He will bestow his blessings and grace upon us.

> **"Hari, the Almighty, is one without a second. He is always vested with infinite power. He is the ocean of *rasa* (the transcendental bliss which forms the essence of any relationship)... Bhakti, devotional service, is the only means of attaining the final object of spiritual existence. *Prema*, pure love of Krsna, is alone the final object of spiritual existence."**[630]
>
> - Srila Bhaktivinoda Thākura, *Śrī Gaurānga-Līlā-Smarana-Mangala-Stotram*, Verse 75.

What is devotion and how can we express it? And how can we love the Divine, when the Divine Being is invisible? In order to express and practice devotion, we have to have an object of devotion. We can, of course, pray to God directly and meditate on

God through His attributes. Thus we can reflect on God's infinite Names and His glory, majesty, might, justice, power, etc. But this will be incomplete unless we also recognize the Fountainhead of Divine Guidance in this material world, which is the Great Teacher, the Prophet, the Messenger, the Buddha, the Avatar, who is the source of all wisdom, truth and guidance. Jesus says: **"I am the way, the truth, and the life: no man cometh unto the Father, but by me."**[631] Krishna, likewise, says: **"Forsake every other religion, and fly to me alone. Grieve not then, for I will deliver thee from all thy transgressions."**[632] At the first, we should recognize these Great Teachers as Perfect Mirrors of the Sun of Truth and Lamps of Divine Light. Jesus says: **"I am in the Father and the Father is in me."**[633] This is essential, as we cannot receive Divine Light unless we recognize the instrument of that Light. We cannot benefit from the Lamp if we are blind and cannot see it. Only by overcoming spiritual blindness, and opening our eyes to Truth can we see the Lamp and recognize its Light. The next step is to recognize the Great Teacher as the Divine Beloved. Ultimately, we should love God above all else, but this cannot be achieved without loving the Perfect Mirror of God, which manifests His Light and power. We should direct all our love, all our devotion, all our longing, towards that Source of love, that abounding Spring of the water of life. For example, we should first recognize Jesus Christ as the Mirror of God, and, next, we should develop a deep love (*'ishq*) for the Person and Teachings of Jesus Christ. By studying His life, by learning His teachings and the tremendous sacrifice He made, we can begin to feel abounding love and devotion for that glorious Personage.

How shall we love these Great Teachers as our true Beloved? We should reflect on this point and consider how we can express our love. The answer lies in devotional service. Krishna gives some practical methods, when he says: **"Occupy thy mind with Me, be devoted to Me, sacrifice to Me, bow down to Me. Thou shalt reach Myself; truly do I promise unto thee, (for) thou art dear to Me."**[634] The first part, **"occupy thy mind with Me"** (Sanskrit *man-manah*), means that we should develop a state of God-consciousness, always remembering God and His Great Teachers.[635] Mantra meditation is one way of achieving this. Another way is to study the lives of the Great Teachers and remember their activities, sufferings, accomplishments, teachings, etc. We can read biographies of the Great Teachers and study these so that we can always bring them to mind. The second thing Krishna advises is that we should **"be devoted to Me"** (Sanskrit *bhava mat-bhaktah*, lit. 'become My devotee'). A *bhakta* is someone who practises *bhakti-yoga*, i.e. devotional service to the Divine.

How can we do this? Krishna answers in verses 68 and 69 of the same chapter of the Bhagavad-Gita (18:68 - 69), where he says: **"He who with supreme devotion to Me will teach this deeply profound philosophy to My devotees, shall doubtless come to Me alone. Nor among men is there any who does dearer service to Me, nor shall there be another on earth dearer to Me, than he."**[636] In other words, the greatest form of devotional service is to teach the message of the Great Teachers, spreading their message and teachings throughout the world. A true lover—a true *bhakta*—then, will

266

prioritize this above all else. Next, Krishna says that the devotee should "sacrifice to Me" (Sanskrit *mat-yaji*) and "bow down to Me" (Sanskrit *mam namaskuru*). The Sanskrit word *yajña* ('sacrifice') refers to a ritual sacrifice, devotion, worship or offering.[637] In the widest sense, therefore, it could mean worship of God and devotion to Him. The word *namaskuru* means to 'offer obeisance',[638] i.e. to show humility and submission to God. A summary of devotional service is also given in the Qur'ān, where He says (glorified be He): **"Serve ye none but God, and to your two parents show kindness, and to your kindred and the orphans and the poor, and speak to men kindly, and be steadfast in prayer, and give alms."** [639] Jesus, likewise, gave two great commandments, which form the basis of devotional service:

"Thou shalt love the Lord thy God with all thy heart, and with all thy soul, and with all thy mind. This is the first and great commandment. And the second is like unto it, Thou shalt love thy neighbour as thyself. On these two commandments hang all the law and the prophets."[640]

- Matthew 22:37 - 40

The essence of this meditation, therefore, is to develop the seed of the love of God, and the love of the Great Teacher as the Divine Beloved, within one's heart, and to cultivate this seed with the water of true devotion and pious service. This devotional service can, in summary, consist of: (1) loving God with all our heart, mind and soul, (2) loving our neighbour(s) as we love ourselves, (3) serving none but God alone, (4) thinking of God and the Great Teacher(s), (5) humility and submission to the Great Teacher(s), (6) teaching the message of the Great Teacher(s), (6) showing kindness to our parents, (7) showing kindness to relatives, (8) showing kindness to orphans and the poor, (9) speaking to others with kindness, (10) praying to God in a steadfast and regular manner, (11) giving alms to the poor, and (12) developing divine virtues and qualities, e.g. patience, tolerance, justice, chastity, truthfulness, mercy, forgiveness, forbearance, etc.

We have already quoted Krishna's summary of the divine virtues above, such as **"fearlessness, singleness of soul, the will always to strive for wisdom; opened hand and governed appetites; and piety... humbleness, uprightness, heed to injure nought which lives, truthfulness, slowness unto wrath, a mind that lightly letteth go what others prize; and equanimity, and charity which spieth no man's faults; and tenderness towards all that suffer; a contented heart, fluttered by no desires; a bearing mind, modest, and grave... with patience, fortitude, and purity; an unrevengeful spirit."**[641] In the Qur'ān, likewise, God says (exalted be His glory): **"Shall I tell you of better things than these, prepared for those who fear God, in His presence?... The patient, and the truthful, the lowly, and the charitable, and they who seek pardon at each daybreak,"**[642] **"And clothe not the truth** with falsehood, and hide not the truth when ye know it,"[643] "O ye who believe! stand fast to justice, when ye bear witness before God, though it be against yourselves, or your parents, or your kindred, whether the party be rich or poor,"[644] "O my people! give measure and weight fairly, and defraud not men of their things; and wreak not wrong in the earth, corrupting it,"[645] "Say to the believers that they cast down their looks and guard their private parts; that is purer for them; verily, God is well aware of what they do,"[646] "And say to my servants that they speak in a kind way."[647]

We can add to these several virtues mentioned by Plato, which he calls the **"goods of the soul,"** viz. **"temperance, justice, courage, quickness of apprehension, memory, magnanimity and the like."** [648] In the Fourth Book of Maccabees (1:14, 16), we find that wisdom (Greek *sofia*) is lauded as **"the knowledge of things, divine and human, and of their causes"** and **"wisdom is manifested under the forms of judgement and justice, and courage, and temperance."**[649] In 1 Corinthians 13:13, St. Paul also lists these three virtues: **"And now abideth faith (*pistis*), hope (*elpis*), charity (*agapē*), these three; but the greatest of these is charity."**[650] The last of these three, 'charity' (Greek *agapē*), is perhaps better translated as 'love' for, as we have already learned, **"He that loveth not knoweth not God; for God is love (*hoti ho Theos agapē estin*)."**[651] Let us, therefore, meditate on this divine—this supreme love, which burns brightly in our hearts like a raging fire, and fill our hearts with the longing, love and desire for the Divine Beloved.

Conclusion

"Seek refuge in the True Illumination! For the light of His Wisdom is infinite.

In all the worlds there is nothing upon which His Light shines not.

Take refuge in the Light universal.

As the Light of His deliverance is boundless, he who is within it is freed from the lie of affirmation or denial.

Seek refuge in That which is beyond understanding,

For His glory is all-embracing as the air. It shineth and pierceth all things, and there is nothing hid from the light thereof."[652]

- Shinrin Shōnin, *Jodo-Wasan, the Psalms of the Pure Land*, Lauding the Infinite One, v. 2 – 4.

In meditating on the Divine, we are meditating on our innermost selves, on the inner ocean of boundless Light which heaves and crashes upon a limitless shore of eternity, within the limitless expanse of our inner being. We are noble beings made in the image and light of our Creator, imbued with divine attributes and hidden knowledge, full of limitless potential and power, and able to access the eternal power and might, grace and mercy, which flow in everlasting splendour from the river of immortality. This river, like the celestial River Ganges, has its origins in the everlasting ocean of the Word of God, which has neither beginning nor end, proceeding from the inscrutable and transcendent Essence of God. The Sufi poet, Mahmūd Shabestarī (1288 – 1340 CE) writes: "In Being's silver sea / lustrous pearls of knowledge are washed up / on the shore of speech... / Each wave that breaks in foaming arcs / casts up a thousand royal pearls / that hold strange murmuring voices, / gems of devotion, joy, and love / Yet though a thousand waves / at every moment rise and fall / scattering pearls and shells, / yet are there ever more and more to come / nor is that sea of Being less by one sheer drop."[653] Within this great ocean that lies at the depths of our hearts, there are hidden gems of wisdom, hidden knowledge and power, which we can only accessed by looking within ourselves. And, within ourselves, we find nothing but the Light of God. We are mirrors, and when we purify these mirrors, we find naught but the Names and Attributes of God.

> **"The highroad by which thy spirit and prayers can travel towards God lies in the polishing of the mirror of the heart... The burnisher of the mirror is your steadfast faith... Thou canst better see thy image in the mirror of thy heart than in thy clay; break loose from the chain thou hast fettered thyself with—for thou wilt be free when thou hast got clear from thy clay; since clay is dark and heart**

is bright, thy clay is a dustbin and thy heart a rose-garden."[654]

- Sanā'ī, *The Hadīqatu'l-Haqīqat,* On Purity of Heart.

The ultimate goal of meditation on the Divine is to find the Divine Beloved and fill our hearts with His love. This is, in reality, the ultimate goal of existence. Love, whether it be called *'ishq* in Arabic or *agapē* in Greek, is the essence of true existence. It feeds our souls and it unites our hearts. It is the basis of family, of community, of civilization. It is the essence of happiness, of inner peace, and true prosperity. It is the fabric which binds the atoms of existence and moves the celestial bodies in the heavens. This is that which truly remains, which endures and continues. When the fire of love has been kindled within the depths of our hearts, we desire nothing but reunion with the true Beloved. And we can find no greater Beloved than the pure and spotless Mirrors of God who appear in every age. Thus, whether we call the Divine Beloved Moses, or Zoroaster, or Krishna, or Buddha, or Jesus, or Muhammad, or many other names, the Beloved is one, and the Beloved is eternal. Even as a lamp lights a darkened room in the depths of night, so too does the Divine Beloved illuminate the farthest reaches of creation in the darkness of eternity. When we kindle the light of love in the core of our heart, which is placeless—beyond time or space—then the Divine Beloved is present within us, standing within the Mirror—the Sun of Truth—the Logos. The Primal Will appears within us, however imperfectly, and we can see Him, depending on how much we have cleansed our hearts from the dust and dross of illusion and attachment. Even as the Great Teacher is a Perfect Mirror of the Divine Sun—the Eternal Being, so are we imperfect mirrors of that same Light.

"I am the light of the world: he that followeth me shall not walk in darkness, but shall have the light of life."[655]

- John 8:12

True love depends upon longing and thirst for the Beloved, who is the one consolation—the only Source of true happiness. Only when the fire of love is kindled can we become moths dancing around the flame. Then, when we extinguish the lower self within us, and embrace the Divine Beloved, can we truly cultivate the higher self and achieve true enkindlement—i.e. true enlightenment. Separation from the Divine Beloved, in the mire and clay of self and passion, is the greatest of pains and most terrible of sufferings. As the Persian poet, Hafez of Shiraz (1325/6 – 1389/90 CE), writes: "My friend has fled! alas, my friend has fled, and left me nought but tears and pain behind!"[656] Hafez calls upon his Beloved to return, so that he may be consoled and achieve the joy of divine reunion. He writes: "Return! That to a heart wounded full sore, valiance and strength may enter in; return! And life shall pause at the deserted door, the cold dead body breathe again and burn. Oh come! and touch mine eyes, of thy sweet grace, for I am blind to all but to thy face. Open the gates and bid me see once more!"[657] This is not a call for some earthly paramour to return. Rather, it is Hafez, in his innermost heart, calling on the Divine Beloved to grant him the joy of spiritual reunion, for he is blind to all material things and his eyes are open only to the vision of the Divine Face. The Divine Beloved is never far away. In reality, He waits within the innermost essence of our hearts. As Jesus says: **"Behold, I stand at the door, and knock: if any man hear my voice, and open the door, I will come in to him, and will sup with him, and he with me."**[658] For more information on the topic of enkindlement and cultivating the love of God within one's heart, please refer to Chapters XIII, XIV and XV of *Mindfulness: Five Ways to Achieve Real Happiness, True Knowledge and Inner Peace*.[659] For now, let us end this chapter with these words:

"When love of God kindles a flame in the inward man,

He burns, and is freed from effects.

He has no need of signs to assure him of Love,

For Love casts its own Light up to heaven."[660]

- Jalālu'd-Dīn Rūmī, *The Masnavi*

Questions for Reflection:

The following are some questions that will help us to reflect on what we have learned in this chapter:

1. What is the highest way, according to Krishna?

2. In what way is a soul a reflection of the Lord, as Madhva Acharya asserts?

3. What is true knowledge, according to the introduction above?

4. What is the highest form of meditation?

5. How should we prepare to meditate on the Divine?

6. How can we practise the second step?

7. How can we practise the third step?

8. How can we practise the fourth step?

9. How can we practise the fifth step?

10. What are some of the elements of devotional service?

11. What are some of the virtues that we should develop?

12. What is *agapē*?

13. What is the ultimate goal of meditation?

14. In what way is love the essence of true existence?

15. What does true love depend upon?

The next chapter is a bonus chapter, focusing on other meditation methods.

∞∞∞∞∞∞∞∞∞∞∞∞∞∞∞∞∞∞∞∞∞∞∞∞∞∞∞

VIII. BONUS CHAPTER – Other Meditation Techniques

"To men, their mind alone is the cause of bondage or emancipation. That mind which is attracted by objects of sense tends to bondage, while that which is not so attracted tends to emancipation. Now inasmuch as to a mind without a desire for sensual objects there is stated to be salvation, therefore an aspirant after emancipation should render his mind ever free from all longing after material objects. When a mind freed from the desires for objects and controlled in the heart attains the reality of *Ātmā*, then is it in the Supreme Seat. Till that which arises in the heart perishes, till then it (*Manas*) should be controlled. This only is (true) wisdom. This only is true *Dhyāna* (meditation)."[661]

- Amrtabindu-Upanishad.

Introduction

The meditation methods mentioned in the previous five chapters represent five methods of mastering one's mind, body and spirit, enabling us to achieve a state of self-mastery, spiritual elevation, mindfulness, equanimity and inner peace. These are not, however, the only meditation methods. In this chapter, we will briefly look at five other methods, and give some recommendations for further study. Whichever methods you choose to pursue, bear in mind that the ultimate goal of meditation is the cultivation and development of one's inner or 'higher' self, i.e. the soul. Three of the practices outlined below, i.e. *vipassanā, zazen and kinhin*, derive from the Buddhist tradition, while *qigong* is a Chinese practice within the tradition of Taoism. The final meditation practice, *kundalini* (or *shakti*) meditation, falls within the Tantra and Shakti schools of Hinduism.

Vipassanā (Insight) Meditation

"The beginner should consider and practise *Dhyana* [44] in two aspects: as cessation of the mind's intellectual activities, and as realisation of insight. To bring all mental states that produce vagrant thinking to a stand is called cessation. To adequately understand the transitory and emptiness and egolessness of all things is insight."[662]

- Gautama Buddha, The Diamond Sutra (*Vajracchedika Sutra*)

The Pali word *vipissanā* (Sanskrit *vipaśyanā*) literally means 'insight', so this method of meditation may be referred to as either *vipissanā* meditation or 'insight meditation.' According to Hart (2012), *vipissanā* is the essence of Gautama Buddha's

---

[44] Meditation.

teachings and the 'actual experience' of the truths which he imparted. Hart furthermore states that the practice of insight meditation is extraordinary for its simplicity, lack of dogma and the results which it offers.[663] *Vipissanā* is usually taught at a retreat over a course of 10 days, during which participants have no contact with the outside world. Not only that, but they also suspend any other religious practices—or other practices—including reading and writing, and are supposed to adhere to certain moral practices, including celibacy and temperance.[664] Furthermore, Hart relates, they are supposed to maintain silence for the first 9 days of the course, except when discussing meditation with their instruction.[665]

> **"He who has an insight into this truth is free from thoughts, from recollections, from attachments; in him there is no deceit and falsehood. This is where the essence of Suchness is by itself. When all things are viewed in the light of wisdom, there is neither attachment nor detachment. This is seeing into one's Nature and attaining the truth of Buddhahood."[666]**

- Hui-Neng (638 – 713 CE), *The Tan-Ching*, v. 27

According to Sayadaw U Pandita (2017), whose article entitled 'How to Pratice Vipassana Meditation' provides step-by-step instructions, states that Vipassana meditation is the predominant Buddhist meditation practice in Sri Lanka and Southeast Asia.[667] Pandita states that we should sit quietly and peacefully with legs crossed and close our eyes. Next, we should close our eyes, placing our attention at the belly—at the abdomen. We should breathe normally at a regular pace. As we breathe in and out, we should become aware of the sensation of breathing and the rise and fall of our abdomen. One way of being mindful of these feelings is to gently and silently say to ourselves, 'rising, rising' and 'falling, falling.' If our mind loses focus, we should be aware that we are thinking. If anything arises which draws away our attention from this constant process of rising and falling, then we should note it clearly in our minds and be mindful of it, perhaps repeating 'hearing, hearing' when we hear a sound. When the distraction subsides, we should return to our focus on the rising and falling of our abdomen and our breathing. We should also note the various feelings within our body, such as heat and warmth, hardness, pressure, motion, etc. Even as mental objects arise, we should label these as 'thinking,' 'imagining,' 'remembering,' 'planning,' 'visualizing', etc. According to U Pandita, this allows us to develop a direct and clear awareness of our mind and body. After about an hour, we can bring this meditation to an end. We should begin by slowly opening our eyes. Before we open them, we say to ourselves 'intending, intending' and 'opening, opening.' We then gradually get up from our seated position. This need not conclude the meditation, however, as we can maintain this level of mindfulness and awareness throughout the day.

For more information, see Joseph Goldstein & Jack Kornfield (2001) *Seeking the Heart of Wisdom: The Path of Insight Meditation,* [668] Larry Rosenberg & David Guy (2004) *Breath by Breath: The Liberating Practice of Insight*

Meditation, [669] Sayagyi U Ba Khin (1997) *The Essentials of Buddha-Dhamma in Meditative Practice,*[670] William Hart (2012) *The Art of Living: Vipassana Meditation as taught by S. N. Goenke,*[671] and S. N. Goenka (2000) *Discourse Summaries.*[672]

Zazen (Seated Zen) Meditation

"Men of the world, in eternal confusion, are attached everywhere to one thing or another, which is called craving. The wise however understand the truth and are not like the ignorant. Their minds abide serenely in the uncreated while the body moves about in accordance with the laws of causation. All things are empty and there is nothing desirable to seek after."[673]

- Bodhidharma, *The Transmission of the Lamp,* XXX.

Zazen is, literally, the practice of sitting in meditation. However, the term is particularly used in relation to the Zen school of Buddhism. The school, called Chán (from the Sanskrit *dhyāna* 'meditation') in Chinese or Zen in Buddhism, was founded by a Buddhist monk by the name of Bodhidharma (5 – 6th century CE), who came from the 'Western Regions' (i.e. regions to the west of China).[674] Chan Buddhism is a variety of Mahayana Buddhism with Taoist influences. [675] According to Kaiten Nukariya in his work, *The Religion of the Samurai:* "The sole means of securing mental calmness is the practice of Zazen, or the sitting in Meditation..."[676] We gave a brief summary of Zazen in Chapter XI of of *Mindfulness: Five Ways to Achieve Real Happiness, True*

Knowledge and Inner Peace, where we defined Zen as "a type of Buddhism which has a strong focus on mental training and solving problems through meditation."[677] For example, Zen practitioners may ask themselves, 'What is Buddha?' and meditate on that problem. The Zen master, Ten Shwai, for example, used to ask himself: "Where does the real nature of the mind exist? How can you be saved when you are on the verge of death? and Where do you go when your body is reduced to the elements?"[678] Instead of theorizing the answers or presenting arguments to these questions, Zen practitioners take up the task of meditating on each one in order gain deep insights and revelations of truth.

According to Shunryū Suzuki (2011), the most important thing to begin with as you practice Zen is to develop and maintain *shoshin*, which means 'a beginner's mind.' The idea is to keep your mind fresh. If you recite a Buddhist sutra once, for instance, you approach it as a beginner. If you recite the same sutra three, four, or five times, you may lose your original attitude towards it. By cultivating the art of *shoshin*, one maintains the 'limitless meaning' of one's original mind. [679] According to Suzuki, this original mind contains everything within us, being always rich and sufficient in itself. He points out that, in the beginner's mind, there are always many possibilities, while, in the expert's, there are few.[680] The next step in mental training is to become the master of external things. When we are attached to worldly pleasures, then we are servants of material things. This world, with all its attractions of fame, gain, suffering and loss, is like a prison cage. According to Nukariya, we must learn to "shut up all our senses, and turn the currents of thoughts inward."[681] We must learn to become masters of ourselves, just as we are masters of our physical domain. It is not enough to control one's personal finances, job or property. If we are subject to the whims of our self and passion, we are nothing more than slaves.

"Good it is to tame the mind, so difficult to control, fickle, and capricious. Blessed is the tamed mind... There is no fear in him, the vigilant one whose mind is not befouled with lust, nor embittered with rage, who cares nought for merit or demerit."[682]

- Gautama Buddha, *The Dhammapada*, § III, v. 35, 39

The practice of Zazen involves, firstly, seating oneself, preferably on a thick cushion. Next, we should keep our body erect so that the tip of our nose is perpendicular with our navel. The recommended posture is to seat oneself cross-legged. As this is not easy for everyone, one could also seat oneself on a chair or with one's back to the wall, a sofa or a cushion. You should keep our eyes open during meditation. Lower your gaze but maintain focus. In his introduction to Zen Buddhism, Qiao Renjie (2017) recommends that we should sit with our eyes half-closed, 'gazing at nothing.' We then put our left palm inside our fist, which is a symbol of non-aggression, and hold our hands on our lap. Our mouth should be closed and we should hold our tongue on the roof of the mouth. This helps to avoid salivation and distraction.[683] We should not breathe through our mouth. Instead, we should swell our abdomen as we breathe through the nose. Breathe in and out at regular intervals, holding each breath from one to ten. If we find this difficult, then we are still distracted. This can be overcome through regular practice. When we learn to control our breathing, we can learn to control our minds. When we have achieved this, we can then pose spiritual questions, such as those mentioned above. We can ask ourselves, for example, about the nature of suffering and impermanence.

"All composite things are impermanent,

They are subject to birth and death;

Put an end to birth and death,

And there is a blissful tranquillity."[684]

- *The Gatha of Impermanence*

One method employed by Zen teachers and practitioners is the use of *kõans*. *Kõans* are stories, dialogues, questions or statements which are used to test a student's progress in their practice. A number of examples can be found in Mumon's *The Gateless Gate*, such as the following: "Kyogen said: 'Zen is like a man hanging in a tree by his teeth over a precipice. His hands grasp no branch, his feet rest on no limb, and under the tree another person asks him: 'Why did Bodhidharma come to China from India?' If the man in the tree does not answer, he fails; and if he does answer, he falls and loses his life. Now what shall he do?"[685] Such a question provokes deep thought, but it does not provide any clear answers. If he answers, he fails, if he does not, he falls and dies. Mumon comments that, in this predicament, the greatest of eloquence and memorized knowledge will prove to be of no avail. And if the man does answer, according to Mumon, "even though your past road was one of death, you open up a new road of life."[686] What does this mean? Is true life greater than the sum of this mortal life? Another example: "A monk asked Nansen: 'Is there a teaching no master ever preached before?' Nansen said: 'Yes, there is.' 'What is it?' asked the monk. Nansen replied: 'It is not mind, it is not Buddha, it is not things.'"[687] What is that teaching? *That* is the subject of profound meditation. Zen is, in essence, about achieving self-realization through intense contemplation within oneself. That is the essence of *dhyāna*, i.e. meditation.

For a short but insightful introduction to Zen meditation, I recommend that you check out Qiao Renjie (2017) *Zen: A Complete Beginner's Guide to Zen Meditation.*[688] Other useful introductions to Zen meditation include Shunryū Suzuki (2010) *Zen Mind, Beginner's Mind,*[689] Alan W. Watts (2011) *The Way of Zen,*[690] Philip Kapleau (2007) *The Three Pillars of Zen,*[691] Dainin Katagiri (2009) *Each Moment is the Universe,*[692] Charlotte Joko Beck (2009) *Everyday Zen,*[693] and Thich Nhat Hanh (1992) *Peace is Every Step: The Path of Mindfulness in Everyday Life.*[694] For more *kōan*s, also check out Koun Yamada & Rube L.F. Habito (2005) *The Gateless Gate: The Classic Book of Zen Koans.*[695]

Walking Meditation (*Kinhin*)

> **"If you walk according to the teaching, for the sake of which noble youths go forth completely from a house to a houseless life, you will soon, on going forth yourselves, realize the transcendent faculties in this life, and will live in the attainment of the aim of the highest religious life."[696]**

- Gautama Buddha, *Buddhist Scriptures*, VI.

In Zen practice, walking meditation is called *kinhin*. According to Qiao Renjie's book on Zen meditation, when we practice walking meditation, we are 'just walking', i.e. we are not moving towards a destination—we are only experiencing.[697] We can fold our hands the same way as in sitting meditation, with the left thumb tucked into the right palm. Instead of walking to 'get anywhere', we are simply walking to experience walking. Walking meditation can be used as a way of taking a break from sitting meditation. It can allow us to stretch our bodies and loosen our muscles. This is not, however, the main aim of walking meditation. As Renjie informs us, deep insights can be gathered from *kinhin*, which is a bridge which helps us to connect our sitting practice (or *zazen*) with real life.[698]

The goal of this meditation, according to Danny & Katherine Dreyer (2012) is to tame the wanderings of the mind. We live in a world of so many distractions which constantly draw our attention.[699] Walking meditation gives the mind a chance to rest, which is essential for it to function at an optimal level.[700] The first step, according to Dreyer, is to do a brief standing meditation.[701] We should start with our feet hip-width apart, balancing our weight evenly on both feet and taking time to feel the firmness of the ground beneath us.[702] Taking a few deep breaths, we then close our eyes and scan our whole bodies, as in mindfulness meditation, starting at the feet and working up to our face and heads.[703]

"Be not thoughtless, watch your thoughts! Draw yourself out of the evil way, like an elephant sunk in mud."[704]

- Gautama Buddha, *The Dhammapada*, § XXIII, v. 327.

In an article on *Mindful.org*, Boyce (2013) provides a simple set of instructions for practising walking meditation. The first step is to stand up, with one's back upright but not stiff.[705] We should feel our feet touching the ground and let our weight balance out, being evenly distributed. The next step is to curl the thumb (of your left hand) and wrap the fingers of your other hand around it, just as outlined by Renjie above.[706] The third step is to lower your gaze slightly, which helps to maintain focus.[707] Next, we should step out with our left foot, feeling it swing and hit the ground, placing the ball on the ground and then the toes.[708] Next, we do the same with the right foot.[709] We should walk at a steady pace, a bit slower than our normal pace.[710] We should continue walking at a steady pace and, when our attention wanders, we should bring it back to the sensation of our feet as they touch the ground.[711]

When we finish, we will feel more relaxed and more mindful, having developed a sense of awareness of ourselves and our surroundings. Walking is, in any case, a healthy activity. But if we can also refresh our minds, as well as our bodies, then we feel a greater sense of tranquillity and peace.

For more information, read Chapter 4 of Qiao Renjie's *Zen: A Complete Beginner's Guide to Zen Meditation*. Other books with information on walking meditation include Nguyen Anh-Huong & Thich Nhat Hanh (2006) *Walking Meditation*,[712] and Thich Nhat Hanh (2011) *The Long Road Turns to Joy: A Guide to Walking Meditation*.[713]

Qigong (Life-energy Cultivation) Meditation

"Keep in mind the fact that there are only two known elements in the whole universe, energy and matter... The human mind is a form of energy, a part of it being spiritual in nature."[714]

- Napoleon Hill (1938) *Think and Grow Rich*, p. 252.

We have already explained that *qi* refers to the eternal life-force which flows through all created things. It is synonymous with the Hindu concept of *prāna*, which is the life force of vital principle of existence. In the *Mahabharata*, Bhrigu says that "prana is the living creature, the universal soul, the eternal Being, and the Mind, Intellect, and Consciousness of all living creatures, as also all the objects of the senses."[715] The purpose of qigong is to cultivate this mystic force, or *qi*. The practice dates back to around

700 BCE, when it was first described in the *Yellow Emperor's Classic of Internal Medicine*.[716] Gaik (2009) describes one simple method of qigong meditation. He writes that, when you catch yourself in a negative thought, you should close your eyes for a moment and visualize a big, red stop sign. Next, you should breathe deeply into the area where you feel tension until you begin to relax. The negative thought should be replaced with a more positive one, visualizing the healing energy of qi (which we can imagine to be like light flowing through us) moving to the spot where you feel tension. Then, take in a deep breath and continue to 'breathe into' the area. When you start to feel better, you should express gratitude for the healing.[717]

> **"The Tao is (like) the emptiness of a vessel; and in our employment of it we must be on our guard against all fulness. How deep and unfathomable it is, as if it were the Honoured Ancestor of all things!"[718]**

\- Laozi, *The Tao Te Ching*, 4

Davis (2015), in his book, *Qigong Through the Seasons*, writes that the foundational practice of qigong meditation is breath counting. This involves counting each breath so we are better able to clear our minds of any distractions.[719] Our internal dialogue, he writes, is often negative, which causes tension in both our body and our mind. As such, we should focus on our breathing as a means of switching off this inner dialogue, instead focusing on peace and inner calm.[720] We should begin, he directs us, by sitting upright on a cushion or chair, holding our spine erect with hands resting on thighs, palms down, or in one's lap with palms facing upwards, one hand resting on the other. If we sit on a meditation cushion, our knees should be bent and legs crossed. Several different seating positions are described in the book.[721] It is useful to use a timer so that one can meditate for a specified period of time, e.g. 10, 20, 30, 40 minutes, etc.[722] We should become aware of our breath as we inhale and exhale. We should not try to control it—instead, just become mindful of each inhalation, each pause, exhalation and pause.[723] Next, we begin to count our exhalations from one to ten. As we do so, many thoughts may pass through our minds, but we should not become attached to them. Rather, we should let them pass through and bring our minds back to the counting. This can serve as a stand-alone meditation or can be used as part of a longer *qigong* meditation.[724]

Qigong offers several methods of meditation, including visualization meditation, which walks you through a forest. The purpose, according to Flood (2017), is to reconnect you with the healing life-energy both inside and around you. It also allows us to create greater harmony within our mind, body and spirit and increase our inner happiness.[725] The first step outlined by Flood in her article on 'forest meditation' is to become present. We can do this by sitting comfortably, closing our eyes, with spine straight yet relaxed. Practise the breathing exercise outlined by Davis (2015) above. Then, allow your attention to descend from your head down through your neck, your shoulders and your arms, as if you feel the earth gently pulling you downwards. You should slowly bring your attention over your torso, then move into your pelvis, through your legs and, finally, into your feet. This is rather similar to mindfulness meditation.[726]

"Restraining all the senses in a forest that is free from noise and that is uninhabited, with mind fixed thereon, one should meditate on the All (or universal Brahman) both outside and inside one's body."[727]

- *The Mahabharata*, Book 14: Aswamedha Parva, Section XIX.

The second step is to enter the forest. Imagine yourself standing in a beautiful and verdant forest. Imagine that you are walking down a path through this forest as sunlight beams through the canopy above and illumines all the trees, leaves and branches with a subtle glow. Feel your feet on the path as you walk through this forest, taking a moment to smell the fresh air and experience it flowing over your skin. Reflect on the beauty and wonder of the forest—the great miracle of God's creation which you can see before your eyes. Imagine how you feel in that moment—every part of your body, as well as your emotions. The third step is to find the river. You hear a river coming up right ahead and see the water shining brightly as it reflects the sunlight. Next, walk towards its sandy bank which warms your feet, and then place your feet in its warm, pellucid water, washing your toes therein. Walk further and further into the river until it reaches your hips. Then, immerse your entire body within the water, feeling how it rejuvenates and purifies your body, mind and soul. Imagine how you feel in that moment. The water will carry away any tensions, worries and cares that might be bothering you and will allow you to feel clean, refreshed and renewed, tranquil and free of any cares. Lastly, we should open our eyes.[728]

For further reading, the following are recommended: Ronald H. Davis (2015) *Qigong Through the Seasons: How to Stay Healthy All Year with Qigong, Meditation, Diet, and Herbs*,[729] Kenneth S. Cohen (1999) *The Way of Qigong: The Art and Science of Chinese Energy Healing*,[730] Jwing-Ming Yang (2016) *The Root of Chinese Qigong: Secrets of Health, Longevity, & Enlightenment*,[731] Jwing-Ming Yang (2016) *Qigong Meditation: Small Circulation*,[732] Jwing-Ming Yang (2016) *Qigong Meditation: Embryonic Breathing*,[733] and Edward Hines (2013) *Moving into Stillness – A Practical Guide to Qigong and Meditation*.[734]

Kundalini (Shakti) Meditation

"It is by the power of Pranayama[45] that the Yogis do the wonderful feats of levitation, walking on water, etc. This is not their goal—they only want liberation—but there is no liberation without awakening the Kundalini."[735]

- Rishi Singh Gherwal, *Kundalini, The Mother of the Universe*, p. 54.

---

45 Controlling one's breath, or *prana*.

What is *kundalinī*? The basic concept is that kundalini is an energy which coils at the base of one's spine, rather like a serpent.[736] Gherwal (1930) defines it as "Divine static and dynamic energy."[737] This untapped energy is creative and spiritual, and the goal of kundalini yoga is to release and hone this energy.[738] Kundalini yoga, also known as *laya yoga*, is a variety of yoga which is influenced by Shakti and Tantra schools of Hinduism.[739] There are a number of Sanskrit texts which deal with the practice of kundalini yoga, including the *Sat-cakra-nirūpana* and the *Pāduka-pañcaka*, which were first introduced to the west in a translation by John Woodroffe (1865 – 1936 CE) in 1919, entitled *The Serpent Power: The Secrets of Tantric and Shaktic Yoga*. The *Yogakundalī-Upanishad*, one of the canonical 108 Upanishads of the sacred Vedas,[46] was also translated into English and published in 1914 by K. Narayanasvami Aiyar.[740] The basic concept of kundalini-yoga is that *shakti* (meaning 'power' or 'empowerment') is the cosmic energy of the universe, which embodies the so-called 'divine feminine' element of creation. Thus, in Hinduism, Shakti is worshipped as the Great Divine Mother, who is regarded as the wife of Shiva. In Shaktism, a variety of Hinduism, she is worshipped as the Supreme Being.[741] This is mentioned here for the purpose of context and historical background, and I would note that I am a strict monotheist. The meditation methods mentioned in this chapter are shared in a descriptive manner, without any judgement on their merits or spiritual value.

---

[46] According to the Muktika canon.

"The *śakti* (mentioned above) is only *kundalinī*. A wise man should take it from its place (*viz.*, the navel, upwards) to the middle of the eyebrows."[742]

- The *Yoga-Kundalī Upanishad*

In the Hindu and Buddhist Tantras, there is a concept that, in addition to the material or gross body, there is an immutable divine body (*divya-deha*).[743] This is the etheric double of the material body, the latter being subject to decay and death, while the former is eternal and divine. The process of Tantra-yoga involves taming, energising and unfolding this subtle body, which is linked to the pure energy of the cosmos.[744] According to Khanna (2004), awakening the inner potency of this body leads not only to the acquisition of spiritual power (called *siddhi*), but it can also slowly transform the substance of the material body. Kundalini, according to Khanna, is an infinite reservoir of *shakti*, and it lies three-and-a-half circles around the central axis of the spine, at its base, within what is called the *muladhara* ('root support') chakra. *Chakra* means 'wheel' in Sanskrit and there are believed to be seven chakras—or spiritual centres—within the body. These are energy points or nodes within the subtle body, which have a profound effect on our physical bodies, which tap into these energies. [745]

One method of releasing our kundalini is called *bhuta shuddhi*. The practice of *bhuta shuddhi* is outlined in an article from Yoga International, which describes it as method to purify one's chakras. It involves, firstly, sitting in a meditative posture, like the ones already described for other methods above. We should close our eyes, focusing our attention on the *muladhara chakra*, which is the abode of the earth element, sitting at the base of the spine. We should visualize a yellow square surrounded by four petals, in the centre of which is the kundalini, which takes the form of a sleeping serpent, as brilliant as a thousand flashes of lightning.[746] There are a series of short mantras which help the practitioner to 'awaken' his or her *kundalini shakti*, followed by three cycles of *pranayama*, i.e. the formal practice of controlling one's breath. For more information, read the article on the Yoga International website (see endnote).[747] Woodroffe describes that *bhuta shuddhi* as a "subtle rite" in which "the worshipper imagines that each of the component elements of the body is absorbed in the next higher element until all are merged in the Supreme Power of whom man, as a compound of such elements, is a limited manifestation."[748]

For more information on Kundalini meditation, see: Qiao Renjie (2017c) *Kundalini: Awaken Shakti through Kundalini Meditation*.[749] This book provides five chapters describing shakti, kundalini, the benefits of kundalini awakening and the practice of kundalini meditation. In addition, it has a bonus chapter on additional methods to awaken kundalini through *pranayama* and *yoga*. Like most of Renjie's works, this is a short book, but it is also quite informative and interesting. In the bonus chapter, four different yoga poses are described and illustrated, and the method introduced by Yogi Bhajan (1929 – 2004) is described.

Also check out: Gopi Krishna (1997) *Kundalini: The Evolutionary Energy in Man*,[750] Gopi Krishna (2014) *Kundalini:*

The Secret of Yoga, [751] Shakti Parwha Kaur Khalsa (1998) *Kundalini Yoga: The Flow of Eternal Power: A Simple Guide to the Yoga of Awareness as taught by Yogi Bhajan, Ph.D.,* [752] Dharma Singh Khalsa & Darryl O'Keeffe (2002) *The Kundalini Yoga Experience: Bringing Body, Mind, and Spirit Together,* [753] and John Woodroffe (2003) *The Serpent Power.* [754]

Questions for Reflection:

The following are some questions that will help us to reflect on what we have learned in this chapter:

1. What does *vipissanā* mean?

2. What is *zazen*?

3. Who was Bodhidharma?

4. What is a *kōan*?

5. What is the goal of walking meditation?

6. What is the foundational practice of qigong meditation?

7. What is visualization meditation?

8. What is *kundalinī*? What is *shakti*?

9. What is a *chakra*?

10. What is the practice of *bhuta shuddhi*?

In the next chapter, we will look at some steps for further improvement in your meditation practice.

∞∞∞∞∞∞∞∞∞∞∞∞∞∞∞∞∞∞∞∞∞∞∞∞∞∞∞

IX. Meditation – Steps for Further Improvement

"Year after year the annual flowers bloom

Upon the bush uninterruptedly.

Thus Buddha lives unchanged; but we, that are

But shows and shadows of the Inner Soul,

Bud, bloom, and die, as changing years roll on."[755]

- Anon., Buddhist Meditations

Introduction

Now that you have studied the five meditation methods which are covered in depth in this volume, as well as the five additional meditation methods mentioned in Chapter VIII, let us reflect on some additional steps we can take to further enhance our meditation practice. There are many different reasons why people choose to meditate, and these are reflected in the different kinds of meditation which are covered in this book. Some people want to simply de-stress and de-clutter their minds. They want to reduce tension, feel more relaxed, overcome depression or achieve a better state of balance and equanimity. To achieve these goals, mindfulness meditation is highly recommended. Likewise, some people want to feel more loving and loved, achieve greater self-confidence, and enhance their meditation practice—taking it to a higher level. Loving-kindness meditation allows us to feel true love for ourselves and love for others, which is the essence of true religion and philosophy. Love, as we have learned, is the essence of existence and God is love (Koine Greek *agapē*). Whether you want to practise one or the other—or both—of these meditation methods is up to you. It depends on what you want to achieve and what your goals are. They may be seen as complementary methods of mastering your mind and achieving a balance within your mind, body and spirit. When you become the master of your own mind and spirit, you can achieve anything, within reason. You will also be able to restrain and overcome your inner self while releasing your higher self from the prison of attachment. This is the greatest freedom, and this is true equanimity. This is the essence of wisdom and the basis of true happiness.

> **"But the virtues of him who proceeds to the contemplative life, consist in a departure from terrestrial concerns. Hence also, they are called purifications, being surveyed in the refraining from corporeal actions, and avoiding sympathies with the body. For these are the virtues of the soul elevating itself to true being."[756]**

- Porphyry, *Auxiliaries to Intelligibles*

The third method of meditation that we covered was mantra meditation, which involves chanting and recitation of the

Names and Attributes of God, as well as other mantras which invoke the Names of the Great Teachers and Messengers of God. Often, the Names of the Great Teachers can also be used as Names of God. We have discussed the benefits of mantra meditation and various methods of performing it. Mantra meditation takes our spiritual practice to the next level, because it allows us to develop the seed of God-consciousness, remembering and reflecting on the Creator of our bodies and souls every day—and at every moment. Not everyone who reads this book will believe in God, and not everyone who takes up meditation wants to develop the *spiritual* element of life—and that is fine. We are all capable of different levels of understanding and spiritual development. Some have been given a carafe, others a medium-sized glass, others a small cup, and yet others a thimble. But we are all capable of receiving the water of life. Not everyone is ready to accept the existence of the Divine, but we can all set foot on the path of Truth. When we abandon all pre-conceptions and seek the Truth without any reservation, then we are on the path of Truth, which is the Straight Path. If we follow this path all the way, then we will come to recognize the existence of God and experience a deep sense of transcendental love, happiness, bliss and joy. True tranquillity and equanimity can only be accomplished when we follow this narrow yet glorious path to perfection.

"Man was generated and constituted, for the purpose of contemplating the reason of the whole of nature, and in order that, being himself the work of wisdom, he might survey the wisdom of the things which exist."[757]

The last two methods—meditation on the Divine Word and meditation on the Divine Being—are interrelated and represent the next steps following mantra meditation. These are higher forms of meditation, which are intended for those who are committed to the spiritual path and have already recognized the existence of the Divine Being. The seed of the love of God has already been planted in our hearts and we are ready to contemplate that All-Knowing and All-Loving Lord within the revealed Word of God and the universe around us. We can even find this Almighty Lord within the innermost depths of our own souls. As we have learned earlier, the whole of creation is a mirror of the Divine, and His attributes are found within the essence of all created things. Everything mirrors the divine attributes, such as love, mercy, fortitude, tolerance, beauty, justice, mercy, etc. And man, above all other creatures, is capable of reflecting all the divine attributes and acquiring these attributes as part of our characters. We are also mines filled with gems of inestimable value and oceans full of pearls of great wisdom and priceless value.[758] The purpose of these latter two meditation methods is to cultivate ourselves—to dig deep within ourselves and find the inner nobility within. As we discover ourselves—as we learn more about our true, higher self, we will find the Lord, our God, standing within us, mighty and powerful, our most Intimate Friend and Divine Beloved.[759] When we cultivate our higher selves and develop virtues—when we burn with the love of God within our innermost hearts—and we take up the path of service and love, then we will achieve true happiness, true wisdom, equanimity and inner peace.[760] The following are some steps for further development:

STEP ONE: GET THE RIGHT EQUIPMENT / LOCATION

"On his arrival there, he would take his seat in a pavilion, on the excellent Buddha-mat which had been spread for him, where he would wait for the priests to finish their meal. When the priests had finished their meal, the body-servant would announce the fact to The Blessed One. Then The Blessed One would enter the perfumed chamber."[761]

- *Buddhism in Translations*, § 11. The Buddha's Daily Habits, p. 93.

When we engage in sitting meditation, it is important that we are seated in an upright posture in a comfortable and quiet location. Swami Vivekananda (1920) recommends that you have a special room, if you can afford it, in which to practise alone. He writes that you should not sleep in this room, keeping it holy, nor should you enter it without bathing, nor even should one think impure thoughts within the room, nor allow any quarrelling or anger to occur in that spot.[762] Vivekananda recommends that this room be beautified with flowers and pleasing pictures. It can also be made to smell nice by burning incense every morning and evening. By preventing material and spiritual impurities from entering the room, it retains an atmosphere of holiness, rather like a temple, mosque or church.[763] For most people, this would be impractical, but I am repeating his suggestion here as it may be useful for some readers.

Figure 17. Swami Vivekananda

A meditation society or club could also do the same by providing a common meditation room with the same rules and atmosphere. Either way, it is useful to meditate in a special place.

---

[47] Image source: Swami Vivekananda. Public domain image. Photograph created 1 December 1896 CE. Available online at: https://upload.wikimedia.org/wikipedia/commons/0/0c/Swami_Viveka nanda_1896.jpg (accessed 15/05/2017).

The concept of sacredness or holiness is an ancient one and usually involves setting something aside as sacred. Émile Durkheim (1858 – 1917 CE) writes that "sacred things" are "things set apart and forbidden."[764] In other words, they have a restricted use and are set apart for a sacred purpose. A church or mosque, for example, is a building which has been set aside for worship. As such, when we enter these buildings, we feel a sense of sacredness which is difficult to explain or describe. Have you ever entered a sacred building and felt a sense of awe, wonder or peacefulness? Exactly. If we choose one particular place to meditate in, and set it aside for that purpose, we can feel the same sense of awe, wonder or peacefulness as we approach that spot.

> **"There is no holier sanctuary than a purified mind, a mind concentrated upon God. There is no more sacred place than the region of peace into which the mind enters when it becomes fixed in the lord. No more sweet-odorous and holy incense is there than the rising of thought unto God."[765]**

- A Disciple, *In the Hours of Meditation*, I, p. 2.

Next, let us ensure that we have the right equipment to meditate. I would highly recommend that you purchase a meditation mat. There are many different kinds of meditation mats, such as buckwheat (or kapok) *zafu* cushions, which are circular (or cylindrical) and thick, like a beanbag; v-shaped meditation cushions; rectangular zen yoga pillows; *seiza* kneeling stools (meditation benches); half-moon bolsters (or wedges) for back support; or *zabuton*s. A *zabuton* is a rectangular-shaped cotton-filled cushion which has a removable cover. This gives extra support for your ankles and knees,[766] especially if your meditation room has a hard-wood or other hard surface.

Figure 18: A Japanese zafu cushion

A *zabuton* can also be used as a yoga bolster—simply fold it up and place it under your knees.[767] One can also use a simple, straw mat or a yoga mat for meditation. It is, really, up to you, according to your preferences/comfort. In addition to meditation mats, there are other products which are useful to give us a sense of mindfulness and relaxation. We can, for example, use a traditional gong to keep us mindful of our meditation and focus. This is particularly useful in group meditation, where one person hits the gong at regular intervals—perhaps every few minutes—in order to keep the rest of the meditators alert and awake. A singing

---

[48] Image source: Black velvet zafu used in Antai-ji zen monastery, Japan. Photograph taken by Dontpanic, 19 May 2013 (CC BY-SA 2.0). Available online at: https://upload.wikimedia.org/wikipedia/commons/5/5f/Japanese_Zafu.jpg (accessed 18/05/2017). For more information on the license, see: http://creativecommons.org/licenses/by-sa/3.0

bowl or bell can also be used at the beginning or end of meditation practice.[768] An electronic meditation timer can be used to time our meditation and ensure that we either meditate long enough or do not go beyond the set time which we have allotted for meditation.

Figure 19. Different types of vajras

769

There are several ritual objects used in Tantric Buddhist meditation and practice. According to Dasgupta (1950), Tantric Buddhism is divided into three schools: Vajrayāna, Kālacakrayāna and Sahajayāna.[770] In Vajrayana Buddhism, the *ghanta* or 'bell' (Tibetan *dril-bu*) is often accompanied by a ritual object called the *vajra* in Sanskrit (*dorje* in Tibetan). Often made of brass or bronze with four prongs at each end, twisted to form a lotus-bud shape, the *vajra* is used in conjunction with the bell in various sacred gestures (called *mudrās*), which are said to have metaphysical power.[771] The *vajra* should be held in the right hand (representing fitness for action and the masculine element), while the bell is held in the left hand (representing intelligence and the feminine). Together, the *ghanta* and *vajra* symbolize the union of wisdom/emptiness (i.e. the *ghanta*) and method/skilful means (i.e. the *vajra*).[772] For more information on the *vajra* and its historical/religious significance, see Robert Beer (2003) *The Handbook of Tibetan Buddhist Symbols*, pp. 87 – 98. According to Dasgupta (1950), *vajra*, as a metaphysical concept, refers to 'perfect void.' In Vajrayana Buddhism, everything is *vajra* (void), and the ultimate goal is realization of one's *vajra*-nature.[773] For more on this, see Shashi Bhusan Dasgupta (1950) *An Introduction to Tāntric Buddhism*, pp. 78 – 85. A detailed explanation of the Tantric ritual involving the *ghanta* and *vajra* can be found in the *Shrīchakrasambhāra Tantra: A Buddhist Tantra*, edited by John Woodroffe (as 'Arthur Avalon') and Kazi Dawa-Samdup (1919).[774]

STEP TWO: JOIN A MEDITATION COURSE / RETREAT

"Come away, for a while, from external things, from the pleasures of the senses, from the arguments of the intellect, from the noise and the excitements of the world, and withdraw yourself into the inmost chamber of your heart, and there, free from the sacrilegious intrusion of all selfish desires, you will find a deep silence, a holy calm, a blissful repose, and if you will rest awhile in that holy place, and will meditate there, the faultless eye of Truth will open within you, and you will see things as they really are. This holy place within you is your real and eternal self; it is the divine within you; and only when you identify yourself with it can you be said to be 'clothed and in your right mind.' It is the abode of peace, the temple of wisdom, the dwelling-place of immortality."[775]

- James Allen, *The Way of Peace.*

So far, we have written about methods of practising meditation by oneself. The purpose of this book, indeed, is to provide a 'how-to' guide to meditation, so that one may teach oneself to meditate alone or in groups. This book can also be used as a companion to a course, or in a book club or reading group. One may use this book with or without a teacher, and the practices described herein do not require additional coaching or instruction. However, not everyone can learn meditation through reading a book, and not everyone is comfortable practising meditation at home. Meditation retreats, therefore, are particularly useful for such individuals, as they allow us to gain practical instruction from meditation experts in a calm, soothing and tranquil environment—away from the distractions of modern technology, the stress of work and work commitments, the comforts of one's home and the noise of the material world around us. It would be impossible, within the scope of this book, to give a detailed list of all the best meditation retreats and courses around the world, nor can we give a detailed list for each country. I recommend that you search for a suitable meditation course or institute near you, wherever you live in the world.

There are several online articles which list some of the best meditation retreats worldwide, so I recommend that you check these out, such as Rebecca Weber's (2013) article on 'The world's best meditation retreats,' [776] Caroline Jones (2015) 'Wellness Holidays: from meditation weekends to high-tech rejuvenation'[777] and (2016) '10 UK holidays that will make you a better person,'[778] Erica Camus (2016) '14 of the best mindfulness retreats,' [779] Carolyn Gregoire (2013) 'Silent Retreats: 10 Fantastic Retreat Centers In The U.S. For Peace & Quiet (PHOTOS),'[780] and Brooke Bobb (2016) 'Beginner-Friendly Meditation Retreats in Some of the World's Most Beautiful Settings.' [781] The College of Vedic Studies at Bhaktivedanta Manor in the UK offers a range of educational, spiritual and practical courses and workshops based on ancient Vedic teachings and the spiritual philosophy of Gaudiya

Vaishnavism.[782] Another Hare Krishna centre, New Govardhana, ISKCON Australia, also offers a Vedic Sanctuary Retreat which allows you to explore the 'intrinsic healing dynamics' of the whole human being.[783] The Hare Krishna movement also has an institute based in Vrindavan, India, called the Vrindavan Institute for Higher Education (VIHE), which offers the annual Govardhan Retreat, also called the 'Holy Name Retreat (Japa & Kirtana)'.[784] This consists of a week of chanting and hearing the names of God in Sanskrit.[785]

STEP THREE: PRACTISE THE METHODS IN THIS BOOK

"'Tis you who must strive: the Blessed Ones are only preachers. They who strive and meditate are freed from Mara's bonds."[786]

- Gautama Buddha, *The Dhammapada*, § XX, v. 276

One of the best ways to cultivate your mindfulness and inner peace, of course, is to *practise* the meditation methods you have studied. There can be no substitute for actual practice. Follow the methods in this book and practice each one according to the step-by-step instructions we have given. You do not have to practice each and every method but focus on the ones which are most suited to your needs and level of spiritual awareness and receptivity. I would recommend that you start with mindfulness meditation, as this is a good, foundational practice. When you have mastered this, move on to loving-kindness meditation, and so on. Thus, as you gradually develop your practice of each of these five key meditation methods, you will gain greater spiritual awareness, greater mindfulness and a greater sense of equanimity, inner balance and tranquillity. For more information on how to enhance your spiritual progress while going through these methods, I would highly recommend that you study the philosophy and spiritual insights contained in the previous book in this series, _Mindfulness: Five Ways to Achieve Real Happiness, True Knowledge and Inner Peace_, which lays out the 'Five Ways to Be'—the core principles of what I call the 'philosophy of equanimity.' Study these 'Ways to Be' in conjunction with the meditation methods of this book, practising them with sincerity and effort, and you will find your inner life transformed. You will find a noticeable change in your character, behaviour and general awareness. Your relationships will improve, you will feel a sense of purpose and inner happiness and joy, and you will begin to develop a relationship of love and devotion to your Creator, the All-Knowing Divine Being—God. Whether we call Him Allāh, Elohim, Jehovah, Gott, Deus, ho Theos or any other Names, He is the Ultimate Principle of existence, and we are created to know, love and worship Him.

> **"Man is created to praise, reverence, and serve God our Lord, and by this means to save his soul. And the other things on the face of the earth are created for man and that they may help him in prosecuting the end for which he is created."[787]**

- St. Ignatius of Loyola, *Spiritual Exercises of St. Ignatius of Loyola*, First   Week.

We should combine our practice, furthermore, with the twin principles of gratitude and magnanimity. Gratitude is thankfulness for everything that we have, being aware that everything we receive is a gift from God. This includes what we perceive as the good and the bad. Everything we receive comes from a Higher Power which moves the universe and sustains it with His all-encompassing power. The more we are grateful, the more blessings we shall receive. Linked to this is the concept of magnanimity—or generosity—which is expressed through the practice of generous giving. When we are generous, we show our love for others, and for God, who is the most Generous of all. Since God has given us everything that we need out of His abiding generosity, should be not also express that same principle of generosity for others? This includes being generous with our time, knowledge and wealth. This can take the form of teaching others, volunteering in the local community, or giving money to charity. I have written a list of recommended charities, which you can find on Equanimity Blog.[788]

STEP FOUR: STUDY THE SCRIPTURES SYSTEMATICALLY

"Without the aid of an understanding cleansed by study of the scriptures and without that true conception of all things which is known by the name of Vijnana, [49] the attainment of Emancipation is impossible."[789]

- Janaka, *The Mahabharata*, Book 12: Santi Parva, Part 3, Section CCCXXVII.

This step is essential for spiritual advancement. We should study the scriptures of the great religions systematically. What does that mean? It would be unreasonable for anyone to expect to study all the scriptures of the divine religions and Great Teachers. Therefore, we should narrow our studies to those key texts which are of most benefit and spiritual significance for the seeker after Truth. Every religion and philosophy has some core texts which provide a succinct and distilled summation of the core principles of that belief-system. In the Old Testament (or *Tanakh*), for instance, the Ten Commandments (Exodus 20:1 – 17), along with the *Shema Yisrael* (Deuteronomy 6:4 – 9; 11:13 – 21; Numbers 15:37 – 41) and Leviticus 19:18, contain the essence of the teachings of the Prophet Moses. Leviticus 19:18 contains the famous verse: **"Thou shalt not avenge, nor bear any grudge against the children of thy people, but thou shalt love thy neighbour as thyself: I am the LORD,"[790]** and Deuteronomy

---

[49] *Vijñāna* is Sanskrit for 'consciousness,' 'life force,' 'mind,' or 'discernment.' See: https://en.wikipedia.org/wiki/Vij%C3%B1%C4%81na (accessed 29/04/2017).

6:4 – 5 states: **"Here, O Israel: The LORD our God is one LORD: And thou shalt love the Lord thy God with all thine heart, and with all thy soul, and with all thy might."**[791] Jesus says: **"On these two commandments hang all the Law and the Prophets."**[792] In the Psalms, there are a number of beautiful passages potent with meaning, such as those already quoted in previous chapters—in particular, Psalms 1, 23, 40, 46, 62, 84 117, 121 and 138.

> **"Truly my soul waiteth upon God: from him cometh my salvation... He only is my rock and my salvation: he is my defence; I shall not be moved. In God is my salvation and my glory: the rock of my strength, and my refuge, is in God... Also unto thee, O Lord, belongeth mercy: for thou renderest to every man according to his work."**[793]
>
> - Psalm 62:1, 6 – 7, 12

In Christianity, there are several core teachings, which are summarized in The Sermon on the Mount (Matthew 5 – 7) and the Parables. There are several key parables taught by Jesus Christ (peace and blessings be upon him), including the Parable of the Sower (Matthew 13:1 – 23), the Hidden Treasure (Matthew 13:44), the Pearl of Great Price (Matthew 13:45 – 46), the Growing Seed (Mark 4:26 – 29), the Mustard Seed (Matthew 13:31 – 32), the Lost Sheep (Matthew 18:12 – 14), the Lost Coin (Luke 15:8 – 10), the Prodigal Son (Luke 15:11 – 32), the Good Samaritan (Luke 10:25 – 37), the Two Debtors (Luke 7:36 – 50), the Unforgiving Servant (Matthew 18:21 – 35), the Friend at Night (Luke 11:5 – 8), the Unjust Judge (Luke 18:1 – 8), the Pharisee and the Publican (Luke 18:9 – 14), the Faithful Servant (Matthew 24:42 – 51), the Wise and Foolish Virgins (Matthew 25:1 – 13), the Great Banquet (Matthew 22:1 – 14), the Rich Fool (Luke 12:13 – 21), the Wicked Husbandmen (Matthew 21:33 – 46), the Wheat and the Tares (Matthew 13:24 – 30), Drawing in the Net (Matthew 13:47 – 52), the Budding Fig Tree (Matthew 24:32 – 35), the Barren Fig Tree (Luke 13:6 – 9), the Wise and the Foolish Builders (Matthew 7:24 – 27), the Lamp under a Bushel (Mark 4:21 – 25), the Unjust Steward (Luke 16:1 – 13), the Rich Man and Lazarus (Luke 16:19 – 31), the Talents (or the Parable of Minas) (Matthew 25:14 – 30), and the Workers in the Vineyard (Matthew 20:1 – 16). By studying the many parables revealed by Jesus Christ, we can come to understand deep spiritual truths. The whole of the Gospel of John is full of mystical truths and spiritual principles, so this Gospel is worthy of particular study. I prefer to use the Authorised Version of the Bible (AV), also known as the 'King James Bible' (KJB) or the 'King James Version' (KJV), but one can use whichever version one prefers.

"Those who are ever watchful, who study day and night, and who strive after Nirvâna, their passions will come to an end."[794]

- Gautama Buddha, *The Dhammapada*, Ch. XVII, v. 226

The whole of the Dhammapada and Bhagavad-Gita can be studied, as these are both very short works. The Dhammapada is an authoritative work within Buddhism as it contains sayings of Gautama Buddha (peace and blessings be upon him) and was

318

originally part of the Khuddaka Nikaya, which is the last of the five nikayas within the Sutta Pitaka. The Sutta Pitaka itself is one of the 'three baskets' of the Pali Tipitaka, which constitute the scriptures of Theravada Buddhism.[795] According to the Buddhist scholar and commentator, Buddhaghosa (5th century CE), each of the sayings in the Dhammapada was made in response to a different situation that arose within Buddha's monastic community.[796] The Dhammadapa, as revealed in Pali, contains some 423 verses divided into 26 chapters.[797] Buddhagosa's commentary on the Dhammapada contains 350 stories which illustrate the teachings of the book. This commentary, therefore, is highly recommended when one wants to study this eternal book of wisdom. These can be found in *The Dhammapada: Verses and Stories* (1986), translated by Daw Mya Tin and edited by the Editorial Committee of the Burma Tipitaka Association.[798] Other translations include *The Dhammapada* (1881), translated by Friedrich Max Müller (1823 – 1900); *The Buddha's Way of Virtue* (1920), translated by W.D.C. Wagiswara and K.J. Saunders; and *The Dhammapada: The Buddha's Path of Wisdom* (1996), translated by Acharya Buddharakkhita.[799] For meditation, the most important parts of the Dhammapada include Chapter III (the 'Mind') [v. 33 – 43], Chapter VI (the 'Wise Man') [v. 76 – 89], Chapter VII (the 'Perfected One') [v. 90 – 99], Chapter XII (the 'Self') [v. 157 – 166], Chapter XIII (the 'World') [v. 167 – 178], Chapter XIV (the 'Buddha') [v. 179 – 196], Chapter XX (the 'Path') [v. 273 – 289], Chapter XXIII (the 'Elephant') [v. 320 – 333], Chapter XXV (the 'Monk') [v. 360 – 382], and Chapter XXVI (the 'Holy Man') [v. 383 – 423]. By studying these key chapters, one can gain an understanding of the essence of Gautama Buddha's teachings, especially as they relate to training the mind and meditation.

> **"And he who will study this sacred dialogue of ours, by him shall I have been worshipped by the Yajna[50] of knowledge; such is My conviction. And even that man who hears this, full of Shraddhâ[51] and free from malice, he too, liberated, shall attain to the happy worlds of those of righteous deeds."[800]**

- Krishna, The Bhagavad-Gita, Ch. XVIII, v. 70 – 71

The Bhagavad-Gita (Sanskrit for 'Song of the Lord') contains 700 verses originally revealed in Sanskrit, which form chapters 23-40 of the 6th book of the Mahabharata—the epic history of ancient India. The book consists of a dialogue between Lord Krishna (may his grace fill us with life and light), an Avatar of Lord Vishnu, and his disciple, Arjuna, as they stand on the battlefield of Kurukshetra. There are numerous translations available of this book, including *Bhagavad-Gītā As It Is* by A.C. Bhaktivedanta Swami Prabhupada, first published in 1968,[801]

---

[50] *jnana* = knowledge, *yajnena* = by sacrifice. See: https://asitis.com/18/70.html (accessed 30/04/2017).

[51] *shraddhavan* = faithful. See: https://asitis.com/18/71.html (accessed 30/04/2017).

which contains extensive commentary according to the Gaudiya Vaishnava school of Hinduism. Other key translations include *Bhagvat-geeta, or Dialogues of Kreeshna and Arjoon* (1785), translated by Sir Charles Wilkins (1749 – 1836);[802] *The Song Celestial or Bhagavad-Gita (From the Mahabharata), Being a Discourse Between Arjuna, Prince of India, and the Supreme Being, Under the Form of Krishna* (1885), translated by Sir Edwin Arnold (1832 – 1904),[803] who was an English poet and journalist; *Srimad-Bhagavad-Gita* (1909), translated by Swarupananda (1871 – 1906),[804] a disciple of Swami Vivekananda (1863 – 1902); and *The Bhagavad-Gita, Krishna's Counsel in Time of War* (2004), translated by Barbara Stoler Miller (1940 – 1993).[805] Within the Bhagavad-Gita, the most important chapter is probably Chapter 9, which contains *guhyataman* (the 'most confidential knowledge'), which is also described as *raja-vidya* (the 'king of education'), *raja-guhyam* (the 'king of confidential knowledge'), and *pavitram* (the 'purest').[806] This chapter, then, we might say, is the heart of the Bhagavad-Gita.

"And with measured tone intone the Koran."[807]

- Qur'ān 73:4

The Qur'ān could be said to contain a wealth of parables and spiritual teachings. In particular, if we are to focus on one or two key parts of the book, then it is advisable to study the last 30th *juz'* (or 'part') of the Qur'ān, which is usually the first section of the holy Book that devotees memorize as children—after learning the first surah. This *juz'* contains all the short surahs of the Qur'ān,

321

from Surah 78 (called 'the Surah of the Great Announcement') to Surah 114 (called 'the Surah of Mankind'). The only other short Surah of the Qur'ān, Surah 1 (called 'The Opening'), is also worthy of much study and memorization. The second Surah of the Qur'ān, called *al-Baqarah* ('the Heifer'), contains all the essential teachings revealed by the Prophet Muhammad (upon whom be peace). There are also parables and many divine teachings contained in Surah 12, called 'the Surah of Joseph,' which is unique in that it contains the complete Biblical story of Joseph. It is also said to contain all the grammatical elements of Arabic, so it is very useful for study if one is learning Arabic. Also of immense importance are the 'Light Verse' (Qur'ān 24:35), the 'Throne Verse' (Qur'ān 2:255) and verses 2 – 3 of Surah 65 (called the 'Surah of Divorce'). There are, furthermore, numerous hadiths extolling the importance of reading Surah 36, called the Surah of *Yā-Sīn* (two Arabic letters). Sir Richard Francis Burton describes this chapter as "one of the most esteemed chapters of the Koran, frequently recited as a *Wazifah* or daily task by religious Moslems in Egypt."[808] This surah has, furthermore, been described as the 'Heart of the Qur'ān,' and its eloquence is traditionally regarded as an example of the miraculous nature of the Qur'ān.[809]

"These are the verses (signs) of the wise Book—a guidance and a mercy to the righteous."[810]

- Qur'ān 31:2 – 3

As for translations into English, the best are probably those by Talal Itani (b. 1961),[811] Arthur John Arberry (1905 – 1969),[812]

Muhammad Asad (1900 – 1992),[813] Muhammad Marmaduke Pickthall (born Marmaduke William Pickthall) (1875 – 1936),[814] Abdullah Yusuf Ali (1872 – 1953),[815] Edward Henry Palmer (1840 – 1882),[816] John Meadows Rodwell (1808 – 1900),[817] and George Sale (1697 – 1736),[818] as well as *The Study Quran: A New Translation and Commentary* (2015),[819] translated by Seyyed Hossein Nasr, Caner K. Dagli, Maria Massi Dakake, Joseph E.B. Lumbard and Mohammed Rustom. This most recent version (Nasr et al 2015) is particularly useful, as it contains a scholarly and comprehensive commentary. I have used the translations of Rodwell, Sale and Palmer within this work, as these are all in the public domain. The entire Qur'ān, with multiple translations of each verse, can be found at the IslamAwakened website.[820] Another useful tool is the Quranic Arabic Corpus, which you can find online (see endnote).[821]

STEP FIVE: STUDY THE LIVES OF THE GREAT TEACHERS

"**Confucius said, 'Those who are born with the possession of knowledge are the highest class of men. Those who learn, and so, readily, get possession of knowledge, are the next.'**"[822]

- Confucius, *Confucian Analects*, Book XVI, Ch. IX.

Lastly, we should study the lives of the Great Teachers. Why is this important? And why is it important for meditation? Meditation on the Divine, as we have already learned, involves focusing our minds on God—seeing His attributes in all created things, seeing them within ourselves and, ultimately, within those Focal Points of Divine Power and Might—the Great Teachers—the Divine Messengers, who come from time to time to bring us wisdom, principles and laws to shape our lives and communities. By turning to these Focal Mirrors, we can come to understand the Divine more directly and more clearly. Their struggles, their words, their lives, their persecution and victories—these things help to draw us closer to the Divine and allow us to understand His Will and His Way. What can we learn from the story of Noah and the Ark? What can we learn from the exile of Abraham? What can we learn from the Exodus of Moses? What can we learn from the wanderings of Jesus and his crucifixion? What can we learn from the persecution of Muhammad and his Hijrah? What can we learn from Buddha, Krishna and the many other Great Teachers and their lives (may the peace and blessings of God be upon them all)? What gems of wisdom can we gather, what patterns can we discern, what glorious attributes can we emulate?

"I am the light of the world: he that followeth me shall not walk in darkness, but shall have the light of life."[823]

- John 8:12

Human beings are in need of patterns—of methods of behaviour—and what greater pattern is there to follow than the example of perfect human beings who lived their entire lives along a perfect path, free from faults or errors, being the perfection of every virtue and good quality. As God, the All-Glorious, says of Muhammad (peace be upon him) in the Qur'ān (53:1 – 4): **"By the star when it falls, your comrade** [Muhammad] **errs not, nor is he deluded!**[824] **Neither doth he speak of his own will.**[825] **It is but an inspiration inspired!"**[826] Also, God says, speaking to Muhammad: **"And thou threwest not when thou didst throw, but it was God Who threw."**[827] Likewise, Jesus Christ (peace be upon him) said: **"I am in my Father, and you are in me, and I am in you"**[828] meaning that the Father (God) can be seen within him, just as we can also reflect the Light of God. And he also said: **"I am the way, the truth, and the life: no man cometh unto the Father, but by me."** In other words, the only way to reach God, the Heavenly Father, is through the Great Teacher, the Perfect Mirror of God, whether he be called Moses, or Jesus, or Muhammad, or Krishna, or Buddha, or Zoroaster, or many other names (may their blessings descend upon us). The important thing is that we recognize the Light in all of these Lamps and recognize every such Lamp, whenever and wherever he may appear, either in the past or the future. Just as there have been many, many such Great Teachers in the past, there are many, many more to come in the future. As the Qur'ān (7:35) says: **"O children of Adam, verily apostles from among you shall come unto you, who shall expound my signs unto you."**[829] So let us look to the lives of these Great Teachers of the recent or distant past, and study their biographies and recorded utterances.

> **"Tathagata** (another name for Buddha) **gives life to all beings, just as the lake Anavatapta gives rise to the four great rivers."**[830]
>
> - *Mahaparinirvana-sutra*

There are many popular biographies of these Great Teachers, including those which I have mentioned in Chapter XV of *Mindfulness: Five Ways to Achieve Real Happiness, True Knowledge and Inner Peace*: "The stories of many of the Judaeo-Christian Prophets can be found in the Bible. The Qur'ān, on the other hand, is not a biographical work or narrative, so it does not contain the life of the Prophet. For that, one must refer to a number of good biographies, such as those of Martin Lings (1983)[831] and Karen Armstrong (1992),[832] which are in English. There is also *Muhammad and the Course of Islam* by HM Balyuzi (1976)[833] and *Muhammad at Mecca* and *Muhammad at Medina*,[834] both by W. Montgomery Watt (1953, 1956). Many biographies of the Prophet have been written throughout the centuries, however, both in the original Arabic and in other languages... There are a number of good books about Gautama Buddha, such as *The God of Buddha* by Jamshed Fozdar (1973) (not a biography but still a very interesting book).[835] Other books can be found on the lives of Zoroaster and Krishna. Krishna's story, though mixed with a lot of mythology and fantastical events, can be found in the *Srimad-Bhagavatam* and the *Mahabharata*, which are both available in English translations.[836] A much shorter account of Krishna's life can be found in *Krsna, The Supreme*

Personality of Godhead, [837] by A.C. Bhaktivedanta Swami Prabhupada (1972)."[838] In addition to these, I would add A.V. Williams Jackson (1899) *Zoroaster, the Prophet of Ancient Iran,*[839] Robert Charles Zaehner (1961) *The Dawn and Twilight of Zoroastrianism,* [840] Vanamali (2012) *The Complete Life of Krishna: Based on the Earliest Oral Traditions and the Sacred Scriptures,* [841] Vraja Kishor (2013) *Beautiful Tales of the All-Attractive: Volume 1,*[842] Reza Aslan (2005) *No god but God: The Origins, Evolution, and Future of Islam,*[843] Bhikkhu Nanamoli (2003) *Life of the Buddha: According to the Pali Canon,*[844] Karen Armstrong (2004) *Buddha,*[845] and (2013) *Muhammad: A Prophet for Our Time.*[846] For much shorter summaries of the lives of these Great Teachers, you may be interested in reading my short biographies of Krishna, Abraham, Moses, Zoroaster, etc. which I wrote in 2004. These can be found <u>at this link</u>.[847]

Some Additional Resources

"And understand with the heart."[848]

- *The Book of Enoch*, Chap. XIV, v. 2, p. 16.

In addition to the books already mentioned above, I would recommend that you check out and read both Equanimity Blog and Crossing the Bridge—my two blogs, which I occasionally update with new content. In particular, you may be interested in reading my article 'How can we achieve true happiness and inner peace?'[849]

Some general books on meditation include Jack Kornfield (2008) *Meditation for Beginners*,[850] Sharon Salzberg (2010) *Real Happiness: The Power of Meditation*,[851] Thich Nhat Hanh (1996) *The Miracle of Mindfulness: An Introduction to the Practice of Meditation*,[852] Jon Kabat-Zinn (2016) *Mindfulness for Beginners: Reclaiming the Present Moment—and Your Life*,[853] Alan W. Watts (2011) *The Way of Zen*,[854] Shunryū Suzuki (2010) *Zen Mind, Beginner's Mind*,[855] and His Divine Grace A.C. Bhaktivedanta Swami Prabhupada (2011) *Chant and Be Happy: The Power of Mantra Meditation*.[856]

I would also recommend the short but concise writings of Qiao Renjie, including Zen: A Complete Beginner's Guide to Zen Meditation, Yoga: A Complete Beginner's Guide to Yoga and Simplify: A Guide to Simple Living: How to Declutter, Organise and Enjoy Your Life—all published in 2017 and available on *Amazon Kindle*.

Conclusion

Now we have come to the end of this book. The following section will contain some quotations for further reflection. I would urge the reader to ponder on what I have written in the pages of this volume and try to reflect on the message contained herein. This book is part of a larger series called the Five Ways to Be series, the purpose of which is to respond to the urgent need for spiritualization which we find in society. The people of the world are hopeless, despairing, drowning in materialism and confusion.

At such a time as this, it is important for humanity to return to its roots—its spiritual roots—to the foundations of human consciousness and meaning. It is time for everyone—everywhere—to come to a realization of our higher selves and our true nature and purpose in this world. Contemplation, or meditation, is one of the main methods we can use to achieve this self-realization, to free ourselves from the attachments of this world, and to open our minds and our hearts to the flowing grace of that Eternal Lord which brought us into being. As Krishna says in the Bhagavad-Gita: **"Mankind are led astray by their reasons being obscured by ignorance; but when that ignorance of their souls is destroyed by the force of reason, their wisdom shineth forth again with the glory of the sun."**[857]

Let us now, as we come to the end of this book, allow the lessons we have learned to sink in and become deeply-rooted in our minds, before we plunge into the ocean of beautiful and inspiring words in the next chapter. May the grace and bounty of the Divine Being descend upon all of you—and all of us—and may His Light fill our hearts, and flow out of our very beings, so that we may become lamps in the darkness—candles shining brightly within the depths of eternity. May the blessings of all the Great Teachers be upon you! May their Light fill you with abiding joy!

Questions for Reflection:

The following are some questions that will help us to reflect on what we have learned in this chapter:

1. 1. What are some of the different kinds of mats and other equipment which can use to enhance our meditation experience?

2. Why is it useful to join a meditation retreat?

3. Why is it important to practise the methods we have learned in this book?

4. Why are thankfulness and magnanimity important?

5. 5. What are some of the scriptures which can study to deepen our spiritual knowledge and understanding?

6. What are the names of some of the important parables of Jesus Christ?

7. Why is it important to study the lives of the Great Teachers?

8. What makes the Great Teachers mentioned above different from ordinary human beings?

9. What does John 14:20 (**"I am in my Father, and you are in me, and I am in you"**) mean?[858]

10. What is the purpose of the Five Ways to Be series?

∞∞∞∞∞∞∞∞∞∞∞∞∞∞∞∞∞∞∞∞∞∞∞∞∞∞

Meditate—search out the truth within thee,

Within thy soul an ocean deep lies hid.

Plant seeds of truth that shall become a tree,

Heed thine inner voice that doth thee bid.

Open up thine heart, that brims with light,

Eternal bliss within thee surges—grows.

Upon the tablet of thy being write

What only mystic lover—seeker—knows.

Happiness—eternal bliss—shall be thine,

When deepest wisdom thou dost truly seek.

Everlasting light shall within thee shine,

When the voice divine doth within thee speak.

- Abú-Jalál NJ Bridgewater

The next section contains some additional quotations to inspire you and give you new insights into meditation and self-realization.

X. Some Other Quotations on Meditation

My name is Ahura (the Lord). My name is Mazdau (the all-knowing). My name is the Holy; my name is the most Holy. My name is the Glorious; my name is the most Glorious... And he who in this material world, O Spitama Zarathustra! shall recite and pronounce those names of mine either by day or by night... That man, neither in that day nor in that night, shall be wounded by the weapons of the foe... It will be as if there were a thousand men watching over one man."[859]

- Zoroaster, *The Zend Avesta*, Part II, I. Ormazd Yast, v. 12, 18 – 19

"And God said, Let us make man in our image, after our likeness: and let them have dominion over the fish of the sea, and over the fowl of the air, and over the cattle, and over all the earth, and over every creeping thing that creepeth upon the earth. So God created man in his own image, in the image of God created he him; male and female created he them. And God blessed them, and God said unto them, Be fruitful, and multiply, and replenish the earth, and subdue it: and have dominion over the fish of the sea, and over the fowl of the air, and over every living thing that moveth upon the earth."[860]

- Genesis 1:26 – 28

"And I appeared unto Abraham, unto Isaac, and unto Jacob, by the name of God Almighty, but by my name JEHOVAH was I not known to them."[861]

- Exodus 6:3

"Here, O Israel: The LORD our God is one LORD: And thou shalt love the Lord thy God with all thine heart, and with all thy soul, and with all thy might. And these words, which I command thee this day, shall be in thine heart: And thou shalt teach them diligently unto thy children, and shalt talk of them when thou sittest in thine house, and when thou walkest by the way, and when thou liest down, and when thou risest up. And thou shalt bind them for a sign upon thine hand, and they shall be as frontlets between thine eyes. And thou shalt write them upon the posts of thy house, and on thy gates."[862]

- Deuteronomy 6:4 – 9

"Blessed is the man that walketh not in the counsel of the ungodly, nor standeth in the way of sinners, nor sitteth in the seat of the scornful. But his delight is in the law of the LORD; and in his law doth he meditate day and night. And he shall be like a tree planted by the rivers of water, that bringeth forth his fruit in his season; his leaf also shall not wither; and whatsoever he doeth shall prosper."[863]

- Psalm 1:1 – 3

"I will meditate also of all thy work, and talk of thy doings. Thy way, O God, is in the sanctuary: who is so great a God as our God? Thou art the God that doest wonders: thou hast declared thy strength among the people."[864]

- Psalm 77:12 – 14

"That men may know that thou, whose name alone is JEHOVAH, art the most high over all the earth."[865]

- Psalm 83:18

"Bless the Lord, O my soul. O Lord my God, thou art very great; thou art clothed with honour and majesty."[866]

- Psalm 104:1

"Blessed be the name of the LORD from this time forth and for evermore. From the rising of the sun unto the going down of the same the LORD's name *is* to be praised. The LORD *is* high above all nations, *and* his glory above the heavens."[867]

- Psalm 113:2 -4

"The heart of the righteous studieth to answer: but the mouth of the wicked poureth out evil things."[868]

- Proverbs 15:28

"Trust ye in the LORD for ever: for in the LORD JEHOVAH is everlasting strength."[869]

- Isaiah 26:4

"I will bring them into the splendid light of those who love my holy name: and I will place each of them on a throne of glory, of glory peculiarly his own, and they shall be at rest during unnumbered periods. Righteous is the judgment of God."[870]

- *The Book of Enoch*, Chap. CV, v. 26, p. 180.

"And he said unto them, He that hath ears to hear, let him hear."[871]

- Mark 4:9

"And he said, Whereunto shall we liken the kingdom of God? or with what comparison shall we compare it? It is like a grain of mustard seed, which, when it is sown in the earth, is less than all the seeds that be in the earth: But when it is sown, it groweth up, and becometh greater than all herbs, and shooteth out great branches; so that the fowls of the air may lodge under the shadow of it."[872]

- Mark 4:30 – 32

"Ye are the light of the world. A city that is set on an hill cannot be hid. Neither do men light a candle, and put it under a bushel, but on a candlestick; and it giveth light unto all that are in the house. Let your light so shine before men, that they may see your good works, and glorify your Father which is in heaven."[873]

- Matthew 5:14 – 16

"And when thou prayest, thou shalt not be as the hypocrites are: for they love to pray standing in the synagogues and in the corners of the streets, that they may be seen of men. Verily I say unto you, They have their reward. But thou, when thou prayest, enter into thy closet, and when thou hast shut thy door, pray to thy Father which is in secret; and thy Father which seeth in secret shall reward thee openly."[874]

- Matthew 6:5 – 6

"Lay not up for yourselves treasures upon earth, where moth and rust doth corrupt, and where thieves break through and steal: But lay up for yourselves treasures in heaven, where neither moth nor rust doth corrupt, and where thieves do not break through nor steal: For where your treasure is, there will your heart be also."[875]

- Matthew 6:19 – 21

"The light of the body is the eye: if therefore thine eye be single, thy whole body shall be full of light. But if thine eye be evil, thy whole body shall be full of darkness. If therefore the light that is in thee be darkness, how great is that darkness!"[876]

- Matthew 6:22 – 23

"He that findeth his life shall lose it: and he that loseth his life for my sake shall find it."[877]

- Matthew 10:39

"Therefore speak I to them in parables: because they seeing see not; and hearing they hear not, neither do they understand... But blessed *are* your eyes, for they see: and your ears, for they hear."[878]

- Matthew 13:13, 16

"But whosoever drinketh of the water that I shall give him shall never thirst; but the water that I shall give him shall be in him a well of water springing up into everlasting life."[879]

- John 4:14

"Then spake Jesus again unto them, saying, I am the light of the world: he that followeth me shall not walk in darkness, but shall have the light of life."[880]

- John 8:12

"Jesus cried and said, He that believeth on me, believeth not on me, but on him that sent me. And he that seeth me seeth him that sent me. I am come a light into the world, that whosoever believeth on me should not abide in darkness. And if any man hear my words, and believe not, I judge him not: for I came not to judge the world, but to save the world."[881]

- John 12:44 - 47

"If ye keep my commandments, ye shall abide in my love; even as I have kept my Father's commandments, and abide in his love. These things have I spoken unto you, that my joy might remain in you, and *that* your joy might be full. This is my commandment, That ye love one another, as I have loved you."[882]

- John 15:10 - 12

"Finally, brethren, whatsoever things are true, whatsoever things are honest, whatsoever things are just, whatsoever things are pure, whatsoever things are lovely, whatsoever things are of good report; if there be any virtue, and if there be any praise, think on these things. Those things, which ye have both learned, and received,

339

and heard, and seen in me, do: and the God of peace shall be with you."[883]

- Philippians 4:8 – 9

"The Spirit itself beareth witness with our spirit, that we are the children of God."[884]

- Romans 8:16

"And he said unto me, It is done. I am Alpha and Omega, the beginning and the end. I will give unto him that is athirst of the fountain of the water of life freely."[885]

- Revelation 21:6

"Why, God is not ashamed to set forth a parable of a gnat, or anything beyond; and as for those who believe, they know that it is truth from the Lord; but as for those who disbelieve, they say, 'What is it that God means by this as a parable? He leads astray many and He guides many;' - but He leads astray only the evildoers."[886]

- Qur'ān 2:26

"God! There is no God but He; the Living, the Eternal; Nor slumber seizeth Him, nor sleep; His, whatsoever is in the Heavens and whatsoever is in the Earth! Who is he that can intercede with Him but by His own permission? He knoweth what hath been before them and what shall be after them; yet nought of His knowledge shall they grasp, save what He willeth. His Throne reacheth over the Heavens and the Earth, and the upholding of both burdeneth Him not; and He is the High, the Great!"[887]

- Qur'ān 2:255 (The Throne Verse)

"Verily, in the creation of the Heavens and of the Earth, and in the succession of the night and of the day, are signs for men of understanding heart,[888] who remember God standing, and sitting, and lying on their sides; and meditate on the creation of heaven and earth."[889]

- Qur'ān 3:190 – 191

"This is no new tale of fiction, but a confirmation of previous scriptures, and an explanation of all things, and guidance and mercy to those who believe."[890]

- Qur'ān 12:111

"And He it is who hath outstretched the earth, and placed on it the firm mountains, and rivers: and of every fruit He hath placed on it two kinds: He causeth the night to enshroud the day. Verily in this are signs for those who reflect."[891]

- Qur'ān 13:3

"This Book have we sent down to thee that by their Lord's permission thou mayest bring men out of darkness into light, into the path of the Mighty, the Glorious."[892]

- Qur'ān 14:1

"We sent them with evident miracles, and written revelations; and We have sent down unto thee this Koran, that thou mayest declare unto mankind that which hath been sent down unto them, and that they may consider."[893]

- Qur'ān 16:44

"God is the LIGHT of the Heavens and of the Earth. His Light is like a niche in which is a lamp - the lamp encased in glass - the glass, as it were, a glistening star. From a blessed tree is it lighted, the olive neither of the East nor of the West, whose oil would well-nigh shine out, even though fire touched it not! It is light upon light. God guideth whom He will to His light, and God setteth forth parables to men, for God knoweth all things."[894]

- Qur'ān 24:35 (The Light Verse)

"And a sign for them is the dead earth which we have quickened and brought forth therefrom seed, and from it do they eat; and we made therein gardens and palms and grapes, and we have caused fountains to gush forth therein, that they may eat from the fruit thereof, and of what their hands have made; will they not then give thanks?"[895]

- Qur'ān 36:33 – 35

"And he hath subjected to you all that is in the Heavens and all that is on the Earth: all is from him. Verily, herein are signs for those who reflect."[896]

- Qur'ān 45:13

"And whoso feareth God, to him will He grant a prosperous issue, and will provide for him whence he reckoned not upon it. And for him who putteth his trust in Him will God be all-sufficient. God truly will attain his purpose. For everything hath God assigned a period."[897]

- Qur'ān 65:2 – 3

"Thy Lord knoweth that thou continuest in prayer and meditation sometimes near two third parts of the night, and sometimes one half thereof, and at other times one third part thereof... Read, therefore, so much of the Koran as may be easy unto you."[898]

- Qur'ān 73:20

"It is good to tame the mind, which is difficult to hold in and flighty, rushing wherever it listeth; a tamed mind brings happiness. Let the wise man guard his thoughts, for they are difficult to perceive, very artful, and they rush wherever they list: thoughts well guarded bring happiness. Those who bridle their mind which travels far, moves about alone, is without a body, and hides in the chamber (of the heart), will be free from the bonds of Mâra (the tempter)... Knowing that this body is (fragile) like a jar, and making this thought firm like a fortress, one should attack Mâra (the tempter) with the weapon of knowledge, one should watch him when conquered, and should never rest."[899]

- Gautama Buddha, *The Dhammapada*, Ch. III, v. 35 - 37, 40

"Wise people, after they have listened to the laws, become serene, like a deep, smooth, and still lake."[900]

- Gautama Buddha, *The Dhammapada*, Ch. VI, v. 82

"There is no suffering for him who has finished his journey, and abandoned grief, who has freed himself on all sides, and thrown off all fetters. They depart with their thoughts well-collected, they are not happy in their abode; like swans who have left their lake, they leave their house and home."[901]

- Gautama Buddha, *The Dhammapada*, Ch. VII, v. 90 – 91

"Self is the lord of self, who else could be the lord? With self well subdued, a man finds a lord such as few can find."[902]

- Gautama Buddha, *The Dhammapada*, Ch. XII, v. 160

"Watching his speech, well restrained in mind, let a man never commit any wrong with his body! Let a man but keep these three roads of action clear, and he will achieve the way which is taught by the wise."[903]

- Gautama Buddha, *The Dhammapada*, Ch. XX, v. 281

"This mind of mine went formerly wandering about as it liked, as it listed, as it pleased; but I shall now hold it in thoroughly, as the rider who holds the hook holds in the furious elephant. Be not thoughtless, watch your thoughts! Draw yourself out of the evil way, like an elephant sunk in mud."[904]

- Gautama Buddha, *The Dhammapada*, Ch. XXIII, v. 326 – 327

"Without knowledge there is no meditation, without meditation there is no knowledge: he who has knowledge and meditation is near unto Nirvâna."[905]

- Gautama Buddha, *The Dhammapada*, Ch. XXV, v. 372

"The sun is bright by day, the moon shines by night, the warrior is bright in his armour, the Brâhmana is bright in his meditation; but Buddha, the Awakened, is bright with splendour day and night."[906]

- Gautama Buddha, *The Dhammapada*, Ch. XXVI, v. 387

"He who is Lord of men and Lord of cattle... By him the heavens are strong and earth is steadfast, by him light's realm and sky-vault are supported: By him the regions in mid-air were measured... He is the God of gods, and none beside him... Ne'er may he harm us who is earth's Begetter, nor he whose laws are sure, the heavens' Creator, He who brought forth the great and lucid waters..."[907]

The Rig-Veda, Hymn CXXI. Ka., v. 3, 5, 8 – 9

"This light is come, amid all lights the fairest; born is the brilliant, far-extending brightness."[908]

The Rig-Veda, Hymn CXIII, Dawn, v. 1

"When thy intellect crosses beyond the taint of illusion, then shalt thou attain to indifference, regarding things heard and things yet to be heard. When thy intellect, tossed about by the conflict of opinions—has become immovable and firmly established in the Self, then thou shalt attain Self-realisation."[909]

- Krishna, *The Bhagavad-Gita*, Ch. II, v. 51 – 52

"He whose mind is not shaken by adversity, who does not hanker after happiness, who has become free from affection, fear, and wrath, is indeed the Muni of steady wisdom. He who is everywhere unattached, not pleased at receiving good, nor vexed at evil, his wisdom is fixed. When also, like the tortoise its limbs, he can completely withdraw the senses from their objects, then his wisdom becomes steady. Objects fall away from the abstinent man, leaving the longing behind. But his longing also ceases, who sees the Supreme."[910]

- Krishna, *The Bhagavad-Gita*, Ch. II, v. 56 – 59

"Thinking of objects, attachment to them is formed in a man. From attachment longing, and from longing anger grows. From anger comes delusion, and from delusion loss of memory. From loss of memory comes the ruin of discrimination, and from the ruin of discrimination he perishes. But the self-controlled man, moving among objects with senses under restraint, and free from attraction and aversion, attains to tranquillity. In tranquillity, all sorrow is destroyed. For the intellect of him who is tranquil-minded, is soon established in firmness."[911]

- Krishna, *The Bhagavad-Gita*, Ch. II, v. 62 – 65

"As into the ocean,—brimful, and still,—flow the waters, even so the Muni into whom enter all desires, he, and not the desirer of desires, attains to peace. That man who lives devoid of longing, abandoning all desires, without the sense of 'I' and 'mine,' he attains to peace."[912]

- Krishna, *The Bhagavad-Gita*, Ch. II, v. 70 – 71

"Freed from attachment, fear and anger, absorbed in Me, taking refuge in Me, purified by the fire of Knowledge, many have attained My Being. In whatever way men worship Me, in the same way do I fulfil their desires: (it is) My path, O son of Prithâ, (that) men tread, in all ways."[913]

- Krishna, *The Bhagavad-Gita*, Ch. IV, v. 10 – 11

"Even if thou be the most sinful among all the sinful, yet by the raft of knowledge alone thou shalt go across all sin. As blazing fire reduces wood into ashes, so, O Arjuna, does the fire of knowledge reduce all Karma to ashes. Verily there exists nothing in this world purifying like knowledge. In good time, having reached perfection in Yoga, one realises that oneself in one's own heart. The man with Shraddhâ, the devoted, the master of one's senses, attains (this) knowledge. Having attained knowledge one goes at once to the Supreme Peace."[914]

- Krishna, *The Bhagavad-Gita*, Ch. IV, v. 36 – 39

"Shutting out external objects, steadying the eyes between the eyebrows, restricting the even currents of Prâna and Apâna inside the nostrils; the senses, mind, and intellect controlled, with Moksha as the supreme goal, freed from desire, fear and anger: such a man of meditation is verily free for ever. Knowing Me as the dispenser of Yajnas and asceticisms, as the Great Lord of all worlds, as the friend of all beings, he attains Peace."[915]

- Krishna, *The Bhagavad-Gita*, Ch. V, v. 27 – 29

"For the man of meditation wishing to attain purification of heart leading to concentration, work is said to be the way: For him, when he has attained such (concentration), inaction is said to be the way. Verily, when there is no attachment, either to sense-objects, or to actions, having renounced all Sankalpas,[52] then is one said to have attained concentration. A man should uplift himself by his own self, so let him not weaken this self. For this self is the friend of oneself, and this self is the enemy of oneself. To the self-controlled and serene, the Supreme Self is, the object of constant realisation, in cold and heat, pleasure and pain, as well as in honour and dishonour. Whose heart is filled with satisfaction by wisdom and realisation, and is changeless, whose senses are

---

[52] "The working of the imaging faculty, forming fancies, making plans and again brushing them aside, conceiving future results, starting afresh on a new line, leading to different issues, and so on and so forth." - Swami Swarupananda (translator) (1909) *Srimad-Bhagavad-Gita*.

conquered, and to whom a lump of earth, stone, and gold are the same: that Yogi is called steadfast."[916]

- Krishna, *The Bhagavad-Gita*, Ch. VI, v. 3 – 8

"He attains excellence who looks with equal regard upon well-wishers, friends, foes, neutrals, arbiters, the hateful, the relatives, and upon the righteous and the unrighteous alike."[917]

- Krishna, *The Bhagavad-Gita*, Ch. VI, v. 9

"The Yogi should constantly practise concentration of the heart, retiring into solitude, alone, with the mind and body subdued, and free from hope and possession... Let him firmly hold his body, head and neck erect and still, (with the eye-balls fixed, as if) gazing at the tip of his nose, and not looking around. With the heart serene and fearless, firm in the vow of a Brahmachâri, with the mind controlled, and ever thinking of Me, let him sit (in Yoga) having Me as his supreme goal. Thus always keeping the mind steadfast, the Yogi of subdued mind attains the peace residing in Me,—the peace which culminates in Nirvâna (Moksha)."[918]

- Krishna, *The Bhagavad-Gita*, Ch. VI, v. 10, 13 – 15, pp. 143 – 146

"When the completely controlled mind rests serenely in the Self alone, free from longing after all desires, then is one called steadfast, (in the Self). 'As a lamp in a spot sheltered from the wind does not flicker,'—even such has been the simile used for a Yogi of subdued mind, practising concentration in the Self."[919]

- Krishna, *The Bhagavad-Gita*, Ch. VI, v. 18 – 19

"He who sees Me in all things, and sees all things in Me, he never becomes separated from Me, nor do I become separated from him. He who being established in unity, worships Me, who am dwelling in all beings, whatever his mode of life, that Yogi abides in Me."[920]

- Krishna, *The Bhagavad-Gita*, Ch. VI, v. 30 – 31

"And he, who at the time of death, meditating on Me alone, goes forth, leaving the body, attains My Being: there is no doubt about this... Therefore, at all times, constantly remember Me, and fight. With mind and intellect absorbed, in Me, thou shalt doubtless come to Me."[921]

- Krishna, *The Bhagavad-Gita*, Ch. VIII, v. 5, 7

"I am the Father of this world, the Mother, the Sustainer, the Grandfather; the Purifier, the (one) thing to be known, (the syllable) Om, and also the Rik, Sâman and Yajus.[922] The Goal, the Supporter, the Lord, the Witness, the Abode, the Refuge, the Friend, the Origin, the Dissolution, the Substratum, the Storehouse, the Seed immutable. (As sun) I give heat: I withhold and send forth rain; I am immortality and also death; being and non-being am I, O Arjuna!"[923]

- Krishna, *The Bhagavad-Gita*, Ch. IX, v. 17 – 19

"Whoever with devotion offers Me a leaf, a flower, a fruit, or water, that I accept—the devout gift of the pure-minded. Whatever thou doest, whatever thou eatest, whatever thou offerest in sacrifice, whatever thou givest away, whatever austerity thou practisest, O son of Kunti, do that as an offering unto Me. Thus shalt thou be freed from the bondages of actions, bearing good and evil results: with the heart steadfast in the Yoga of renunciation, and liberated, thou shalt come unto Me."[924]

- Krishna, *The Bhagavad-Gita*, Ch. IX, v. 26 – 28

"Fill thy mind with Me, be My devotee, sacrifice unto Me, bow down to Me; thus having made thy heart steadfast in Me, taking Me as the Supreme Goal, thou shalt come to Me."[925]

- Krishna, *The Bhagavad-Gita*, Ch. IX, v. 34, p. 218

"I am the origin of all, from Me everything evolves;—thus thinking the wise worship Me with loving consciousness. With their minds wholly in Me, with their senses absorbed in Me, enlightening one another, and always speaking of Me, they are satisfied and delighted."[926]

- Krishna, *The Bhagavad-Gita*, Ch. X, v. 8 – 9

"And whatsoever is the seed of all beings, that also am I, O Arjuna. There is no being, whether moving or unmoving, that can exist without Me. There is no end of My divine attributes, O scorcher of foes; but this is a brief statement by Me of the particulars of My divine attributes. Whatever being there is great, prosperous or powerful, that know thou to be a product of a part of My splendour."[927]

- Krishna, *The Bhagavad-Gita*, Ch. X, v. 39 – 41

"Thou art the Primal Deva, the Ancient Purusha; Thou art the Supreme Refuge of this universe, Thou art the Knower, and the One Thing to be known; Thou art the Supreme Goal. By Thee is the universe pervaded, O Boundless Form."[928]

- Krishna, *The Bhagavad-Gita*, Ch. XI, v. 38

"But those who worship Me, resigning all actions in Me, regarding Me as the Supreme Goal, meditating on Me with single-minded Yoga,—to these whose mind is set on Me, verily, I become ere long, O son of Prithâ, the Saviour out of the ocean of the mortal Samsâra."[929]

- Krishna, *The Bhagavad-Gita*, Ch. XII, v. 6 – 7

"I shall describe that which has to be known, knowing which one attains to immortality, the beginningless Supreme Brahman. It is called neither being nor non-being... The Light even of lights, It is said to be beyond darkness; Knowledge, and the One Thing to be known, the Goal of' knowledge, dwelling in the hearts of all."[930]

- Krishna, *The Bhagavad-Gita*, Ch. XIII, v. 12, 17

"He sees, who sees the Lord Supreme, existing equally in all beings, deathless in the dying. Since seeing the Lord equally existent everywhere, he injures not Self by self, and so goes to the highest Goal."[931]

- Krishna, *The Bhagavad-Gita*, Ch. XIII, v. 27 – 28

"He who free from delusion thus knows Me, the Highest Spirit, he knowing all, worships Me with all his heart, O descendant of Bharata."[932]

- Krishna, *The Bhagavad-Gita*, Ch. XV, v. 19

"Wherefore, O Arjoon, having made thyself acquainted with the precepts of the *Sāstra*,[53] in the establishment of what is fit and unfit to be done, thou shouldst perform those works which are declared by the commandments of the *Sāstra* [scriptures]."[933]

- Krishna, *The Bhagavad-Gita*, Ch. XVI, v. 24

---

[53] Scriptures.

"By devotion he knows Me in reality, what and who I am; then having known Me in reality, he forthwith enters into Me. Even doing all actions always, taking refuge in Me,—by My grace he attains to the eternal, immutable State... Fixing thy mind on Me, thou shalt, by My grace, overcome all obstacles; but if from self-conceit thou wilt not hear Me, thou shalt perish."[934]

- Krishna, *The Bhagavad-Gita*, Ch. XVIII, v. 55- 56, 58

"Hear thou again My supreme word, the profoundest of all; because thou art dearly beloved of Me, therefore will I speak what is good to thee. Occupy thy mind with Me, be devoted to Me, sacrifice to Me, bow down to Me. Thou shalt reach Myself; truly do I promise unto thee, (for) thou art dear to Me. Relinquishing all Dharmas[54] take refuge in Me alone; I will liberate thee from all sins; grieve not."[935]

- Krishna, *The Bhagavad-Gita*, Ch. XVIII, v. 64 – 66

"He who with supreme devotion to Me will teach this deeply profound philosophy to My devotees, shall doubtless come to Me alone. Nor among men is there any who does dearer service to Me, nor shall there be another on earth dearer to Me, than he."[936]

- Krishna, *The Bhagavad-Gita*, Ch. XVIII, v. 68 – 69

---

[54] Religions.

"The suppliant will I ne'er forsake,

Nor my protecting aid refuse

When one in name of friendship sues.

Though faults and folly blot his fame,

Pity and help he still may claim."[937]

- Rāma, *The Ramayana*, Book VI, Ch. XVIII.

"I always declare 'no fear' unto all creatures, whenever any, approaching me, says, 'I am thine' and seeketh my shelter. Even this is my pious observance."[938]

- Rāma, *The Ramayana*, Yuddhakāndam, Section XVIII, p. 1151.

"The effulgent ray exists in one's Soul and not anywhere else. It exists equally in all creatures. One can see it oneself if one's heart be devoted to Yoga. When a person lives in such a way that another is not inspired with fear at his sight, and when a person is not himself inspired with fear at the sight of others, when a person ceases to cherish desire and hate, he is then said to attain to Brahma. When a person ceases to entertain a sinful attitude towards all creatures in thought, word, and deed, he is then said to attain to Brahma. By restraining the mind and the soul, by casting off malice that stupefies the mind, and by throwing off desire and stupefaction, one is said to attain to Brahma... As a house enveloped in darkness is capable of being seen with the aid of a lighted lamp, after the same manner can the soul be seen with the aid of the lamp of the understanding. O foremost of intelligent persons, I see that all this knowledge that I am communicating to thee dwells in thee."[939]

- Janaka, *The Mahabharata*, Book 12: Santi Parva, Part 3, Section CCCXXVII.

"The sage who would bring his mind into a fit state for the performance of devout contemplation must be devoid of desire, and observe invariably continence, compassion, truth, honesty, and disinterestedness: he must fix his mind intently on the supreme Brahma, practising holy study, purification, contentment, penance, and self-control."[940]

- *The Vishnu Purana*, Chapter VII, pp. 652 – 653.

"Therefore, let him meditate on the Lord as (his) abode and guide; he who meditates on the Lord only, as his abode and light, has his works (rendered) undecaying; and through the grace of that Lord, his work creates for him whatever he desires."[941]

- *Brihadaranyaka Upanishad*, III, 4. 15, quoted by Madhva Acharya.

"When the consciousness is firmly fixed in God, the conception of diversity naturally drops away; because the One Cosmic Existence shines through all things. As we gain the light of wisdom, we cease to cling to the unrealities of this world and we find all our joy in the realm of Reality."942

- *Isa-Upanishad*, I.

"The wise, who by means of the highest meditation on the Self knows the Ancient One, difficult to perceive, seated in the innermost recess, hidden in the cave of the heart, dwelling in the depth of inner being, (he who knows that One) as God, is liberated from the fetters of joy and sorrow."943

- *Katha Upanishad*, XII.

"OM. Manas (mind) is said to be of two kinds, the pure and the impure. That which is associated with the thought of desire is the impure, while that which is without desire is the pure. To men, their mind alone is the cause of bondage or emancipation. That mind which is attracted by objects of sense tends to bondage, while that which is not so attracted tends to emancipation. Now inasmuch as to a mind without a desire for sensual objects there is stated to be salvation, therefore an aspirant after emancipation should render his mind ever free from all longing after material objects. When a mind freed from the desires for objects and controlled in the heart attains the reality of Ātmā, then is it in the Supreme Seat. Till that which arises in the heart perishes, till then it (Manas) should be controlled. This only is (true) wisdom. This only is true Dhyāna (meditation)."944

- *Thirty Minor Upanishads*, Amrtabindu-Upanishad of Krshna-Yajurveda

"And what is Jñāna (wisdom)? It is self-light. It is that which illuminates all. It is that Absolute Consciousness which is without any obscuration. It is that Consciousness which is without any obscuration. It is that which is not subject to the six changes (*viz.*, birth, growth, manhood, decay, old age and death). It is free from all Upādhis. It is that Consciousness which, being all full and without destruction, permeates the created universe composed of Avyakta and others, like the earth and the modifications of clay, the gold in the modifications of gold, and thread in the modifications of thread."[945]

- *Thirty Minor Upanishads*, Sarvasāra-Upanishad of Krshna-Yajurveda, v. 10

"Now, then, the praise of the study (of the scriptures). The study and teaching (of the Veda) are a source of pleasure to him, he becomes ready-minded, and independent of others, and day by day he acquires wealth. He sleeps peacefully; he is the best physician for himself; and (peculiar) to him are restraint of the senses, delight in the one thing, growth of intelligence, fame, and the (task of) perfecting the people."[946]

- *The Satapatha Brahmana*, Part V, XI, 5.7, Seventh Brâhmana

"As the Supreme Being of His own accord shows Himself in consideration of the soul's devotion and bestows upon him final beatitude; devotion becomes the foremost of all the means, and consequently it is spoken of as the only means. This is also said in the Maya Vaibhava: 'The Supreme Being Vishnu is in devotion and by devotion brings him under His influence and in consideration of devotion He discovers Himself and bestows final beatitude (on the devotee). The intense love which proceeding from a knowledge of His greatness becomes the tie between the Lord and the soul, is called devotion; and that indeed is the (chief) instrument of the Supreme Ruler.' (Even the word 'devotion' in the Sruti is the name of the Lord), because all the words have been shown to declare Brahman."[947]

- Madhva Acharya, *Commentary on the Vedanta-Sutras*, Adhyaya III, Third Pada

"All the powers in the universe are already ours. It is we who have put our hands before our eyes, and cry that it is dark. Know that there is no darkness round us. Take the hands off and there is light from the beginning. Darkness never existed, weakness never existed."[948]

- Swami Vivekananda, *Vedânta Philosophy*, XII, Part I.

"Of all good virtues, lovingkindness stands foremost.... It is the source of all merit.... It is the mother of all Buddhas.... It induces others to take refuge in the incomparable Bodhi. The loving heart of a Bodhisattva is annoyed by one thing, that all beings are constantly tortured and threatened by all sorts of pain."[949]

- Devala's Mahâpurusa, quoted in *Outlines of Mahayana Buddhism*, pp. 365 – 366.

"The man that has true light, no darkness dwells

Within his soul. Who shall describe the peace

Of that Pure Land, where this true light doth shine?"[950]

- Jichin, Buddhist Meditations, *The Open Court* (magazine), p. 556.

"Always without desire we must be found,

If its deep mystery we would sound;

But if desire always within us be,

Its outer fringe is all that we shall see.

"Under these two aspects, it is really the same; but as development takes place, it receives the different names. Together we call them the Mystery. Where the Mystery is the deepest is the gate of all that

is subtle and wonderful."[951]

- Laozi, *The Tao Te Ching*, 1

"The Tao is (like) the emptiness of a vessel; and in our

employment of it we must be on our guard against all fullness. How

deep and unfathomable it is, as if it were the Honoured Ancestor of

all things!

"We should blunt our sharp points, and unravel the complications of

things; we should attemper our brightness, and bring ourselves into

agreement with the obscurity of others. How pure and still the Tao

is, as if it would ever so continue!"[952]

- Laozi, *The Tao Te Ching*, 4

"All things are produced by the Tao, and nourished by its outflowing operation. They receive their forms according to the nature of each, and are completed according to the circumstances of

their condition. Therefore all things without exception honour the

Tao, and exalt its outflowing operation."[953]

- Laozi, *The Tao Te Ching*, 51

"The Master said, 'Am I indeed possessed of knowledge? I am not knowing. But if a mean person, who appears quite empty-like, ask anything of me, I set it forth from one end to the other, and exhaust it.'"[954]

- Confucius, *Confucian Analects*, Book IX, Ch. VII.

"The Master said, 'They who know the truth are not equal to those who love it, and they who love it are not equal to those who delight in it.'"[955]

- Confucius, *Confucian Analects*, Book VI, Ch. XVIII.

"You hear not with the ears, but with the mind; not with the mind, but with your soul. But let hearing stop with the ears. Let the working of the mind stop with itself. Then the soul will be a negative experience, only TAO can abide. And that negative state is the fasting of the heart."[956]

- Confucius, *Chuang Tzu, Mystic, Moralist, and Social Reformer*, Chapter IV, p. 43.

"A man does not seek to see himself in running water, but in still water. For only what is itself still can instil stillness into others... By nourishment of physical courage, the sense of fear may be so eliminated that a man will, single-handed, brave a whole army. And if such a result can be achieved in search of fame, how much more by one who extends his sway over heaven and earth and influences all things; and who, lodging within the confines of a body with its channels of sight and sound, brings his knowledge to know that all things are ONE, and that his soul endures for ever! Besides, he awaits his appointed hour, and men flock to him of their own accord. He makes no effort to attract them."[957]

- Confucius, *Chuang Tzu, Mystic, Moralist, and Social Reformer*, Chapter V, p. 58.

"In a water-level, the water is in a most perfect state of repose. Let that be your model. The water remains quietly within, and does not overflow. It is from the cultivation of such harmony that virtue results. And if virtue takes no outward form, man will not be able to keep aloof from it."[958]

- Confucius, *Chuang Tzu, Mystic, Moralist, and Social Reformer*, Chapter V, p. 64.

"The principle which the superior man holds is that of personal cultivation, but the kingdom is thereby tranquillized. The disease of men is this:— that they neglect their own fields, and go to weed the fields of others, and that what they require from others is great, while what they lay upon themselves is light."[959]

- Mencius, Book 7, Part II, Chapter 32, v. 2 - 3

"Mencius said, 'To nourish the mind there is nothing better than to make the desires few. Here is a man whose desires are few:– in some things he may not be able to keep his heart, but they will be few. Here is a man whose desires are many:– in some things he may be able to keep his heart, but they will be few.'"[960]

- Mencius, Book 7, Part II, Chapter 35.

"My life has a limit, but my knowledge is without limit."[961]

- Zhuangzi, *Chuang Tzu, Mystic, Moralist, and Social Reformer,* Chapter III, p. 33.

"He who knows what God is, and who knows what Man is, has attained. Knowing what God is, he knows that he himself proceeded therefrom. Knowing what Man is, he rests in the knowledge of the known, waiting for the knowledge of the unknown. Working out one's allotted span, and not perishing in mid career,—this is the fullness of knowledge. God is a principle which exists by virtue of its own intrinsicality, and operates spontaneously, without self-manifestation."[962]

- Zhuangzi, *Chuang Tzu, Mystic, Moralist, and Social Reformer,*
Chapter VI, p. 68.

"The man of complete virtue remains blankly passive as regards what goes on around him. He is as originally by nature, and his knowledge extends to the supernatural. Thus, his virtue expands his heart, which goes forth to all who come to take refuge therein. Without TAO, form cannot be endued with life. Without virtue, life cannot be endued with intelligence. To preserve one's form, live out one's life, establish one's virtue, and realise TAO,—is not this complete virtue? Issuing forth spontaneously, moving without premeditation, all things following in his wake,—such is the man of complete virtue! He can see where all is dark. He can hear where all is still. In the darkness he alone can see light. In the stillness he alone can detect harmony. He can sink to the lowest depths of materialism. To the highest heights of spirituality he can soar. This because he stands in due relation to all things. Through a mere abstraction, he can minister to their wants, and ever and anon receive them into rest,—the great, the small, the long, the short, for ever without end."[963]

- Zhuangzi, *Chuang Tzu, Mystic, Moralist, and Social Reformer,*
Chapter XII, pp. 138 – 139.

"Never suffer sleep to close thy eyelids, after thy going to bed, till thou hast examined by thy reason all thy actions of the day. Wherein have I done amiss? What have I done? What have I

366

omitted that I ought to have done? If in this examination thou find that thou hast done amiss, reprimand thyself severely for it; And if thou hast done any good, rejoice. Practise thoroughly all these things; meditate on them well; thou oughtest to love them with all thy heart. 'Tis they that will put thee in the way of divine virtue."[964]

- Pythagoras, *The Golden Verses of Pythagoras*, v. 40 – 46, p. 5.

"Then reflect, Cebes: is not the conclusion of the whole matter this?—that the soul is in the very likeness of the divine, and immortal, and intelligible, and uniform, and indissoluble, and unchangeable; and the body is in the very likeness of the human, and mortal, and unintelligible, and multiform, and dissoluble, and changeable. Can this, my dear Cebes, be denied?"[965]

- Plato, *The Dialogues of Plato*, Phaedo

"But I will do my utmost to inform you, and do you follow if you can. For he who would proceed aright in this matter should begin in youth to visit beautiful forms; and first, if he be guided by his instructor aright, to love one such form only—out of that he should create fair thoughts; and soon he will of himself perceive that the beauty of one form is akin to the beauty of another; and then if beauty of form in general is his pursuit, how foolish would he be not to recognize that the beauty in every form is and the same!... drawing towards and contemplating the vast sea of beauty, he will create many fair and noble thoughts and notions in boundless love of wisdom; until on that shore he grows and waxes strong, and at last the vision is revealed to him of a single science, which is the science of beauty everywhere. To this I will proceed; please to give me your very best attention: He who has been instructed thus far in the things of love, and who has learned to see the beautiful in due order and succession, when he comes toward the end will suddenly perceive a nature of wondrous beauty (and this, Socrates, is the final cause of all our former toils)—a nature which in the first place is everlasting, not growing and decaying, or waxing and waning... And the true order of going, or being led by another, to the things of love, is to begin from the beauties of earth and mount upwards for the sake of that other beauty, using these as steps only, and from one going on to two, and from two to all fair forms, and from fair forms to fair practices, and from fair practices to fair notions, until from fair notions he arrives at the notion of absolute beauty, and at last knows what the essence of beauty is. This, my dear Socrates, is that life above all others which man should live, in the contemplation of beauty absolute."[966]

- Plato, *The Dialogues of Plato*, Symposium

"Thou canst remove out of the way many useless things among those which disturb thee, for they lie entirely in thy opinion; and thou wilt then gain for thyself ample space by comprehending the whole universe in thy mind, and by contemplating the eternity of time, and observing the rapid change of every several thing, how short is the time from birth to dissolution, and the illimitable time before birth as well as the equally boundless time after dissolution."[967]

- Marcus Aurelius, *The Meditations of Marcus Aurelius*, Book I.

"Begin the morning by saying to thyself, I shall meet with the busy-body, the ungrateful, arrogant, deceitful, envious, unsocial. All these things happen to them by reason of their ignorance of what is good and evil. But I who have seen the nature of the good that it is beautiful, and of the bad that it is ugly, and the nature of him who does wrong, that it is akin to me, not only of the same blood or seed, but that it participates in the same intelligence and the same portion of the divinity, I can neither be injured by any of them, for no one can fix on me what is ugly, nor can I be angry with my kinsman, nor hate him, For we are made for co-operation, like feet, like hands, like eyelids, like the rows of the upper and lower teeth. To act against one another then is contrary to nature; and it is acting against one another to be vexed and to turn away."[968]

- Marcus Aurelius, *The Meditations of Marcus Aurelius*, Book I.

"Observe, then, that when you are silently conversing with yourself, this very process is carried on within you by your reason, which meets you with a word at every movement of your thought, at every impulse of your conception. Whatever you think, there is a word; whatever you conceive, there is reason. You must needs speak it in your mind; and while you are speaking, you admit speech as an interlocutor with you, involved in which there is this very reason, whereby, while in thought you are holding converse with your word, you are (by reciprocal action) producing thought by means of that converse with your word."[969]

- Tertullian, *Ante-Nicene Fathers*, Vol. III.

"For freedom is secured not by the fulfilling of men's desires, but by the removal of desire. To learn the truth of what I say, you must spend your pains on these new studies instead of your studies in the past: sit up late that you may acquire a judgement that makes you free: pay your attentions not to a rich old man, but to a philosopher, and be seen about his doors: to be so seen will not do you discredit: you will not depart empty or without profit, if you approach in the right spirit. If you doubt my word, do but try: there is no disgrace in trying."[970]

- Epictetus, *The Discourses of Epictetus*, Book IV, Chapter I.

"As speech is the echo of the thought in the Soul, so thought in the Soul is an echo from elsewhere: that is to say, as the uttered thought is an image of the soul-thought, so the soul-thought images a thought above itself and is the interpreter of the higher sphere."[971]

- Plotinus, *The Six Enneads*, The First Ennead: Second Tractate, Section 3.

"Keep thyself as a stranger and a pilgrim upon the earth, to whom the things of the world appertain not. Keep thine heart free, and lifted up towards God, for here have we no continuing city. To Him direct thy daily prayers with crying and tears, that thy spirit may be found worthy to pass happily after death unto its Lord."[972]

- Thomas à Kempis, *The Imitation of Christ*, Book I, Chapter XXIV, 9

"If I love heaven, I gladly meditate on heavenly things. If I love the world, I rejoice in the delights of the world, and am made sorry by its adversities. If I love the flesh, I am continually imagining the things which belong to the flesh; if I love the spirit, I am delighted by meditating on spiritual things."[973]

- Thomas à Kempis, *The Imitation of Christ*, Book III, Chapter XLVIII, 6

"Let thy contemplation be on the Most High, and let thy supplication be directed unto Christ without ceasing."[974]

- Thomas à Kempis, *The Imitation of Christ*, Book II, Chapter I, 4

"If thou rejectest outward comfort thou wilt be able to contemplate heavenly things and frequently to be joyful inwardly."[975]

- Thomas à Kempis, *The Imitation of Christ*, Book II, Chapter I, 8

"For this it is necessary to make ourselves indifferent to all created things in all that is allowed to the choice of our free will and is not prohibited to it; so that, on our part, we want not health rather than sickness, riches rather than poverty, honor rather than dishonor, long rather than short life, and so in all the rest; desiring and choosing only what is most conducive for us to the end for which we are created."[976]

- St. Ignatius of Loyola, *Spiritual Exercises of St. Ignatius of Loyola*, First Week

"I call it consolation when some interior movement in the soul is caused, through which the soul comes to be inflamed with love of its Creator and Lord; and when it can in consequence love no created thing on the face of the earth in itself, but in the Creator of them all."[977]

- St. Ignatius of Loyola, *Spiritual Exercises of St. Ignatius of Loyola*, Rules for Perceiving and Knowing in Some Manner the Different Movements which are caused in the Soul: Third Rule

"The more our soul finds itself alone and isolated, the more apt it makes itself to approach and to reach its Creator and Lord, and the more it so approaches Him, the more it disposes itself to receive graces and gifts from His Divine and Sovereign Goodness."[978]

- St. Ignatius of Loyola, *Spiritual Exercises of St. Ignatius of Loyola*, Twentieth Annotation

"Now the rational soul in man abounds in, marvels, both of knowledge and power. By means of it he masters arts and sciences, can pass in a flash from earth to heaven and back again, can map out the skies and measure the distances between the stars. By it also he can draw the fish from the sea and the birds from the air, and can subdue to his service animals, like the elephant, the camel, and the horse. His five senses are like five doors opening on the external world; but, more wonderful than this, his heart has a window which opens on the unseen world of spirits. In the state of sleep, when the avenues of the senses are closed, this window is opened and man receives impressions from the unseen world and sometimes foreshadowings of the future. His heart is then like a mirror which reflects what is pictured in the Tablet of Fate."[979]

- Al-Ghazali, *The Alchemy of Happiness*, Chapter I.

"There was the Door to which I found no Key:

There was the Veil through which I could not see:

Some little talk awhile of Me and Thee

There was – and then no more of Thee and Me."[980]

- Omar Khayyam, *The Rubaiyat of Omar Khayyam*, XXXIII.

"The Hearts of those Two Lovers fill with Blood.

For Lov'd and Lover are not but by Thee,

Nor Beauty;—Mortal Beauty but the Veil

Thy Heavenly hides behind, and from itself

Feeds, and our Hearts yearn after as a Bride

That glances past us Veil'd—but ever so

As none the Beauty from the Veil may know.

How long wilt thou continue thus the World

To cozen with the Fantom of a Veil

From which Thou only peepest?—Time it is

To unfold thy perfect Beauty. I would be

Thy Lover, and Thine only—I, mine Eyes

Seal'd in the Light of Thee to all but Thee,

Yea, in the Revelation of Thyself

Self-Lost, and Conscience-quit of Good and Evil."[981]

- Jāmī, *Salámán and Absál*, prologue, pp. 1 – 2.

"'No longer think of Rhyme, but think of Me!' —

Of Whom?—of Him whose Palace The Soul is,

And Treasure-House—who notices and knows

Its Income and Out-going, and then comes

To fill it when the Stranger is departed.

Whose Shadow being Kings—whose Attributes

The Type of Theirs—their Wrath and Favour His

Lo! in the Celebration of His Glory.

The King Himself come on me unaware,

And suddenly arrests me for his own."982

- Jāmī, *Salámán and Absál*, II, p. 5.

"My heart has become capable of every form: it is a pasture for gazelles and a convent for Christian monks, and a temple for idols and the pilgrim's Ka'ba and the tables of the Tora and the book of the Koran. I follow the religion of Love: whatever way Love's camels take, that is my religion and my faith."983

- Ibn al-'Arabī, *The Tarjumān al-Ashwāq*, XI., v. 13 – 15

"Give me the cup! a voice rings in mine ears

Crying: 'Bear patiently the bitter years!

For all thine ills, I send thee heavenly grace.

God the Creator mirrored in thy face

Thine eyes shall see, God's image in the glass

I send to thee.'"984

- Hafez, *Teachings of Hafiz*, III.

"Before their face the holy teachers stood erect,—

The mirrors of the soul;—than mirror more correct.

Their breasts they've polished with the acts of thought and praise,

That, mirror-like, they catch each image facts may raise.

Each object born in nature with a lovely mien

Should always have a mirror set to catch its sheen.

A beauteous face enamoured is with mirror's glance;

Heart's piety" the polish best the soul can chance."[985]

- Jalālu'd-Dīn Rūmī, *The Mesnavī*, XII. Joseph and the Mirror

"O bird of the morning, learn love from the moth

Because it burnt, lost its life, and found no voice.

These pretenders are ignorantly in search of Him,

Because he who obtained knowledge has not returned."[986]

- Saadi, *The Gulistan*, Introductory

"When He admits thee in His court, ask from Him no object of desire,—ask Himself; when thy Lord has chosen thee for friendship, thy unabashed eye has seen all there is to see. The

376

world of love suffers not duality, —what talk is this of Me and Thee?"[987]

- Sanā'ī, *The Hadîqatu'l-Haqîqat*, On Affection and Isolation

"Yet   he   who   reigns   within   himself,   and   rules
Passions,   desires,   and   fears,   is   more   a   king—
Which every wise and virtuous man attains...

To   know,   and,   knowing,   worship   God   aright,
Is   yet   more   kingly.   This   attracts   the   soul,
Governs the inner man, the nobler part;

That other o'er the body only reigns."[988]

- John Milton, *Paradise Regained*, Second Book

"Be Homer's works your study and delight,

Read them by day, and meditate by night;

Thence form your judgment, thence your maxims bring,

And trace the Muses upward to their spring."[989]

- Alexander Pope, *An Essay on Criticism*, Part 1

"Blest! who can unconcern'dly find

Hours, days, and years slide soft away,

In health of body, peace of mind,

Quiet by day,

Sound sleep by night; study and ease

Together mix'd; sweet recreation,

And innocence, which most does please,

With meditation."[990]

- Alexander Pope, *On Solitude*

"And all must love the human form

In heathen, turk or jew.

Where Mercy, Love and Pity dwell

There God is dwelling too."[991]

- William Blake, *The Divine Image*

"Not that the heart can be good without knowledge, for without that the heart is naught. There are, therefore, two sorts of knowledge, knowledge that resteth in the bare speculation of things, and knowledge that is accompanied with the grace of faith and love, which puts a man upon doing even the will of God from the heart."[992]

- John Bunyan, *Pilgrim's Progress*, The Fifth Stage

"God that made the world and all things in it, dwells not in temples made with hands, neither will be worshipped with men's inventions."993

- George Fox, *Gospel Truth Demonstrated*, p. 25.

"And as the light opens and exerciseth thy conscience, it will open to thee parables and figures, and it will let thee see invisible things, which are clearly seen by that which is invisible in thee, which are clearly seen since the creation of the world, that doth declare the eternal power and Godhead; that which is invisible is the light within thee, which he who is invisible hath given thee a measure of... this light lets thee see... as a candle lighted up in the house without thee, the candle is lighted up in thy heart, which is the spirit of the Lord, and thou wilt see the house foul, there is thy figure... These are all figures; as the sun without thee, so the sun of righteousness arising with healing wings within thee. All who mind the measure which God hath given you, it will open unto you these outward figures which God spake, and will teach you... Now this light will shew you these figures: here thou mayest read scriptures thou that lovest the light; thou that hatest the light canst not see these figures. But it is the invisible that opens these, that gave them forth; and here thou that are unlearned in the letter, mayest read the scripture, and as the secret chambers without thee, hearken to the light within thee; and it will let thee see the secret places, where the retired place, the secret chambers are; and as a prison without thee, so there is a prison within, where the seed of God lies."994

- George Fox, *Gospel Truth Demonstrated*, pp. 34 – 36.

"The light of God which gave forth the scripture, this light of God according to its measure will open the scripture to thee... that man may look upon the creation with that which is invisible, and there read himself; there thou mayest see wherever thou goest."[995]

- George Fox, *Gospel Truth Demonstrated*, p. 37.

"That which the people called *Quakers* lay down as a main fundamental in religion is this— *That God, through Christ, hath placed a principle in every man, to inform him of his duty, and to enable him to do it...* By this *principle* they understand something that is *divine;* and though in man, *yet not of man,* but of God; and that it came from him, and leads to him all those that will be led by it... It is to this principle of Light, Life, and Grace, that this People refer all: for they say it is the great Agent in Religion; *that,* without which, there is no *Conviction,* so no *Conversion,* or *Regeneration;* and consequently no entering into the Kingdom of God."[996]

- William Penn, *Primitive Christianity Revived*, Chapter 1, § 1. - 4.

"A most pregnant instance of the *virtue* and authority of the light. *First,* it is that which men ought to examine themselves by. *Secondly,* it gives a *true discerning* betwixt good and bad, *what is of God, from what is not of God.* And, *lastly,* it is a judge, and condemned or acquitteth, *reproveth* or *comforteth*, the soul of man, as he rejects or obeys it. That must needs be *divine* or *efficacious,* which is able to discover to man, what is of God, from what is not of God; and which gives him a *distinct* knowledge, in himself, of what is wrought in God, from what is not wrought in God. By which it appears, that this place does not only regard the discovery of man and his works, but, in some measure, *it manifesteth God, and his works also,* which is yet something higher; forasmuch as it gives the *obedient* man a discovery of what is wrought or performed by *God's power, and after his will,* from what is the mere workings of the creature of himself."997

- William Penn, *Primitive Christianity Revived*, Chapter IV, § 2.

"He that now loves God, that delights and rejoices in him with an humble joy, and holy delight, and an obedient love, is a child of God; But I thus love, delight, and rejoice in God; Therefore, I am a child of God... The manner how the divine testimony is manifested to the heart, I do not take upon me to explain. Such knowledge is too wonderful and excellent for me: I cannot attain unto it. The wind bloweth, and I hear the sound thereof; but I cannot tell how it cometh, or whither it goeth. As no one knoweth the things of a man, save the spirit of a man that is in him; so the manner of the things of God knoweth no one, save the Spirit of God. But the fact we know; namely, that the Spirit of God does give a believer such a testimony of his adoption that while it is present to the soul, he can no more doubt the reality of his sonship, than he can doubt of the shining of the sun, while he stands full blaze of his beams."[998]

- John Wesley, *Wesley's Standard Sermons*, Sermon 10, Discourse 1, 11 – 12.

"Spiritual meditation is the pathway to Divinity. It is the mystic ladder which reaches from earth to heaven, from error to Truth, from pain to peace."[999]

- James Allen, *The Way of Peace*

"As, by the power of meditation, you grow in wisdom, you will relinquish, more and more, your selfish desires which are fickle, impermanent, and productive of sorrow and pain; and will take your stand, with increasing steadfastness and trust, upon unchangeable principles, and will realize heavenly rest."[1000]

- James Allen, *The Way of Peace*

"He who earnestly meditates first perceives a truth, as it were, afar off, and then realizes it by daily practice. It is only the doer of the Word of Truth that can know of the doctrine of Truth, for though by pure thought the Truth is perceived, it is only actualized by practice."[1001]

- James Allen, *The Way of Peace*

"There is no way to the acquirement of spiritual power except by that inward illumination and enlightenment which is the realization of spiritual principles; and those principles can only be realized by constant practice and application."[1002]

- James Allen, *The Way of Peace*

"Hidden deep in every human heart, though frequently covered up with a mass of hard and almost impenetrable accretions, is the spirit of Divine Love, whose holy and spotless essence is undying and eternal. It is the Truth in man; it is that which belongs to the Supreme: that which is real and immortal. All else changes and passes away; this alone is permanent and imperishable; and to realize this Love by ceaseless diligence in the practice of the highest righteousness, to live in it and to become fully conscious in it, is to enter into immortality here and now, is to become one with Truth, one with God, one with the central Heart of all things, and to know our own divine and eternal nature."[1003]

- James Allen, *The Way of Peace*

"And this Love, this Wisdom, this Peace, this tranquil state of mind and heart may be attained to, may be realized by all who are willing and ready to yield up self, and who are prepared to humbly enter into a comprehension of all that the giving up of self involves."[1004]

- James Allen, *The Way of Peace*

"Retreat from the world! It is the embodiment of dreams."[1005]

- A Disciple, *In the Hours of Meditation*, II.

"Before man attempts to solve the secrets of the Universe without, he should master the Universe within—the Kingdom of the Self. When he has accomplished this, then he may, and should, go forth to gain the outer knowledge as a Master demanding its secrets, rather than as a slave begging for the crumbs from the table of knowledge. The first knowledge for the candidate is the knowledge of the Self."[1006]

- Atkinson, *Series of Lessons in Raja Yoga*, p. 1.

"That which is the Real Self of Man is the Divine Spark sent forth from the Sacred Flame. It is the Child of the Divine Parent. It is Immortal—Eternal—Indestructible—Invincible. It possesses within itself Power, Wisdom, and Reality. But like the infant that contains within itself the sometime Man, the mind of Man is unaware of its latent and potential qualities, and does not know itself. As it awakens and unfolds into the knowledge of its real nature, it manifests its qualities, and realizes what the Absolute has given it."[1007]

- Atkinson, *Series of Lessons in Raja Yoga*, p. 3.

"Place yourself in the State of Meditation, and think of YOURSELF—the Real 'I'—as being independent of the body, but using the body as a covering and an instrument. Think of the body as you might of a suit of clothes... Think of yourself as mastering and controlling the body that you occupy, and using it to the best advantage, making it healthy, strong and vigorous, but still being merely a shell or covering for the real 'You.'... In meditating further, ignore the body entirely, and place your thought upon the Real 'I' that you are beginning to feel to be 'you,' and you will find that your identity—your 'I'—is something entirely apart from the body."[1008]

- Atkinson, *Series of Lessons in Raja Yoga*, pp. 16 – 17.

"Meditation is not dreaming. Meditation is not for the spirit only, nor for the mind only; it is for the whole man. Meditation will help open every window of the life to the Light from heaven, and that means that every power of the consecrated body and mind and spirit shall be quickened and strengthened... Meditation will give *power of vision*. Nothing is more important to soul growth. To have the vision that apprehends God, and sees all things in their true relation to God, is worth striving for."[1009]

- J. W. Mahood, *The Lost Art of Meditation*, p. 31.

This concludes *Meditation: Five Ways to Master your Mind, Body and Spirit*. May the grace of God and all His Prophets and Messengers fill you with happiness, love and joy!

∞∞∞∞∞∞∞∞∞∞∞∞∞∞∞∞∞∞∞∞∞∞∞∞∞∞∞∞

Other Books by the Author

Check these other books by NJ Bridgewater!

MINDFULNESS / MEDITATION / SELF-HELP

SCIENCE FICTION / FANTASY

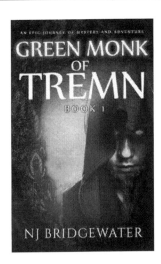

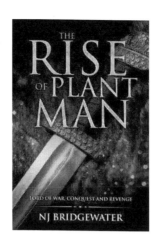

MONEY-MAKING / INVESTMENT

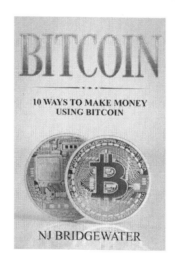

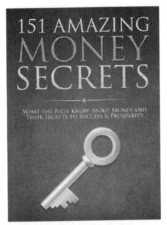

NJ BRIDGEWATER

NJ BRIDGEWATER

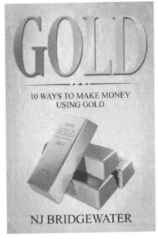

NJ BRIDGEWATER

FULL LIST OF BOOKS BY NJ BRIDGEWATER:

Science Fiction / Fantasy:

NJ Bridgewater (2017) *Green Monk of Tremn, Part I: An Epic Journey of Mystery and Adventure (Coins of Amon-Ra Saga, Book 1)* (Abergavenny, UK: Jaha Publishing). Paperback. Published: January 31, 2017. URL: https://www.amazon.com/Green-Monk-Tremn-Book-Adventure/dp/0995736901/

Mindfulness / Meditation / Self-Help:

NJ Bridgewater (2017) *Mindfulness: Five Ways to Achieve Real Happiness, True Knowledge and Inner Peace (Five Ways to Be, Book 1)* (Abergavenny, UK: Jaha Publishing). Paperback. Published: February 23, 2017. URL: https://www.amazon.com/Mindfulness-Achieve-Happiness-Knowledge-Inner/dp/099573691X/

Money-Making / Investment:

NJ Bridgewater (2017) *Bitcoin: 10 Ways to Make Money Using Bitcoin (Business Mastery Secrets)* (Luxembourg: Amazon EU S.à.r.l.). Kindle Edition. Published: November 18, 2017. URL: https://www.amazon.com/Bitcoin-Money-Business-Mastery-Secrets-ebook/dp/B077M1WJR2/

NJ Bridgewater (2017) *Information Products: 10 Ways to Make Money Using Information Products (Business Mastery Secrets)*. Published on Gumroad.com, 28 November 2017. URL: https://gumroad.com/l/vvHYL

NJ Bridgewater (2017) *Gold: 10 Ways to Make Money Using Gold (Business Mastery Secrets)*. Published on Gumroad.com, 28 November 2017. URL: https://gumroad.com/l/eYACw

NJ Bridgewater (2017) *151 Amazing Money Secrets: What the Rich Know about Money and Their Secrets to Success & Prosperity (Business Mastery Secrets)* (Luxembourg: Amazon EU S.à.r.l.). Kindle Edition. Published: December 6, 2017. URL: https://www.amazon.com/151-Amazing-Money-Secrets-Prosperity-ebook/dp/B077Z2RG87/

Also available for FREE at: https://151amazingmoneysecrets.com/

* Also, please make sure to <u>subscribe to our mailing list</u> for updates on future articles or publications, including any other books in the *Five Ways to Be* series.

* You can also follow the author, NJ Bridgewater, <u>@Nicholas19 on Twitter</u>, <u>Facebook</u> and <u>YouTube</u>.[55]

---

[55]   See: https://twitter.com/Nicholas19   ; https://www.facebook.com/NJBridgewater/   & https://www.youtube.com/channel/UCcMdGAbxcBf_so1WbhLDwog/.

Bibliography

Biographies

Karen Armstrong (1992) *Muhammad: A Biography of the Prophet* (San Francisco, Calif.: Harper San Francisco)

Karen Armstrong (2004) *Buddha* (New York; Toronto: Penguin Books)

Karen Armstrong (2013) *Muhammad: A Prophet for Our Time* (New York: HarperCollins)

H M Balyuzi (2002) *Muhammad and the Course of Islam* (Oxford: George Ronald)

NJ Bridgewater (2004) Founders of the Divine Religions, 1 January 2004. Available online at: http://klausjames.tripod.com/bahai3.html (accessed 29/04/2017)

André Ferdinand Hérold (author), Paul C. Blum (translator) (1929) *The Life of Buddha according to the legends of ancient India* (London: Thornton Butterworth). Available online at: http://www.sacred-texts.com/bud/lob/index.htm (accessed 20/03/2017)

Edith Holland (1918) *The Story of the Buddha* (London: George C. Harrap & Co.). Available online at: https://archive.org/details/storyofbuddha00holl (06/05/2017)

A.V. Williams Jackson (1899) *Zoroaster, the Prophet of Ancient Iran* (New York: Macmillan). URL: https://ia600205.us.archive.org/17/items/zoroasterprophet00jack/zoroasterprophet00jack.pdf (accessed 29/04/2017)

Vraja Kishor (Vic Dicara) (2013) *Beautiful Tales of the All-Attractive: Volume 1* (North Charleston, SC: CreateSpace Independent Publishing Platform)

Martin Lings (1983) *Muhammad: His Life Based on the Earliest Sources* (London: Islamic Texts Society/G. Allen & Unwin)

Bhikkhu Nanamoli (2003) *Life of the Buddha: According to the Pali Canon* (Kandy, Sri Lanka: Buddhist Publication Company)

Thera Nyanaponika, Hellmuth Hecker (2012) *Great Disciples of the Buddha: Their Lives, Their Works, Their Legacy* (New York: Wisdom Publications)

His Divine Grace A.C. Bhaktivedenta Swami Prabhupāda (1972) *Krsna, the supreme personality of Godhead: a summary study of Srila Vyasadeva's 'Śrīmad-Bhāgavatam, tenth canto'. Vol. 3* (New York; London: Bhaktivedanta Book Trust)

Vanamali (2012) *The Complete Life of Krishna: Based on the Earliest Oral Traditions and the Sacred Scriptures* (Rochester, VT: Inner Traditions)

W. Montgomery Watt (1953) *Muhammad at Mecca* (Oxford: The Clarendon Press)

W. Montgomery Watt (1956) *Muhammad at Medina* (Oxford: The Clarendon Press)

Robert Charles Zaehner (1961) *The Dawn and Twilight of Zoroastrianism* (New York: Putnam)

Meditation

Alexander C. N., Langer E. J., Newman R. I., Chandler H. M., Davies J. L. (1989) Transcendental meditation, mindfulness, and longevity: an experimental study with the elderly. *J. Pers. Soc. Psychol.* 57, 950–96410.1037/0022-3514.57.6.950.   Available   online   at: https://www.ncbi.nlm.nih.gov/pubmed/2693686 (accessed 05/05/2017)

Shamash Alidina (2015) *Mindfulness for Dummies* (Hoboken: John Wiley)

Bhikku Anālayo (2003) *Satipatthāna: The Direct Path to Realization* (Birmingham: Windhorse Publications)

Nguyen Anh-Huong, Thich Nhat Hanh (2006) *Walking Meditation* (Boulder: Sounds True)

William Walker Atkinson (1907) *A series of lessons in Gnani yoga (the yoga of wisdom)* (Chicago, IL.: The Yogi Publication Society). Available online at: https://archive.org/details/cu31924022985422 (accessed 04/03/2017)

Klaus B. Bærentsen (2015) Patanjali and neuroscientific research on meditation. *Frontiers in Psychology*,   Vol   6,   Jul   3,   2015.   Available   online   at: http://journal.frontiersin.org.oxfordbrookes.idm.oclc.org/article/10.3389/fpsyg.2015.00915/full#B42 (accessed 16/03/2017)

Charlotte Joko Beck (2009) *Everyday Zen: Love and Work* (New York: HarperCollins)

Charlotte Bell (2015) How to Choose a Meditation Cushion. *Hugger Mugger Yoga Products*. Available online at: http://www.huggermugger.com/blog/2015/meditation-cushion/ (accessed 28/04/2017)

Brooke Bobb (2016) Beginner-Friendly Meditation Retreats in Some of the World's Most Beautiful Settings.   *Vogue*,   February   17,   2016   6:33   PM.   Available   online   at: http://www.vogue.com/article/beginner-meditation-retreats-beginners-italy-california-bali   (accessed 28/04/2017)

Bhikku Bodhi (2013) What does mindfulness really mean? A canonical perspective. In J. Mark G. Williams & Jon Kabat-Zinn (editors) (2013) *Mindfulness: Diverse Perspectives on its Meaning, Origins and Applications* (London; New York: Routledge)

Barry Boyce (2013) Walk This Way. *Mindful.org*, April 3, 2017. The article also appeared in the June 2013 issue of *Mindful* magazine. Available online at: http://www.mindful.org/walk-this-way/ (accessed 16/04/2017)

NJ Bridgewater (2017) *Mindfulness: Five Ways to Achieve Real Happiness, True Knowledge and Inner Peace* (Abergavenny: Jaha Publishing)

NJ Bridgewater (2017b) How can we achieve true happiness and inner peace? *Equanimity Blog*, February 8, 2017. Available online at: https://fivewaystobe.wordpress.com/2017/02/08/how-can-we-achieve-true-happiness-and-inner-peace/ (accessed 29/04/2017)

Kirk Warren Brown, J. David Creswell, Richard M. Ryan (2015) *Handbook of Mindfulness: Theory, Research, and Practice* (New York; London: The Guilford Press)

Erica Camus (2016) 14 of the best mindfulness retreats. *Metro.co.uk*, 15 August 2016 2PM. Available online at: http://metro.co.uk/2016/08/15/14-of-the-best-mindfulness-retreats-6036485/ (accessed 28/04/2017)

Elise Dirlam Ching, Kaleo Ching (2014) *Chi and Creativity: Vital Energy and Your Inner Artist* (Berkeley, California: Blue Snake Books)

Kenneth S. Cohen (1999) *The Way of Qigong: The Art and Science of Chinese Energy Healing* (New York: Ballantine Books)

392

Krishna Rupa Devi dasi (2011) Powerful Meaning of the Hare Krishna Mahamantra by Srila Jiva Goswami. March 14, 2011, 7:46 pm, *ISKCON Desire Tree – Devotee Network*. Available online at: http://www.iskcondesiretree.com/forum/topics/powerful-meaning-of-the-hare (accessed 15/04/2017)

Ronald H. Davis (2015) *Qigong Through the Seasons: How to Stay Healthy All Year with Qigong, Meditation, Diet, and Herbs* (London; Philadelphia: Singing Dragon)

A Disciple (1921) *In the Hours of Meditation* (Calcutta: S. C. Majumdah). Available online at: https://archive.org/details/inhoursofmeditatoodiscrich (accessed 22/02/2017)

R.S. Crane, J. Brewer, C. Feldman, J. Kabat-Zinn, S. Santorelli, J.M.G. Williams and W. Kuyken (2016) What defines mindfulness-based programs? The warp and the weft. *Psychological Medicine*, 2017 Apr; 47(6):990-999. Available online at: http://mbct.com/wp-content/uploads/What-defines-mindfulness-based-programs.pdf (accessed 20/03/2017)

Danny & Katherine Dreyer (2012) Walking as Meditation: Quiet Your Mind as You Improve Your Health. The Blog, *Huffington Post*, Oct 23, 2012 12:06 am ET. Available online at: http://www.huffingtonpost.com/danny-and-katherine-dreyer/walking-meditation_b_1790035.html (accessed 16/04/2017)

Melissa Eisler (2015) How to Sit for Meditation: 8 Options. *Mindful Minutes*, June 12, 2015. https://mindfulminutes.com/how-to-sit-for-meditation/ (18/05/2017).

Ekai, called Mu-mon (author) Nyogen Senzaki, Paul Reps (translators) (1934) *The Gateless Gate* (Los Angeles: John Murray). Copyright not renewed. Available online at: http://www.sacred-texts.com/bud/glg/glg00.htm (accessed 16/04/2017)

Joseph Emet (2012) *Buddha's Book of Sleep: Sleep Better in Seven Weeks with Mindfulness Meditation* (New York: Jeremy P. Tarcher)

Georg Feuerstein (2006) Yoga and Meditation (Dhyana). *Moksha Journal – The Journal of Knowledge, Enlightenment & Freedom*, Issue I, 2006. Available online at: http://www.santosha.com/moksha/meditation1.html (accessed 16/03/2017)

Lucy Flood (2017) How to Practice Qi Gong's Forest Meditation. *The Chopra Center*. Available online at: http://www.chopra.com/articles/how-to-practice-qi-gong%E2%80%99s-forest-meditation#sm.0001bms3lb1svcnwuqm1qb8z6p3d6 (accessed 16/04/2017)

David Fortuna, Ingrid Slack (2007) *Teaching Meditation to Children: The Practical Guide to the Use and Benefits of Meditation Techniques* (London: Watkins; New York: Sterling Publishing Co.)

Fran Gaik (2009) *Managing Depression with Qigong* (London: Jessica Kingsley Publications)

Rishi Singh Gherwal (1930) *Kundalini, The Mother of the Universe: The Mystery of Piercing the Six Chakras* (Santa Barbara, Calif.: Published by the Author). Public domain in the US because its copyright was not renewed in a timely fashion at the US Copyright Office. Available online at: http://www.sacred-texts.com/hin/kmu/kmu00.htm (accessed 05/05/2017)

S. N. Goenka (2000) *Discourse Summaries: Talks from a Ten-day Course in Vipassana Meditation* (Chicago: Pariyatti Publishing)

Joseph Goldstein & Jack Kornfield (2001) *Seeking the Heart of Wisdom: The Path of Insight Meditation* (Boston: Shambhala)

Joseph Goldstein (2013) *Mindfulness: A Practical Guide to Awakening* (Boulder, CO: Sounds True)

Carolyn Gregoire (2013) Silent Retreats: 10 Fantastic Retreat Centers In The U.S. For Peace & Quiet (PHOTOS). *Huffington Post*, 02/28/2013 07:24 AM ET. Updated Feb 28, 2013. Available online at: http://www.huffingtonpost.com/2013/02/28/silent-retreats-america_n_2727408.html (accessed 28/04/2017)

Thich Nhat Hanh (1992) *Peace is Every Step: The Path of Mindfulness in Everyday Life* (New York: Bantam Books)

Thich Nhat Hanh (1996) *The Miracle of Mindfulness: An Introduction to the Practice of Meditation* (Boston: Beacon Press)

Thich Nhat Hanh (2011) *The Long Road Turns to Joy: A Guide to Walking Meditation* (Berkeley, Calif.: Parallax Press)

William Hart (2012) *The Art of Living: Vipassana Meditation as taught by S. N. Goenke* (Maharashtra, India: Vipassana Research Institute)

Virginia Heffernan (2015) The Muddied Meaning of 'Mindfulness'. *The New York Times Magazine*, April 14, 2015. Available online at: https://www.nytimes.com/2015/04/19/magazine/the-muddied-meaning-of-mindfulness.html?_r=0 (accessed 20/03/2017)

Edward Hines (2013) *Moving into Stillness – A Practical Guide to Qigong and Meditation* (North Charleston, SC: CreateSpace Independent Publishing Platform)

Caroline Sylger Jones (2015) Wellness Holidays: from meditation weekends to high-tech rejuvenation. *The Independent*, 9 January 2015 11:11 GMT. Available online at: http://www.independent.co.uk/travel/news-and-advice/wellness-holidays-from-meditation-weekends-to-high-tech-rejuvenation-9967413.html (accessed 28/04/2017)

Caroline Sylger Jones (2016) 10 UK holidays that will make you a better person. *The Telegraph*, 5 September 2016 11:15 AM. Available online at: http://www.telegraph.co.uk/travel/destinations/europe/united-kingdom/articles/the-best-body-and-soul-holidays-in-britain/ (accessed 28/04/2017)

Jon Kabat-Zinn (2001) *Mindfulness Meditation for Everyday Life* (London: Piatkus Books). Available online at: http://chadpearce.com/home/BOOKS/97291641-Mindfulness-Meditation-for-Everyday-Life-Kabat-Zinn-Jon.pdf (accessed 20/03/2017)

Jon Kabat-Zinn (2016) *Mindfulness for Beginners: Reclaiming the Present Moment—and Your Life* (Boulder, CO: Sounds True)

Aryeh Kaplan (1988) *Meditation and the Bible* (Boston: Weiser Books)

Philip Kapleau (2007) *The Three Pillars of Zen: Teaching, Practice and Enlightenment* (New York: Anchor Books)

Dainin Katagiri (2009) *Each Moment is the Universe: Zen and the way of being time* (Boston, Mass.: Shambhala)

Dharma Singh Khalsa, Darryl O'Keeffe (2002) *The Kundalini Yoga Experience: Bringing Body, Mind, and Spirit Together* (New York: Simon & Schuster)

Shakti Parwha Kaur Khalsa (1998) *Kundalini Yoga: The Flow of Eternal Power: A Simple Guide to the Yoga of Awareness as taught by Yogi Bhajan, Ph.D.* (New York: Berkley Pub. Group)

Madhu Khanna (2004) A Journey into Cosmic Consciousness: Kundalini Shakti. *India International Centre Quarterly*, Vol. 30, No. 3/4, JOURNEYS HEROES, PILGRIMS, EXPLORERS (WINTER 2003-SPRING 2004), pp. 224-238. Available online at: http://www.jstor.org/stable/23006136 (accessed 17/04/2017)

394

Sayagyi U Ba Khin (1997) *The Essentials of Buddha-Dhamma in Meditative Practice* (Onalaska, WA: Vipassana Research Publications)

Jack Kornfield (2008) *Meditation for Beginners* (Boulder, Colo.: Sounds True)

Jack Kornfield (2010) *Living Dharma: Teachings and Meditation from Twelve Theravada Masters* (Boston: Shambhala). See also: https://jackkornfield.com/factors-enlightenment/ (accessed 23/03/2017)

Gopi Krishna (1997) *Kundalini: The Evolutionary Energy in Man* (Boston: Shambhala)

Gopi Krishna (2014) *Kundalini: The Secret of Yoga* (Los Gatos: Smashwords Edition)

John Wilmot Mahood (1911) *The Lost Art of Meditation* (New York, Chicago: Fleming H. Revell Company). Available online at: https://archive.org/details/lostartofmeditat00maho (accessed 22/02/2017)

Shirin Mehdi (2016) How To Do The Sukhasana And What Are Its Benefits. *StyleCraze*, May 13, 2016. Available online at: http://www.stylecraze.com/articles/sukhasana-easy-pose/#gref (accessed 21/03/2017)

Jonathan Mermis-Cava (2009) An Anchor and a Sail: Christian Meditation as the Mechanism for a Pluralist Religious Identity. *Sociology of Religion*, Vol. 70, No. 4 (Winter, 2009), pp. 432-453. Available online at: https://www.jstor.org/stable/pdf/40376095.pdf (accessed 18/03/2017)

The Editor, The Open Court (1908) Buddhist Meditations, In *The Open Court – A Monthly Magazine Devoted to the Science of Religion, the Religion of Science, and the Extension of the Religious Parliament Idea*, Vol. XXII (Chicago: The Open Court Publishing Company), Anon., Buddhist Meditations, *The Open Court* (magazine). Available online at: http://www.sacred-texts.com/journals/oc/budmed.htm (accessed 14/03/2017).

Sayadaw U Pandita (2017) How to Practice Vipassana Insight Meditation, *Lion's Roar: Buddhist Wisdom for Our Time*, April 8, 2017. Available online at: https://www.lionsroar.com/how-to-practice-vipassana-insight-meditation/ (accessed 16/04/2017)

Ven Pannyavaro (1996-2017) Loving-Kindness Meditation, BuddhaNet Basic Buddhism Guide. *Buddhist Studies: Buddha Dharma Education Association & BuddhaNet*. Available online at: http://www.buddhanet.net/e-learning/loving-kindness.htm (accessed 26/03/2017)

Patañjali (author), Ganganatha Jha (translator) (1907) *The Yoga-darśana: The Sutras of Patañjali with the Bhāsya of Vyasa* (Bombay: Rajaram Tukaram Tatya). Available online at: https://archive.org/details/yogadaranasutra00patagoog (accessed 04/03/2017)

His Divine Grace A.C. Bhaktivedanta Swami Prabhupada (2011) *Chant and Be Happy: The Power of Mantra Meditation* (Los Angeles: Bhaktivedanta Book Trust)

Qiao Renjie (2017) *Zen: A Complete Beginner's Guide to Zen Meditation* (Meditation, Yoga and Health series) (Kindle ebook). Available online at: https://www.amazon.com/Zen-Complete-Beginners-Meditation-Mindfulness-ebook/dp/B06WGQM8T7/ (accessed 16/04/2017)

Qiao Renjie (2017b) *Yoga: 25 Yoga Poses for Weight Loss, Health, and Inner Peace* (ebook). Available online at: https://www.amazon.com/dp/B071F9Y6CY/ (accessed 18/05/2017)

Qiao Renjie (2017c) *Kundalini: Awaken Shakti through Kundalini Meditation* (Meditation, Yoga and Health series) (Kindle ebook). Available online at: https://www.amazon.com/dp/B071VTSPYF/ (accessed 18/05/2017)

Lodro Rinzler (2015) Everything You Need to Know About Meditation Posture. *Yoga Journal / Meditation*. Available online at: http://www.yogajournal.com/meditation/everything-need-know-meditation-posture/ (accessed 21/03/2017)

Larry Rosenberg & David Guy (2004) *Breath by Breath: The Liberating Practice of Insight Meditation* (Boston, MA: Shambhala)

Dza Kilung Rinpoche (2015) *The Relaxed Mind: A Seven-Step Method for Deepening Meditation Practice* (Boston: Shambhala)

Sharon Salzberg (2004) *Loving-Kindness: The Revolutionary Art of Happiness* (Boston: Shambhala)

Sharon Salzberg (2010) *Real Happiness: The Power of Meditation* (New York: Workman Pub.)

Sharon Salzberg (2015) The Concentric Circles of Connection and Lovingkindness, *On Being* (blog), September 25, 2015. Available online at: https://onbeing.org/blog/the-concentric-circles-of-connection-and-lovingkindness/ (accessed 09/04/2017)

Sukanya Sarbadhikary (2015) Listening to Vrindavan: Chanting and Musical Experience as Embodying a Devotional Soundscape. In *Place of Devotion: Sitting and Experiencing Divinity in Bengal-Vaishnavism* (Oakland: California: University of California Press). Available online at: http://www.jstor.org/stable/10.1525/j.ctt1ffjn1f.10 (accessed 15/04/2017)

Venerable Pa-Auk Sayadaw (1995) *Mindfulness of Breathing & Four Elements Meditation* (Kuala Lumpur: Buddha Dharma Education Association, Inc.). Available online at: http://www.buddhanet.net/pdf_file/fourelements.pdf (accessed 12/03/2017)

Kathleen C. Spadaro (2008) *Weight Loss: Exploring Self-regulation Through Mindfulness Meditation.* Submitted to the Graduate Faculty of School of Nursing in partial fulfilment of the requirements for the degree of Doctor of Philosophy, University of Pittsburgh.

Springs Steele (2000) Christian Insight Meditation: A Test Case on Interreligious Spirituality. *Buddhist-Christian Studies*, Vol. 20 (2000), pp. 217-229. Available online at: http://www.jstor.org/stable/1390332 (accessed 25/03/2017)

Ales Stuchlik, Tomiki Sumiyoshi (editors) (2015) Cognitive deficits in schizophrenia and other neuropsychiatric disorders: convergence of preclinical and clinical evidence, *Frontiers in Behavioral Neuroscience*, January 2014, Volume 8, Article 17 (Lausanne, Switzerland: Frontiers Research Foundation)

Shunryū Suzuki (2011) *Zen Mind, Beginner's Mind* (Boston, Mass.: Shambhala Publications)

Phra Thepyanmongkol (2012) *A Study Guide for Right Practice of the Three Trainings* (Ratchaburi, Thailand: National Center of Provincial Meditation Institutes of Thailand, Wat Luang Phor Sodh Dhammakayaram)

Nyanaponika Thera (2005) *The Heart of Buddhist Meditation: Satipatthāna: a Handbook of Mental Training Based on the Buddha's Way of Mindfulness, with an Anthology of Relevant Texts Translated from the Pali and Sanskrit* (Kandy, Sri Lanka: Buddhist Publication Society)

Soma Thera (translator) (2013) The Way of Mindfulness: The Satipatthana Sutta and Its Commentary. *Access to Insight (Legacy Edition)*, 30 November 2013. Available online at: http://www.accesstoinsight.org/lib/authors/soma/wayof.html#mental (accessed 21/03/2017)

Tulku Thondup (2009) *The Healing Power of Loving-kindness: A Guided Buddhist Meditation* (Boston, Mass.: Shambhala)

Swami Vivekananda (1902), *Vedânta philosophy; lectures by the Swâmi Vivekânanda on jnâna yoga* (New York: The Vedânta Society). Available online at: https://archive.org/details/vedntaphilosopo0ovive (accessed 21/03/2017)

Swami Vivekananda (1920) *Râja Yoga: Being lectures by the Swâmi Vivekânanda* (New York: Brentano's). Available online at: https://archive.org/details/raajayogabeingleo0oviveuoft (accessed 21/03/2017)

B. Alan Wallace (2014) *Mind in the Balance: Meditation in Science, Buddhism, and Christianity* (New York: Columbia University Press)

Alan W. Watts (2011) *The Way of Zen* (New York: Vintage Books)

Rebecca L. Weber (2013) The world's best meditation retreats. *CNN.com*, June 25, 2013. Available online at: http://www.cnn.com/2013/06/25/travel/best-meditation-retreats/ (accessed 28/04/2017)

Leigh Weingus (2016) I Tried Kundalini Yoga. Here's Everything You Need to Know. *Mindbodygreen.com*, July 7, 2016 3:48 AM. Available online at: https://www.mindbodygreen.com/0-25810/i-tried-kundalini-yoga-heres-everything-you-need-to-know.html (accessed 17/04/2017)

J. Mark G. Williams, Jon Kabat-Zinn (editors) (2013) *Mindfulness: Diverse Perspectives on its Meaning, Origins and Applications* (London; New York: Routledge)

Sir John Woodroffe (Arthur Avalon) (1918) *Shakti and Shâkta: Essays and Addresses on the Shâkta tantrashâstra* (London: Luzac &Co.). Available online at: http://www.mysticknowledge.org/Shakti_and_Shakta-By_Arthur_Avalon.pdf (accessed 17/04/2017)

Sir John Woodroffe (2003) *The Serpent Power* (Madras: Ganesh & Co.)

J.H. Woods (1927/2003) *The Yoga-Sutra of Patanjali* (New York, NY: Dover)

Alexander Wynne (2007) *The Origin of Buddhist Meditation* (London: Routledge). Available online at: http://www.ahandfulofleaves.org/documents/The%20Origin%20of%20Buddhist%20Meditation_Alexande%20Wynne.pdf (accessed 12/03/2017)

Koun Yamada & Rube L.F. Habito (2005) *The Gateless Gate: The Classic Book of Zen Koans* (Somerville: Wisdom Publications)

Jwing-Ming Yang (2003) *Qigong Meditation: Embryonic Breathing* (Wolfeboro, NH: YMAA Publication Center)

Jwing-Ming Yang (2016) *Qigong Meditation: Small Circulation* (Wolfeboro, NH: YMAA Publication Center)

Jwing-Ming Yang (2016) *The Root of Chinese Qigong: Secrets of Health, Longevity, & Enlightenment* (Wolfeboro, NH: YMAA Publication Center)

Yoga International (2013) Purify Your Chakras, Part 4: How to Practice Bhuta Shuddhi. *Yoga International*, June 5, 2013. Available online at: https://yogainternational.com/article/view/purify-your-chakras-part-4-how-to-practice-bhuta-shuddhi (accessed 17/04/2017)

Philosophy

Aristotle (author), William David Ross (translator) (1908) *The Nicomachean Ethics of Aristotle* (Oxford: The Clarendon Press). Available online at: http://www.sacred-texts.com/cla/ari/nico/index.htm (accessed 20/03/2017)

397

Marcus Aurelius Antoninus Augustus (author), George Long (translator) (1890) *The thoughts of the Emperor Marcus Aurelius Antoninus* (Boston: Little, Brown). Available online at: http://classics.mit.edu/Antoninus/meditations.html (accessed 05/05/2017)

Hereward Carrington (1920) *Higher Psychical Development (Yoga Philosophy) an Outline of the Secret Hindu Teachings* (New York: Dodd, Mead and Company). Available online at: https://archive.org/details/higherpsychical00carrg00g (accessed 04/03/2017)

Confucius (author), James Legge (translator) (1861) *The Chinese Classics (Confucian Analects)* (London: Trübner & Co.). Available online at: http://www.gutenberg.org/ebooks/3330 (accessed 29/04/2017)

René Descartes (author), John Veitch (translator) (1910) *Discourse on the method of rightly conducting reason, and seeking truth in the sciences* (Chicago: The Open Court Publishing Co.). Available online at: https://ebooks.adelaide.edu.au/d/descartes/rene/d44dm/index.html (last updated 17/12/2014 13:08) (accessed 15/03/2017)

Epictetus (author), P.E. Matheson (translator) (1916) *The Discourses of Epictetus: The Discourses and Manual, together with fragments of his writings* (Oxford: Clarendon Press). Available online at: http://www.sacred-texts.com/cla/dep/index.htm (accessed 19/03/2017)

Iamblichus (author), Thomas Taylor (translator) (1818) *Iamblichus' Life of Pythagoras or Pythagoric Life, accompanied by Fragments of the Ethical Writings of Certain Pythagoreans in the Doric Dialect; and a Collection of Pythagoric Sentences from Stobæus and Others, which are omitted by Gale in his Opuscula Mythologica, and have not been noticed by any editor* (London: J.M. Watkins)

Lao-Tse (Laozi) (author), James Legge (translator) (1891) *The Tâo Teh King, or The Tao and Its Characteristics* (Oxford: Clarendon Press). Available online at: http://www.gutenberg.org/ebooks/216 (accessed 05/05/2017)

Liezi (author), Lionel Giles (translator) (1912) *Taoist Teachings Translated from the Book of Lieh-Tzü, with Introduction and Notes* (London: Murray). Available online at: http://www.sacred-texts.com/tao/tt/index.htm (accessed 16/03/2017)

Linda Johnsen (2016) *Lost Masters: Rediscovering the Mysticism of the Ancient Greek Philosophers* (Novato, California: New World Library)

Mencius (Mengzi / Meng Ke) (author), James Legge (translator) (1895) *The Works of Mencius* (Oxford: Clarendon Press). Available online at: http://nothingistic.org/library/mencius/ (accessed 27/3/2017)

Plato (author), Benjamin Jowett (translator) (1892) *The Dialogues of Plato, translated into English with Analyses and Introductions, Vol. II* (New York: Oxford University Press, American Branch; London: Henry Frowde). Available online at: http://classics.mit.edu/Plato/phaedo.html ; https://archive.org/details/dialoguesofplato18922plat (accessed 03/05/2017)

Plato (author), Benjamin Jowett (translator) (1910) *Socrates. Plato's apology of Socrates and Crito, with part of his Phaedo* (Portland, Maine: Thomas B. Mosher). Available online at: http://www.gutenberg.org/ebooks/1656 (accessed 14/03/2017)

Plotinus (author), Kenneth Sylvan Guthrie (translator (1918) *Plotinus, Complete Works, Vol. II. Amelio-Porphyrian Books, 22–33* (Grantwood, N.J.: Comparative Literature Press)

Plotinus (author), Stephen MacKenna & B.S. Page (translators) (1917 – 1930) *The Six Enneads* (London; Boston: Medici Society). Available online at: http://www.sacred-texts.com/cla/plotenn/index.htm (accessed 22/03/2017)

Pythagoras (author), Florence M. Firth (translator) (1904) *The Golden Verses of Pythagoras, And Other Pythagorean Fragments* (London: Theosophical Publishing Society). Available online at: http://sacred-texts.com/cla/gvp/index.htm (accessed 03/05/2017)

Christoph Riedweg (author), Steven Rendall, Andreas Schatzmann (translators) (2008) *Pythagoras: His Life, Teaching, and Influence* (Ithaca, NY; London: Cornell University Press)

Geoffrey Samuel (2008) *The Origins of Yoga and Tantra* (Cambridge: Cambridge University Press)

Edouard Shuré (1906) *Pythagoras and the Delphic Mysteries* (London: Philip Wellby). Available online at: http://www.sacred-texts.com/cla/pdm/pdm00.htm (accessed 19/03/2017)

Zhuangzi (author), Herbert Allen Giles (translator) (1889) *Chuang Tzu, Mystic, Moralist, and Social Reformer* (London: B. Quaritch). Available online at: https://archive.org/details/chuangtzumysticm00chua (accessed 16/03/2017).

Poetry

William Blake (1901) *Songs of Innocence and Songs of Experience* (London: R. Brimley Johnson). Available online at: http://www.gutenberg.org/ebooks/1934 (accessed 22/04/2017)

Faith Citlak (2007) *Rumi and the Sufi Path of Love* (Lanham: Tughra Books)

F. Hadland Davis (1920) *Jalálu'd-Dín Rúmí* (London: John Murray). Available online at: http://www.gutenberg.org/ebooks/45159 (accessed 05/05/2017)

Khwāja Shamsu'd-Dīn Muhammad (Hafez of Shiraz) (author), Gertrude Lowthian Bell (translator) (1897a) *Teachings of Hafiz* (London: W. Heinemann). Available online at: http://www.sacred-texts.com/isl/hafiz.htm (accessed 17/03/2017)

Khwāja Shamsu'd-Dīn Muhammad (Hafez of Shiraz) (author), Gertrude Lowthian Bell (translator) (1897b) *Poems from the Divan of Hafiz* (London: Heinemann). Available online at: http://sacred-texts.com/isl/pdh/index.htm (accessed 19/12/2016)

Abū 'Abdu'llāh Muhammad ibn 'Alī ibn Muhammad ibn 'Arabī (Ibn al-'Arabī) (author), Reynold A. Nicholson (translator) (1911) *The Tarjumán al-Ashwáq: A Collection of Mystical Odes by Muhyi'ddin ibn Al-'Arabi* (London: Theosophical Publishing House Ltd.). Available online at: http://www.sacred-texts.com/isl/taa/index.htm (available online at: 03/05/2017)

Nūr al-Dīn 'Abd al-Rahmān Jāmī (author), Edward Fitzgerald (translator) (1904) *Miscellanies of Edward Fitzgerald* (London: George Routledge and Sons, Ltd.). Available online at: http://www.sacred-texts.com/isl/saab/index.htm ; https://archive.org/details/miscellaniesedw01fitzg00g (accessed 03/05/2017)

Omar Khayyam (author), Edward FitzGerald (1859) *The Rubáiyàt of Omar Khayyám, the astronomer-poet of Persia, translated into English verse* (London: B. Quaritch). Available online at: http://www.sacred-texts.com/isl/khayyam.txt (accessed 03/05/2017)

John Milton (c 1900) *Paradise Regained* (New York, Boston: H.M. Caldwell Co.). Available online at: http://www.gutenberg.org/ebooks/58 (accessed 04/05/2017)

Alexander Pope (1762) *A Collection of Essays: Epistles and Odes. Epistles to several persons. Epistles to several persons. Eloisa to Abelard. The rape of the lock. Messiah. A sacred Eclogue. The temple of fame. Ode for music on St. Cecilia's Day. Ode on solitude. Essay on criticism. The universal prayer. By Alexander Pope, Esq.* (London: Printed for J. James, in New-Bond Street). Available online at: https://www.poetryfoundation.org/poems-and-poets/poems/detail/44896 (accessed 04/05/2017)

Alexander Pope (author), Thomas Marc Parrott (editor) (1906) *Pope's The Rape of the Lock and other poems* (Boston, Mass.: Ginn & Co.). Available online at: https://en.wikipedia.org/wiki/Ode_on_Solitude ; http://www.gutenberg.org/ebooks/9800 (accessed 04/05/2017)

Jalāl ad-Dīn Rūmī (author), Shams ad-Dīn Ahmad (author), James W. Redhouse (translator) (1881) *The Mesnavī (usually known as the Mesneviyi Sheríf) of Mevlānā (our lord) Jelālu-'d-Dīn, Muhammed, Er-*

399

Rūmī. Book the First. Together with some accounts of the life and acts of the author, of his ancestors, and of his descendants; illustrated by a selection of characteristic anecdotes, as collected by their historian, Mevlānā Shemsu-'d-Dīn Ahmed, El Eflākī, El 'Ārifī (London: Trübner & Co.). Available online at: http://www.sacred-texts.com/isl/mes/index.htm (accessed 15/04/2017)

Jalālu'd-Dīn Rūmī (author), E.H. Whinfield (translator) (1898) *The Masnavi I Ma'navi – The Spiritual Couplets of Maulana Jalalu'd-Din Muhammad Rumi* (London: Kegan Paul, Trench, Trubner). Available online at: http://www.sacred-texts.com/isl/masnavi/index.htm (accessed 19/03/2017)

Jalālu'd-Dīn Muhammad Rūmī (author), Reynold A. Nicholson (translator) (1898) *Selected Poems from the Divani Shamsi Tabriz* (London: Cambridge University Press). Available online at: https://sourcebooks.fordham.edu/source/1270rumi-poems1.asp (accessed 15/03/2017)

Abū-Muhammad Muslihu'd-Dīn bin 'Abdu'llāh Shīrāzī (Saadi) (author), Sir Edwin Arnold (translator) (1899) *The Gulistân of Musle-huddeen Shaik Sady of Sheeraz* (London: T. Burleigh). Available online at: http://www.sacred-texts.com/isl/gulistan.txt (accessed 17/03/2017)

Hakīm Abu'l-Majd Majdūd Sanā'ī (author), J. Stephenson (translator) (1910) *The Hadîqatu'l-Haqîqat (The Enclosed Garden of the Truth)* (Calcutta: Baptist Mission Press). Available online at: http://www.sacred-texts.com/isl/egt/index.htm (accessed 03/05/2017).

Mahmūd Shabestarī (author), Florence Lederer (translator) (1920) *The Secret Rose Garden* (London: J. Murray). Available online at: http://www.sacred-texts.com/isl/srg/index.htm (accessed 24/04/2017)

Alfred Tennyson (author), H.W. Shryock (editor) (1910) *Tennyson's Princess* (New York: American Book Company), The Higher Pantheism. Available online at: https://en.wikisource.org/wiki/The_Higher_Pantheism ; https://archive.org/details/tennysonsprinces04tenn (accessed 22/04/2017)

Religion and Spirituality

Hamid Algar (2002) Hadith iv. In Sufism, *Encyclopædia Iranica* (Online Edition). Available online at: http://www.iranicaonline.org/articles/hadith-iv (accessed 15/03/2017)

Yusuf Ali (1934) *The Holy Quran* (Kashmiri Bazar, Lahore: Shaik Muhammad Ashraf). Available online at: http://www.sacred-texts.com/isl/yaq/index.htm (accessed 30/03/2017)

Thomas Aquinas (author), Fathers of the English Dominican Province (translators) (1920) *Summa Theologica* (London: Burns Oates & Washbourne). Available online at: http://web.mnstate.edu/gracyk/courses/web%20publishing/aquinasFiveWays.htm (accessed 15/03/2017)

Arthur John Arberry (1953) *The Holy Koran* (London: G. Allen). Available online at: http://www.theonlyquran.com/quran/Al-Fathiha/English_Arthur_John_Arberry (accessed 12/05/2017)

Arthur John Arberry (2013) *Sufism: An Account of the Mystics of Islam* (Taylor & Francis)

Muhammad Asad (1980) *The Message of the Qur'ān: the full account of the revealed Arabic text accompanied by parallel transliteration* (Gibraltar: Dar al-Andalus). Available online at: http://muhammad-asad.com/Message-of-Quran.pdf ; https://archive.org/details/TheMessageOfTheQuran_20140419 (accessed 12/05/2017)

Reza Aslan (2005) *No god but God: The Origins, Evolution, and Future of Islam* (New York: Ember)

Bahá'u'lláh (author), Shoghi Effendi (translator) (1985) *The Hidden Words of Bahá'u'lláh* (Wilmette, Illinois: US Bahá'í Publishing Trust). Available online at: http://reference.bahai.org/en/t/b/HW/index.html (accessed 06/07/2018)

400

Bahá'u'lláh (author), Shoghi Effendi (translator) (1990) *Gleanings from the Writings of Bahá'u'lláh* (Wilmette, Illinois: US Bahá'í Publishing Trust). Available online at: http://reference.bahai.org/en/t/b/GWB/index.html (accessed 06/07/2018)

Bahá'u'lláh (author), Alí Kuli Khán, Marzieh Gail (translators) (1991) *The Seven Valleys And the Four Valleys* (Wilmette, Illinois: US Bahá'í Publishing Trust). Available online at: http://reference.bahai.org/en/t/b/SVFV/index.html (accessed 06/07/2018)

BBC (2011) Prophet Muhammad (570-632), *BBC Religions*, 2011-07-08. Available online at: http://www.bbc.co.uk/religion/religions/islam/history/muhammad_1.shtml (accessed 18/03/2017)

Robert Beer (2003) *The Handbook of Tibetan Buddhist Symbols* (Chicago, London: Serindia)

St. Benedict (author), Rev. Boniface Verheyen (translator) (1902) *The holy rule of our most holy Father St. Benedict: in Latin and English* (Atchison: Abbey Student Print). Available online at: http://www.documentacatholicaomnia.eu/03d/0480-0547,_Benedictus_Nursinus,_Regola,_EN.pdf (accessed 18/03/2017)

Sri Kedarnath Dutt Bhaktivinod (1896) *Srigouranga Smaranamangala or Chaitanya Mahaprabhu: His Life and Precepts* (Calcutta: Mookerjee & Co. at the Calcutta Press), *Śrī Gaurānga-Līlā-Smarana-Mangala-Stotram*, 75, p. 36. Available online at: http://www.krishnapath.org/Library/Goswami-books/Bhaktivinoda-Thakura/Bhaktivinoda_Thakura_Gauranga_Lila.pdf (accessed 22/04/2017)

Matheiu Boisvert (1992) A Comparison of the Early Forms of Buddhist and Christian Monastic Traditions. *Buddhist-Christian Studies*, Vol. 12 (1992), pp. 123-141. Available online at: https://www.jstor.org/stable/pdf/1389959.pdf (accessed 18/03/2017)

Siddhartha Gautama Buddha (author), D.J. Gogerly (translator) (1872) Four Short Suttas, translated by D. J. Gogerly, published posthumously. *Journal Asiatique our recuil de mémoires d'extraits et de notices relatifs a l'histoire , a la philosophie, aux langues et la littérature de peoples orientaux et publié par la Société Asiatique*, sixième série, tome XX. Kara.nîya-Metta-Sutta, The Discourse Named Kara.nîya-Metta, v. 3 – 8, pp. 230 – 231. Available online: http://www.sacred-texts.com/journals/ja/tbg.htm (accessed 24/03/2017)

Siddhartha Gautama Buddha (author), Max Müller (translator) (1881) *The Dhammapada, a Collection of Verses; being one of the canonical books of the Buddhists* (Oxford: The Clarendon Press). Available online at: http://www.sacred-texts.com/bud/sbe10/index.htm (accessed 05/05/2017)

Siddhartha Gautama Buddha (author), T.W. Rhys Davids (translator) (1881) *Buddhist Suttas, translated from the Pâli* (Oxford: The Clarendon Press). Available online at: http://www.sacred-texts.com/bud/sbe11/index.htm (accessed 05/05/2017)

Siddhartha Gautama Buddha (author), Henry Clarke Warren (translator) (1896) *Buddhism in Translations: Passages Selected from the Buddhist Sacred Books and Translated from the Original Pâli into English* (Cambridge, Mass.: Harvard University Press). Available online at: http://www.sacred-texts.com/bud/bits/index.htm (accessed 29/03/2017)

Siddhartha Gautama Buddha (author), Dawsonne Melanchthon Strong (translator) (1902) *The Udâna, Translated from the Pali* (London: Luzac & Co.). Available online at: http://sacred-texts.com/bud/udn/index.htm (accessed 05/05/2017)

Siddhartha Gautama Buddha (author), E.J. Thomas (translator) (1913) *Buddhist Scriptures: A Selection from the Pali with an Introduction* (London: John Murray). Available online at: http://www.sacred-texts.com/bud/busc/index.htm (accessed 17/04/2017)

Siddhartha Gautama Buddha (author), W.D.C. Wagiswara, K.J. Saunders (translators) (1920) *The Buddha's Way of Virtue* (A Translation of the Dhammapada) (London: J. Murray). Available online at: http://www.sacred-texts.com/bud/wov/index.htm (accessed 19/03/2017)

Siddhartha Gautama Buddha (author), Buddhaghosa (commentator), Daw Mya Tin (translator), Editorial Committee, Burma Tipitaka Association (editors) (1986) *The Dhammapada: Verses and Stories* (Rangoon, Burma). Available online at: http://www.tipitaka.net/tipitaka/dhp/ (accessed 28/04/2017)

Siddhartha Gautama Buddha (author), Acharya Buddharakkhita (translator) (1996) *The Dhammapada: The Buddha's Path of Wisdom* (Kandy, Sri Lanka: Buddhist Publication Society). Available online at: http://www.accesstoinsight.org/tipitaka/kn/dhp/dhp.intro.budd.html (accessed 28/04/2017)

John Bunyan (1853) *The Pilgrim's Progress From This World to That Which is to Come; Delivered under the Similitude of a Dream* (Auburn: Derby & Miller; Buffalo: Geo. H. Derby and Co.). Available online at: https://www.ccel.org/ccel/bunyan/pilgrim.iv.v.html (accessed 05/05/2017)

Sir Richard Francis Burton (1893) *Personal Narrative of a Pilgrimage to Al-Madinah and Meccah, Volume I* (Memorial Edition) (London: Tylston and Edwards). Available online at: http://www.gutenberg.org/ebooks/4657 ; https://archive.org/details/in.ernet.dli.2015.38756 (accessed 28/04/2017)

Paul Carus (1894) *Buddha, The Gospel* (Chicago: The Open Court Publishing Company), Jetavana, The Vihara. Available online at: http://www.sacred-texts.com/bud/btg/index.htm (accessed 17/03/2017)

Paul Carus (1915) *The Gospel of Buddha Compiled from Ancient Records* (Chicago, London: The Open Court Publishing Company)

Robert Chalmers (translator), E.B. Cowell (editor) (1895) *The Jātaka, or Stories of the Buddha's Former Births, Volume I* (Cambridge: Cambridge University Press). Available online at: http://www.sacred-texts.com/bud/j1/index.htm (accessed 19/03/2017)

William C. Chittick (1975/1976) Ibn 'Arabi's own summary of the *Fusûs*, "The Imprint of the Bezels of the Wisdom". The translation first appeared in Sophia Perennis (*Tehran*) Vol. 1, No. 2 (Autumn 1975) and Vol. 2, No. 1 (Spring 1976). It was reprinted in the *Journal of the Muhyiddin Ibn 'Arabi Society* Vol. 1, 1982. Available online at: http://www.ibnarabisociety.org/articlespdf/naqshalfusus.pdf (accessed 15/03/2017).

William C. Chittick (1993) The Spiritual Path of Love in Ibn al-'Arabi and Rumi. *Mystics Quarterly*, Vol. 19, No. 1 (March 1993), pp. 4-16. Available online at: https://www.jstor.org/stable/pdf/20717149.pdf (accessed 15/03/2017).

William C. Chittick (2005) *The Sufi Doctrines of Rumi* (Bloomington, Indiana: World Wisdom, Inc.)

Mark Cobb, Christina M Puchalski, Bruce Rumbold (2014) *Oxford Textbook of Spirituality in Healthcare* (Oxford: Oxford Univiersity Press)

Shashi Bhusan Dasgupta (1950) *An Introduction to Tāntric Buddhism* (Calcutta: University of Calcutta). Available online at: https://archive.org/details/in.ernet.dli.2015.28797?q=vajra (accessed 28/04/2017)

Émile Durkheim (author), Joseph Ward Swain (translator) (1915) *The Elementary Forms of the Religious Life* (London: George Allen & Unwin). Available online at: https://archive.org/details/elementaryformso00durk (accessed 28/04/2017). See also: http://www.gutenberg.org/ebooks/41360 (accessed 28/04/2017)

Glenys Eddy (2012) *Becoming Buddhist: Experiences of Socialization and Self-Transformation in Two Australian Buddhist Centres* (London: Continuum International Publ. Group)

Julius Eggeling (translator) (1900) *The Satapatha Brahmana, according to the text of the Mâdhyandina School, Part V* (Sacred Books of the East, Vol. 44) (Oxford: The Clarendon Press). Available online at: http://www.sacred-texts.com/hin/sbr/sbe44/index.htm (accessed 29/04/2017)

Jamshed K. Fozdar (1995) *The God of Buddha* (Ariccia: Casa Editrice Bahá'í Srl)

George Fox (1706) *Gospel Truth Demonstrated in A Collection of Doctrinal Books, given forth by that faithful minister of Jesus Christ, George Fox: containing principles essential to Christianity and salvation, held among the people called Quakers* (London: T. Sowle, in White-Hart-Court, in Gracious-Street). Available online at: http://www.hallvworthington.com/Original%20PDFs/Works_4_Doctrine1.pdf (accessed 03/05/2017)

Rupert Gethin (2011) Mindfulness: diverse perspectives on its meaning, origins, and multiple applications at the intersection of science and dharma. *Contemporary Buddhism: An Interdisciplinary Journal*, Vol. 12, 2011, Issue 1, pp. 263-279. Published online: 14 Jun 2011. Available online at: http://www.tandfonline.com/doi/full/10.1080/14639947.2011.564843?scroll=top&needAccess=true (accessed 20/03/2017)

Abū Hāmid Muhamad ibn Muhammad Al-Ghazālī (author), Claud Field (translator) (1909) *The Alchemy of Happiness* (London: J. Murray). Available online at: http://www.sacred-texts.com/isl/tah/index.htm (accessed 24/04/2017)

Abū Hāmid Muhamad ibn Muhammad Al-Ghazālī (author), W.H.T. Gairdner (1924) *Mishkât Al-Anwar (The Niche for Lights)* (London: Royal Asiatic Society). Available online at: http://www.sacred-texts.com/isl/mishkat/index.htm (accessed 24/04/2017)

Dwight Goddard (translator) (1932) *A Buddhist Bible: The Favorite Scriptures of the Zen Sect* (Thetford, Vermont). [First Edition; published in 1932 – copyright not renewed]. Available online at: http://www.sacred-texts.com/bud/bb/index.htm (accessed 19/03/2017)

S.A. Kapadia (1905) *The Teachings of Zoroaster, and The Philosophy of the Parsi Religion* (London: John Murray), p. 56. Available online at: http://www.sacred-texts.com/zor/toz/index.htm (accessed 21/04/2017)

Shree Shreemat Krishnadasa Kaviraja Goswamee (author), Nihar Ranjan Banerjee (translator) (1925) *Shree Shree Chaitanya Charitamritam* (Calcutta: Bhudeb Publishing House), p. 206. Available online at: https://archive.org/details/in.ernet.dli.2015.20750 (accessed 28/03/2017).

Sri Sri Krishnadasa Kaviraja Goswamin (author) Sanjib Kumar Chaudhari (translator) (1954) *Sri Sri Chaitanya Charitamrita* (Calcutta: Biraj Mohan De). Available online at: https://archive.org/details/in.ernet.dli.2015.425626 (accessed 30/03/2017)

Shree Shreemad Jeeva Goswāmi (commentator), Bhaktisiddhānta Sarasvatī Goswāmi (translator, commentator) (1932) *Srī Brahma-Samhitā (Shree Brahma-Samhitā)* (Madras: Shree Gaudiya Math). Available online at: https://archive.org/details/brahmasamhita (accessed 03/05/2017).

Satsvarūpa Dāsa Gosvāmī (2003) *Prabhupāda: Your Ever Well-Wisher* (Watford: The Bhaktivedanta Book Trust)

Akira Hirakawa (2007) *A History of Indian Buddhism: From Śākyamuni to Early Mahāyāna* (Delhi: Motilal Banarsidass)

Qamar-ul Huda (2003) *Striving for Divine Union: Spiritual Exercises for Suhrawardī Sūfis* (London: RoutledgeCurzon)

Talal Itani (2014) *The Quran in English* (Dallas, Tex.: ClearQuran). Available online at: http://www.clearquran.com/ ; http://www.quranful.com/ (accessed 12/05/2017)

Thomas à Kempis (author), William Benham (translator) (1886) *The Imitation of Christ* (London: Elliot Stock). Available online at: http://www.sacred-texts.com/chr//ioc/index.htm (accessed 17/03/2017)

H. Kern (1884) *Saddharma-Pundarîka or, The Lotus of the True Law.* Sacred Books of the East (Clarendon Press: Oxford), Vol XXI, Chapter XXIV, v. 25 – 26. Available online at: http://www.sacred-texts.com/bud/lotus/index.htm (accessed 25/03/2017)

The King James Version (KJV) (1611), also known as the Authorized Version (AV), or the King James Bible (KJB). URL: http://www.gutenberg.org/ebooks/10 (accessed 05/05/2017)

Leonard Lewisohn (2015) Sufism's religion of love, from Rābi'a to Ibn 'Arabī. In Lloyd Ridgeon (editor) (2015) *The Cambridge Companion to Sufism* (Cambridge: Cambridge University Press)

St. Ignatius of Loyola (Íñigo López de Loyola) (author), Elder Mullan (translator) (1914) *Spiritual Exercises of St. Ignatius of Loyola* (New York: Kennedy). Available online at: http://www.sacred-texts.com/chr/seil/ (accessed 29/04/2017)

Madhvācārya (Ānanda Tīrtha) (author), S. Subba Rau (translator) (1904) *The Vedanta-Sutras with the Commentary by Sri Madhwacharya – A Complete Translation* (Madras: Thompson & Co. at the 'Minerva' Press). Available online at: https://archive.org/details/BrahmasutraMadhvaEnglish (accessed 21/04/2017)

'Allāmah Majlisī (author) *Bihār al-Anwār*. See: 'Merits of 'Tasbih' of Syeda Fatema Zehra (a.s)', *Duas.org*. Available online at: https://www.duas.org/tasbihzehra.htm (accessed 15/04/2017)

Svayambhuva Manu (author), George Bühler (translator) (1886) *The Laws of Manu, Translated with Extracts from Seven Commentaries* (Oxford: Clarendon Press). Available online at: http://www.sacred-texts.com/hin/manu.htm ; https://archive.org/details/lawsofmanu00bh (accessed 16/03/2017)

Freda Matchett (2014) *Krsna: Lord or Avatara?: The Relationship Between Krsna and Visnu* (London: Routledge)

Friedrich Max Müller (1879) *The Upanishads, Part 2* (Oxford: The Clarendon Press). Available online at: https://archive.org/details/upanishads01ml (accessed 05/05/2017)

Bhikkhu Ñānamoli, Bhikkhu Bodhi (translators) (2015) *The Middle Length Discourses of the Buddha: A Translation of the Majjhima-Nikaya* (Boston: Wisdom Publications, in association with the Barre Center for Buddhist Studies). Available online at: http://www.wisdompubs.org/landing/satipatthana-sutta (accessed 21/03/2017)

P. Lakshmi Narasu (1907) *The Essence of Buddhism* (Madras: Srinivasa Varadachari), pp. 54 – 55. Available online at: https://archive.org/details/essenceofbuddhis00laksrich (accessed 30/03/2017)

Richard Laurence (translator) (1883) *The Book of Enoch The Prophet, Translated from the Ethiopic Ms. In the Bodleian Library* (London: Kegan Paul, Trench & Co.). Available online at: http://www.sacred-texts.com/bib/bep/index.htm (accessed 30/04/2017)

Donald Lopez (2004) *Buddhist Scriptures* (London: Penguin)

Seyyed Hossein Nasr, Caner K. Dagli, Maria Massi Dakake, Joseph E.B. Lumbard and Mohammed Rustom (2015) *The Study Quran: A New Translation and Commentary* (New York, NY: HarperCollins Publishers)

Ian Richard Netton (2000) *Sufi Ritual: The Parallel Universe* (Richmond, England: Curzon Press)

Nicodemus, Makarios, G.E.H. Palmer, Philip Sherrard, Kallistos (1979) *The Philokalia of the Neptic Saints gathered from our Holy Theophoric Father, through which, by means of the philosophy of ascetic practice and contemplation, the intellect is purified, illumined, and made perfect* (London; Boston: Faber and Faber), A Discourse on Abba Philimon. The Philokalia was first compiled by St. Nikodemos of the Holy Mountain and St. Makarios of Corinth and published in 1782. Available online at: http://desertfathers.blogspot.com/2011/06/abba-philimonexcerpts-from-philokalia.html (accessed 15/04/2017)

Nimatullahi Sufi Order (2011-2014) *Spiritual Method, Nimatullahi Sufi Order*. Available online at: http://www.nimatullahi.org/our-order/practices/spiritual-method.php (accessed 12/04/2017)

Kaiten Nukariya (1913) *The Religion of the Samurai: A Study of Zen Philosophy and Discipline in China and Japan* (Auckland: The Floating Press). Available online at: http://www.sacred-texts.com/bud/rosa/index.htm (accessed 19/03/2017)

Yejitsu Okusa (1915) *Principal Teachings of The True Sect of Pure Land* (Kyōto: The Ōtaniha Hongwanji). Available online at: http://www.sacred-texts.com/bud/ptpl/index.htm (accessed 30/12/2016)

Edward Henry Palmer (translator) (1880) *The sacred books of the east translated by various oriental scholars and edited by F. Max Müller. Vol. 6, The Qur'ân, Part I: I-XVI & Vol. 9, Part II: XVII-CXIV* (Oxford: At the Clarendon Press). Available online at: http://www.sacred-texts.com/isl/sbe06/index.htm (accessed 15/03/2017)

William Penn (1792) *Fruits of a father's love: being the advice of William Penn to his children, relating to their civil and religious conduct* (Philadelphia: Printed by Benjamin Johnson). Available online at: http://www.qhpress.org/quakerpages/qwhp/qwhp.htm (accessed 31/12/2016)

William Penn (1857) *Primitive Christianity Revived in the faith and practice of the people called Quakers; written in testimony to the present dispensation of God through them to the world; that prejudices may be removed, the simple informed, the well-inclined encouraged, and the truth and its innocent friends rightly represented* (Philadelphia: Miller & Burlock). Available online at: http://www.strecorsoc.org/penn/title.html (accessed 04/05/2017)

Muhammad Marmaduke Pickthall (1938) *The Meaning of the Glorious Quran* (Hyderabad-Deccan: Government Central Press). Available online at: http://www.sacred-texts.com/isl/pick/ (accessed 12/05/2017)

His Divine Grace A.C. Bhaktivedanta Swami Prabhupada (1968a) *Bhagavad-Gītā As It Is* (New York: ISKCON). Available online at: https://asitis.com/9 (accessed 28/04/2017)

His Divine Grace A.C. Bhaktivedanta Swami Prabhupāda (1968b) *The Science of Self-Realization* (Los Angeles: Bhaktivedanta Book Trust). Available online at: http://www.krishnapath.org/free-ebooks-audiobooks-of-srila-prabhupada/the-science-of-self-realization/ (accessed 15/04/2017)

His Divine Grace A.C. Bhaktivedanta Swami Prabhupāda (1974) Maha-mantra Includes Lord Rama, A lecture by His Divine Grace A.C. Bhaktivedanta Swami Prabhupāda, delivered in Bombay, April 1, 1974, *The Prabhupada Connection*. Available online at: http://www.prabhupadaconnect.com/Lecture75.html (accessed 15/04/2017)

His Divine Grace A.C. Bhaktivedenta Swami Prabhupāda (1977) *Śrīmad Bhaġavatam: Tenth Canto: "the summum bonum": (part one--chapters 1-5): with the original Sanskrit text, its Roman transliteration, synonyms, translation and elaborate purports* (New York: Bhaktivedanta Book Trust)

J. M. Rodwell (1876) *El-Kor'ân, or, The Koran* (London: B. Quaritch). URL: http://www.sacred-texts.com/isl/qr/index.htm; http://www.gutenberg.org/ebooks/3434 (accessed 05/05/2017)

George Sale (1734) *The Koran, commonly called the Alcoran of Mohammed: translated into English immediately from the original Arabic; with explanatory notes, taken from the most approved commentators. To which is prefixed a preliminary discourse* (London: J. Wilcox). Available online at: http://web.archive.org/web/20130510213544/http://arthursbookshelf.com/koran/The%20Qur'an%20tranlated%20oby%20George%20Sale-h.html ; http://www.gutenberg.org/ebooks/7440 ; http://oll.libertyfund.org/people/4376 (accessed 12/05/2017).

Mark Sedgwick (2016) *Western Sufism: From the Abbasids to the New Age* (Oxford: Oxford University Press)

Soyen Shaku (author), Daisetz Teitaro Suzuki (translator) (1906) *Sermons of a Buddhist Abbot [Zen for Americans]* (Chicago: Open Court Publishing Co.). Available online at: http://www.sacred-texts.com/bud/zfa/index.htm (accessed 19/03/2017)

Shinrin Shōnin (author), S. Yamabe, L. Adams Beck (translators) (1921) *Buddhist Psalms translated from the Japanese of Shinran Shōnin* (London: John Murray). Available online at: http://www.sacred-texts.com/bud/bups/index.htm (accessed 24/04/2017)

Daisetz Teitaro Suzuki (1908) *Outlines of Mahayana Buddhism* (Chicago: Open Court). Available online at: https://archive.org/details/outlinesofmahayoosuzurich/ (accessed 11/04/2017)

Daisetz Teitaro Suzuki (1935) *Manual of Zen Buddhism* (Kyoto: Pl. XV. Kyoto). Available online at: http://www.sacred-texts.com/bud/mzb/index.htm (accessed 17/04/2017). The book is in the public domain as it was not properly copyrighted in its earlier editions.

Daisetz Teitaro Suzuki (1957) *Mysticism, Christian and Buddhist* (Volume Twelve of the World Perspective Series) (New York: Harper & Brothers Publishers)

Sahl ibn 'Abd Allāh al-Tustarī (author), Annabel Keeler, Ali Keeler (translators) (2011) *Tafsīr al-Tustarī* (Great Commentaries on the Holy Qur'ān) (Louisville, KY: Fons Vitae). Available online at: https://archive.org/details/TafsirAlQuranAlAzimBySahlAlTustari/ (accessed 12/04/2017)

Tertullian (author), Allan Menzies (translator) (1885-96) *Ante-Nicene Fathers, Vol. III.* (Grand Rapids, Michigan: WM. B. Eerdmans Publishing Company). Available online at: http://www.sacred-texts.com/chr/ecf/003/index.htm (accessed 30/03/2017)

Vālmīki (author), Ralph T.H. Griffith (translator) (1870-74) *The Rámáyan of Válmíki translated into English verse* (London: Trübner). Available online at: http://www.sacred-texts.com/hin/rama/ (accessed 11/03/2017)

Vālmīki (author), Manmatha Nath Dutt (translator) (1893) *The Ramayana, translated into English Prose from the Original Sanskrit of Valmiki, Volume VI. Yuddha Kandam* (Calcutta: Elysium Press). Available online at: https://archive.org/details/Valmiki_Ramayana_English_Prose_Translation_7_volumes_by_Manmatha_Nath_Dutt_1891_to_1894 (accessed 07/05/2017)

Various (authors), Rutherford H. Platt, Jr. (translator) (1926) *The Lost Books of the Bible* (New York: Alpha House). Available online at: http://sacred-texts.com/bib/lbob/index.htm (accessed 05/05/2017)

Various (authors), Rutherford H. Platt, Jr. (editor) (1926) *The Forgotten Books of Eden* (New York: L. Copeland). Available online at: http://www.sacred-texts.com/bib/fbe/index.htm (accessed 23/04/2017)

Veda-Vyāsa (author), Wilkins (translator) (1785) *The Bhagvat-Geetā or Dialogues of Kreeshna and Arjoon* (London: C. Nourse). Available online at: http://oll.libertyfund.org/titles/wilkins-the-bhagvat-geeta-or-dialogues-of-kreeshna-and-arjoon (accessed 05/05/2017)

Veda-Vyāsa (author), Horace Hayman Wilson (translator) (1840) *The Vishnu Purána: A System of Hindu Mythology and Tradition, Translated from the Original Sanscrit* (London: John Murray). Available online at: http://www.sacred-texts.com/hin/vp/index.htm (accessed 19/03/2017)

Veda-Vyāsa (author), Kisari Mohan Ganguli (translator) (1883-96) *The Mahabharata of Krishna-Dwaipayana Vyasa* (Calcutta: Bharata Press). Available online at: http://www.sacred-texts.com/hin/maha/index.htm (accessed 20/03/2017)

Veda-Vyāsa (author), Sir Edwin Arnold (translator) (1885) *The Song celestial or Bhagavad-gítá (from the Mahābhârata), Translated from the Sanskrit Text* (London: Trübner & Co.). Available online at: http://www.sacred-texts.com/hin/gita/index.htm (accessed 16/03/2017)

Veda-Vyāsa (author), Ralph T.H. Griffith (translator) (1896) *The Hymns of the Rig-Veda, translated with a popular commentary* (Benares: E.J. Lazaarus). Available online at: http://www.sacred-texts.com/hin/rigveda/index.htm (accessed 12/04/2017)

Veda-Vyāsa (author), Swami Swarupananda (translator) (1909) *Srimad-Bhagavad-Gita* (Mayavati, Himalayas: Prabuddha Bharata Press). Available online at: http://www.sacred-texts.com/hin/sbg/index.htm (accessed 19/03/2017)

Veda-Vyāsa (author), Ernest Wood, S.V. Subhrahmanyam (translators) (1911) *The Garuda Purāna (Sāroddhāra) with English Translation* (Allahabad: Pānini Office). Available online at: http://www.sacred-texts.com/hin/gpu/gpu00.htm (accessed 05/05/2017)

Veda-Vyāsa (author), K. Narayanasvami Aiyar (translator) (1914) *Thirty Minor Upanishads* (Madras: Annie Besant at the Vasantā Press). Available online at: http://www.sacred-texts.com/hin/tmu/tmu00.htm (accessed 17/04/2017)

Veda-Vyāsa (author), Swami Vijñanananda (translator) (1921-22) *The S'rîmad Devî Bhâgawatam.* Available online at: http://www.sacred-texts.com/hin/db/index.htm (accessed 16/03/2017)

Veda-Vyāsa (author), S. Subba Rau (translator) (1928) *Srimad Bhagavatam, Translated into Easy English Prose, embodying the interpretations of the Three leading Schools of Thought, (Advaita, Visistadvaita and Dvaita)* (Tirupati: Sri Vyasa Press). Available online at: https://archive.org/details/in.ernet.dli.2015.272624 (accessed 22/04/2017)

Veda-Vyāsa (author), Barbara Stoler Miller (translator) (2004) *The Bhagavad-Gita, Krishna's Counsel in Time of War* (New York: Bantam Books)

Veda-Vyāsa (author), Eknath Easwaran (translator) (2007) *The Bhagavad Gita* (Tomales, CA: Nilgiri Press)

John Wesley (author), Edward H. Sugden (editor) (1920), *Wesley's Standard Sermons, consisting of Forty-Four Discourses, Published in Four Volumes, Volume I* (Nashville: M.E. Church, South). Available online at: http://www.godrules.net/library/wesley/wesley.htm#john-wesley-sermons ; https://archive.org/details/10305045.76.emory.edu (accessed 03/05/2017)

Robert J. Wilkinson (2015) *Tetragrammaton: Western Christians and the Hebrew Name of God: From the Beginnings to the Seventeenth Century* (Boston: BRILL)

John Woodroffe (Arthur Avalon), Kazi Dawa-Samdup (editors) (1919) *Shrīchakrasambhāra Tantra: A Buddhist Tantra, Tantrik Texts, Vol. VII* (London, Calcutta: Luzac & Co.). Available online at: https://archive.org/details/Tantric_Texts_Series_Edited_by_Arthur_Avalon_John_Woodroffe?q=vajr a (accessed 28/04/2017)

Sidi Fadi Qutub Zada (2014) The Fiqh of Voluntary (Nafl) Prayers, *SeekersHub*, July 14, 2014. Available online at: http://seekershub.org/ans-blog/2014/07/14/the-fiqh-of-voluntary-nafl-prayers/ (accessed 18/03/2017)

Waleed Ziad (2017) Transporting Knowledge in the Durrani Empire: Two Manuals of Naqshbandi-Mujaddidi Sufi Practice, In *Afghanistan's Islam: From Conversion to the Taliban* (Oakland, California: University of California Press). Available online at: http://www.jstor.org/stable/pdf/10.1525/j.ctt1kc6k3q.11.pdf (accessed 13/04/2017)

Zoroaster (author), James Darmesteter (translator) (1882) *The Zend Avesta, Part II: The The Sîrôzahs, Yasts and Nyâyis* (Oxford: Oxford University Press). Available online at: http://sacred-texts.com/zor/sbe23/index.htm (accessed 05/05/2017)

Zoroaster (author), Maneckji Nusservanji Dhalla (translator), A.V. Williams Jackson (editor) (1908) *The Nyaishes or Zoroastrian Litanies: Avestan Text with the Pahlavi, Sanskrit, Persian and Gujarati Versions, Khordah Avesta, Part I* (New York: The Columbia University Press). Available online at: http://www.sacred-texts.com/zor/sbe23/ka.htm (accessed 15/04/2017)

Other Sources

James Allen (1907) *From Poverty to Power: The Path to prosperity and The Way of Peace* (Albuquerque, NM: Sun Pub. Co.). Available online at: http://www.gutenberg.org/ebooks/10740 (accessed 22/02/2017)

Arthur Llewellyn Basham (1954) *The wonder that was India: a survey of the culture of the Indian subcontinent before the coming of the Muslims* (New York: Grove Press)

NJ Bridgewater (2017c) Recommended Charities & Charitable Organizations. *Equanimity Blog*, February 6, 2017. Available online at: https://fivewaystobe.wordpress.com/2017/02/06/recommended-charities-charitable-organizations/ (accessed 28/04/2017)

Yan Y. Dhyansky (1987) The Indus Valley Origin of a Yoga Practice. *Artibus Asiae*, Vol. 48, No. 1/2 (1987), pp. 89-108. Available online at: http://www.jstor.org/stable/3249853 (accessed 08/03/2017)

The Editors of Encyclopædia Britannica (2010) Amitabha: Buddhism. *Encyclopædia Britannica*. Available online at: https://www.britannica.com/topic/Amitabha-Buddhism (accessed 30/12/2016)

The Editors of Encyclopædia Britannica (2015) Ishvara (article), *Encyclopædia Britannica*, last updated 2-19-2015. Available online at: https://global.britannica.com/topic/Ishvara (accessed 25/03/2017)

The Editors of Encyclopædia Britannica (1998) Vajra, Buddhist Ritual Object. *Encyclopædia Britannica Online*. Available online at: https://www.britannica.com/topic/vajra (accessed 28/04/2017)

Louis H. Feldman, Meyer Reinhold (1996) *Jewish Life and Thought Among Greeks and Romans: Primary Readings* (Minneapolis: Fortress Press)

Lexi Finnigan (2016) Number of UK Muslims exceeds three million for first time. *The Telegraph*, 31 Jan 2016 4:59PM GMT. Available online at: http://www.telegraph.co.uk/news/uknews/12132641/Number-of-UK-Muslims-exceeds-three-million-for-first-time.html (accessed 18/03/2017)

Michael J. Gelb (2014) *Creativity on Demand: How to Ignite and Sustain the Fire of Genius* (Boulder, CO: Sounds True, Inc.)

Russell E. Gmirkin (2006) *Berossus and Genesis, Manetho and Exodus: Hellenistic Histories and the Date of the Pentateuch* (New York: Bloomsbury Publishing)

Francis Hamilton (1819) *Genealogies Tables of the Hindus, extracted from their Sacred Writings; with an Introduction and Alphabetical Index* (Edinburgh: Printed for the Author). Available online at: https://archive.org/details/genealogieshindoounkngoog (accessed 11/03/2017)

Gary W. Hartz (2012) *Spirituality and Mental Health: Clinical Applications* (Hoboken: Taylor and Francis)

Napoleon Hill (1938) *Think and Grow Rich* (Meriden, Conn.: The Ralston Society). Available online at: http://www.sacred-texts.com/nth/tgr/tgr00.htm (accessed 17/04/2017). Public domain in the US as its copyright was not renewed at the US Copyright Office in a timely fashion.

John Horgan (2013) Scientific Materialism "Almost Certainly False"? *Scientific American*, January 30, 2013. Available online at: https://blogs.scientificamerican.com/cross-check/is-scientific-materialism-almost-certainly-false/ (accessed 19/03/2017)

Robert C. Koons, George Bealer (2010) *The Waning of Materialism* (Oxford: Oxford University Press)

Michael Lipka (2017) Muslims and Islam: Key findings in the U.S. and around the world. *PewResearch Center*. Available online at: http://www.pewresearch.org/fact-tank/2017/02/27/muslims-and-islam-key-findings-in-the-u-s-and-around-the-world/ (accessed 18/03/2017)

Robert Madigan (2015) *How Memory Works—And How to Make It Work for You* (New York: Guilford Publications)

Carol A. Miller (2013) *Fast Facts for Health Promotion in Nursing: Promoting Wellness in a Nutshell* (New York: Springer Pub. Co.)

V.S. Misra (2007) *Ancient Indian Dynasties* (Mumbai: Bharatiya Vidya Bhavan)

New World Encyclopaedia (NEW) (2016) Bhagavad Gita (article), *New World Encyclopedia*. Available online at: http://www.newworldencyclopedia.org/entry/Bhagavad_Gita (accessed 11/03/2017)

B.A. Robinson (2015) Numbers of adherents of major religions, their geographical distribution, date founded, and sacred texts, *Religious Tolerance – Ontario Consultants on Religious Tolerance*. Last update: 2015-DEC-02. Available online at: http://www.religioustolerance.org/worldrel.htm (accessed 18/03/2017)

Upinder Singh, Nayanjot Lahiri (2009) *Ancient India: New Research* (Delhi: Oxford University Press)

George Smith (1876) *The Chaldean Account of Genesis* (London: S. Low, Marston, Searle, and Rivington). Available online at: http://www.sacred-texts.com/ane/caog/index.htm (accessed 12/03/2017)

Noah Webster; Thomas Herbert Russell, Albert C. Bean, L. Brent Vaughan (1913) *Webster's modern English dictionary unabridged, comprising the authoritative unabridged dictionary by Noah Webster, LL. D.* (New York Syndicate Pub. Co.). Available online at: http://mikefinch.com/md/art/dm.htm (accessed 16/03/2017)

∞∞∞∞∞∞∞∞∞∞∞∞∞∞∞∞∞∞∞∞∞∞∞∞∞∞∞

References

1 René Descartes (author), John Veitch (translator) (1910) *Discourse on the method of rightly conducting reason, and seeking truth in the sciences* (Chicago: The Open Court Publishing Co.), Part 4. Available online at: https://ebooks.adelaide.edu.au/d/descartes/rene/d44dm/index.html (last updated 17/12/2014 13:08) (accessed 15/03/2017).

2 René Descartes (author), John Veitch (translator) (1910), Part 4.

3 Thomas Aquinas (author), Fathers of the English Dominican Province (translators) (1920) *Summa Theologica* (London: Burns Oates & Washbourne), First part, a, Question 2, Article 3. Available online at: http://web.mnstate.edu/gracyk/courses/web%20publishing/aquinasFiveWays.htm (accessed 15/03/2017).

4 Critics of Sufism, such as Ibn Taymiyyah (d. 1328 CE), have argued that the hadith has a weak chain of transmission. However, as Algar (2002) points out, there is nothing in the content of the hadith to warrant its rejection, and it is cited in a number of Sufi works. See: Hamid Algar (2002) Hadith iv. In Sufism, *Encyclopædia Iranica* (Online Edition). Available online at: http://www.iranicaonline.org/articles/hadith-iv (accessed 15/03/2017).

5 Jalālu'd-Dīn Muhammad Rūmī (author), Reynold A. Nicholson (translator) (1898) *Selected Poems from the Divani Shamsi Tabriz* (London: Cambridge University Press). Available online at: https://sourcebooks.fordham.edu/source/1270rumi-poems1.asp (accessed 15/03/2017).

6 William C. Chittick (1993) The Spiritual Path of Love in Ibn al-'Arabi and Rumi. *Mystics Quarterly*, Vol. 19, No. 1 (March 1993), pp. 4-16. Available online at: https://www.jstor.org/stable/pdf/20717149.pdf (accessed 15/03/2017).

7 Qur'ān 57:4 (Rodwell translation).

8 Chittick (1993).

9 Qur'ān 28:88 (Palmer translation). Edward Henry Palmer (translator) (1880) *The sacred books of the east translated by various oriental scholars and edited by F. Max Müller. Vol. 6, The Qur'ân, Part I: I-XVI & Vol. 9, Part II: XVII-CXIV.*, (Oxford: At the Clarendon Press). Available online at: http://www.sacred-texts.com/isl/sbe06/index.htm (accessed 15/03/2017).

10 William C. Chittick (2005) *The Sufi Doctrines of Rumi* (Bloomington, Indiana: World Wisdom, Inc.), p. 37.

11 Genesis 1:26 (King James Version).

12 William C. Chittick (1975/1976) Ibn 'Arabi's own summary of the *Fusûs*, "The Imprint of the Bezels of the Wisdom". The translation first appeared in Sophia Perennis (*Tehran*) Vol. 1, No. 2 (Autumn 1975) and Vol. 2, No. 1 (Spring 1976). It was reprinted in the *Journal of the Muhyiddin Ibn 'Arabi Society* Vol. 1, 1982. Available online at: http://www.ibnarabisociety.org/articlespdf/naqshalfusus.pdf (accessed 15/03/2017).

13 Qur'ān 2:31 (Rodwell translation).

[14] Liezi (author), Lionel Giles (translator) (1912) *Taoist Teachings Translated from the Book of Lieh-Tzü, with Introduction and Notes*, Book I: Cosmogony, p. 25. Available online at: http://www.sacred-texts.com/tao/tt/index.htm (accessed 16/03/2017).

[15] Svayambhuva Manu (author), George Bühler (translator) (1886) *The Laws of Manu, Translated with Extracts from Seven Commentaries* (Oxford: Clarendon Press). Available online at: http://www.sacred-texts.com/hin/manu.htm ; https://archive.org/details/lawsofmanu00bh (accessed 16/03/2017).

[16] Noah Webster; Thomas Herbert Russell, Albert C. Bean, L. Brent Vaughan (1913) *Webster's modern English dictionary unabridged, comprising the authoritative unabridged dictionary by Noah Webster, LL. D.* (New York Syndicate Pub. Co.). See: Definitions of Mediation. Available online at: http://mikefinch.com/md/art/dm.htm (accessed 16/03/2017).

[17] Georg Feuerstein (2006) Yoga and Meditation (Dhyana). *Moksha Journal – The Journal of Knowledge, Enlightenment & Freedom*, Issue I, 2006. Available online at: http://www.santosha.com/moksha/meditation1.html (accessed 16/03/2017).

[18] Veda-Vyāsa (author), Swami Vijñanananda (translator) (1921-22) *The S'rîmad Devî Bhâgawatam*, Book I, Chapter XVII, p. 63. Available online at: http://www.sacred-texts.com/hin/db/index.htm (accessed 16/03/2017).

[19] Veda-Vyāsa (author), Swami Vijñanananda (translator) (1921-22) *The S'rîmad Devî Bhâgawatam*, Book I, Chapter XVII, pp. 63 – 64.

[20] Paul Carus (1894) *Buddha, The Gospel* (Chicago: The Open Court Publishing Company), Jetavana, The Vihara. Available online at: http://www.sacred-texts.com/bud/btg/index.htm (accessed 17/03/2017).

[21] Patañjali (author), Ganganatha Jha (translator) (1907) *The Yoga-darśana: The Sutras of Patañjali with the Bhāsya of Vyasa* (Bombay: Rajaram Tukaram Tatya), p. 2. Available online at: https://archive.org/details/yogadaranasutra00patagoog (accessed 04/03/2017).

[22] J.H. Woods (1927/2003) *The Yoga-Sutra of Patanjali* (New York, NY: Dover).

[23] Klaus B. Bærentsen (2015) Patanjali and neuroscientific research on meditation. *Frontiers in Psychology*, Vol 6, Jul 3, 2015. Available online at: http://journal.frontiersin.org.oxfordbrookes.idm.oclc.org/article/10.3389/fpsyg.2015.00915/full#B42 (accessed 16/03/2017).

[24] Veda-Vyāsa (author), Sir Edwin Arnold (translator) (1885) *The Song celestial or Bhagavad-gîtâ (from the Mahâbhârata), Translated from the Sanskrit Text* (London: Trübner & Co.), Chapter VII – Of Religion by Devotion to the One Supreme God. Available online at: http://www.sacred-texts.com/hin/gita/index.htm (accessed 16/03/2017).

[25] Krishna (author) Sir Edwin Arnold (translator) (1885), Chapter V – Of Religion by Renouncing Fruit of Works.

[26] Friedrich Max Müller (1879) *The Upanishads, Part 2* (Oxford: The Clarendon Press), Maitrâyana Brâhmana Upanishad, Fourth Prapâthaka, v. 4, p. 301. Available online at: https://archive.org/details/upanishads01ml (accessed 16/03/2017).

[27] NJ Bridgewater (2017) *Mindfulness: Five Ways to Achieve Real Happiness, True Knowledge and Inner Peace* (Abergavenny: Jaha Publishing), p. 6.

[28] NJ Bridgewater (2017), p. 7.

[29] Thomas à Kempis (author), William Benham (translator) (1886) *The Imitation of Christ* (London: Elliot Stock), Chapter XVI, v. 2- 3. Available online at: http://www.sacred-texts.com/chr//ioc/index.htm (accessed 17/03/2017).

[30] Zhuangzi (author), Herbert Allen Giles (translator) (1889) *Chuang Tzu, Mystic, Moralist, and Social Reformer* (London: B. Quaritch), Chapter IV, pp. 38 – 45. Available online at: https://archive.org/details/chuangtzumysticm00chua (accessed 16/03/2017).

[31] Abū-Muhammad Muslihu'd-Dīn bin 'Abdu'llāh Shīrāzī (Saadi) (author), Sir Edwin Arnold (translator) (1899) *The Gulistân of Musle-huddeen Shaik Sady of Sheeraz* (London: T. Burleigh), Story 9. Available online at: http://www.sacred-texts.com/isl/gulistan.txt (accessed 17/03/2017).

32 Shamsu'd-Dīn Muhammad Hāfez-e-Shīrāzī (author), Gertrude Lowthian Bell (translator) (1897) *Teachings of Hafiz* (London: W. Heinemann), XXIX. Available online at: http://www.sacred-texts.com/isl/hafiz.htm (accessed 17/03/2017).

33 Yan Y. Dhyansky (1987) The Indus Valley Origin of a Yoga Practice. *Artibus Asiae*, Vol. 48, No. 1/2 (1987), pp. 89-108. Available online at: http://www.jstor.org/stable/3249853 (accessed 08/03/2017).

34 Dhyansky (1987).

35 Russell E. Gmirkin (2006) *Berossus and Genesis, Manetho and Exodus: Hellenistic Histories and the Date of the Pentateuch* (New York: Bloomsbury Publishing), p. 109.

36 Extract from Alexander Polyhistor, quoted in George Smith (1876) *The Chaldean Account of Genesis* (London: S. Low, Marston, Searle, and Rivington), Chapter III – Chaldean Legens Transmitted through Berosus and Other Ancient Authors, pp. 39 – 40. Available online at: http://www.sacred-texts.com/ane/caog/index.htm (accesssed 12/03/2017).

37 Freda Matchett (2014) *Krsna: Lord or Avatara?: The Relationship Between Krsna and Visnu* (London: Routledge), p. 159.

38 NJ Bridgewater (2017) *Mindfulness: Five Ways to Achieve Real Happiness, True Knowledge and Inner Peace* (Abergavenny: Jaha Publishing), pp. 68 – 69.

39 Vālmīki (author), Ralph T.H. Griffith (translator) (1870-74) *The Rámáyan of Válmíki translated into English verse* (London: Trübner), Canto CV. Available online at: http://www.sacred-texts.com/hin/rama/ (accessed 11/03/2017).

40 Veda-Vyāsa (author), Sir Edwin Arnold (translator) (1885) *The Song celestial or Bhagavad-gítâ (from the Mahâbhârata), Translated from the Sanskrit Text* (London: Trübner & Co.), Chapter II – Of Doctrines. Available online at: http://www.sacred-texts.com/hin/gita/index.htm (accessed 11/03/2017).

41 New World Encyclopedia (NEW) (2016) Bhagavad Gita (article), *New World Encyclopedia*. Available online at: http://www.newworldencyclopedia.org/entry/Bhagavad_Gita (accessed 11/03/2017).

42 Arthur Llewellyn Basham (1954) *The wonder that was India: a survey of the culture of the Indian sub-continent before the coming of the Muslims* (New York: Grove Press), pp. 39 – 40.

43 Upinder Singh, Nayanjot Lahiri (2009) *Ancient India: New Research* (Delhi: Oxford University Press), p. 19.

44 Friedrich Max Müller (1879) *The Upanishads* (Oxford: The Clarendon Press), Khândogya-Upanishad, Seventeenth Khanda, v. 6, pp. 52 - 53. Available online at: https://archive.org/details/upanishads01ml (accessed 11/03/2017).

45 Müller (1879), p. 53.

46 Müller (1879), Thirteenth Khanda, v. 7, p. 47

47 Müller (1879), First Prapâthaka, First Khanda, v. 1, p. 1; Ninth Khanda, v. 4, p. 17.

48 Müller (1879), Talavakâra-Upanishad, First Khanda, v. 4 – 6; Second Khanda, v. 3 - 4, pp. 147 – 148.

49 Müller (1879), Kaushîtaki-Upanishad, 1 Adhyâya, v. 6 – 7, pp. 278 – 279.

50 See: Yoga (*Wikipedia* article). URL: https://en.wikipedia.org/wiki/Yoga (accessed 11/03/2017).

51 Geoffrey Samuel (2008) *The Origins of Yoga and Tantra* (Cambridge: Cambridge University Press), p. 8.

52 Śramana (*Wikipedia* article). URL: https://en.wikipedia.org/wiki/%C5%9Arama%E1%B9%87a (accessed 11/03/2017).

53 Patañjali (author), Ganganatha Jha (translator) (1907) *The Yoga-darśana: The Sutras of Patañjali with the Bhāsya of Vyasa* (Bombay: Rajaram Tukaram Tatya), p. 1. Available online at: https://archive.org/details/yogadaranasutra00patagoog (accessed 04/03/2017).

54 Patañjali (author), Ganganatha Jha (translator) (1907), p. 2.

[55] Yoga_Sutras_of_Patanjali (*Wikipedia* article). URL: https://en.wikipedia.org/wiki/Yoga_Sutras_of_Patanjali (accessed 11/03/2017).

[56] Müller (1879), The *Vâgasaneyi-Samhitâ-Upanishad (Îsâvâsya/Îsâ-Upanishad)*, v. 11 – 12, 14 – 15, pp. 312 – 313.

[57] Hereward Carrington (1920) *Higher Psychical Development (Yoga Philosophy) an Outline of the Secret Hindu Teachings* (New York: Dodd, Mead and Company), p. 4. Available online at: https://archive.org/details/higherpsychicaloocarrgoog (accessed 04/03/2017).

[58] Carrington (1920), p. 5.

[59] Müller (1879), Aitareya-Âranyaka, Fourth Adhyâya, First Khanda, v. 1 – 2, p. 237.

[60] NJ Bridgewater (2017), pp. 19 – 22.

[61] Biography.com Editors (2015) Buddha Biography, Religious Figure (c. 600 BCE-c. 300 BCE), *Biography.com*. Last updated: January 24, 2015. Available online at: http://www.biography.com/people/buddha-9230587 (accessed 11/03/2017).

[62] Gautama Buddha (*Wikipedia* article). Available online at: https://en.wikipedia.org/wiki/Gautama_Buddha (accessed 11/03/2017).

[63] Gautama Buddha (*Wikipedia* article).

[64] V.S. Misra (2007) *Ancient Indian Dynasties* (Mumbai: Bharatiya Vidya Bhavan), pp. 283 – 8, 384. See also: The Buddha's Ancestors – The Gotamagotta (Gotama Family) of the Sakiya (Sakya) Clan. URL: http://theravada.triratna.info/Gotama-Family-Tree.html (accessed 11/03/2017).

[65] Francis Hamilton (1819) *Genealogies Tables of the Hindus, extracted from their Sacred Writings; with an Introduction and Alphabetical Index* (Edinburgh: Printed for the Author). Available online at: https://archive.org/details/genealogieshindoounkngoog (accessed 11/03/2017).

[66] Edith Holland (1918) *The Story of the Buddha* (London: George C. Harrap & Co.), p. 28.

[67] Holland (1918), pp. 39 – 45.

[68] Holland (1918), pp. 62 – 65.

[69] Paul Carus (1915) *The Gospel of Buddha Compiled from Ancient Records* (Chicago, London: The Open Court Publishing Company), p. 52. Available online at: http://www.gutenberg.org/ebooks/35895 (accessed 12/03/2017).

[70] NJ Bridgewater (2017), pp. 29 – 48.

[71] Alexander Wynne (2007) *The Origin of Buddhist Meditation* (London: Routledge), p. 24. Available online at: http://www.ahandfulofleaves.org/documents/The%20Origin%20of%20Buddhist%20Meditation_Alexa nde%20Wynne.pdf (accessed 12/03/2017).

[72] Arūpajhāna (*Wikipedia* article). Available online at: https://en.wikipedia.org/wiki/Ar%C5%ABpajh%C4%81na (accessed 12/03/2017).

[73] Wynn (2007).

[74] Venerable Pa-Auk Sayadaw (1995) *Mindfulness of Breathing & Four Elements Meditation* (Kuala Lumpur: Buddha Dharma Education Association, Inc.), p. 19. Available online at: http://www.buddhanet.net/pdf_file/fourelements.pdf (accessed 12/03/2017).

[75] Akira Hirakawa (2007) *A History of Indian Buddhism: From Śākyamuni to Early Mahāyāna* (Delhi: Motilal Banarsidass), p. 25.

[76] Plato (author), Benjamin Jowett (translator) (1910) *Socrates. Plato's apology of Socrates and Crito, with part of his Phaedo* (Portland, Maine: Thomas B. Mosher). Available online at: http://www.gutenberg.org/ebooks/1656 (accessed 14/03/2017).

[77] Plato (author), Benjamin Jowett (translator) (1910).

78 Plato (author), Benjamin Jowett (translator) (1921) *The Republic of Plato* (Oxford: The Clarendon Press), Book VI. Available online at: http://www.gutenberg.org/ebooks/1497 (accessed 14/03/2017).

79 Linda Johnsen (2016) *Lost Masters: Rediscovering the Mysticism of the Ancient Greek Philosophers* (Novato, California: New World Library), p. 2.

80 Johnsen (2016), p. 2.

81 Plotinus (author), Kenneth Sylvan Guthrie (translator (1918) *Plotinus, Complete Works, Vol. II. Amelio-Porphyrian Books, 22–33* (Grantwood, N.J.: Comparative Literature Press), Fifth Ennead, Book V, 11, p. 592. Available online at: http://www.gutenberg.org/ebooks/42930 (accessed 14/03/2017).

82 Pythagoras (Wikipedia article). Available online at: https://en.wikipedia.org/wiki/Pythagoras (accessed 14/03/2017).

83 Iamblichus (author), Thomas Taylor (translator) (1818) *Iamblichus' Life of Pythagoras or Pythagoric Life, accompanied by Fragments of the Ethical Writings of Certain Pythagoreans in the Doric Dialect; and a Collection of Pythagoric Sentences from Stobæus and Others, which are omitted by Gale in his Opuscula Mythologica, and have not been noticed by any editor* (London: J.M. Watkins), p. 28. Available online at: https://classicalastrologer.files.wordpress.com/2012/12/iamblichus-the-pythagorean-life-1.pdf (accessed 14/03/2017).

84 Christoph Riedweg (author), Steven Rendall, Andreas Schatzmann (translators) (2008) *Pythagoras: His Life, Teaching, and Influence* (Ithaca, NY; London: Cornell University Press), p. 33.

85 Florence M. Firth (translator) (1904) *The Golden Verses of Pythagoras, And Other Pythagorean Fragments* (London: Theosophical Publishing Society), v. 40 – 41. Available online at: http://sacred-texts.com/cla/gvp/index.htm (accessed 14/03/2017).

86 NJ Bridgewater (2017), pp. 98 – 99.

87 Pythagoreans celebrating sunrise, by Fyodor Bronnikov (1827 – 1902). Available online at: https://upload.wikimedia.org/wikipedia/commons/5/56/Bronnikov_gimnpifagoreizev.jpg (accessed 18/03/2017).

88 Riedweg (2008), p. 33.

89 Firth (1904), v. 64 – 66.

90 B. Alan Wallace (2014) *Mind in the Balance: Meditation in Science, Buddhism, and Christianity* (New York: Columbia University Press), pp. 8 – 9.

91 Louis H. Feldman, Meyer Reinhold (1996) *Jewish Life and Thought Among Greeks and Romans: Primary Readings* (Minneapolis: Fortress Press), p. 13.

92 Iamblichus (author), Thomas Taylor (translator) (1818), p. 7.

93 Iamblichus (author), Thomas Taylor (translator) (1818), p. 7.

94 Aryeh Kaplan (1988) *Meditation and the Bible* (Boston: Weiser Books), pp. 111 – 112.

95 King James Bible.

96 King James Bible.

97 King James Bible.

98 Kaplan (1988), p. 112.

99 Psalm 92:1 – 3 (King James Version).

100 Kaplan (1988), p. 112.

101 Matthew 2:1.

102 Matthew 1:18 – 25.

103 Luke 2:41 – 52.

104 Matthew 5 – 6.

[105] John 14:21 (King James Bible).

[106] John 14:6 (King James Bible).

[107] Revelation 3:20 (King James Bible).

[108] Matthew 18:20 (King James Bible).

[109] e.g. Luke 22:19; 1 Corinthians 11:24.

[110] John 6:35 (King James Bible).

[111] John 6:51 (King James Bible).

[112] John 11:26 (King James Bible).

[113] King James Bible.

[114] Matthew 6:9 – 13 (King James Bible).

[115] Matthew 6:6, 19 – 22 (King James Bible).

[116] Jonathan Mermis-Cava (2009) An Anchor and a Sail: Christian Meditation as the Mechanism for a Pluralist Religious. *Sociology of Religion*, Vol. 70, No. 4 (Winter, 2009), pp. 432-453. Available online at: https://www.jstor.org/stable/pdf/40376095.pdf (accessed 18/03/2017).

[117] Matheiu Boisvert (1992) A Comparison of the Early Forms of Buddhist and Christian Monastic Traditions. *Buddhist-Christian Studies*, Vol. 12 (1992), pp. 123-141. Available online at: https://www.jstor.org/stable/pdf/1389959.pdf (accessed 18/03/2017).

[118] Bened. Reg. 4,47. See: St. Benedict (author), Rev. Boniface Verheyen (translator) (1902) *The holy rule of our most holy Father St. Benedict: in Latin and English* (Atchison: Abbey Student Print). Available online at: http://www.documentacatholicaomnia.eu/03d/0480-0547,_Benedictus_Nursinus,_Regola,_EN.pdf (accessed 18/03/2017).

[119] Michael Lipka (2017) Muslims and Islam: Key findings in the U.S. and around the world. *PewResearch Center*. Available online at: http://www.pewresearch.org/fact-tank/2017/02/27/muslims-and-islam-key-findings-in-the-u-s-and-around-the-world/ (accessed 18/03/2017).

[120] Lipka (2017).

[121] Lexi Finnigan (2016) Number of UK Muslims exceeds three million for first time. *The Telegraph*, 31 Jan 2016 4:59PM GMT. Available online at: http://www.telegraph.co.uk/news/uknews/12132641/Number-of-UK-Muslims-exceeds-three-million-for-first-time.html (accessed 18/03/2017).

[122] B.A. Robinson (2015) Numbers of adherents of major religions, their geographical distribution, date founded, and sacred texts, *Religious Tolerance – Ontario Consultants on Religious Tolerance*. Last update: 2015-DEC-02. Available online at: http://www.religioustolerance.org/worldrel.htm (accessed 18/03/2017).

[123] Martin Lings (1983) *Muhammad: His Life Based on the Earliest Sources* (London: Islamic Texts Society/G. Allen & Unwin) 53 53 , p. 16. Available online at: http://www.icorlando.org/pdfs/muhammad_martin_Lings.pdf (accessed 18/03/2017).

[124] Lings (1983), pp. 43 – 44.

[125] Qur'ān 96:1 – 5 (Rodwell translation).

[126] Luke 1:26 – 38.

[127] Sidi Fadi Qutub Zada (2014) The Fiqh of Voluntary (Nafl) Prayers, *SeekersHub*, July 14, 2014. Available online at: http://seekershub.org/ans-blog/2014/07/14/the-fiqh-of-voluntary-nafl-prayers/ (accessed 18/03/2017).

[128] BBC (2011) Prophet Muhammad (570-632), *BBC Religions*, 2011-07-08. Available online at: http://www.bbc.co.uk/religion/religions/islam/history/muhammad_1.shtml (accessed 18/03/2017).

[129] Nile Green (2012) *Sufism: A Global History* (Malden, MA: Wiley-Blackwee), p. 17.

[130] Green (2012), p. 18.

[131] A.J. Arberry (2013) *Sufism: An Account of the Mystics of Islam* (Taylor & Francis), p. 58.

[132] Qur'ān 28:88 (Rodwell translation).

[133] Arberry (2013), p. 58.

[134] Shamsu'd-Dīn Muhammad Hāfez-e-Shīrāzī (author), Gertrude Lowthian Bell (translator) (1897), XXXIII.

[135] Bridgewater (2017), p. 217.

[136] Veda-Vyāsa (author), Kisari Mohan Ganguli (translator) (1883-96) *The Mahabharata of Krishna-Dwaipayana Vyasa* (Calcutta: Bharata Press), Book 12: Santi Parva, Section CXCV, pp. 51 – 52. Available online at: http://www.sacred-texts.com/hin/maha/index.htm (accessed 20/03/2017).

[137] Aristotle (author), William David Ross (translator) (1908) *The Nicomachean Ethics of Aristotle* (Oxford: The Clarendon Press), Chapter 7. Available online at: http://www.sacred-texts.com/cla/ari/nico/index.htm (accessed 20/03/2017).

[138] J.H. Woods (1927/2003).

[139] The Diamond Sutra, printed on the 11th of May 868 CE (image in the public domain). This document is stored in the British Library. Available online at: https://upload.wikimedia.org/wikipedia/commons/d/d2/Jingangjing.jpg (accessed 19/03/2017).

[140] Dwight Goddard (translator) (1932) *A Buddhist Bible: The Favorite Scriptures of the Zen Sect* (Thetford, Vermont), The Diamond Sutra (*Vajracchedika Sutra*), p. 197. [First Edition; published in 1932 – copyright not renewed]. Available online at: http://www.sacred-texts.com/bud/bb/index.htm (accessed 19/03/2017).

[141] Goddard (1932), p. 197.

[142] David Fortuna, Ingrid Slack (2007) *Teaching Meditation to Children: The Practical Guide to the Use and Benefits of Meditation Techniques* (London: Watkins; New York: Sterling Publishing Co.).

[143] Soyen Shaku (author), Daisetz Teitaro Suzuki (translator) (1906) *Sermons of a Buddhist Abbot [Zen for Americans]* (Chicago: Open Court Publishing Co.), p. 151. Available online at: http://www.sacred-texts.com/bud/zfa/index.htm (accessed 19/03/2017).

[144] Feuerstein (2006).

[145] Shaku (1906), p. 151.

[146] Feuerstein (2006).

[147] J. Mark G. Williams, Jon Kabat-Zinn (2013) Mindfulness: diverse perspectives on its meaning, origins, and multiple applications at the intersection of science and dharma. In J. Mark G. Williams & Jon Kabat-Zinn (editors) (2013) *Mindfulness: Diverse Perspectives on its Meaning, Origins and Applications* (London; New York: Routledge).

[148] Williams & Kabat-Zinn (2013).

[149] Bhikku Bodhi (2013) What does mindfulness really mean? A canonical perspective. In J. Mark G. Williams & Jon Kabat-Zinn (editors) (2013) *Mindfulness: Diverse Perspectives on its Meaning, Origins and Applications* (London; New York: Routledge).

[150] Carus (1894), The Mustard Seed.

[151] Fontana & Slack (2007).

[152] Fontana & Slack (2007).

[153] Bridgewater (2017), pp. 9 – 10.

[154] Robert C. Koons, George Bealer (2010) *The Waning of Materialism* (Oxford: Oxford University Press).

[155] John Horgan (2013) Scientific Materialism "Almost Certainly False"? *Scientific American*, January 30, 2013. Available online at: https://blogs.scientificamerican.com/cross-check/is-scientific-materialism-almost-certainly-false/ (accessed 19/03/2017).

[156] Goddard (1932), p. 196.

[157] Jalālu'd-Dīn Rūmī (author), E.H. Whinfield (translator) (1898) *The Masnavi I Ma'navi – The Spiritual Couplets of Maulana Jalalu'd-Din Muhammad Rumi* (London: Kegan Paul, Trench, Trubner), Book I., Story XI. Available online at: http://www.sacred-texts.com/isl/masnavi/index.htm (accessed 19/03/2017).

[158] Jalālu'd-Dīn Rūmī (author), E.H. Whinfield (translator) (1898), Book I., Story XIV.

[159] Proverbs 14:8 (King James Bible).

[160] Edouard Shuré (1906) *Pythagoras and the Delphic Mysteries* (London: Philip Wellby). Available online at: http://www.sacred-texts.com/cla/pdm/pdm00.htm (accessed 19/03/2017).

[161] Veda-Vyāsa (author), Swami Swarupananda (translator) (1909) *Srimad-Bhagavad-Gita* (Mayavati, Himalayas: Prabuddha Bharata Press), Ch. VI, v. 18 - 19, p. 147. Available online at: http://www.sacred-texts.com/hin/sbg/index.htm (accessed 19/03/2017).

[162] John 6:20 (King James Bible).

[163] See: OUP (Oxford University Press) (2017) *Oxford Living Dictionaries*. Available online at: https://en.oxforddictionaries.com/definition/ego (accessed 19/03/2017).

[164] Robert Chalmers (translator), E.B. Cowell (editor) (1895) *The Jātaka, or Stories of the Buddha's Former Births, Volume I* (Cambridge: Cambridge University Press), No. 95. Mahāsudassana-Jātaka , p. 231. Available online at: http://www.sacred-texts.com/bud/j1/index.htm (accessed 19/03/2017).

[165] Luke 17:21 (King James Bible).

[166] John 14:20 (King James Bible).

[167] Gautama Buddha (author), W.D.C. Wagiswara, K.J. Saunders (translators) (1920) *The Buddha's Way of Virtue* (A Translation of the Dhammapada) (London: J. Murray), § XIX, v. 261. Available online at: http://www.sacred-texts.com/bud/wov/index.htm (accessed 19/03/2017).

[168] Liezi (author), Lionel Giles (translator), Book VII., p. 98.

[169] Kaiten Nukariya (1913) *The Religion of the Samurai: A Study of Zen Philosophy and Discipline in China and Japan* (Auckland: The Floating Press), Chapter VIII. The Training of the Mind and the Practice of Meditation. Available online at: http://www.sacred-texts.com/bud/rosa/index.htm (accessed 19/03/2017).

[170] Nukariya (1913), Chapter VIII.

[171] Epictetus (author), P.E. Matheson (translator) (1916) *The Discourses of Epictetus: The Discourses and Manual, together with fragments of his writings* (Oxford: Clarendon Press), Book IV, Chapter I. On Freedom, p. 422. Available online at: http://www.sacred-texts.com/cla/dep/index.htm (accessed 19/03/2017).

[172] Veda-Vyāsa (author), Swami Swarupananda (translator) (1909) *Srimad-Bhagavad-Gita*, Chapter VI., v. 4, p. 139.

[173] Veda-Vyāsa (author), Swami Swarupananda (translator) (1909) *Srimad-Bhagavad-Gita*, Chapter VI., v. 10, p. 143.

[174] Fontana & Slack (2007).

[175] Robert Madigan (2015) *How Memory Works—And How to Make It Work for You* (New York: Guilford Publications), p. 89.

[176] Madigan (2015), p. 89.

[177] Alexander C. N., Langer E. J., Newman R. I., Chandler H. M., Davies J. L. (1989). Transcendental meditation, mindfulness, and longevity: an experimental study with the elderly. *J. Pers. Soc. Psychol.* 57, 950–96410.1037/0022-3514.57.6.950.

[178] Rafat Marciniak, Katerina Sheardova, Pavla Čermáková, Daniel Hudeček, Rastislav Šumec, Jakob Hort (2014), Effect of meditation on cognitive functions in context of aging and neurodegenerative disease. In Ales Stuchlik, Tomiki Sumiyoshi (editors) (2015) Cognitive deficits in schizophrenia and other neuropsychiatric disorders: convergence of preclinical and clinical evidence, *Frontiers in Behavioral Neuroscience*, January 2014, Volume 8, Article 17 (Lausanne, Switzerland: Frontiers Research Foundation), p. 196.

[179] Marieke K. van Vugt (2015) Cognitive Benefits of Mindfulness Meditation. In Kirk Warren Brown, J. David Creswell, Richard M. Ryan (2015) *Handbook of Mindfulness: Theory, Research, and Practice* (New York; London: The Guilford Press), p. 199.

[180] Michael J. Gelb (2014) *Creativity on Demand: How to Ignite and Sustain the Fire of Genius* (Boulder, CO: Sounds True, Inc.).

[181] Merriam-Webster (2017) "Qi, variant spelling of CHI", *Merriam-Webster.com*. Available online at: https://www.merriam-webster.com/dictionary/qi (accessed 20/03/2017).

[182] Gelb (2014).

[183] Gelb (2014).

[184] Elise Dirlam Ching, Kaleo Ching (2014) *Chi and Creativity: Vital Energy and Your Inner Artist* (Berkeley, California: Blue Snake Books), p. 42.

[185] Ching & Ching (2014), p. xxii.

[186] Michael Sinclair, Josie Seydel (2016) *Working with Mindfulness: Keeping calm and focused to get the job done* (Harlow, England: Pearson).

[187] Sinclair & Seydel (2016).

[188] Dwight Goddard (1932) *A Buddhist Bible* (Thetford, Vermont), The Lankāvatāra Sutra, Chapter IX. The Fruit of Self-Realization, p. 133. [1932, copyright not renewed]. Available online at: http://www.sacred-texts.com/bud/bb/index.htm (accessed 20/03/2017).

[189] André Ferdinand Hérold (author), Paul C. Blum (translator) (1929) *The Life of Buddha according to the legends of ancient India* (London: Thornton Butterworth), 14. The Buddha Teaches the Doctrine, p. 272. Available online at: http://www.sacred-texts.com/bud/lob/index.htm (accessed 20/03/2017). The work is public domain in the US because it was published before 1964 and the copyright was not renewed. See: https://en.wikisource.org/wiki/The_Life_of_Buddha (accessed 20/03/2017).

[190] Matthew 5:9 (King James Bible).

[191] See: John 6:33, 6:35, 6:48, 6:51; Revelation 22:1; John 4:14.

[192] Kathleen Gregory (2014) Buddhism: perspective for the contemporary world. In Mark Cobb, Christina M Puchalski, Bruce Rumbold (2014) *Oxford Textbook of Spirituality in Healthcare* (Oxford: Oxford Univiersity Press), p. 13.

[193] Carol A. Miller (2013) *Fast Facts for Health Promotion in Nursing: Promoting Wellness in a Nutshell* (New York: Springer Pub. Co.), pp. 68 – 69.

[194] Miller (2013), p. 63.

[195] Gary W. Hartz (2012) *Spirituality and Mental Health: Clinical Applications* (Hoboken: Taylor and Francis), p. 52.

[196] Kathleen C. Spadaro (2008) *Weight Loss: Exploring Self-regulation Through Mindfulness Meditation*. Submitted to the Graduate Faculty of School of Nursing in partial fulfilment of the requirements for the degree of Doctor of Philosophy, University of Pittsburgh, p. 91.

[197] Joseph Emet (2012) *Buddha's Book of Sleep: Sleep Better in Seven Weeks with Mindfulness Meditation* (New York: Jeremy P. Tarcher), p. 63.

[198] Gautama Buddha (author), F. Max Müller (translator) (1881) *The Dhammapada* (Oxford: The Clarendon Press), Chapter XXV., v. 372, 374, 381.

[199] Gautama Buddha (author), T.W. Rhys Davids (translator) (1881) *Buddhist Suttas, translated from Pâli, Vol. IX of The Sacred Books of the East* (Oxford: The Clarendon Press), *Mahâ-Parinibbâna-*

Suttanta (Book of the Great Decease), Chapter II, v. 13 – 15, pp. 28 – 29. Available online at: http://sacred-texts.com/bud/sbe11/index.htm (accessed 21/03/2017).

[200] NJ Bridgewater (2017b) 'How can we achieve true happiness and inner peace?' *Equanimity Blog*, February 8, 2017. Available online at: https://fivewaystobc.wordpress.com/2017/02/08/how-can-we-achieve-true-happiness-and-inner-peace/ (accessed 20/03/2017).

[201] Rupert Gethin (2011) Mindfulness: diverse perspectives on its meaning, origins, and multiple applications at the intersection of science and dharma. *Contemporary Buddhism: An Interdisciplinary Journal*, Vol. 12, 2011, Issue 1, pp. 263-279. Published online: 14 Jun 2011. Available online at: http://www.tandfonline.com/doi/full/10.1080/14639947.2011.564843?scroll=top&needAccess=true (accessed 20/03/2017).

[202] Gethin (2011).

[203] T.W. Rhys Davids (1881) *Buddhist suttas* (Oxford: Clarendon Press), p. 145.

[204] Gethin (2011).

[205] Various (authors), Rutherford H. Platt, Jr. (translator) (1926) *The Lost Books of the Bible* (New York: Alpha House), The Second Book of Hermas, Command IV, v. 2- - 3, p. 214.

[206] Gethin (2011).

[207] Gethin (2011).

[208] Gethin (2011).

[209] Gethin (2011).

[210] Bridgewater (2017), Chapters II & III, pp. 26 – 65.

[211] Gautama Buddha (author), T.W. Rhys Davids (translator) (1881), *Dhamma-Kakka-Ppavattana-Sutta (The Foundation of the Kingdom of Righteousness)*, v. 2 – 4, pp. 146 - 148

[212] Virginia Heffernan (2015) The Muddied Meaning of 'Mindfulness'. *The New York Times Magazine*, April 14, 2015. Available online at: https://www.nytimes.com/2015/04/19/magazine/the-muddied-meaning-of-mindfulness.html?_r=0 (accessed 20/03/2017).

[213] Heffernan (2005).

[214] Jon Kabat-Zinn (2001) *Mindfulness Meditation for Everyday Life* (London: Piatkus Books), p. 24. Available online at: http://chadpearce.com/home/BOOKS/97291641-Mindfulness-Meditation-for-Everyday-Life-Kabat-Zinn-Jon.pdf (accessed 20/03/2017).

[215] Kabat-Zinn (2001), p. 25.

[216] Kabat-Zinn (2001), p. 25.

[217] Kabat-Zinn (2001), pp. 35 – 44.

[218] R.S. Crane, J. Brewer, C. Feldman, J. Kabat-Zinn, S. Santorelli, J.M.G. Williams and W. Kuyken (2016) What defines mindfulness-based programs? The warp and the weft. *Psychological Medicine*, 2017 Apr; 47(6):990-999. Available online at: http://mbct.com/wp-content/uploads/What-defines-mindfulness-based-programs.pdf (accessed 20/03/2017).

[219] Crane et al. (2006).

[220] Cranet et al. (2006).

[221] Gethin (2011).

[222] Gethin (2011).

[223] Nyanaponika Thera (2005) *The Heart of Buddhist Meditation: Satipatthāna: a Handbook of Mental Training Based on the Buddha's Way of Mindfulness, with an Anthology of Relevant Texts Translated from the Pali and Sanskrit* (Kandy, Sri Lanka: Buddhist Publication Society), p. 7.

[224] Thera (2005), p. 8.

[225] Thera (2005), p. 21.

[226] Müller (1881), *The Dhammapada*, Chapter I. The Twin-Verses, v. 1 - 2, pp. 3 -4.

[227] Thera (2005), p. 24.

[228] Thích Nhât Hanh (*Wikipedia* article). Available online at: https://en.wikipedia.org/wiki/Th%C3%ADch_Nh%E1%BA%A5t_H%E1%BA%A1nh (accessed 21/03/2017).

[229] Chan Buddhism (*Wikipedia* article). Available online at: https://en.wikipedia.org/wiki/Chan_Buddhism (accessed 21/03/2017).

[230] Dhyāna in Buddhism (*Wikipedia* article). Available online at: https://en.wikipedia.org/wiki/Dhy%C4%81na_in_Buddhism (accessed 21/03/2017).

[231] Veda-Vyāsa (author), Edwin Arnold (translator) (1885) *The Bhagavad Gita: Or, The Song Celestial* (Auckland: Floating Press), Chapter VI. Of Religion and Self-Restraint. Available online at: http://www.sacred-texts.com/hin/gita/index.htm (accessed 21/03/2017).

[232] Rinzler (2015).

[233] Shirin Mehdi (2016) How To Do The Sukhasana And What Are Its Benefits. *StyleCraze*, May 13, 2016. Available online at: http://www.stylecraze.com/articles/sukhasana-easy-pose/#gref (accessed 21/03/2017).

[234] Lodro Rinzler (2015) Everything You Need to Know About Meditation Posture. *Yoga Journal / Meditation*. Available online at: http://www.yogajournal.com/meditation/everything-need-know-meditation-posture/ (accessed 21/03/2017).

[235] Kaiten Nukariya (1913) *The Religion of the Samurai: A Study of Zen Philosophy and Discipline in China and Japan* (Auckland: The Floating Press), Chapter VIII, The Training of the Mind and the Practice of Meditation, 5. Zazen, or the Sitting in Meditation. Available online at: http://www.sacred-texts.com/bud/rosa/rosa10.htm (accessed 21/03/2017).

[236] Available online at: Melissa Eisler (2015) How to Sit for Meditation: 8 Options. *Mindful Minutes*, June 12, 2015. https://mindfulminutes.com/how-to-sit-for-meditation/ (18/05/2017).

[237] Lodro Rinzler (2015) Everything You Need to Know About Meditation Posture. *Yoga Journal / Meditation*. Available online at: http://www.yogajournal.com/meditation/everything-need-know-meditation-posture/ (accessed 21/03/2017).

[238] See: http://www.yogajournal.com/pose/hero-pose/ (accessed 21/03/2017).

[239] Nukariya (1913), Chapter VIII.

[240] Rinzler (2015).

[241] Nukariya (1913), Chapter VIII.

[242] Dza Kilung Rinpoche (2015) *The Relaxed Mind: A Seven-Step Method for Deepening Meditation Practice* (Boston: Shambhala), p. 12. See also: Rinzler (2015).

[243] Rinpoche (2015)

[244] Rinpoche (2015).

[245] Rinzler (2015).

[246] Jalālu'd-Dīn Rūmī (author), E.H. Whinfield (translator) (1898) *The Masnavī*, Book VI., Story V.

[247] Henry Clarke Warren (translator) (1896) *Buddhism in Translations, Harvard Oriental Series, Vol. III* (Cambridge, Mass: Harvard University) § 74. The Four Intent Contemplations {Mahâ-Satipatthāna-Sutta}, Translated from the Digha-Nikâya, and constituting Sutta 22, p. 354. Available online at: http://www.sacred-texts.com/bud/bits/index.htm (accessed 22/03/2017).

[248] Gautama Buddha (author), Henry Clarke Warren (translator), p. 355.

[249] Gautama Buddha (author), Henry Clarke Warren (translator), p. 356.

[250] Hanh (2015).

[251] Thera (2005), p. 68.

[252] Thera (2005), p. 69.

[253] Hanh (2015).

[254] Gautama Buddha (author), Henry Clarke Warren (translator), p. 356.

[255] Vivekananda (1920), p. 29.

[256] Vivekananda (1920), pp. 29 – 30.

[257] Vivekananda (1920), p. 33.

[258] Vivekananda (1920), p. 56.

[259] Hanh (2015).

[260] Gautama Buddha (author), Henry Clarke Warren (translator), pp. 357 - 359.

[261] Hanh (2015).

[262] Joseph Goldstein (2013) *Mindfulness: A Practical Guide to Awakening* (Boulder, CO: Sounds True).

[263] Goldstein (2013).

[264] Thera (2005), p. 71.

[265] Gautama Buddha (author), Henry Clarke Warren (translator), p. 359.

[266] Goldstein (2013).

[267] Thera (2005), p. 50.

[268] Bridgewater (2017), p. 35.

[269] Goldstein (2013).

[270] Thera (2005), p. 72.

[271] Gautama Buddha (author), Henry Clarke Warren (translator), pp. 359 – 360.

[272] Goldstein (2013).

[273] Vyāsadeva (author), Edwin Arnold (translator) (1885), Chapter XIII.

[274] Gautama Buddha (author), Henry Clarke Warren (translator), pp. 360 – 361.

[275] Thera (2005), p. 74.

[276] Gautama Buddha (author), Henry Clarke Warren (translator), p. 361.

[277] Gautama Buddha (author), W.D.C. Wagiswara, K.J. Saunders (translators) (1920) *The Buddha's Way of Virtue: A Translation of the Dhammapada from the Pāli text* (London: J. Murray), § III., v. 41, p. 27. Available online at: http://www.sacred-texts.com/bud/wov/index.htm (accessed 23/03/2017).

[278] Goldstein (2013).

[279] Plotinus (author), Stephen MacKenna & B.S. Page (translators) (1917 – 1930) *The Six Enneads* (London; Boston: Medici Society), The Fifth Ennead: Ninth Tractate, Section 3, par. 3. Available online at: http://www.sacred-texts.com/cla/plotenn/index.htm (accessed 22/03/2017).

[280] Thera (2005), pp. 75 - 76.

[281] Thera (2005), p. 76.

[282] Gautama Buddha (author), Henry Clarke Warren (translator), p. 363.

[283] Goldstein (2013).

284 Vyāsadeva (author), Edwin Arnold (translator) (1885), Chapter II.

285 Buddha (author), Müller (1881), *The Dhammapada*, v. 239.

286 Gautama Buddha (author), Henry Clarke Warren (translator), pp. 363 – 364.

287 Thera (2005), p. 79.

288 Thera (2005), p. 80.

289 Goldstein (2013).

290 Bhikku Anālayo (2003) *Satipatthāna: The Direct Path to Realization* (Birmingham: Windhorse Publications), p. 174.

291 Phra Thepyanmongkol (2012) *A Study Guide for Right Practice of the Three Trainings* (Ratchaburi, Thailand: National Center of Provincial Meditation Institutes of Thailand, Wat Luang Phor Sodh Dhammakayaram), p. 439.

292 Thera Nyanaponika, Hellmuth Hecker (2012) *Great Disciples of the Buddha: Their Lives, Their Works, Their Legacy* (New York: Wisdom Publications), p. 196.

293 Anālayo (2003), pp. 179 – 180.

294 Vyāsadeva (author), Edwin Arnold (translator) (1885), Chapter II.

295 Thera (2005), p. 81.

296 Bhikkhu Ñānamoli, Bhikkhu Bodhi (translators) (2015) *The Middle Length Discourses of the Buddha: A Translation of the Majjhima-Nikaya* (Boston: Wisdom Publications, in association with the Barre Center for Buddhist Studies), The Satipatthana Sutta: The Foundations of Mindfulness. Available online at: http://www.wisdompubs.org/landing/satipatthana-sutta (accessed 21/03/2017).

297 Bridgewater (2017), pp. 16 – 17.

298 Gautama Buddha (author), Henry Clarke Warren (translator), pp. 364 – 365.

299 Soma Thera (translator) (2013) The Way of Mindfulness: The Satipatthana Sutta and Its Commentary. *Access to Insight (Legacy Edition)*, 30 November 2013. Available online at: http://www.accesstoinsight.org/lib/authors/soma/wayof.html#mental (accessed 21/03/2017).

300 Gautama Buddha (author), Henry Clarke Warren (translator), p. 366.

301 Thera (2013); Ñānamoli & Bodhi (2015).

302 Jack Kornfield (2010) *Living Dharma: Teachings and Meditation from Twelve Theravada Masters* (Boston: Shambhala). See also: https://jackkornfield.com/factors-enlightenment/ (accessed 23/03/2017).

303 Thera (2013); Ñānamoli & Bodhi (2015).

304 Matthew 7:14 (King James Bible).

305 Gautama Buddha (author), Henry Clarke Warren (translator), pp. 368 – 372.

306 Glenys Eddy (2012) *Becoming Buddhist: Experiences of Socialization and Self-Transformation in Two Australian Buddhist Centres* (London: Continuum International Publ. Group), p. 87.

307 Luke 13:18 – 19 (King James Bible).

308 Carus (1894) *Buddha, The Gospel*, The Buddha Replies to the Deva.

309 Buddha (author), Wagiswara, Saunders (translators) (1920) v. 33, 35 – 36, 39 - 40, pp. 26 – 27.

310 Buddha (author), Wagiswara, Saunders (translators) (1920) v. 2, pp. 21 – 22.

311 Gautama Buddha (author), D.J. Gogerly (translator) (1872) Four Short Suttas, translated by D. J. Gogerly, published posthumously. *Journal Asiatique our recuil de mémoires d'extraits et de notices relatifs a l'histoire , a la philosophie, aux langues et la littérature de peoples orientaux et publié par la Société Asiatique*, sixième série, tome XX. Kara.nîya-Metta-Sutta, The Discourse Named Kara.nîya-

Metta, v. 3 – 8, pp. 230 – 231. Available online: http://www.sacred-texts.com/journals/ja/tbg.htm (accessed 24/03/2017).

[312] Leonard Lewisohn (2015) Sufism's religion of love, from Rābiʻa to Ibn ʻArabī. In Lloyd Ridgeon (editor) (2015) *The Cambridge Companion to Sufism* (Cambridge: Cambridge University Press), p. 171.

[313] Mettā (Wikipedia article). Available online at: https://en.wikipedia.org/wiki/Mett%C4%81 (accessed 24/03/2017).

[314] Tulku Thondup (2009) *The Healing Power of Loving-kindness: A Guided Buddhist Meditation* (Boston, Mass.: Shambhala), p. 3.

[315] Lewisohn (2015), p. 171.

[316] Carus (1894), The Sermon at Rajagaha.

[317] Luke 6:35 (King James Bible).

[318] Matthew 5:39, 5:44 - 45 (King James Bible).

[319] Thondup (2009), p. 3.

[320] Thondup (2009), p. 4.

[321] Thondup (2009), p. 5.

[322] H. Kern (1884) *Saddharma-Pundarîka or, The Lotus of the True Law*. Sacred Books of the East (Clarendon Press: Oxford), Vol XXI, Chapter XXIV, v. 25 – 26. Available online at: http://www.sacred-texts.com/bud/lotus/index.htm (accessed 25/03/2017).

[323] Avalokitesvara (*Wikipedia* article). Available online at: https://en.wikipedia.org/wiki/Avalokiteśvara (accessed 25/03/2017).

[324] The Editors of Encyclopædia Britannica (2015) Ishvara (article), *Encyclopædia Britannica*, last updated 2-19-2015. Available online at: https://global.britannica.com/topic/Ishvara (accessed 25/03/2017).

[325] Carus (1894), The Three Characteristics And The Uncreated.

[326] Springs Steele (2000) Christian Insight Meditation: A Test Case on Interreligious Spirituality. *Buddhist-Christian Studies*, Vol. 20 (2000), pp. 217-229. Available online at: http://www.jstor.org/stable/1390332 (accessed 25/03/2017).

[327] Galatians 2:20 (King James Bible). This connection was identified by Donald K. Swearer (1999) Buddha Loves Me! This I Know, for the Dharma Tells Me So. *Buddhist-Christian Studies*, Vol. 19 (1999), pp. 113-120. Available online at: http://www.jstor.org/stable/1390527 (accessed 26/03/2017).

[328] Qur'ān 112:2 – 4 (Rodwell translation).

[329] Müller (1881), *The Dhammapada*, Ch. XXV, v. 368, p. 86.

[330] Sharon Salzberg (2004) *Loving-Kindness: The Revolutionary Art of Happiness* (Boston: Shambhala), p. 2.

[331] Salzberg (2004), p. 23.

[332] Salzberg (2004), pp. 27 – 28.

[333] Salzberg (2004), p. 28.

[334] Carus (1894), Sermon at Benares.

[335] P. Lakshmi Narasu (1907) *The Essence of Buddhism* (Madras: Srinivasa Varadachari), pp. 54 – 55. Available online at: https://archive.org/details/essenceofbuddhis00laksrich (accessed 30/03/2017).

[336] Bridgewater (2017), pp. 166 – 170.

[337] Salzberg (2004).

338 Ven Pannyavaro (1996-2017) Loving-Kindness Meditation, BuddhaNet Basic Buddhism Guide. *Buddhist Studies: Buddha Dharma Education Association & BuddhaNet.* Available online at: http://www.buddhanet.net/e-learning/loving-kindness.htm (accessed 26/03/2017).

339 Pannyavaro (1996-2017).

340 Salzberg (2004), p. 36.

341 Salzberg (2004), pp. 36 – 37.

342 NJ Bridgewater (2017), pp. 167 - 169.

343 Genesis 1:27 (King James Bible).

344 Krishna (author), Edwin Arnold (1885), Chapter X. Of Religion by the Heavenly Perfections.

345 Epictetus (author), Matheson (translator) (1916), Chapter VIII, p. 295.

346 Qur'ān 84:14 (Yusuf Ali translation). Yusuf Ali (1934) *The Holy Quran* (Kashmiri Bazar, Lahore: Shaik Muhammad Ashraf). Available online at: http://www.sacred-texts.com/isl/yaq/index.htm (accessed 30/03/2017).

347 Pannyavaro (1996-2017).

348 Pannyavaro (1996-2017).

349 Shamash Alidina (2015) *Mindfulness for Dummies* (Hoboken: John Wiley), Part III: Practising Mindfulness, p. 116.

350 See: Alidina (2015), p. 116.

351 See: Alidina (2015), p. 116.

352 Sharon Salzberg (2015) The Concentric Circles of Connection and Lovingkindness, *On Being* (blog), September 25, 2015. Available online at: https://onbeing.org/blog/the-concentric-circles-of-connection-and-lovingkindness/ (accessed 09/04/2017).

353 Thomas à Kempis (author), William Benham (translator) (1886), Chapter X. Gratitude for the Grace of God, par. 5.

354 Veda-Vyāsa (author), Kisari Mohan Ganguli (translator) (1883-1896) *The Mahabharata*, Book 12: Santi Parva, Part I, Rajadharmanusasana Parva, Section CVIII, p. 236. Available online at: http://www.sacred-texts.com/hin/m12/index.htm (accessed 10/04/2017).

355 Govinda means the 'Divine Cowherd', Syāmasundara refers to his dark complexion and Muralīdhara means 'Holder of the Flute.' See: *Srī Brahma-Samhitā*, p. 69.

356 See: Bhakti: the means and the goal (article), *Krishna.com*. URL: http://www.krishna.com/bhakti-means-and-goal (accessed 10/04/2017).

357 Devala's Mahâpurusa, quoted in Daisetz Teitaro Suzuki (1908) *Outlines of Mahayana Buddhism* (Chicago: Open Court), pp. 365 – 366. Available online at: https://archive.org/details/outlinesofmahayoosuzurich/ (accessed 11/04/2017).

358 James Allen (1907) *From Poverty to Power: The Path to prosperity and The Way of Peace* (Albuquerque, NM: Sun Pub. Co.). Available online at: http://www.gutenberg.org/ebooks/10740 (accessed 22/02/2017).

359 Veda-Vyāsa (author), Swami Swarupananda (translator) (1909), Chapter VI, v. 29, p. 152.

360 Veda-Vyāsa (author), Swami Swarupananda (translator) (1909), Chapter VI, v. 9, p. 143.

361 Veda-Vyāsa (author), Swami Swarupananda (translator) (1909), Chapter VI, v. 30 - 31, p. 153.

362 Allen (1907).

363 Luke 6:27 – 36 (King James Bible).

364 Ignatius of Antioch (author), Epistle to the Ephesians, Chap III, v. 1 – 2. In Rutherford H. Platt (translator) (1926) *The Lost Books of the Bible* (New York: Alpha House).

[365] Ignatius of Antioch (author), Epistle to the Smyrnæans, Chap III, v. 19.

[366] Ignatius of Antioch (author), Epistle to the Trallians, Chap II, v. 7.

[367] Veda-Vyāsa (author), Swami Swarupananda (translator) (1909), Chapter VI, v. 9, p. 143.

[368] Matthew 5:44 – 45 (King James Bible).

[369] Qur'ān 5:8 (Palmer translation).

[370] NJ Bridgewater (2017), p. 169.

[371] Barnabus (author), The General Epistle of Barnabus, Chap. V, v. 18. In In Rutherford H. Platt (translator) (1926) *The Lost Books of the Bible* (New York: Alpha House).

[372] Gautama Buddha (author), D.J. Gogerly (translator) (1872) *Four Short Suttas*, Karanīya-Metta-Sutta, v. 3 – 8.

[373] Gautama Buddha (author), H. Kern (translator) (1884) *Saddharma-Puntarîka or, The Lotus of the True Law*, Chapter XXIV. v. 27, 22.

[374] Mencius (Mengzi / Meng Ke) (author), James Legge (translator) (1895) *The Works of Mencius* (Oxford: Clarendon Press), Book 7, Part II, Chapter 25, v. 4 – 8. Available online at: http://nothingistic.org/library/mencius/ (accessed 27/3/2017).

[375] Martin Lings (1983) *Muhammad: His Life Based on the Earliest Sources* (Cambridge: Islamic Texts Society), p. 98.

[376] Lings (1983), p. 98.

[377] 1 John 4:7 – 8, 11 (King James Bible).

[378] Psalm 26:3; 63:3 (King James Bible).

[379] Qur'ān 17:110 (Rodwell translation).

[380] Qur'ān 7:180 (Sale translation). George Sale (1734) *The Koran, commonly called the Alcoran of Mohammed: translated into English immediately from the original Arabic; with explanatory notes, taken from the most approved commentators. To which is prefixed a preliminary discourse* (London: J. Wilcox).

[381] Qur'ān 17:44 (Sale translation).

[382] Qur'ān 59:1 (Rodwell translation).

[383] Psalm 113:1 – 4 (King James Bible).

[384] Veda-Vyāsa (author), Ernest Wood, S.V. Subhrahmanyam (translators) (1911) *The Garuda Purāna (Sāroddhāra) with English Translation* (Allahabad: Pānini Office), Chapter VIII, v. 9 – 12, 14, 17, pp. 62 – 63.

. Available online at: http://www.sacred-texts.com/hin/gpu/index.htm (accessed 11/04/2017).

[385] *Thirty Minor Upanishads*, Ātmabodha-Upanishad of Rgveda, p. 37.

[386] From the Indo-European root *ēt-men*, meaning 'essence, breath, soul.' See: Ātman (*Wikipedia* article). Available online at: https://en.wikipedia.org/wiki/%C4%80tman_(Buddhism) (accessed 12/04/2017).

[387] Jamshed K. Fozdar (1995) *The God of Buddha* (Ariccia: Casa Editrice Bahá'í Srl), p. 70.

[388] Müller (1881), *The Dhammapada*, Chapter XII., v. 160.

[389] John 1:1 - 3 (King James Bible).

[390] *Thirty Minor Upanishads*, Sarvasāra-Upanishad of Krshna-Yajurveda, v. 10, p. 16.

[391] Gautama Buddha (author), Dawsonne Melanchthon Strong (translator) (1902) *The Udâna, Translated from the Pali* (London: Luzac & Co.), Chapter VIII. Patalagami, v. 3. Also, see: Carus (1894) *Buddha, The Gospel*, The Three Characteristics of the Uncreated. The translation used in Carus is:

"There is, O monks, an unborn, unoriginated, uncreated, unformed. Were there not, O monks, this unborn, unoriginated, uncreated, unformed, there would be no escape from the world of the born, originated, created, formed. Since, O monks, there is an unborn, unoriginated, uncreated and unformed, therefore is there an escape from the born, originated, created, formed."

392 Fozdar (1995), p. 130.

393 Fozdar (1995), p. 132.

394 Veda-Vyāsa (author), Swami Swarupananda (translator) (1909) *Srimad-Bhagavad-Gita*, Thirteenth Chapter, v. 12, 15, 17, pp. 296 – 297.

395 Veda-Vyāsa (author), Ralph T.H. Griffith (translator) (1896) *The Hymns of the Rgveda* (Benares: E.J. Lazaarus), Book 10, Hymn LXXXII. Visvakarman, v. 6. Available online at: http://www.sacred-texts.com/hin/rigveda/index.htm (accessed 12/04/2017).

396 Qur'ān 2:31 (Rodwell translation).

397 Genesis 1:27 (King James Bible).

398 Veda-Vyāsa (author), Swami Swarupananda (translator) (1909) *Srimad-Bhagavad-Gita*, Thirteenth Chapter, v. 27 - 28, p. 304.

399 Qur'ān 59:24 (George Sale translation).

400 The Haribhakti-Vilasa, 11-2819, Padmapurana, quoted in Sri Sri Krishnadasa Kaviraja Goswamin (author) Sanjib Kumar Chaudhuri (translator) (1954) *Sri Sri Chaitanya Charitamrita* (Calcutta: Biraj Mohan De), Ch. 3, p. 54. Available online at: https://archive.org/details/in.ernet.dli.2015.425626 (accessed 30/03/2017).

401 Krsnādasa Kavirāja (1954), Ch. 3, p. 54.

402 Bhaktirasamrita Sindhu, Part I, Bibhag I, Sec. 52, quoted in Krsnādasa Kavirāja (1954), Ch. 3, p. 54.

403 Krsnādasa Kavirāja (1954), Ch. 3, p. 54.

404 Veda-Vyāsa, *The Mahabharata*, Book 12: Santi Parva, Part 3, Section CCCL, p. 198.

405 See: Vishnu (*Wikipedia* article). Available online at: https://en.wikipedia.org/wiki/Vishnu (accessed 11/04/2017).

406 Ralph T. H. Griffith (1889) *Rig-Veda* (1896), Book I, Hymn CLIV. Visnu, v. 1.

407 Rig-Veda, Book I, Hymn CLIV. Visnu, v. 6.

408 Veda-Vyāsa (author), Wood, Subhrahmanyam (translators) (1911) *The Garuda Purāna*, v. 12 – 13, p. 62.

409 His Divine Grace A.C. Bhaktivedanta Swami Prabhupāda (1968*) The Science of Self-Realization* (Los Angeles: Bhaktivedanta Book Trust), p. 19. Available online at: http://www.krishnapath.org/free-ebooks-audiobooks-of-srila-prabhupada/the-science-of-self-realization/ (accessed 15/04/2017).

410 Veda-Vyāsa (author), Kisari Mohan Gangulia (translator) (1919) *The Mahabharata of Krishna-Dwaipayana Vyasa*, Book 5: Udyoga Parva, Sanat-sujata Parva Section LXX, p. 152.

411 Bhaktisiddhanta Sarasvati (1932), republished in ..., p. 12. Available online at: (accessed 08/04/2017).

412 Veda-Vyāsa (author), Kisari Mohan Gangulia (translator) (1919) *The Mahabharata of Krishna-Dwaipayana Vyasa*, Book 12 (Part one of three): Santi Parva. Translated into English Prose from the Original Sanskrit Text (Calcutta: D. Bose & Co.), Part 3, Section CCCXLIII, p. 165. Available online at: http://www.sacred-texts.com/hin/m12/index.htm (accessed 30/12/2016).

413 The Most Revered Shree Shreemat Krishnadasa Kaviraja Goswamee (author), Nihar Ranjan Banerjee (translator) (1925) *Shree Shree Chaitanya Charitamritam* (Calcutta: Bhudeb Publishing House), p. 206. Available online at: https://archive.org/details/in.ernet.dli.2015.20750 (accessed 28/03/2017).

414 NJ Bridgewater (2017), p. 165.

[415] Hare Krishna (mantra) (*Wikipedia* article). Available online at: https://en.wikipedia.org/wiki/Hare_Krishna_(mantra) (accessed 30/12/2016 18:06).

[416] See: 'The Meaning of the Hare Krishna Mantra—1966 MP3 Audio Lecture.' Available online at: https://krishna.org/the-meaning-of-the-hare-krishna-mantra-1966-mp3-audio-lecture/ (accessed 15/04/2017).

[417] Satsvarūpa Dāsa Gosvāmī (2003) *Prabhupāda: Your Ever Well-Wisher* (Watford: The Bhaktivedanta Book Trust), p. 73.

[418] A.C. Bhaktivedanta Swami Prabhupāda (1974) Maha-mantra Includes Lord Rama, A lecture by His Divine Grace A.C. Bhaktivedanta Swami Prabhupāda, delivered in Bombay, April 1, 1974, *The Prabhupada Connection*. Available online at: http://www.prabhupadaconnect.com/Lecture75.html (accessed 15/04/2017).

[419] Krishna Rupa Devi dasi (2011) Powerful Meaning of the Hare Krishna *Mahamantra by Srsila Jiva Goswami, March 14, 2011, 7:46 pm, ISKCON* Desire Tree – Devotee Network. Available online at: http://www.iskcondesiretree.com/forum/topics/powerful-meaning-of-the-hare (accessed 15/04/2017).

[420] Veda-Vyāsa (author), Wood, Subhrahmanyam (translators) (1911) *The Garuda Purāna*, v. 8 – 9, 14, 25, pp. 62 – 64.

[421] *Thirty Minor Upanishads*, Kalisantārana-Upanishad, pp. 130 – 131.

[422] In the Mahabharata, he says: "My complexion also is of that foremost of gems called Harit. It is for these reasons that I am called by the name of Hari." Veda-Vyāsa (author), Kisari Mohan Gangulia (translator) (1919), Part 3, Section CCCXLIII, p. 160.

[423] Sri Sri Krishnadasa Kaviraja Goswamin (author) Sanjib Kumar Chaudhari (translator) (1954) *Sri Sri Chaitanya Charitamrita* (Calcutta: Biraj Mohan De), pp. 56 - 62. Available online at: https://archive.org/details/in.ernet.dli.2015.425626 (accessed 30/03/2017).

[424] Krsnadāsa Kavirāja (author), Chaudhari (translator) (1954), p. 59.

[425] Krsnadāsa Kavirāja (author), Chaudhari (translator) (1954), p. 60.

[426] Krsnadāsa Kavirāja (author), Chaudhari (translator) (1954), pp. 60 – 61.

[427] Krsnadāsa Kavirāja (author), Chaudhari (translator) (1954), p. 61.

[428] Krsnadāsa Kavirāja (author), Chaudhari (translator) (1954), p. 62.

[429] Krsnadāsa Kavirāja (author), Chaudhari (translator) (1954), p. 62.

[430] Veda-Vyāsa, *The Mahabharata*, Book 12: Santi Parva, Part 3, Section CCCXLII, p. 151.

[431] Veda-Vyāsa, *The Mahabharata*, Book 13: Anusasana Parva, Part 2, Section CXLIX, pp. 327 – 328.

[432] Donald S. Lopez, Jr. (editor) (2004) *Buddhist Scriptures* (London: Penguin), p. 379.

[433] Lopez (2004), p. 379.

[434] Lopez (2004), p. 379.

[435] Lopez (2004), p. 380.

[436] Lopez (2004), p. 380.

[437] Lopez (2004), p. 380.

[438] Translated by Dennis Hirota (1971), originally published in Ōhashi Shunnō (ed.) (1971) *Hōnen Ippen*, Nihon shisō taikei, vol. 10 (Tokyo: Iwanami shoten). In Lopez (2004), p. 386.

[439] Gautama Buddha (author), E.B. Cowell, F. Max Müller, J. Takakusu (translators) (1894) *Buddhist Mahâyâna Texts* (Oxford: The Clarendon Press), The Larger Sukhâvatî-Vyûha, Description of Sukhâvatî, The Land of Bliss, § 39, p. 59.

[440] Fozdar (1995), p. 110.

[441] NJ Bridgewater (2017), p. 162.

[442] See: The Editors of Encyclopædia Britannica (2010) Amitabha: Buddhism. *Encyclopædia Britannica.* Available online at: https://www.britannica.com/topic/Amitabha-Buddhism (accessed 30/12/2016).

[443] Yejitsu Okusa (1915) *Principal Teachings of The True Sect of Pure Land* (Kyōto: The Ōtaniha Hongwanji), Chapter IV. Salvation, pp. 70 – 71. Available online at: http://www.sacred-texts.com/bud/ptpl/index.htm (accessed 30/12/2016).

[444] Saichi Asahara, quoted in Daisetz Teitaro Suzuki (1957) *Mysticism, Christian and Buddhist* (Volume Twelve of the World Perspective Series) (New York: Harper & Brothers Publishers), Appendices VIII. Notes on "Namu-amida-butsu", p. 163. Copyright not renewed.

[445] Lopez (2004), p. 61.

[446] Lopez (2004), pp. 62 – 63.

[447] Lopez (2004), pp. 62 – 63.

[448] Lopez (2004), p. 65.

[449] Amitābha (*Wikipedia* article). Available online at: https://en.wikipedia.org/wiki/Amitābha (accessed 30/12/2016 17:39).

[450] Nianfo (*Wikipedia* article). Available online at: https://en.wikipedia.org/wiki/Nianfo (accessed 30/12/2016 17:41).

[451] Nianfo (*Wikipedia* article).

[452] NJ Bridgewater (2017), p. 164.

[453] Okusa (1915), p. 77.

[454] Paul Carus (author), Olga Kopetzky (illustrator) (1915) *The Gospel of Buddha, Compiled from Ancient Records*, LX – Amitabha, pp. 173 – 174.

[455] NJ Bridgewater (2017), p. 164.

[456] Luke 18:13 (King James Bible).

[457] Matthew 6:6 (King James Bible).

[458] 1 Thessalonians 5:16 – 18 (King James Bible).

[459] Luke 18:11 - 12 (King James Bible).

[460] Luke 18:13 (King James Bible).

[461] John 14:13 - 14 (King James Bible).

[462] See: Jesus Prayer (*Wikipedia* article). Available online at: https://en.wikipedia.org/wiki/Jesus_Prayer (accessed 15/04/2017).

[463] A Discourse on Abba Philimon, excerpt from *The Philokalia of the Neptic Saints gathered from our Holy Theophoric Father, through which, by means of the philosophy of ascetic practice and contemplation, the intellect is purified, illumined, and made perfect.* The Philokalia was first compiled by St. Nikodemos of the Holy Mountain and St. Makarios of Corinth and published in 1782. Available online at: http://desertfathers.blogspot.com/2011/06/abba-philimonexcerpts-from-philokalia.html (accessed 15/04/2017).

[464] A Discourse on Abba Philimon.

[465] Qur'ān 55:78 (Rodwell translation).

[466] Qur'ān 24:35 (Rodwell translation).

[467] NJ Bridgewater (2017), pp. 14 – 65.

[468] Jalāl ad-Dīn Rūmī (author), E.H. Whinfield (tranaslator) (1898) *The Spiritual Couplets of Maulana Jalalu'd-Din Muhammad Rumi*, Book I.

[469] See: Nimatullahi Sufi Order (2011-2014) *Spiritual Method, Nimatullahi Sufi Order*. Available online at: http://www.nimatullahi.org/our-order/practices/spiritual-method.php (accessed 12/04/2017).

[470] Ian Richard Netton (2000) *Sufi Ritual: The Parallel Universe* (Richmond, England: Curzon Press), p. 166.

[471] Mark Sedgwick (2016) *Western Sufism: From the Abbasids to the New Age* (Oxford: Oxford University Press), p. 38.

[472] Sedgwick (2016), p. 38.

[473] Sedgwick (2016), pp. 38 – 39.

[474] Sahl ibn 'Abd Allāh al-Tustarī (author), Annabel Keeler, Ali Keeler (translators) (2011) *Tafsīr al-Tustarī* (Great Commentaries on the Holy Qur'ān) (Louisville, KY: Fons Vitae), p. xv. Available online at: https://archive.org/details/TafsirAlQuranAlAzimBySahlAlTustari/ (accessed 12/04/2017).

[475] Qur'ān 39:36 (Sale translation).

[476] Qur'ān 50:16 (Sale translation).

[477] Qur'ān 49:18 (Rodwell translation).

[478] Qur'ān 4:79 (Palmer translation).

[479] Waleed Ziad (2017) Transporting Knowledge in the Durrani Empire: Two Manuals of Naqshbandi-Mujaddidi Sufi Practice, In *Afghanistan's Islam: From Conversion to the Taliban* (Oakland, California: University of California Press), pp. 117 – 118. Available online at: http://www.jstor.org/stable/pdf/10.1525/j.ctt1kc6k3q.11.pdf (accessed 13/04/2017).

[480] Ziad (2017), p. 118.

[481] Qamar-ul Huda (2003) *Striving for Divine Union: Spiritual Exercises for Suhrawardī Sūfis* (London: RoutledgeCurzon), pp. 169 – 172.

[482] Huda (2003), p. 172.

[483] Huda (2003), p. 168.

[484] Rodwell had 'slay the victims' but many other translations simply say 'sacrifice'.

[485] Qur'ān 108 (Rodwell; Sale translations).

[486] Jalāl ad-Dīn Rūmī (author), Shams ad-Dīn Ahmad (author), James W. Redhouse (translator) (1881) *The Mesnavi (usually known as the Mesneviyi Sherīf) of Mevlānā (our lord) Jelālu-'d-Dīn, Muhammed, Er-Rūmī. Book the First. Together with some accounts of the life and acts of the author, of his ancestors, and of his descendants; illustrated by a selection of characteristic anecdotes, as collected by their historian, Mevlānā Shemsu-'d-Dīn Ahmed, El Eflākī, El 'Ārifī* (London: Trübner & Co.), Chapter III, par. 4, p. 20. Available online at: http://www.sacred-texts.com/isl/mes/index.htm (accessed 15/04/2017).

[487] Redhouse (1881), p. 20.

[488] Sezai Küçük (2007) Sama and the Spiritual Signs Within. In Faith Citlak (2007) *Rumi and the Sufi Path of Love* (Lanham: Tughra Books).

[489] Küçük (2007).

[490] Zoroaster (author), Maneckji Nusservanji Dhalla (translator), A.V. Williams Jackson (editor) (1908) *The Nyaishes or Zoroastrian Litanies: Avestan Text with the Pahlavi, Sanskrit, Persian and Gujarati Versions, Khordah Avesta, Part I* (New York: The Columia University Press), Khwarshed Niyayesh (Sun Litany), v. 0. Available online at: http://www.sacred-texts.com/zor/sbe23/ka.htm (accessed 15/04/2017).

[491] Veda-Vyāsa (author), Eknath Easwaran (translator) (2007) *The Bhagavad Gita* (Tomales, CA: Nilgiri Press), p. 113.

[492] Qur'ān 24:35 (Rodwell translation).

[493] Robert J. Wilkinson (2015) *Tetragrammaton: Western Christians and the Hebrew Name of God: From the Beginnings to the Seventeenth Century* (Boston: BRILL), p. 109.

[494] Sukanya Sarbadhikary (2015) Listening to Vrindavan: Chanting and Musical Experience as Embodying a Devotional Soundscape. In *Place of Devotion: Sitting and Experiencing Divinity in Bengal-Vaishnavism* (Oakland: California: University of California Press). Available online at: http://www.jstor.org/stable/10.1525/j.ctt1ffjn1f.10 (accessed 15/04/2017).

[495] 'Allāmah Majlisī (author) *Bihār al-Anwār*, vol. 85, p. 334. See: 'Merits of 'Tasbih' of Syeda Fatema Zehra (a.s)', *Duas.org*. Available online at: https://www.duas.org/tasbihzehra.htm (accessed 15/04/2017).

[496] Muhammad ibn Ya'qūb al-Kulaynī (author) *Al-Kāfī*, Kitābu s-Salāt, p. 342.. See: 'Merits of 'Tasbih' of Syeda Fatema Zehra (a.s)', *Duas.org*. Available online at: https://www.duas.org/tasbihzehra.htm (accessed 15/04/2017).

[497] 1 Thessalonians 5:17 (King James Bible).

[498] Luke 1:49 (King James Bible).

[499] Psalm 135:3, 13 (King James Bible).

[500] Jalāl ad-Dīn Rūmī (author), E.H. Whinfield (tranaslator) (1898) *The Spiritual Couplets of Maulana Jalalu'd-Din Muhammad Rumi*, Book I, Story IX. The Arab and his wife.

[501] Krsnādasa Kavirāja (1954), Ch. 3, p. 54.

[502] A Discourse on Abba Philimon.

[503] Isaiah 40:8 (King James Bible).

[504] Qur'ān 3:3 – 4 (Rodwell translation).

[505] Qur'ān 16:89 (Palmer translation).

[506] Qur'ān 14:1 (Rodwell translation).

[507] *Thirty Minor Upanishads*, Nārāyana-Upanishad, pp. 128 – 129.

[508] Madhvacharya writes: "The word Brahman is properly used to denote Vishnu the highest Lord and never any other; for all others (souls) are imperfect.. The Lord is spoken of as Brahman, Paramatman (the perfect self), Bagavan (the Almighty)." – *The Vedanta Sutras with the commentary of Sri Madhvacharya*, p. 18.

[509] **"That which is beyond these, (viz.,) Parabrahman which is beyond (the above *mātrās*), the pure, the all-pervading, beyond *kalās*, the ever resplendent and the source of all *jyoṭ is* (light) should be known."** – Nādabindu-Upanishad of Rig-Veda, *Thirty Minor Upanishads*, p. 256.

[510] **"The one Purusha, however, of whom I am thinking, transcends all Purushas and is invisible. The many Purushas that exist in the universe have that one Purusha as their basis."** – *The Mahabharata*, Book 12: Santi Parva, Part 3, Section CCCLI, p. 200.

[511] Qur'ān 6:73 (Palmer translation).

[512] Qur'ān 57:25 (Palmer translation).

[513] Thomas à Kempis, *The Imitation of Christ*, Ch. XXXIV, 1.

[514] Qur'ān 31:27 (Rodwell translation).

[515] Thomas à Kempis, *The Imitation of Christ*, Ch. V.

[516] Thomas à Kempis, *The Imitation of Christ*, Ch. V.

[517] John 6:63 (King James Bible).

[518] Matthew 13:13 (King James Bible).

[519] NJ Bridgewater (2017), pp. 179 – 180.

[520] Qur'ān 65:2 – 3 (Rodwell translation).

[521] Matthew 6:25 – 26 (King James Bible).

[522] Qur'ān 24:35 (Rodwell translation).

[523] Psalm 27:1 (King James Bible).

[524] *"There are also celestial bodies, and bodies terrestrial: but the glory of the celestial is one, and the glory of the terrestrial is another."* 1 Corinthians 15:40 (King James Bible).

[525] Matthew 5:3 – 16 (King James Bible).

[526] John 3:3 (King James Bible).

[527] Matthew 3:11 (King James Bible).

[528] John 6:51 (King James Bible).

[529] Zoroaster (author) *The Zend-Avesta*, Part I. The Vendîdâd, Fargard X, 19 (38). In S.A. Kapadia (1905) *The Teachings of Zoroaster, and The Philosophy of the Parsi Religion* (London: John Murray), p. 56. Available online at: http://www.sacred-texts.com/zor/toz/index.htm (accessed 21/04/2017).

[530] John 6:50 (King James Bible).

[531] Luke 9:60 (King James Bible).

[532] Qur'ān 12:111 (Rodwell translation).

[533] 1 Corinthians 6:19 (King James Bible).

[534] Philippians 4:8 (King James Bible).

[535] 1 Timothy 4:13 (King James Bible).

[536] Qur'ān 17:82 (Rodwell translation).

[537] Qur'ān 96:1, 3 – 5 (Rodwell translation).

[538] Proverbs 16:3 (King James Bible).

[539] Psalm 4:4 (King James Bible).

[540] Genesis 7:7 (King James Bible).

[541] Qur'ān 71:1 – 4 (Palmer translation).

[542] Qur'ān 59:21 (Sale translation).

[543] Matthew 13:13 (King James Bible).

[544] John 14:15 (King James Bible).

[545] Matthew 15:17 – 18 (King James Bible).

[546] Matthew 15:3 (King James Bible).

[547] Matthew 15:8 – 9 (King James Bible).

[548] John 13:35 (King James Bible).

[549] Veda-Vyāsa (author), Ganguli (translator) (1883-1896) *The Mahabharata*, Book 12: Santi Parva, Part 1: Rajadharmanusasana Parva, Section CIX.

[550] NJ Bridgewater (2017), p. 17.

[551] S. Subba Rau (translator) (1904) *The Vedanta-Sutras with the Commentary by Sri Madhwacharya – A Complete Translation* (Madras: Thompson & Co. at the 'Minerva' Press), Vedanta-Sutras with Madhwa Bhashya, p. 228. Available online at: https://archive.org/details/BrahmasutraMadhvaEnglish (accessed 21/04/2017).

[552] John 3:3 (King James Bible).

[553] Veda-Vyāsa (author), Ganguli (translator) (1883 – 1896) *The Mahabharata*, Book 18: Svargarohanika Parva, Section 5.

[554] Hebrews 4:12 (King James Bible).

[555] 2 Timothy 3:16 (King James Bible).

[556] *Srimad-Bhagavad-Gita*, Chapter II. v. 7, p. 70.

[557] Joshua 1:8 (King James Bible).

[558] William Blake (1901) *Songs of Innocence and Songs of Experience* (London: R. Brimley Johnson), The Divine Image, p. 17. Available online at: http://www.gutenberg.org/ebooks/1934 (accessed 22/04/2017).

[559] Alfred Tennyson (author), H.W. Shryock (editor) (1910) *Tennyson's Princess* (New York: American Book Company), The Higher Pantheism. Available online at: https://en.wikisource.org/wiki/The_Higher_Pantheism ; https://archive.org/details/tennysonsprinces04tenn (accessed 22/04/2017).

[560] Thomas à Kempis, *The Imitation of Christ*, Ch. III, 2.

[561] Veda-Vyāsa (author), S. Subba Rau (translator) (1928) *Srimad Bhagavatam, Translated into Easy English Prose, embodying the interpretations of the Three leading Schools of Thought, (Advaita, Visistadvaita and Dvaita)* (Tirupati: Sri Vyasa Press), First Skandha, Adhyaya 1, p. 1. Available online at: https://archive.org/details/in.ernet.dli.2015.272624 (accessed 22/04/2017).

[562] Patañjali (author), Ganganatha Jha (translator) (1907).

[563] Veda-Vyāsa (author), Arnold (translator) (1885) *The Song celestial or Bhagavad-gitâ*, Chapter VII.

[564] Jalāl ad-Dīn Rūmī (author), E.H. Whinfield (translator) (1898) *The Masnavi I Ma'navi* (London: Kegan Paul, Trench, Trubner), Book I, Prologue. Available online at: http://www.sacred-texts.com/isl/masnavi/index.htm (accessed 23/04/2017).

[565] Rv. VI. 47. 18. Quoted in Madhvacharya (author), S. Subba Rau (translator) (1904) *The Vedanta-Sutras with the Commentary by Sri Madhvacharya. A Complete Translation* (Madras: Thompson & Co. at the 'Minerva' Press), Vedanta-Sutras with Madhwa Bhashya, Second Adhyaya, Third Pada. Available online at: https://archive.org/details/BrahmasutraMadhvaEnglish (accessed 21/04/2017). See also: http://www.sacred-texts.com/hin/rigveda/rv06047.htm (accessed 22/04/2017).

[566] Qur'ān 23:84 (Rodwell translation).

[567] Madhvacharya (author), S. Subba Rau (translator) (1904), Fourth Adhyaya, First Pada, pp. 261 – 262.

[568] Madhvacharya (author), S. Subba Rau (translator) (1904), Fourth Adhyaya, First Pada, p. 263.

[569] Madhvacharya (author), S. Subba Rau (translator) (1904), First Adhyaya, Fourth Pada, p. 75.

[570] Genesis 1:27 (King James Bible).

[571] 1 John 4:8 (King James Bible).

[572] 1 John 4:7 (King James Bible).

[573] John 14:20 (King James Bible).

[574] NJ Bridgewater (2017), p. 184.

[575] NJ Bridgewater (2017), p. 184.

[576] Madhvacharya (author), S. Subba Rau (translator) (1904), Third Adhyaya, Third Pada, pp. 206 – 207.

[577] Madhvacharya (author), S. Subba Rau (translator) (1904), Third Adhyaya, Third Pada, pp. 209 – 210.

[578] Madhvacharya (author), S. Subba Rau (translator) (1904), Third Adhyaya, Third Pada, pp. 209 – 210.

[579] Qur'ān 47:3 (Sale translation).

[580] Qur'ān 62:1 (Rodwell translation).

[581] Veda-Vyāsa (author), Ralph T.H. Griffith (translator) (1896) *The Hymns of the Rig-Veda, translated with a popular commentary* (Benares: E.J. Lazarus and Co.), Book 6, Hymn LXIV. Available online at: http://www.sacred-texts.com/hin/rigveda/index.htm (accessed 24/04/2017). See also: https://archive.org/details/hymnsrigveda02grifgoog (accessed 24/04/2017).

[582] William Penn's Advice to His Children, at *The Quaker Writings Home Page*. Available online at: http://www.qhpress.org/quakerpages/qwhp/qwhp.htm (accessed 31/12/2016).

[583] Psalm 57:8 - 9 (1599 Geneva Bible). See also: Psalm 108:2 – 3.

[584] Qur'ān 30:17 (Rodwell translation).

[585] Madhvacharya (author), S. Subba Rau (translator) (1904), Fourth Adhyaya, First Pada, p. 263.

[586] Madhvacharya (author), S. Subba Rau (translator) (1904), Fourth Adhyaya, First Pada, pp. 261 – 262.

[587] *Thirty Minor Upanishads*, Ātmabodha-Upanishad of Rgveda, p. 37.

[588] *Thirty Minor Upanishads*, Kalisantārana-Upanishad, pp. 130 – 131.

[589] *Thirty Minor Upanishads*, Kalisantārana-Upanishad, pp. 130 – 131.

[590] See: NJ Bridgewater (2017), p. 173.

[591] Proverbs 18:10 (King James Bible).

[592] Psalm 61:8 (1599 Geneva Bible).

[593] Psalm 106:1 (King James Bible).

[594] Psalm 150:6 (King James Bible).

[595] Matthew 6:9 (King James Bible).

[596] Qur'ān 3:51 (Palmer translation).

[597] Qur'ān 1:1 (Rodwell translation).

[598] Qur'ān 55:78 (Rodwell translation).

[599] Qur'ān 2:255 (Sale translation).

[600] Qur'ān 24:35 (Palmer translation).

[601] Qur'ān 2:164 (Rodwell translation).

[602] Madhvacharya (author), S. Subba Rau (translator) (1904), Third Adhyaya, Third Pada, pp. 206 – 207.

[603] Madhvacharya (author), S. Subba Rau (translator) (1904), Third Adhyaya, Third Pada, pp. 209 – 210.

[604] *The Mahabharata*, Book 13: Anusasana Parva, Part 1, Anusasanika Parva, Section XVII.

[605] Veda-Vyāsa (author), Sir Edwin Arnold (translator) (1900) *The Song Celestial; Or, Bhagavad-Gîtâ (from the Mahâbhârata): Being a Discourse Between Arjuna, Prince of India, and the Supreme Being, Under the Form of Krishna*, Ch. XVI.

[606] Rv. VI. 47. 18. Quoted in Madhvacharya (author), S. Subba Rau (translator) (1904) *The Vedanta-Sutras with the Commentary by Sri Madhwacharya. A Complete Translation* (Madras: Thompson & Co. at the 'Minerva' Press), Vedanta-Sutras with Madhwa Bhashya, Second Adhyaya, Third Pada. Available online at: https://archive.org/details/BrahmasutraMadhvaEnglish (accessed 21/04/2017). See also: http://www.sacred-texts.com/hin/rigveda/rv06047.htm (accessed 22/04/2017).

[607] Qur'ān 45:12 – 13 (Rodwell translation).

[608] Jalāl ad-Dīn Rūmī (author), Whinfield (translator) (1898) *The Masnavi*, Book I, Story VI. Omar and the Ambassador.

[609] Abū Hāmid Muhamad ibn Muhammad Al-Ghazālī (author), Claud Field (translator) (1909) *The Alchemy of Happiness* (London: J. Murray), Chapter I, p. 19. Available online at: http://www.sacred-texts.com/isl/tah/index.htm (accessed 24/04/2017).

[610] Jalāl ad-Dīn Rūmī (author), Whinfield (translator) (1898) *The Masnavi*, Book I, Story VI. Omar and the Ambassador.

[611] Hakīm Abu'l-Majd Majdūd Sanā'ī (author), J. Stephenson (translator) (1910) *The Hadîqatu'l-Haqîqat (The Enclosed Garden of the Truth)* (Calcutta: Baptist Mission Press), On Intimate Friendship and Attachment, p. 103.

[612] Jalāl ad-Dīn Rūmī (author), Whinfield (translator) (1898) *The Masnavi*, Book I, Prologue.

[613] Matthew 11:15 (King James Bible).

[614] Mark 8:18 (King James Bible).

[615] Gautama Buddha (author), H. Kern (translator) (1884) *Saddharma-Pundarîka, or, the Lotus of the True Law*. In F. Max Müller (editor) (1884) *The Sacred Books of the East, translated by various Oriental scholars, Vol. XXI*. (Oxford: At the Clarendon Press), Chapter XXIV., v. 25 – 26. Available online at: http://www.sacred-texts.com/bud/lotus/index.htm (accessed 24/04/2017). See also: https://archive.org/details/sacredbookofthee025071mbp (accessed 24/04/2017).

[616] Veda-Vyāsa (author), Charles Wilkins (1785) *Bhagvat-geeta, or Dialogues of Kreeshna and Arjoon* (London: Nourse), p. 52. URL: http://lf-oll.s3.amazonaws.com/titles/2369/Wilkins_Bhagvat_Geeta_1785.pdf (accessed 23/04/2017).

[617] For the Sanskrit text, see: https://asitis.com/4/7.html (accessed 23/04/2017).

[618] John 1:1, 1:14 (King James Bible).

[619] Charles Wilkins (1785), p. 52.

[620] John 9:39 (King James Bible).

[621] Al-Ghazzali (author), W.H.T. Gairdner (1924) *Mishkât Al-Anwar (The Niche for Lights)* (London: Royal Asiatic Society), Part I. Light, and Lights: Preliminary Studies, p. 93. Available online at: http://www.sacred-texts.com/isl/mishkat/index.htm (accessed 24/04/2017).

[622] Carus (1894) *Buddha, The Gospel*, Sermon at Benares.

[623] Qur'ān 33:40 (Rodwell translation).

[624] Al-Ghazzali (author), W.H.T. Gairdner (1924), p. 111.

[625] John 5:46 (King James Bible).

[626] Qur'an 2:285 (Rodwell translation).

[627] Jalāl ad-Dīn Rūmī (author), Whinfield (translator) (1898) *The Masnavi*, Book I, Prologue.

[628] Madhvacharya (author), S. Subba Rau (translator) (1904), Third Adhyaya, Third Pada, p. 228.

[629] Madhvacharya (author), S. Subba Rau (translator) (1904), Third Adhyaya, Third Pada, p. 229.

[630] Sri Kedarnath Dutt Bhaktivinod (1896) *Srigouranga Smaranamangala or Chaitanya Mahaprabhu: His Life and Precepts* (Calcutta: Mookerjee & Co. at the Calcutta Press), *Śrī Gaurānga-Līlā-Smarana-Mangala-Stotram*, 75, p. 36. Available online at: http://www.krishnapath.org/Library/Goswami-books/Bhaktivinoda-Thakura/Bhaktivinoda_Thakura_Gauranga_Lila.pdf (accessed 22/04/2017).

[631] John 14:6 (King James Bible).

[632] Veda-Vyāsa (author), Wilkins (1785), Lecture XVIII, p. 133.

[633] John 14:11 (King James Bible).

[634] Veda-Vyāsa (author), Swarupananda (1909) *Srimad-Bhagavad-Gita*, Eighteenth Chapter, v. 65, p. 397. Wilkins (1785: 133) translates this as: **"Be of my mind, be my servant, offer unto me alone and bow down humbly before me, and thou shalt verily come unto me."**

[635] See the Sanskrit original here: https://asitis.com/18/65.html (accessed 23/04/2017).

[636] Veda-Vyāsa (author), Swarupananda (1909), Eighteenth Chapter, v. 68 – 69, pp. 399 – 400.

[637] See: Yajna (*Wikipedia* article). Available online at: https://en.wikipedia.org/wiki/Yajna (accessed 23/04/2017).

[638] See: https://asitis.com/18/65.html (accessed 23/04/2017).

[639] Qur'ān 2:83 (Palmer translation).

[640] Matthew 22:37 – 40 (King James Bible).

[641] Veda-Vyāsa (author), Sir Edwin Arnold (translator) (1900), Ch. XVI.

[642] Qur'ān 3:15, 17 (Rodwell translation).

[643] Qur'ān 2:42 (Rodwell translation).

[644] Qur'ān 4:135 (Rodwell translation).

[645] Qur'ān 11:85 (Palmer translation).

[646] Qur'ān 24:30 (Palmer translation).

[647] Qur'ān 17:53 (Palmer translation).

[648] Plato (author), Benjamin Jowett (translator) (1892) *The Dialogues of Plato, translated into English with Analyses and Introductions, Vol. II* (New York: Oxford University Press, American Branch; London: Henry Frowde), Meno. Available online at: http://classics.mit.edu/Plato/meno.1b.txt ; https://archive.org/details/dialoguesofplato18922plat (accessed 28/03/2017).

[649] 4 Maccabees 1:14, 16. In Rutherford H. Platt, Jr. (editor) (1926) *The Forgotten Books of Eden* (New York: L. Copeland). Available online at: http://www.sacred-texts.com/bib/fbe/index.htm (accessed 23/04/2017).

[650] 1 Corinthians 13:13 (King James Bible). For the Greek text, see: http://biblehub.com/text/1_corinthians/13-13.htm (accessed 23/04/2017).

[651] 1 John 4:8 (King James Bible). For the Greek text, see: http://biblehub.com/text/1_john/4-8.htm (accessed 23/04/2017).

[652] Shinrin Shōnin (author), S. Yamabe, L. Adams Beck (translators) (1921) *Buddhist Psalms translated from the Japanese of Shinran Shōnin* (London: John Murray), Lauding the Infinite One, v. 2 – 4, p. 19. Available online at: http://www.sacred-texts.com/bud/bups/index.htm (accessed 24/04/2017).

[653] Mahmūd Shabestarī (author), Florence Lederer (translator) (1920) *The Secret Rose Garden* (London: J. Murray), Part III. The Sea and Its Pearls, p. 37. Available online at: http://www.sacred-texts.com/isl/srg/index.htm (accessed 24/04/2017).

[654] Sanā'ī (author), Stephenson (translator) (1910), On Purity of Heart, pp. 11 – 12.

[655] John 8:12 (King James Bible).

[656] Khwāja Shamsu'd-Dīn Hafez-e-Shīrāzī (author), Gertrude Lowthian Bell (translator) (1897) *Poems from the Divan of Hafez* (London: Heinemann), XXVII.

[657] Hafez (author), Bell (translator) (1897), XV.

[658] Revelation 3:20 (King James Bible).

[659] NJ Bridgewater (2017), Chapters XIII – XV, pp. 189 – 228.

[660] F. Hadland Davis (1920) *Jalálu'd-Dín Rúmí*.

[661] Veda-Vyāsa (author), K. Narayanasvami Aiyar (translator) (1914) *Thirty Minor Upanishads* (Madras: Annie Besant at the Vasantā Press), Amrtabindu-Upanishad of Krshna-Yajurveda, p. 34. Available online at: http://www.sacred-texts.com/hin/tmu/tmu00.htm (accessed 17/04/2017).

662 Gautama Buddha, The Diamond Sutra (*Vajracchedika Sutra*), Based on William Gemmell's Translation, Edited, Rearranged and Interpreted. In Dwight Goddard (1932) *A Buddhist Bible*, p. 196. Copyright not renewed.

663 William Hart (2012) *The Art of Living: Vipissana Meditation as Taught by S.N. Goenka* (Maharashtra, India: Vipissana Research Institute), p. 6.

664 Hart (2012), p. 6.

665 Hart (2012), p. 6.

666 Hui-Neng, *The Tan-Ching*, v. 27. Quoted in Daisetz Teitaro Suzuki (1935) *Manual of Zen Buddhism* (Kyoto: Pl. XV. Kyoto), IV. From the Chinese Zen Masters, III. From Hui-Neng's Tan-Ching. Available online at: http://www.sacred-texts.com/bud/mzb/index.htm (accessed 17/04/2017). The book is in the public domain as it was not properly copyrighted in its earlier editions.

667 Sayadaw U Pandita (2017) How to Practice Vipassana Insight Meditation, *Lion's Roar: Buddhist Wisdom for Our Time*, April 8, 2017. Available online at: https://www.lionsroar.com/how-to-practice-vipassana-insight-meditation/ (accessed 16/04/2017).

668 Joseph Goldstein & Jack Kornfield (2001) *Seeking the Heart of Wisdom: The Path of Insight Meditation* (Boston: Shambhala).

669 Larry Rosenberg & David Guy (2004) *Breath by Breath: The Liberating Practice of Insight Meditation* (Boston, MA: Shambhala).

670 Sayagyi U Ba Khin (1997) *The Essentials of Buddha-Dhamma in Meditative Practice* (Onalaska, WA: Vipassana Research Publications).

671 William Hart (2012) *The Art of Living: Vipassana Meditation as taught by S. N. Goenke* (Maharashtra, India: Vipassana Research Institute).

672 S. N. Goenka (2000) *Discourse Summaries: Talks from a Ten-day Course in Vipassana Meditation* (Chicago: Pariyatti Publishing).

673 Bodhidharma, *The Transmission of the Lamp*, XXX. In Daisetz Teitaro Suzuki (1935), IV. From the Chinese Zen Masters, I. Bodhidharma on the Twofold Entrance to the Tao.

674 Bodhidharma (*Wikipedia* article). Available online at: https://en.wikipedia.org/wiki/Bodhidharma (accessed 16/04/2017).

675 Chan Buddhism (*Wikipedia* article). Available online at: https://en.wikipedia.org/wiki/Chan_Buddhism (accessed 16/04/2017).

676 Kaiten Nukariya (1913) *The Religion of the Samurai, A Study of Zen Philosophy and Discipline in China and Japan* (Auckland: Floating Press), Ch. VIII. Available online at: http://www.sacred-texts.com/bud/rosa/index.htm (accessed 26/12/2016).

677 NJ Bridgewater (2017), p. 161.

678 NJ Bridgewater (2017), pp. 161 – 162.

679 Shunryū Suzuki (2011) *Zen Mind, Beginner's Mind* (Boston, Mass.: Shambhala Publications), p. 1.

680 Suzuki (2011), p. 2.

681 Kaiten Nukariya (1913) *The Religion of the Samurai, A Study of Zen Philosophy and Discipline in China and Japan*, Ch. VIII.

682 Gautama Buddha (author), W.D.C. Wagiswara, K.J. Saunders (1920) *The Buddha's Way of Virtue*, § III, v. 35, 39, pp. 26 – 27.

683 Qiao Renjie (2017a) *Zen: A Complete Beginner's Guide to Zen Meditation* (Meditation, Yoga and Health series) (Kindle ebook), p. 11. Available online at: https://www.amazon.com/Zen-Complete-Beginners-Meditation-Mindfulness-ebook/dp/B06WGQM8T7/ (accessed 16/04/2017).

684 Suzuki (1935) *Manual of Zen Buddhism*, I. Gathas and Prayers. VII. The Gatha of Impermanence.

[685] Ekai, called Mu-mon (author) Nyogen Senzaki, Paul Reps (translators) (1934) *The Gateless Gate* (Los Angeles: John Murray), 5. Kyogen Mounts the Tree. Copyright not renewed. Available online at: http://www.sacred-texts.com/bud/glg/glg00.htm (accessed 16/04/2017).

[686] Ekai (author), Senzaki, Reps (translators).

[687] Ekai (author), Nyogen Senzaki, Paul Reps (translators) (1934), 27. It is Not Mind, It Is Not Buddha, It Is Not Things.

[688] Qiao Renjie (2017a) *Zen: A Complete Beginner's Guide to Zen Meditation* (Meditation, Yoga and Health series) (Kindle ebook). Available online at: https://www.amazon.com/Zen-Complete-Beginners-Meditation-Mindfulness-ebook/dp/B06WGQM8T7/ (accessed 16/04/2017).

[689] Shunryū Suzuki (2011) *Zen Mind, Beginner's Mind* (Boston, Mass.: Shambhala Publications).

[690] Alan W. Watts (2011) *The Way of Zen* (New York: Vintage Books).

[691] Philip Kapleau (2007) *The Three Pillars of Zen: Teaching, Practice and Enlightenment* (New York: Anchor Books).

[692] Dainin Katagiri (2009) *Each Moment is the Universe: Zen and the way of being time* (Boston, Mass.: Shambhala).

[693] Charlotte Joko Beck (2009) *Everyday Zen: Love and Work* (New York: HarperCollins).

[694] Thich Nhat Hanh (1992) *Peace is Every Step: The Path of Mindfulness in Everyday Life* (New York: Bantam Books).

[695] Koun Yamada & Rube L.F. Habito (2005) *The Gateless Gate: The Classic Book of Zen Koans* (Somerville: Wisdom Publications).

[696] Gautama Buddha (author), E.J. Thomas (translator) (1913) *Buddhist Scriptures: A Selection from the Pali with an Introduction* (London: John Murray), VI. The Beginning of the Buddha's Preaching, p. 41. Available online at: http://www.sacred-texts.com/bud/busc/index.htm (accessed 17/04/2017).

[697] Qiao Renjie (2017a), p. 13.

[698] Renjie (2017), p. 13.

[699] Danny & Katherine Dreyer (2012) Walking as Meditation: Quiet Your Mind as You Improve Your Health. The Blog, *Huffington Post*, Oct 23, 2012 12:06 am ET. Available online at: http://www.huffingtonpost.com/danny-and-katherine-dreyer/walking-meditation_b_1790035.html (accessed 16/04/2017).

[700] Dreyer & Dreyer (2012).

[701] Dreyer & Dreyer (2012).

[702] Dreyer & Dreyer (2012).

[703] Dreyer & Dreyer (2012).

[704] Gautama Buddha (author), W.D.C. Wagiswara, K.J. Saunders (1920) *The Buddha's Way of Virtue*, § XXIII, v. 327, p. 78.

[705] Barry Boyce (2013) Walk This Way. *Mindful.org*, April 3, 2017. The article also appeared in the June 2013 issue of Mindful magazine. Available online at: http://www.mindful.org/walk-this-way/ (accessed 16/04/2017).

[706] Boyce (2013).

[707] Boyce (2013).

[708] Boyce (2013).

[709] Boyce (2013).

[710] Boyce (2013).

[711] Boyce (2013).

[712] Nguyen Anh-Huong & Thich Nhat Hanh (2006) *Walking Meditation* (Boulder: Sounds True).

[713] Thich Nhat Hanh (2011) *The Long Road Turns to Joy: A Guide to Walking Meditation* (Berkeley, Calif.: Parallax Press).

[714] Napoleon Hill (1938) *Think and Grow Rich* (Meriden, Conn.: The Ralston Society), Chapter 10 – Power of the Master Mind, p. 252. Available online at: http://www.sacred-texts.com/nth/tgr/tgr00.htm (accessed 17/04/2017). Public domain in the US as its copyright was not renewed at the US Copyright office in a timely fashion.

[715] Veda-Vyāsa (author), Ganguli (translator) (1883-1896) *The Mahabharata*, Book 12: Santi Parva, Section CLXXXV, p. 28.

[716] Fran Gaik (2009) *Managing Depression with Qigong* (London: Jessica Kingsley Publications), p. 48.

[717] Gaik (2009), p. 39.

[718] Laozi (author) Tao Te Ching. In J. Legge (translator) (1891) *The Texts of Taoism* Sacred Books of the East, Vol. 39) (Oxford: Oxford University Press), 4. Available online at: http://www.sacred-texts.com/tao/sbe39/sbe39000.htm (accessed 17/04/2017).

[719] Ronald H. Davis (2015) *Qigong Through the Seasons: How to Stay Healthy All Year with Qigong, Meditation, Diet, and Herbs* (London; Philadelphia: Singing Dragon), pp. 58 – 59.

[720] Davis (2015), p. 59.

[721] Davis (2015), p. 59.

[722] Davis (2015), p. 59.

[723] Davis (2015), p. 59.

[724] Davis (2015), p. 59.

[725] Lucy Flood (2017) How to Practice Qi Gong's Forest Meditation, *The Chopra Center*. Available online at: http://www.chopra.com/articles/how-to-practice-qi-gong%E2%80%99s-forest-meditation#sm.0001bms3lb1svcnwuqm1qb8z6p3d6 (accessed 16/04/2017).

[726] Flood (2017).

[727] Veda-Vyāsa (author), Ganguli (translator) (1883-1896) *The Mahabharata*, Book 14: Aswamedha Parva, Anugita Parva, Section XIX, p. 34.

[728] Flood (2017).

[729] Ronald H. Davis (2015) *Qigong Through the Seasons: How to Stay Healthy All Year with Qigong, Meditation, Diet, and Herbs* (London; Philadelphia: Singing Dragon).

[730] Kenneth S. Cohen (1999) *The Way of Qigong: The Art and Science of Chinese Energy Healing* (New York: Ballantine Books).

[731] Jwing-Ming Yang (2016) *The Root of Chinese Qigong: Secrets of Health, Longevity, & Enlightenment* (Wolfeboro, NH: YMAA Publication Center).

[732] Jwing-Ming Yang (2016) *Qigong Meditation: Small Circulation* (Wolfeboro, NH: YMAA Publication Center).

[733] Jwing-Ming Yang (2003) *Qigong Meditation: Embryonic Breathing* (Wolfeboro, NH: YMAA Publication Center).

[734] Edward Hines (2013) *Moving into Stillness – A Practical Guide to Qigong and Meditation* (North Charleston, SC: CreateSpace Independent Publishing Platform).

[735] Rishi Singh Gherwal (1930) *Kundalini, The Mother of the Universe: The Mystery of Piercing the Six Chakras* (Santa Barbara, Calif.: Published by the Author), p. 54. Public domain in the US because its copyright was not renewed in a timely fashion at the US Copyright Office.

[736] See: Leigh Weingus (2016) I Tried Kundalini Yoga. Here's Everything You Need to Know. *Mindbodygreen.com*, July 7, 2016 3:48 AM. Available online at: https://www.mindbodygreen.com/0-25810/i-tried-kundalini-yoga-heres-everything-you-need-to-know.html (accessed 17/04/2017).

[737] Rishi Singh Gherwal (1930), p.22.

[738] Weingus (2016).

[739] Kundalini yoga (*Wikipedia* article). Available online at: https://en.wikipedia.org/wiki/Kundalini_yoga (accessed 17/04/2017).

[740] Veda-Vyāsa (author), K. Narayanasvami Aiyar (translator) (1914) Yogakundalī-Upanishad of Krshna-Yajurveda, pp. 260 - 272.

[741] Shakti (*Wikipedia* article). Available online at: https://en.wikipedia.org/wiki/Shakti (accessed 17/04/2017).

[742] Veda-Vyāsa (author), K. Narayanasvami Aiyar (translator) (1914) Yogakundalī-Upanishad of Krshna-Yajurveda.

[743] Madhu Khanna (2004) A Journey into Cosmic Consciousness: Kundalini Shakti. *India International Centre Quarterly*, Vol. 30, No. 3/4, JOURNEYS HEROES, PILGRIMS, EXPLORERS (WINTER 2003-SPRING 2004), pp. 224-238. Available online at: http://www.jstor.org/stable/23006136 (accessed 17/04/2017).

[744] Khanna (2004).

[745] Chakra (*Wikipedia* article). Available online at: https://en.wikipedia.org/wiki/Chakra (accessed 17/04/2017).

[746] Yoga International (2013) Purify Your Chakras, Part 4: How to Practice Bhuta Shuddhi. *Yoga International*, June 5, 2013. Available online at: https://yogainternational.com/article/view/purify-your-chakras-part-4-how-to-practice-bhuta-shuddhi (accessed 17/04/2017).

[747] See: https://yogainternational.com/article/view/purify-your-chakras-part-4-how-to-practice-bhuta-shuddhi

[748] Arthur Avalon (Sir John Woodroffe) (1918) *Shakti and Shâkta: Essays and Addresses on the Shâkta tantrashâstra* (London: Luzac &Co.), p. 240. Available online at: http://www.mysticknowledge.org/Shakti_and_Shakta-By_Arthur_Avalon.pdf (accessed 17/04/2017).

[749] Qiao Renjie (2017c) *Kundalini: Awaken Shakti through Kundalini Meditation* (Meditation, Yoga and Health series) (Kindle ebook). Available online at: https://www.amazon.com/dp/B071VTSPYF/ (accessed 18/05/2017).

[750] Gopi Krishna (1997) *Kundalini: The Evolutionary Energy in Man* (Boston: Shambhala).

[751] Gopi Krishna (2014) *Kundalini: The Secret of Yoga* (Los Gatos: Smashwords Edition).

[752] Shakti Parwha Kaur Khalsa (1998) *Kundalini Yoga: The Flow of Eternal Power: A Simple Guide to the Yoga of Awareness as taught by Yogi Bhajan, Ph.D.* (New York: Berkley Pub. Group).

[753] Dharma Singh Khalsa, Darryl O'Keeffe (2002) *The Kundalini Yoga Experience: Bringing Body, Mind, and Spirit Together* (New York: Simon & Schuster).

[754] John Woodroffe (2003) *The Serpent Power* (Madras: Ganesh & Co.).

[755] The Editor (1908) Buddhist Meditations, In *The Open Court – A Monthly Magazine Devoted to the Science of Religion, the Religion of Science, and the Extension of the Religious Parliament Idea*, Vol. XXII (Chicago: The Open Court Publishing Company), Anon., Buddhist Meditations, *The Open Court* (magazine), p. 559. Available online at: http://www.sacred-texts.com/journals/oc/budmed.htm (accessed 14/03/2017).

[756] Quoted in Iamblichus, *Life of Pythagoras or Pythagoric Life*, Protreptics, or Exhortations to Philosophy, Ch. III, p. 247.

[757] Quoted in Iamblichus, *Life of Pythagoras or Pythagoric Life*, Protreptics, or Exhortations to Philosophy, Ch. III, par. 3, p. 184.

[758] See: Bahá'u'lláh (author), Shoghi Effendi (translator) (1990) *Gleanings from the Writings of Bahá'u'lláh* (Wilmette, Illinois: US Bahá'í Publishing Trust), CXII, p. 260. Available online at: http://reference.bahai.org/en/t/b/GWB/index.html (accessed 06/07/2018). See also: the 'Parable of the Pearl of Great Price' (Matthew 13:45 – 46).

[759] See: Bahá'u'lláh (author), Shoghi Effendi (translator) (1985) *The Hidden Words of Bahá'u'lláh* (Wilmette, Illinois: US Bahá'í Publishing Trust), Arabic #13. Available online at: http://reference.bahai.org/en/t/b/HW/index.html (accessed 06/07/2018).

[760] See: Bahá'u'lláh (author), Alí Kuli Khán, Marzieh Gail (translators) (1991) *The Seven Valleys And the Four Valleys* (Wilmette, Illinois: US Bahá'í Publishing Trust), Seven Valleys, The Valley of Love, p. 11. Available online at: http://reference.bahai.org/en/t/b/SVFV/index.html (accessed 06/07/2018).

[761] Henry Clarke Warren (1896) *Buddhism in Translations: Passages Selected from the Buddhist Sacred Books and Translated from the Original Pâli into English* (Cambridge, Mass.: Harvard University Press), § 11. The Buddha's Daily Habits, p. 93. Available online at: http://www.sacred-texts.com/bud/bits/index.htm (accessed 29/03/2017).

[762] Swami Vivekananda (1920) *Râja Yoga: Being lectures by the Swâmi Vivekânanda* (New York: Brentano's), p. 27. Available online at: https://archive.org/details/raajayogabeingleoooviveuoft (accessed 21/03/2017).

[763] Vivekananda (1920), pp. 26 – 27.

[764] Émile Durkheim (author), Joseph Ward Swain (translator) (1915) *The Elementary Forms of the Religious Life* (London: George Allen & Unwin), p. 47. Available online at: https://archive.org/details/elementaryformsooodurk (accessed 28/04/2017). See also: http://www.gutenberg.org/ebooks/41360 (accessed 28/04/2017).

[765] A Disciple (1921) *In the Hours of Meditation* (Calcutta: S. C. Majumdah) I, p. 2. Available online at: https://archive.org/details/inhoursofmeditatoodiscrich (accessed 22/02/2017).

[766] See: Charlotte Bell (2015) How to Choose a Meditation Cushion. *Hugger Mugger Yoga Products*. Available online at: http://www.huggermugger.com/blog/2015/meditation-cushion/ (accessed 28/04/2017).

[767] See: Which Meditation Cushion Is Best for You? *Yoga Outlet*. Available online at: https://www.yogaoutlet.com/guides/which-meditation-cushion-is-best-for-you (accessed 28/04/2017).

[768] See: Singing bowl (Wikipedia article). Available online at: https://en.wikipedia.org/wiki/Singing_bowl (accessed 28/04/2017).

[769] Image source: Imperial Japanese Commission to the Panama-Pacific International Exposition - Japanese Temples and their Treasures (The Shimbi Shoin 1915). URL: https://upload.wikimedia.org/wikipedia/commons/c/c9/Itsukushima_Jinsha_Bronze_Vadjras_and_B ell_%28477%29.jpg (accessed 28/04/2017). Image is in the public domain.

[770] Shashi Bhusan Dasgupta (1950) *An Introduction to Tāntric Buddhism* (Calcutta: University of Calcutta), p. 72. Available online at: https://archive.org/details/in.ernet.dli.2015.28797?q=vajra (accessed 28/04/2017).

[771] The Editors of Encyclopædia Britannica (1998) Vajra, Buddhist Ritual Object. *Encyclopædia Britannica Online*. Available online at: https://www.britannica.com/topic/vajra (accessed 28/04/2017).

[772] Robert Beer (2003) *The Handbook of Tibetan Buddhist Symbols* (Chicago, London: Serindia), p. 92.

[773] Dasgupta (1950), p. 78.

[774] John Woodroffe (Arthur Avalon), Kazi Dawa-Samdup (editors) (1919) *Shrīchakrasambhāra Tantra: A Buddhist Tantra, Tantrik Texts, Vol. VII* (London, Calcutta: Luzac & Co.). Available online at: https://archive.org/details/Tantric_Texts_Series_Edited_by_Arthur_Avalon_John_Woodroffe?q=vajr a (accessed 28/04/2017).

[775] James Allen (1907) *From Poverty to Power: The Path to prosperity and The Way of Peace* (Albuquerque, NM: Sun Pub. Co.). Available online at: http://www.gutenberg.org/ebooks/10740 (accessed 22/02/2017).

[776] Rebecca L. Weber (2013) The world's best meditation retreats. *CNN.com*, June 25, 2013. Available online at: http://www.cnn.com/2013/06/25/travel/best-meditation-retreats/ (accessed 28/04/2017).

[777] Caroline Sylger Jones (2015) Wellness Holidays: from meditation weekends to high-tech rejuvenation. *The Independent*, 9 January 2015 11:11 GMT. Available online at: http://www.independent.co.uk/travel/news-and-advice/wellness-holidays-from-meditation-weekends-to-high-tech-rejuvenation-9967413.html (accessed 28/04/2017).

[778] Caroline Sylger Jones (2016) 10 UK holidays that will make you a better person. *The Telegraph*, 5 September 2016 11:15 AM. Available online at: http://www.telegraph.co.uk/travel/destinations/europe/united-kingdom/articles/the-best-body-and-soul-holidays-in-britain/ (accessed 28/04/2017).

[779] Erica Camus (2016) 14 of the best mindfulness retreats. *Metro.co.uk*, 15 August 2016 2PM. Available online at: http://metro.co.uk/2016/08/15/14-of-the-best-mindfulness-retreats-6036485/ (accessed 28/04/2017).

[780] Carolyn Gregoire (2013) Silent Retreats: 10 Fantastic Retreat Centers In The U.S. For Peace & Quiet (PHOTOS). *Huffington Post*, 02/28/2013 07:24 AM ET. Updated Feb 28, 2013. Available online at: http://www.huffingtonpost.com/2013/02/28/silent-retreats-america_n_2727408.html (accessed 28/04/2017).

[781] Brooke Bobb (2016) Beginner-Friendly Meditation Retreats in Some of the World's Most Beautiful Settings. *Vogue*, February 17, 2016 6:33 PM. Available online at: http://www.vogue.com/article/beginner-meditation-retreats-beginners-italy-california-bali (accessed 28/04/2017).

[782] See: Bhaktivedanta Manor, The College of Vedic Studies. Available online at: http://krishnacollege.co.uk/ (accessed 28/04/2017).

[783] See: ISKCON New Govardhana Australia (2014) 'New Govardhana Weddings and Retreats,' *New Govardhana Australia, ISKCON*. Available online at: http://www.krishnafarm.net/new-govardhana-retreats/ (accessed 28/04/2017).

[784] See: VIHE (2017) Vrindavan Institute for Higher Education (VIHE). Available online at: http://vihe.org/ (accessed 28/04/2017).

[785] VIHE (2017).

[786] Gautama Buddha (author), W.D.C. Wagiswara, K.J. Saunders (translators) (1920) *The Buddha's Way of Virtue*, § XX. The Path, v. 276 , p. 63.

[787] St. Ignatius of Loyola (author), Elder Mullan (translator) (1914) *Spiritual Exercises of St. Ignatius of Loyola* (New York: Kennedy), First Week. Available online at: http://www.sacred-texts.com/chr/seil/ (accessed 29/04/2017).

[788] NJ Bridgewater (2017c) Recommended Charities & Charitable Organizations. *Equanimity Blog*, February 6, 2017. Available online at: https://fivewaystobe.wordpress.com/2017/02/06/recommended-charities-charitable-organizations/ (accessed 28/04/2017).

[789] Veda-Vyāsa (author), Ganguli (translator) (1883-1896) *The Mahabharata*, Book 12: Santi Parva, Part 3, Section CCCXXVII, p. 89.

[790] Leviticus 19:18 (King James Bible).

[791] Deuteronomy 6:4 – 5 (King James Bible).

[792] Matthew 22:40 (King James Bible).

[793] Psalm 62:1, 6 – 7, 12 (King James Bible).

[794] Gautama Buddha (author), Müller (1881) *The Dhammapada*, Ch. XVII, v. 226, p. 58.

[795] See: Khuddaka Nikaya (*Wikipedia* article). Available online at: https://en.wikipedia.org/wiki/Khuddaka_Nikaya (accessed 28/04/2017).

[796] Dhammapada (*Wikipedia* article). Available online at: https://en.wikipedia.org/wiki/Dhammapada (accessed 28/04/2017).

797 Dhammapada (*Wikipedia* article).

798 Gautama Buddha (author), Buddhaghosa (commentator), Daw Mya Tin (translator), Editorial Committee, Burma Tipitaka Association (editors) (1986) *The Dhammapada: Verses and Stories* (Rangoon, Burma). Available online at: http://www.tipitaka.net/tipitaka/dhp/ (accessed 28/04/2017).

799 Gautama Buddha (author), Acharya Buddharakkhita (translator) (1996) *The Dhammapada: The Buddha's Path of Wisdom* (Kandy, Sri Lanka: Buddhist Publication Society). Available online at: http://www.accesstoinsight.org/tipitaka/kn/dhp/dhp.intro.budd.html (accessed 28/04/2017).

800 Veda-Vyāsa (author), Swami Swarupananda (translator) (1909) *Srimad-Bhagavad-Gita*, Ch. XVIII, v. 70 – 71, pp. 400 – 401.

801 His Divine Grace A.C. Bhaktivedanta Swami Prabhupada (1968a) *Bhagavad-Gītā As It Is* (New York: ISKCON).

802 Veda-Vyāsa (author), Wilkins (translator) (1785) *The Bhagvat-Geetā or Dialogues of Kreeshna and Arjoon* (London: C. Nourse). Available online at: http://oll.libertyfund.org/titles/wilkins-the-bhagvat-geeta-or-dialogues-of-kreeshna-and-arjoon (accessed 05/05/2017).

803 Veda-Vyāsa (author), Sir Edwin Arnold (translator) (1885) *The Song celestial or Bhagavad-gîtâ (from the Mahâbhârata), Translated from the Sanskrit Text* (London: Trübner & Co.). Available online at: http://www.sacred-texts.com/hin/gita/index.htm (accessed 16/03/2017).

804 Veda-Vyāsa (author), Swami Swarupananda (translator) (1909) *Srimad-Bhagavad-Gita* (Mayavati, Himalayas: Prabuddha Bharata Press). Available online at: http://www.sacred-texts.com/hin/sbg/index.htm (accessed 19/03/2017).

805 Veda-Vyāsa (author), Barbara Stoler Miller (translator) (2004) *The Bhagavad-Gita, Krishna's Counsel in Time of War* (New York: Bantam Books).

806 See: A.C. Bhaktivedanta Swami Prabhupada (1968) *Bhagavad-Gītā As It Is*, Chapter 9: The Most Confidential Knowledge. Available online at: https://asitis.com/9 (accessed 28/04/2017).

807 Qur'ān 73:4 (Rodwell translation).

808 Sir Richard Francis Burton (1893) *Personal Narrative of a Pilgrimage to Al-Madinah and Meccah, Volume I* (Memorial Edition) (London: Tylston and Edwards), Chapter IV. Life in the Wakalah, p. 68, Footnote 29. Available online at: http://www.gutenberg.org/ebooks/4657 ; https://archive.org/details/in.ernet.dli.2015.38756 (accessed 28/04/2017).

809 See: Ya Sin (*Wikipedia* article). Available online at: https://en.wikipedia.org/wiki/Ya_Sin (accessed 28/04/2017).

810 Qur'ān 31:2 – 3 (Rodwell translation).

811 Talal Itani (2014) *The Quran in English* (Dallas, Tex.: ClearQuran). Available online at: http://www.clearquran.com/ ; http://www.quranful.com/ (accessed 12/05/2017).

812 Arthur John Arberry (1953) *The Holy Koran* (London: G. Allen). Available online at: http://www.theonlyquran.com/quran/Al-Fathiha/English_Arthur_John_Arberry (accessed 12/05/2017).

813 Muhammad Asad (1980) *The Message of the Qur'ān: the full account of the revealed Arabic text accompanied by parallel transliteration* (Gibraltar: Dar al-Andalus). Available online at: http://muhammad-asad.com/Message-of-Quran.pdf ; https://archive.org/details/TheMessageOfTheQuran_20140419 (accessed 12/05/2017).

814 Muhammad Marmaduke Pickthall (1938) *The Meaning of the Glorious Quran* (Hyderabad-Deccan: Government Central Press). Available online at: http://www.sacred-texts.com/isl/pick/ (accessed 12/05/2017).

815 Abdullah Yusuf Ali (1934) *The Meaning of the Glorious Qur'ân: Text, Translation and Commentary* (Cairo: Dar al-Kitab Al-Masri). Available online at: http://www.sacred-texts.com/isl/yaq/index.htm (accessed 12/05/2017).

816 Edward Henry Palmer (translator) (1880) *The sacred books of the east translated by various oriental scholars and edited by F. Max Müller. Vol. 6, The Qur'ân, Part I: I-XVI & Vol. 9, Part II: XVII-CXIV*

(Oxford: At the Clarendon Press). Available online at: http://www.sacred-texts.com/isl/sbe06/index.htm (accessed 15/03/2017).

[817] J. M. Rodwell (1876) *El-Kor'ân, or, The Koran* (London: B. Quaritch). URL: http://www.sacred-texts.com/isl/qr/index.htm; http://www.gutenberg.org/ebooks/3434 (accessed 05/05/2017).

[818] George Sale (1734) *The Koran, commonly called the Alcoran of Mohammed: translated into English immediately from the original Arabic; with explanatory notes, taken from the most approved commentators. To which is prefixed a preliminary discourse* (London: J. Wilcox). Available online at: http://web.archive.org/web/20130510213544/http://arthursbookshelf.com/koran/The%20Qur'an%20tranlated%20by%20George%20Sale-h.html ; http://www.gutenberg.org/ebooks/7440 ; http://oll.libertyfund.org/people/4376 (accessed 12/05/2017).

[819] Seyyed Hossein Nasr, Caner K. Dagli, Maria Massi Dakake, Joseph E.B. Lumbard and Mohammed Rustom (2015) *The Study Quran: A New Translation and Commentary* (New York, NY: HarperCollins Publishers).

[820] See: http://www.islamawakened.com/index.php/qur-an (accessed 12/05/2017).

[821][821] See: http://corpus.quran.com/ (accessed 12/05/2017).

[822] Confucius (author), James Legge (translator) (1861) *The Chinese Classics (Confucian Analects)* (London: Trübner & Co.), Book XVI, Ch. IX. Available online at: http://www.gutenberg.org/ebooks/3330 (accessed 29/04/2017).

[823] John 8:12 (King James Bible)

[824] Qur'ān 53:1 – 2 (Palmer translation).

[825] Qur'ān 53:3 (Sale translation).

[826] Qur'ān 53:4 (Palmer translation).

[827] Qur'ān 8:17 (Sale translation).

[828] John 14:20 (King James Bible).

[829] Qur'ān 7:35 (Sale translation).

[830] *Mahaparinirvana-sutra*, quoted in Kaiten Nukariya (1913) *The Religion of the Samurai*, Chapter IV.

[831] Martin Lings (1983) *Muhammad: His Life Based on the Earliest Sources* (New York: Inner Traditions International).

[832] Karen Armstrong (1992) *Muhammad: A Biography of the Prophet* (San Francisco, Calif.: Harper San Fransisco).

[833] H M Balyuzi (2002) *Muhammad and the Course of Islam* (Oxford: George Ronald).

[834] W. Montgomery Watt (1953) *Muhammad at Mecca* (Oxford: The Clarendon Press); W. Montgomery Watt (1956) *Muhammad at Medina* (Oxford: The Clarendon Press).

[835] Jamshed Fozdar (1979) *The God of Buddha* (New York: Asia Pub. House).

[836] A.C. Bhaktivedenta Swami Prabhupāda (1977) *Śrīmad Bhāgavatam: Tenth Canto: "the summum bonum": (part one--chapters 1-5): with the original Sanskrit text, its Roman transliteration, synonyms, translation and elaborate purports* (New York: Bhaktivedanta Book Trust).

[837] A.C. Bhaktivedenta Swami Prabhupāda (1972) *Krsna, the supreme personality of Godhead : a summary study of Srila Vyasadeva's 'Śrīmad-Bhāgavatam, tenth canto'. Vol. 3* (New York; London: Bhaktivedanta Book Trust).

[838] NJ Bridgewater (2017), p. 222 – 223.

[839] A.V. Williams Jackson (1899) *Zoroaster, the Prophet of Ancient Iran* (New York: Macmillan). URL: https://ia600205.us.archive.org/17/items/zoroasterprophet00jack/zoroasterprophet00jack.pdf (accessed 29/04/2017).

[840] Robert Charles Zaehner (1961) *The Dawn and Twilight of Zoroastrianism* (New York: Putnam).

[841] Vanamali (2012) *The Complete Life of Krishna: Based on the Earliest Oral Traditions and the Sacred Scriptures* (Rochester, VT: Inner Traditions).

[842] Vraja Kishor (Vic Dicara) (2013) *Beautiful Tales of the All-Attractive: Volume 1* (North Charleston, SC: CreateSpace Independent Publishing Platform).

[843] Reza Aslan (2005) *No god but God: The Origins, Evolution, and Future of Islam* (New York: Ember).

[844] Bhikkhu Nanamoli (2003) *Life of the Buddha: According to the Pali Canon* (Kandy, Sri Lanka: Buddhist Publication Company).

[845] Karen Armstrong (2004) *Buddha* (New York; Toronto: Penguin Books).

[846] Karen Armstrong (2013) *Muhammad: A Prophet for Our Time* (New York: HarperCollins).

[847] NJ Bridgewater (2004) Founders of the Divine Religions, 1 January 2004. Available online at: http://klausjames.tripod.com/bahai3.html (accessed 29/04/2017).

[848] Richard Laurence (translator) (1883) *The Book of Enoch The Prophet, Translated from the Ethiopic Ms. In the Bodleian Library* (London: Kegan Paul, Trench & Co.), Chap. XIV, 2, p. 16. Available online at: http://www.sacred-texts.com/bib/bep/index.htm (accessed 30/04/2017).

[849] NJ Bridgewater (2017b) How can we achieve true happiness and inner peace? *Equanimity Blog*, February 8, 2017. Available online at: https://fivewaystobe.wordpress.com/2017/02/08/how-can-we-achieve-true-happiness-and-inner-peace/ (accessed 29/04/2017).

[850] Jack Kornfield (2008) *Meditation for Beginners* (Boulder, Colo.: Sounds True).

[851] Sharon Salzberg (2010) *Real Happiness: The Power of Meditation* (New York: Workman Pub.).

[852] Thich Nhat Hanh (1996) *The Miracle of Mindfulness: An Introduction to the Practice of Meditation* (Boston: Beacon Press).

[853] Jon Kabat-Zinn (2016) *Mindfulness for Beginners: Reclaiming the Present Moment—and Your Life* (Boulder, CO: Sounds True).

[854] Alan W. Watts (2011) *The Way of Zen* (New York: Vintage Books).

[855] Shunryū Suzuki (2010) *Zen Mind, Beginner's Mind* (Boston: Shambhala).

[856] His Divine Grace A.C. Bhaktivedanta Swami Prabhupada (2011) *Chant and Be Happy: The Power of Mantra Meditation* (Los Angeles: Bhaktivedanta Book Trust).

[857] Veda-Vyāsa (author), Charles Wilkins (translator) (1785), Lecture V. Of Forsaking the Fruits of Works, p. 59.

[858] John 14:20 (King James Bible).

[859] Zoroaster (author), James Darmesteter (translator) (1882) *The Zend Avesta, Part II: The The Sîrôzahs, Yasts and Nyâyis* (Oxford: Oxford University Press), I. Ormazd Yast, v. 12, 18 - 19, pp. 27, 29.

[860] Genesis 1:26 – 28 (King James Bible).

[861] Exodus 6:3 (King James Bible).

[862] Deuteronomy 6:4 – 9 (King James Bible).

[863] Psalm 1:1 – 3 (King James Bible).

[864] Psalm 77:12 – 14 (King James Bible).

[865] Psalm 83:18 (King James Bible).

[866] Psalm 104:1 (King James Bible).

[867] Psalm 113:2 -4 (King James Bible).

[868] Proverbs 15:28 (King James Bible).

[869] Isaiah 26:4 (King James Bible).

[870] Richard Laurence (translator) (1883) *The Book of Enoch The Prophet, Translated from the Ethiopic Ms. In the Bodleian Library* (London: Kegan Paul, Trench & Co.), Chap. CV, v. 26, p. 180. Available online at: http://www.sacred-texts.com/bib/bep/index.htm (accessed 30/04/2017).

[871] Mark 4:9 (King James Bible).

[872] Mark 4:30 – 32 (King James Bible).

[873] Matthew 5:14 – 16 (King James Bible).

[874] Matthew 6:5 – 6 (King James Bible).

[875] Matthew 6:19 – 21 (King James Bible).

[876] Matthew 6:22 - 23 (King James Bible).

[877] Matthew 10:39 King James Bible).

[878] Matthew 13:13, 16 (King James Bible).

[879] John 4:14 (King James Bible).

[880] John 8:12 (King James Bible).

[881] John 12:44 – 47 (King James Bible).

[882] John 15:10 – 12 (King James Bible).

[883] Philippians 4:8 – 9 (King James Bible).

[884] Romans 8:16 (King James Bible).

[885] Revelation 21:6 (King James Bible).

[886] Qur'ān 2:26 (Palmer translation).

[887] Qur'ān 2:255 (Rodwell translation).

[888] Qur'ān 3:190 (Rodwell translation).

[889] Qur'ān 3:191 (Sale translation).

[890] Qur'ān 12:111 (Rodwell translation).

[891] Qur'ān 13:3 (Rodwell translation).

[892] Qur'ān 14:1 (Rodwell translation).

[893] Qur'ān 16:44 (Sale translation).

[894] Qur'ān 24:35 (Rodwell translation).

[895] Qur'ān 36:33 – 35 (Palmer translation).

[896] Qur'ān 45:13 (Rodwell translation).

[897] Qur'ān 65:2 - 3 (Rodwell translation).

[898] Qur'ān 73:20 (Sale translation).

[899] Gautama Buddha (author), Müller (1881) *The Dhammapada*, Ch. III, v. 35 - 37, 40, pp. 12 - 14.

[900] Gautama Buddha (author), Müller (1881) *The Dhammapada*, Ch. VI, v. 82, p. 24.

[901] Gautama Buddha (author), Müller (1881) *The Dhammapada*, Ch. VII, v. 90 – 91, p. 27.

[902] Gautama Buddha (author), Müller (1881) *The Dhammapada*, Ch. XII, v. 160, p. 45.

[903] Gautama Buddha (author), Müller (1881) *The Dhammapada*, Ch. XX, v. 281, p. 68.

[904] Gautama Buddha (author), Müller (1881) *The Dhammapada*, Ch. XXIII, v. 326 - 327, p. 78.

905 Gautama Buddha (author), Müller (1881) *The Dhammapada*, Ch. XXV, v. 372, p. 87.

906 Gautama Buddha (author), Müller (1881) *The Dhammapada*, Ch. XXVI, v. 387, p. 89.

907 Veda-Vyāsa (author), Ralph T.H. Griffith (translator) (1896) *The Hymns of the Rig-Veda, translated with a popular commentary* (Benares: E.J. Lazaarus), Hymn CXXI. Ka., v. 3, 5, 8 – 9. Available online at: http://www.sacred-texts.com/hin/rigveda/index.htm (accessed 12/04/2017).

908 Veda-Vyāsa (author), Ralph T.H. Griffith (translator) (1896), Hymn CXIII, Dawn, v. 1.

909 Veda-Vyāsa (author), Swami Swarupananda (translator) (1909) *Srimad-Bhagavad-Gita* (Mayavati, Himalayas: Prabuddha Bharata Press), Ch. II, v. 51 – 52, pp. 60 – 61. Available online at: http://www.sacred-texts.com/hin/sbg/index.htm (accessed 19/03/2017).

910 Veda-Vyāsa (author), Swami Swarupananda (translator) (1909) *Srimad-Bhagavad-Gita*, Ch. II, v. 56 – 59, pp. 63 – 64.

911 Veda-Vyāsa (author), Swami Swarupananda (translator) (1909) *Srimad-Bhagavad-Gita*, Ch. II, v. 62 – 65, pp. 66 - 67.

912 Veda-Vyāsa (author), Swami Swarupananda (translator) (1909) *Srimad-Bhagavad-Gita*, Ch. II, v. 70 – 71, pp. 70 - 71.

913 Veda-Vyāsa (author), Swami Swarupananda (translator) (1909) *Srimad-Bhagavad-Gita*, Ch. IV, v. 10 – 11, pp. 101 – 102.

914 Veda-Vyāsa (author), Swami Swarupananda (translator) (1909) *Srimad-Bhagavad-Gita*, Ch. IV, v. 36 – 39, pp. 116 – 117.

915 Veda-Vyāsa (author), Swami Swarupananda (translator) (1909) *Srimad-Bhagavad-Gita*, Ch. V, v. 27 – 29, pp. 135 – 136.

916 Veda-Vyāsa (author), Swami Swarupananda (translator) (1909) *Srimad-Bhagavad-Gita*, Ch. VI, v. 3 – 8, pp. 139 – 142.

917 Veda-Vyāsa (author), Swami Swarupananda (translator) (1909) *Srimad-Bhagavad-Gita*, Ch. VI, v. 9 – 10, p. 143.

918 Veda-Vyāsa (author), Swami Swarupananda (translator) (1909) *Srimad-Bhagavad-Gita*, Ch. VI, v. 10, 13 – 15, pp. 143 – 146.

919 Veda-Vyāsa (author), Swami Swarupananda (translator) (1909) *Srimad-Bhagavad-Gita*, Ch. VI, v. 18 – 19, p. 147.

920 Veda-Vyāsa (author), Swami Swarupananda (translator) (1909) *Srimad-Bhagavad-Gita*, Ch. VI, v. 30 – 31, pp. 152 – 153.

921 Veda-Vyāsa (author), Swami Swarupananda (translator) (1909) *Srimad-Bhagavad-Gita*, Ch. VIII, v. 5, 7, pp. 182 – 183.

922 Three Vedas.

923 Veda-Vyāsa (author), Swami Swarupananda (translator) (1909) *Srimad-Bhagavad-Gita*, Ch. IX, v. 17 – 19, pp. 207 – 208.

924 Veda-Vyāsa (author), Swami Swarupananda (translator) (1909) *Srimad-Bhagavad-Gita*, Ch. IX, v. 26 – 28, pp. 213 – 214.

925 Veda-Vyāsa (author), Swami Swarupananda (translator) (1909) *Srimad-Bhagavad-Gita*, Ch. IX, v. 34, p. 218.

926 Veda-Vyāsa (author), Swami Swarupananda (translator) (1909) *Srimad-Bhagavad-Gita*, Ch. X, v. 8 – 9, p. 223.

927 Veda-Vyāsa (author), Swami Swarupananda (translator) (1909) *Srimad-Bhagavad-Gita*, Ch. X, v. 39 – 41, pp. 239 – 240.

928 Veda-Vyāsa (author), Swami Swarupananda (translator) (1909) *Srimad-Bhagavad-Gita*, Ch. XI, v. 38, p. 264.

[929] Veda-Vyāsa (author), Swami Swarupananda (translator) (1909) *Srimad-Bhagavad-Gita*, Ch. XII, v. 6 – 7, pp. 279 – 280.

[930] Veda-Vyāsa (author), Swami Swarupananda (translator) (1909) *Srimad-Bhagavad-Gita*, Ch. XIII, v. 12, 17, pp. 296, 298.

[931] Veda-Vyāsa (author), Swami Swarupananda (translator) (1909) *Srimad-Bhagavad-Gita*, Ch. XIII, v. 27 – 28, p. 304.

[932] Veda-Vyāsa (author), Swami Swarupananda (translator) (1909) *Srimad-Bhagavad-Gita*, Ch. XV, v. 19, p. 335.

[933] Veda-Vyāsa (author), Wilkins (translator) (1785) *The Bhagvat-Geetā or Dialogues of Kreeshna and Arjoon*, Lecture XVI. Of Good and Evil Destiny, v. 24, p. 118.

[934] Veda-Vyāsa (author), Swami Swarupananda (translator) (1909) *Srimad-Bhagavad-Gita*, Ch. XVIII, v. 55- 56, 58, pp. 392 – 394.

[935] Veda-Vyāsa (author), Swami Swarupananda (translator) (1909) *Srimad-Bhagavad-Gita*, Ch. XVIII, v. 64 – 66, pp. 396 – 398.

[936] Veda-Vyāsa (author), Swami Swarupananda (translator) (1909) *Srimad-Bhagavad-Gita*, Ch. XVIII, v. 68 – 69, pp. 399 – 400.

[937] Vālmīki (author), Ralph T.H. Griffith (translator) (1870-74) *The Rámáyan of Válmíki translated into English verse* (London: Trübner), Book VI, Ch. XVIII. Available online at: http://www.sacred-texts.com/hin/rama/ (accessed 11/03/2017).

[938] Vālmīki (author), Manmatha Nath Dutt (translator) (1893) *The Ramayana, translated into English Prose from the Original Sanskrit of Valmiki, Volume VI. Yuddha Kandam* (Calcutta: Elysium Press), Section XVIII, p. 1151. Available online at: https://archive.org/details/Valmiki_Ramayana_English_Prose_Translation_7_volumes_by_Manmath a_Nath_Dutt_1891_to_1894 (accessed 07/05/2017).

[939] Veda-Vyāsa (author), Ganguli (translator) (1883-1896) *The Mahabharata*, Book 12: Santi Parva, Part 3, Section CCCXXVII, pp. 89 – 90.

[940] Veda-Vyāsa (author), Horace Hayman Wilson (translator) (1840) *The Vishnu Purána: A System of Hindu Mythology and Tradition, Translated from the Original Sanscrit* (London: John Murray), Chapter VII, pp. 652 – 653. Available online at: http://www.sacred-texts.com/hin/vp/index.htm (accessed 19/03/2017).

[941] Madhva Acharya (author), S. Subba Rau (translator) (1904) *The Vedanta-Sutras with the Commentary by Sri Madhwachary – A Complete Translation* (Madras: Thompson & Co. at the 'Minerva' Press), Vedanta-Sutras with Madhwa Bhashya, Third Adhyaya, First Pada, pp. 171 - 172. Available online at: https://archive.org/details/BrahmasutraMadhvaEnglish (accessed 21/04/2017).

[942] Swami Paramananda (1919) *The Upanishads, Translated and Commentated by Swami Paramananda, From the Original Sanskrit Text* (Boston: Vedanta Centre), Isa-Upanishad, I. Available online at: http://www.gutenberg.org/ebooks/3283 (accessed 02/05/2017).

[943] Swami Paramananda (1919), *Katha Upanishad*, XII.

[944] Veda-Vyāsa (author), Narayanasvami Aiyar (translator) (1914) *Thirty Minor Upanishads* (Madras: Printed by Annie Besant at the Vasanta Press), Amrtabindu-Upanishad of Krshna-Yajurveda, p. 34. Available online at: http://sacred-texts.com/hin/tmu/index.htm (accessed 29/04/2017). See also: https://archive.org/details/thirtyminorupanioooxxxxuoft (accessed 29/04/2017).

[945] *Thirty Minor Upanishads*, Sarvasāra-Upanishad of Krshna-Yajurveda, v. 10, pp. 16 – 17.

[946] Julius Eggeling (translator) (1900) *The Satapatha Brahmana, according to the text of the Mâdhyandina School, Part V* (Sacred Books of the East, Vol. 44) (Oxford: The Clarendon Press), XI. 5.7, Seventh Brâhmana, v. 1, p. 99. Available online at: http://www.sacred-texts.com/hin/sbr/sbe44/index.htm (accessed 29/04/2017).

[947] Madhva Acharya (author), S. Subba Rau (translator) (1904), Third Adhyaya, Third Pada, p. 229.

948 Swami Vivekananda (1902), *Vedânta philosophy; lectures by the Swâmi Vivekânanda on jnâna yoga*, XII. Practical Vedânta, Part I, p. 206. New York: The Vedânta Society. Available online at: https://archive.org/details/vedntaphilosopo0vive (accessed 21/03/2017).

949 Daisetz Teitaro Suzuki (1908) *Outlines of Mahayana Buddhism* (Chicago: Open Court), pp. 365 – 366.

950 The Editor (1908) Buddhist Meditations, In *The Open Court – A Monthly Magazine Devoted to the Science of Religion, the Religion of Science, and the Extension of the Religious Parliament Idea*, Vol. XXII (Chicago: The Open Court Publishing Company), p. 556. Available online at: http://www.sacred-texts.com/journals/oc/budmed.htm (accessed 14/03/2017).

951 Laozi (author), J. Legge (translator) (1891) *The Tao Te Ching* (London: Oxford University Press), v. 1. Available online at: http://www.sacred-texts.com/tao/taote.htm (accessed 29/04/2017).

952 Laozi (author), J. Legge (translator) (1891), v. 4.

953 Laozi (author), J. Legge (translator) (1891), v. 51.

954 Confucius (author), James Legge (translator) (1861) *The Chinese Classics (Confucian Analects)* (London: Trübner & Co.), Book IX, Ch. VII. Available online at: http://www.gutenberg.org/ebooks/3330 (accessed 29/04/2017).

955 Confucius (author), James Legge (translator) (1861), Book VI, Ch. XVIII.

956 Zhuangzi, *Chuang Tzu, Mystic, Moralist, and Social Reformer*, Chapter IV, p. 43.

957 Zhuangzi, *Chuang Tzu, Mystic, Moralist, and Social Reformer*, Chapter V, p. 58.

958 Zhuangzi, *Chuang Tzu, Mystic, Moralist, and Social Reformer*, Chapter V, p. 64.

959 Mencius (author), James Legge (translator) (1895) *The Works of Mencius, Vol. 2* (Oxford: Clarendon Press), Book 7, Part II, Chapter 32, v. 2 - 3. Available online at: http://nothingistic.org/library/mencius/ (accessed 02/05/2017).

960 Mencius (author), James Legge (translator) (1895), Book 7, Part II, Chapter 35.

961 Zhuangzi (author), Herbert Allen Giles (translator) (1889) *Chuang Tzu, Mystic, Moralist, and Social Reformer* (London: B. Quaritch), Chapter III, p. 33.. Available online at: https://archive.org/details/chuangtzumysticmoochua (accessed 02/05/2017).

962 Zhuangzi (author), Herbert Allen Giles (translator) (1889) *Chuang Tzu, Mystic, Moralist, and Social Reformer* (London: B. Quaritch), Chapter VI, p. 68.

963 Zhuangzi (author), Herbert Allen Giles (translator) (1889) *Chuang Tzu, Mystic, Moralist, and Social Reformer* (London: B. Quaritch), Chapter XII, pp. 138 – 139.

964 Florence M. Firth (translator) (1904) *The Golden Verses of Pythagoras, And Other Pythagorean Fragments* (London: Theosophical Publishing Society), v. 40 – 46, p. 5. Available online at: http://sacred-texts.com/cla/gvp/index.htm (accessed 03/05/2017).

965 Plato (author), Benjamin Jowett (translator) (1892) *The Dialogues of Plato, translated into English with Analyses and Introductions, Vol. II* (New York: Oxford University Press, American Branch; London: Henry Frowde), Phaedo. Available online at: http://classics.mit.edu/Plato/phaedo.html ; https://archive.org/details/dialoguesofplato18922plat (accessed 03/05/2017).

966 Plato (author), Benjamin Jowett (translator) (1892), Symposium. See also: http://classics.mit.edu/Plato/symposium.html (accessed 03/05/2017).

967 Marcus Aurelius (author), George Long (translator) (192-?) *The Meditations of Marcus Aurelius* (London, Glasgow: Collins' Clear-Type Press), Book I. Available online at: http://www.sacred-texts.com/cla/aurelmed.htm (accessed 20/03/2017).

968 Marcus Aurelius (author), George Long (translator) (192-?) *The Meditations of Marcus Aurelius* (London, Glasgow: Collins' Clear-Type Press), Book II.

969 Tertullian (author), Allan Menzies (translator) (1885-96) *Ante-Nicene Fathers, Vol. III.* (Grand Rapids, Michigan: WM. B. Eerdmans Publishing Company), Chapter V, pp. 600 – 601. Available online at: http://www.sacred-texts.com/chr/ecf/003/index.htm (accessed 30/03/2017).

⁹⁷⁰ Epictetus (author), P.E. Matheson (translator) (1916) *The Discourses of Epictetus: The Discourses and Manual, together with fragments of his writings* (Oxford: Clarendon Press), Book IV, Chapter I, pp. 422 – 423. Available online at: http://www.sacred-texts.com/cla/dep/index.htm (accessed 19/03/2017)

⁹⁷¹ Plotinus (author), Stephen MacKenna & B.S. Page (translators) (1917 – 1930) *The Six Enneads* (London; Boston: Medici Society), The First Ennead: Second Tractate, Section 3. Available online at: http://www.sacred-texts.com/cla/plotenn/index.htm (accessed 22/03/2017).

⁹⁷² Thomas à Kempis (author), Rev. William Benham (translator) (1877) *The Imitation of Christ* (Leipzig: B. Tauchnitz), Book I, Chapter XXIV, 9. Available online at: http://www.gutenberg.org/ebooks/1653 (accessed 22/02/2017).

⁹⁷³ Thomas à Kempis (author), Rev. William Benham (translator) (1877), Chapter XLVIII, 6.

⁹⁷⁴ Thomas à Kempis (author), Rev. William Benham (translator) (1877), Book II, Chapter I, 4.

⁹⁷⁵ Thomas à Kempis (author), Rev. William Benham (translator) (1877), Book II, Chapter I, 8.

⁹⁷⁶ St. Ignatius of Loyola (author), Elder Mullan (translator) (1914) *Spiritual Exercises of St. Ignatius of Loyola* (New York: Kennedy), First Week. Available online at: http://www.sacred-texts.com/chr/seil/ (accessed 29/04/2017).

⁹⁷⁷ St. Ignatius of Loyola (author), Elder Mullan (translator) (1914), Rules for Perceiving and Knowing in Some Manner the Different Movements which are caused in the Soul: Third Rule.

⁹⁷⁸ St. Ignatius of Loyola (author), Elder Mullan (translator) (1914), Twentieth Annotation.

⁹⁷⁹ Abū Hāmid Muhammad ibn Muhammad Al-Ghazālī (author), Claud Field (translator) *The Alchemy of Happiness by Al Ghazzali, Translated from the Hindustani* (London: John Murray, Albermarle Street), Chapter I. Available online at: https://en.wikisource.org/wiki/The_Alchemy_of_Happiness_(Field) (accessed 02/05/2017).

⁹⁸⁰ Omar Khayyam (author), Edward FitzGerald (1859) *The Rubáiyàt of Omar Khayyám, the astronomer-poet of Persia, translated into English verse* (London: B. Quaritch), XXXIII. Available online at: http://www.sacred-texts.com/isl/khayyam.txt (accessed 03/05/2017).

⁹⁸¹ Nūr al-Dīn 'Abd al-Rahmān Jāmī (author), Edward Fitzgerald (translator) (1904) *Miscellanies of Edward Fitzgerald* (London: George Routledge and Sons, Ltd.), *Salámán and Absál*, Prologue, pp. 1 - 2. Available online at: http://www.sacred-texts.com/isl/saab/index.htm ; https://archive.org/details/miscellaniesedw01fitzgoog (accessed 03/05/2017).

⁹⁸² Nūr al-Dīn 'Abd al-Rahmān Jāmī (author), Edward Fitzgerald (translator) (1904) *Salámán and Absál*, II, p. 5.

⁹⁸³ Abū 'Abdu'llāh Muhammad ibn 'Alī ibn Muhammad ibn 'Arabī (Ibn al-'Arabī) (author), Reynold A. Nicholson (1911) *The Tarjumán al-Ashwáq: A Collection of Mystical Odes by Muhyi'ddin ibn Al-'Arabi* (London: Theosophical Publishing House Ltd.), XI., v. 13 – 15. Available online at: http://www.sacred-texts.com/isl/taa/index.htm (available online at: 03/05/2017).

⁹⁸⁴ Shamsu'd-Dīn Muhammad Hāfez-e-Shīrāzī (author), Gertrude Lowthian Bell (translator) (1897) *Teachings of Hafiz* (London: W. Heinemann), III. Available online at: http://www.sacred-texts.com/isl/hafiz.htm (accessed 17/03/2017).

⁹⁸⁵ Jalāl ad-Dīn Rūmī (author), Shams ad-Dīn Ahmad (author), James W. Redhouse (translator) (1881) *The Mesnavi (usually known as the Mesneviyi Sherif) of Mevlānā (our lord) Jelālu-'d-Dīn, Muhammed, Er-Rūmī. Book the First. Together with some accounts of the life and acts of the author, of his ancestors, and of his descendants; illustrated by a selection of characteristic anecdotes, as collected by their historian, Mevlānā Shemsu-'d-Dīn Ahmed, El Eflākī, El 'Ārifi* (London: Trübner & Co.), XII. Joseph and the Mirror. Available online at: http://www.sacred-texts.com/isl/mes/index.htm (accessed 15/04/2017).

⁹⁸⁶ Abū-Muhammad Muslihu'd-Dīn bin 'Abdu'llāh Shīrāzī (Saadi) (author), Sir Edwin Arnold (translator) (1899) *The Gulistân of Musle-huddeen Shaik Sady of Sheeraz* (London: T. Burleigh), Introductory. Available online at: http://www.sacred-texts.com/isl/gulistan.txt (accessed 17/03/2017).

⁹⁸⁷ Hakīm Abu'l-Majd Majdūd Sanā'ī (author), J. Stephenson (translator) (1910) *The Hadîqatu'l-Haqîqat (The Enclosed Garden of the Truth)* (Calcutta: Baptist Mission Press), On Affection and Isolation, p. 70. Available online at: http://www.sacred-texts.com/isl/egt/index.htm (accessed 03/05/2017).

[988] John Milton (c.1900) *Paradise Regained* (New York, Boston: H.M. Caldwell Co.), Second Book, v. 466 - 468, 475 - 478. Available online at: http://www.gutenberg.org/ebooks/58 (accessed 04/05/2017).

[989] Alexander Pope (1762) *A Collection of Essays: Epistles and Odes. Epistles to several persons. Epistles to several persons. Eloisa to Abelard. The rape of the lock. Messiah. A sacred Eclogue. The temple of fame. Ode for music on St. Cecilia's Day. Ode on solitude. Essay on criticism. The universal prayer. By Alexander Pope, Esq.* (London: Printed for J. James, in New-Bond Street), An Essay on Criticism, Part 1. Available online at: https://www.poetryfoundation.org/poems-and-poets/poems/detail/44896 (accessed 04/05/2017).

[990] Alexander Pope (author), Thomas Marc Parrott (editor) (1906) *Pope's The Rape of the Lock and other poems* (Boston, Mass.: Ginn & Co.), On Solitude. Available online at: https://en.wikipedia.org/wiki/Ode_on_Solitude ; http://www.gutenberg.org/ebooks/9800 (accessed 04/05/2017).

[991] William Blake (1901) *Songs of Innocence and Songs of Experience* (London: R. Brimley Johnson), The Divine Image. Available online at: http://www.gutenberg.org/ebooks/1934 (accessed 22/04/2017).

[992] John Bunyan (1853) *The Pilgrim's Progress From This World to That Which is to Come; Delivered under the Similitude of a Dream* (Auburn: Derby & Miller; Buffalo: Geo. H. Derby and Co.), The Fifth Stage. Available online at: https://www.ccel.org/ccel/bunyan/pilgrim.iv.v.html (accessed 05/05/2017).

[993] George Fox (1706) *Gospel Truth Demonstrated in A Collection of Doctrinal Books, given forth by that faithful minister of Jesus Christ, George Fox: containing principles essential to Christianity and salvation, held among the people called Quakers* (London: T. Sowle, in White-Hart-Court, in Gracious-Street), p. 25. Available online at: http://www.hallvworthington.com/Original%20PDFs/Works_4_Doctrine1.pdf (accessed 03/05/2017).

[994] George Fox (1706), pp. 34 - 36.

[995] George Fox (1706), p. 37.

[996] William Penn (1857) *Primitive Christianity Revived in the faith and practice of the people called Quakers; written in testimony to the present dispensation of God through them to the world; that prejudices may be removed, the simple informed, the well-inclined encouraged, and the truth and its innocent friends rightly represented* (Philadelphia: Miller & Burlock), Chapter 1, § 1. - 4. Available online at: http://www.strecorsoc.org/penn/title.html (accessed 04/05/2017).

[997] William Penn (1857), Chapter IV, § 2.

[998] John Wesley (author), Edward H. Sugden (editor) (1920), *Wesley's Standard Sermons, consisting of Forty-Four Discourses, Published in Four Volumes, Volume I* (Nashville: M.E. Church, South), Sermon 10: The Witness of the Spirit, Discourse 1, 11 - 12. Available online at: http://www.godrules.net/library/wesley/wesley.htm#john-wesley-sermons ; https://archive.org/details/10305045.76.emory.edu (accessed 03/05/2017).

[999] James Allen (1907) *From Poverty to Power: The Path to prosperity and The Way of Peace* (Albuquerque, NM: Sun Pub. Co.). Available online at: http://www.gutenberg.org/ebooks/10740 (accessed 22/02/2017).

[1000] Allen (1907).

[1001] Allen (1907).

[1002] Allen (1907).

[1003] Allen (1907).

[1004] Allen (1907).

[1005] A Disciple (1921) *In the Hours of Meditation* (Calcutta: S. C. Majumdah), II, p. 7. Available online at: https://archive.org/details/inhoursofmeditatoodiscrich (accessed 22/02/2017).

[1006] William Walker Atkinson (1907) *A series of lessons in Gnani yoga (the yoga of wisdom)* (Chicago, IL.: The Yogi Publication Society), p. 1. Available online at: https://archive.org/details/cu31924022985422 (accessed 04/03/2017).

[1007] Atkinson (1907), p. 3.

[1008] Atkinson (1907), pp. 16 – 17.

[1009] John Wilmot Mahood (1911) *The Lost Art of Meditation* (New York, Chicago: Fleming H. Revell Company), p. 31. Available online at: https://archive.org/details/lostartofmeditatoomaho (accessed 22/02/2017).

98307665R00251

Made in the USA
Lexington, KY
06 September 2018